understanding educational leadership

Also available from Bloomsbury

Global Education Policy and International Development: New Agendas, Issues and Policies, edited by Antoni Verger, Hulya K. Altinyelken and Mario Novelli.

Knowledge and the Future School: Curriculum and Social Justice, edited by Michael Young, David Lambert, Carolyn Roberts and Martin Roberts.

An Intellectual History of School Leadership Practice and Research, Helen M. Gunter.

understanding educational leadership

critical perspectives and approaches

Edited by
Steven J. Courtney, Helen M. Gunter, Richard Niesche, Tina Trujillo

BLOOMSBURY ACADEMIC
LONDON • NEW YORK • OXFORD • NEW DELHI • SYDNEY

BLOOMSBURY ACADEMIC
Bloomsbury Publishing Plc
50 Bedford Square, London, WC1B 3DP, UK
1385 Broadway, New York, NY 10018, USA
29 Earlsfort Terrace, Dublin 2, Ireland

BLOOMSBURY, BLOOMSBURY ACADEMIC and the Diana logo are trademarks of
Bloomsbury Publishing Plc

First published in Great Britain 2021

Cover design by Charlotte James

A catalogue record for this book is available from the British Library.

Library of Congress Cataloging-in-Publication Data
Names: Courtney, Steven J., editor. | Gunter, Helen, editor. | Niesche, Richard, editor. |
Trujillo, Tina M., editor.
Title: Understanding educational leadership : critical perspectives and approaches / edited
by Steven J. Courtney, Helen M. Gunter, Richard Niesche, Tina Trujillo.
Description: London ; New York : Bloomsbury Academic, 2020. | Includes bibliographical
references and index.
Identifiers: LCCN 2020038827 (print) | LCCN 2020038828 (ebook) |
ISBN 9781350081819 (paperback) | ISBN 9781350081826 (hardback) |
ISBN 9781350081840 (pdf) | ISBN 9781350081833 (epub)
Subjects: LCSH: Educational leadership.
Classification: LCC LB2806 .U35 2021 (print) | LCC LB2806 (ebook) | DDC 371.2/011—dc23
LC record available at https://lccn.loc.gov/2020038827
LC ebook record available at https://lccn.loc.gov/2020038828

ISBN: HB: 978-1-3500-8182-6
        PB: 978-1-3500-8181-9
        ePDF: 978-1-3500-8184-0
        eBook: 978-1-3500-8183-3

Typeset by RefineCatch Limited, Bungay, Suffolk
Printed and bound in Great Britain

To find out more about our authors and books visit www.bloomsbury.com
and sign up for our newsletters.

Contents

Notes on contributors   viii
Foreword by John Smyth   xvii

Introduction: Taking critical perspectives and using critical approaches
in educational leadership *Steven J. Courtney, Helen M. Gunter,*
Richard Niesche and Tina Trujillo   1

Part one Critical perspectives and approaches across the world

1 Critical perspectives in and approaches to educational leadership
in the United States *Tina Trujillo and Sonya Douglass Horsford*   15
2 Critical perspectives in and approaches to educational leadership
in England *Ruth McGinity and Kay Fuller*   29
3 Critical perspectives in and approaches to educational leadership
in Australia *Martin Mills and Glenda McGregor*   45
4 Critical perspectives in and approaches to educational leadership
in South Africa *Pontso Moorosi and Jan Heystek*   59
5 Critical perspectives in and approaches to educational leadership
in China *Ting Wang and Kai Yu*   75
6 Critical perspectives in and approaches to educational leadership
in Indonesia *Zulfa Sakhiyya and Tanya Fitzgerald*   91
7 Critical perspectives in and approaches to educational leadership
in two Nordic countries *Jorunn Møller and Linda Rönnberg*   105

8   Critical perspectives in and approaches to educational leadership
    in Chile *Alejandro Carrasco and Germán Fromm, with
    Helen M. Gunter*   121

Part two Critical perspectives on models and methods in educational leadership

9   Leading and managing in educational organizations
    Helen M. Gunter and Emiliano Grimaldi   139
10 Using theory in educational leadership, management and
    administration research *Pat Thomson and Amanda Heffernan*   155
11 Research methods in educational leadership *Scott Eacott
    and Gus Riveros*   171
12 A historical deconstruction of leadership style *Fenwick W. English
    and Lisa Catherine Ehrich*   187
13 Distributed leadership *Howard Youngs and Linda Evans*   203
14 Educational and instructional leadership *Scott Eacott and
    Richard Niesche*   221
15 Educational reform and leading school change
    Jill Blackmore and Rachel McNae   237

Part three Critical perspectives and approaches to contemporary issues in educational leadership

16 Gender and educational leadership *Jane Wilkinson, Anar Purvee
    and Katrina MacDonald*   255
17 Sexual identity and educational leadership *Catherine A. Lugg
    and Robin Roscigno*   269
18 Race and educational leadership *Mark A. Gooden and Victoria Showunmi* 281
19 Socio-economic class and educational leadership
    Helen M. Gunter and Steven J. Courtney   295
20 Governance and educational leadership *Andrew Wilkins
    and Brad Gobby*   309

21 Performativity, managerialism and educational leadership
    Tanya Fitzgerald and David Hall   323

22 Corporatization and educational leadership *Kenneth Saltman*
    and Alexander J. Means   339

23 Leading in a genetics-informed education market
    Steven Jones, Steven J. Courtney and Helen M. Gunter   355

Conclusion: Putting critical approaches to work in educational
leadership *Helen M. Gunter, Steven J. Courtney,*
Richard Niesche and Tina Trujillo   **371**

Index   383

Notes on contributors

Jill Blackmore is Alfred Deakin Professor and Personal Chair in Education in the Faculty of Arts and Education at Deakin University, Australia, founding Director of Centre for Research in Educational Futures and Innovation (2010–2015) and Fellow of the Academy of Social Sciences, Australia. Her research interests include, from a feminist perspective, globalization, education policy and governance; international and intercultural education; educational restructuring, leadership and organizational change; spatial redesign and innovative pedagogies; and teachers' and academics' work, focusing on equity. Her current research is on international students in schools; school autonomy; disengagement with – and homogeneity in – university leadership; international education; and graduate employability.

Alejandro Carrasco is Associate Professor in the Faculty of Education at the Pontificia Universidad Católica de Chile, Chile. His work focuses on school choice and admission systems, and the impact of accountability-regime-based reforms. His recent paper with Gunter (2019) is 'The "private" in the privatization of schools: the case of Chile', in the *Journal of Educational Review*. His previous books are: *Contrasting dynamics in education politics of extremes: school choice in Chile and Finland*, with Piia Seppänen and others (2015); *Mercado escolar y oportunidad educacional* (2016), and *De la Reforma a la Transformación* (2019).

Steven J. Courtney is Senior Lecturer in Management and Leadership and Research Coordinator in the Manchester Institute of Education, University of Manchester, UK. He uses critical sociological approaches to explore the interplay between agency and structure in education policy and leadership. His research has been recognized with awards from AERA Division A, BERA, BELMAS and the British Academy. His co-edited collection was published in 2017, *Educational leadership: theorising professional practice in neoliberal times*. He is an editor of *Critical Studies in Education* and co-convenor of the BELMAS Critical Education Policy and Leadership Studies research interest group.

Scott Eacott is Associate Professor of Educational Leadership in the School of Education, University of New South Wales Sydney, Australia, and Adjunct Professor in the Department of Educational Administration at the University of Saskatchewan, Canada. His research interests and contributions fall into three areas: (1) developing a relational approach to organizational theory; (2) educational leadership; and (3) school reform. Current projects include regional school consolidation reform, high-impact leadership and school autonomy. His most recent book is *Beyond leadership: a relational approach to organisational theory in education* (2018).

Lisa Catherine Ehrich is a mentoring and leadership consultant as well as Adjunct Associate Professor in the Faculty of Education at Queensland University of Technology (QUT), Australia. Formerly, she served for twenty-four years at QUT. In 2014, she was recognized for her contribution to Australian leadership when she received a Queensland Fellowship and a National Fellowship of the Australian Council for Educational Leaders (ACEL). Her research areas include mentoring for professionals and the aesthetics of educational leadership. Her most recent book, co-authored with Fenwick English, is *Leading beautifully: educational leadership as connoisseurship*, published 2016.

Fenwick W. English is Professor and Department Chair of Educational Leadership of Teachers College at Ball State University, United States. He is past president of the University Council of Educational Administration (UCEA) and the International Council of Professors of Educational Leadership (ICPEL formerly NCPEA) from which he received the Living Legend Award in 2013. His major interest is in the epistemology of professional practice and ideology. He is the author or co-author of more than forty books, including *Leading beautifully: educational leadership as connoisseurship* with Lisa Catherine Ehrich, published in 2016.

Linda Evans is Professor of Education at the University of Manchester, UK, and has worked at the Universities of Warwick and Leeds. A former student of French, she has lived in France as visiting professor at the Institut Français de l'Education in Lyon. She researches working life in education contexts, with a particular focus on work-related attitudes, professionalism, professional development and leadership. She has published nine books, including *Teacher morale, job satisfaction and motivation* (1998), *Reflective practice in educational research: developing advanced skills* (2002), and *Professors as academic leaders: expectations, enacted professionalism and evolving roles* (2018).

Tanya Fitzgerald is Professor of Higher Education and Dean of the Graduate School of Education at the University of Western Australia, Australia. She holds visiting professor roles at universities in South Africa, Malaysia and North America. Her research interests span the history of women's higher education, higher education policy and leadership, and educational biography. She is Editor-in-Chief of the *International handbook of historical studies in education* (2020), and her scholarly publications include numerous books, book chapters and journal articles. Tanya is currently working on a history of scholarly women, academic diplomacy and the International Federation of University Women.

Germán Fromm is an Associated Researcher in the Center for Advanced Research in Education at the University of Chile. He focuses on educational leadership, specifically training and schools' organizational change and development. His current research project is titled 'Development of change management in in-service training for educational leaders'. His most recent publications are 'Social justice accountability for educational leaders' in 2019, a chapter of the book *Education and poverty*, and co-author in 2018 of 'Longitudinal evaluation of the educational leadership training in public schools' [original in Spanish] by Centro de Liderazgo para la Mejora Escolar, Chile.

Kay Fuller is Associate Professor of Educational Leadership in the Centre for Research in Educational Leadership and Management at the University of Nottingham, UK. She is co-convener of the BELMAS Gender and Leadership Research Interest Group and a member of international networks, *Women Leading Education Across the Continents* and *#WomenEd*. Her work focuses on women and gender in educational leadership. Her books include: *Gender, identity and educational leadership* in 2013, *Gender and leadership in education* (co-edited with Judith Harford) by Peter Lang in 2016. She is currently working on *Feminist perspectives in contemporary educational leadership*.

Brad Gobby is Senior Lecturer in the School of Education at Curtin University, Western Australia. He has published widely on the topics of education policy, politics and school autonomy in peer-reviewed international journals and edited books, and is an editorial board member of the *Journal of Educational Administration and History*. His recent books include *Powers of curriculum: sociological perspectives on education* (co-editor) in 2017, and *Teaching: dilemmas, challenges and opportunities* (co-author) in 2019.

Mark A. Gooden is the Christian Johnson Endeavor Professor in Education Leadership and Director of the Endeavor Leadership Initiative in the Department of Organization and Leadership at Teachers College, Columbia University, United States. His research focuses on culturally responsive school leadership with specific interests in the principalship, anti-racist leadership, urban educational leadership and legal issues in education. Mark is 2017 recipient of the Jay D. Scribner Mentoring Award. His research has appeared in a range of outlets including *American Educational Research Journal*, *Educational Administration Quarterly*, *Teachers College Record*, *Review of Educational Research*, *The Journal of Negro Education* and *Urban Education*.

Emiliano Grimaldi is Professor of Sociology of Education in the Department of Social Sciences at the University of Naples Federico II, Italy. He is a co-convenor of the Network 28 Sociologies of Education of the EERA. His research focuses on governmentality and social epistemology in the fields of education and education policy. His most recent book is: *An archaeology of educational evaluation: epistemological spaces and political paradoxes* in 2019.

Helen M. Gunter is Professor of Education Policy in the Manchester Institute of Education at the University of Manchester, UK. She is a Fellow of the Academy of Social Sciences, and recipient of the BELMAS Distinguished Service Award 2016. Her work focuses on the politics of education policy and knowledge production in the field of school leadership. She has published twenty books, including: *An intellectual history of school leadership practice and research* (2016); *Consultants and consultancy: the case of education,* co-authored with Colin Mills (2017); and *The politics of public education* (2018).

David Hall is Professor of Education Policy and Head of the Graduate School of Education at the University of Exeter, UK. His research has principally focused upon large-scale, public-sector reform and its re-contextualization within educational institutions and by educational practitioners. David's research has been funded by organizations including the Economic and Social Research Council, the Department for Education and the EU, and has been published in a range of international journals and books.

Amanda Heffernan is a Lecturer in Leadership in the Faculty of Education at Monash University in Melbourne, Australia. In 2019, she was awarded the Hedley Beare Award for Educational Writing from the Australian Council for Educational Leaders, for an outstanding piece of educational leadership writing that has made a significant contribution to the field. Her work takes a critical perspective towards school leadership, education policy, and the everyday experiences of educational leaders' work. Her book, *The principal and school improvement: theorising discourse, policy, and practice*, was published in 2018.

Jan Heystek is Professor in Education Leadership, and Governance and Research Director of the research entity of Edu-Lead (education leadership), at the Faculty of Education at the North-West University, South Africa. His work focuses on leadership in schools and specifically in school improvement in deprived schools in low socio-economic contexts in South Africa. The most recent outputs have been published electronically in 2019: Chingara and Heystek 'Leadership as agency in the context of structure' in *International Journal of Educational Management*; and Du Plessis and Heystek 'The emergence of decentralised-centralism in the South African education governance system' in *Journal of Southern African Studies* (JASAS).

Sonya Douglass Horsford is Associate Professor of Education Leadership in the Department of Organization and Leadership at Teachers College, Columbia University, United States. Her work focuses on the politics of race, education policy and urban school leadership and has been published in *Educational Administration Quarterly*, *Educational Policy*, *Teachers College Record*, *Urban Education* and *The Urban Review*. She is editor of three books and author of *Learning in a burning house: educational inequality, ideology, and (dis)integration* (2011) and *The politics of education policy in an era of inequality: possibilities for democratic schooling* (2019) with Janelle Scott and Gary Anderson.

Steven Jones is Professor of Higher Education in the Manchester Institute of Education at the University of Manchester, UK. He conducts research into policy and practice in post-compulsory education, and has co-authored reports for the Sutton Trust, the Joseph Rowntree Foundation and HEFCE that explore how socially disadvantaged young people conceptualize, engage with and perform at university. He is particularly interested in how students' cultural and social capital affect their HE experiences. He has presented research findings to Universities UK, HM Treasury, the ASCL and the Sunday Times Festival of Education, and given evidence to the All-Party Parliamentary University Group in the House of Commons.

Catherine A. Lugg is Professor of Education at Rutgers, the State University of New Jersey, United States. She researches the relationship between social movements, political ideology, history and educational politics and policy. She has written three books, including *Kitsch: from education to public policy* (1999), and *US public schools and the politics of queer erasure* (2016). Honours include: Paul S. Silver Award (outstanding article in the *Journal of Cases in Educational Leadership*, with Tooms-Cypres), Scholar-Activist Award (AERA-Queer Studies SIG), William J. Davis Award (outstanding article in *Educational Administration Quarterly*, with Tooms-Cypres and Bogotch) and the Jay D. Scribner Mentoring Award.

Katrina MacDonald is Post-Doctoral Research Fellow at the Research for Educational Impact Research Centre at Deakin University, Australia. Her research and teaching interests are in educational leadership, social justice and the sociology of education. She has recently completed her doctoral study examining the social-justice understandings and practices of principals working in some of the most disadvantaged locations in Australia. She is a former anthropologist, archaeologist and primary and secondary teacher in Victoria, Australia.

Ruth McGinity is Lecturer in Educational Leadership and Policy at UCL Institute of Education, University College London, UK. Through a critical sociological approach, her research considers the ways in which policy and leadership interact in educational sites, and the extent to which theories of power and identity can help make sense of professional practice during periods of rapid and intense reform. Ruth is part of a research team at UCL IOE to be awarded £296,943 from the Nuffield Foundation for a project investing the competitive effects of free schools in England on student outcomes in neighbouring schools, commencing in 2020.

Glenda McGregor is Senior Lecturer in the School of Education and Professional Studies at Griffith University, Australia. She has been a Chief Investigator on Australian Research Council grants and government consultancies. Her research focuses on educational (re)engagement, schooling reform and social justice. In 2019 she was appointed Honorary Associate Professor, University College London, Institute of Education and was a founding board member of the Australian Association for Flexible & Inclusive Education. Her work is exemplified in her book: McGregor, Mills, te Riele, Baroutsis and Hayes, *Re-imagining schooling for education: socially just alternatives* (2017).

Rachel McNae is Associate Professor and Director of the Centre for Educational Leadership Research at the University of Waikato, New Zealand, and is National President of NZEALs. In 2015, she received the Meritorious Service Award for service to leadership and the New Zealand Education Administration and Leadership Society Presidential Research Award. In 2016, she received the International Emerald-European Foundation for Management and Development Outstanding Research Award for Leadership and Strategy, and in 2018, she was appointed as New Zealand Educational Leadership Society Visiting Scholar. Recently published books include *Educational leadership for social justice in Aotearoa New Zealand* (2017).

Alexander J. Means is Assistant Professor of Educational Policy with Global Perspectives, and Graduate Chair in the Department of Educational Foundations, at the University of Hawai'i at Mānoa, United States. He is the author of *Learning to save the future: rethinking education and work in the era digital capitalism* (2018); *Educational commons in theory and practice: global pedagogy and politics* (2017); and co-editor with Kenneth Saltman of *The Wiley handbook of global education reform* (2018). His research examines educational policy and organization in relation to political, economic, cultural and social change.

Martin Mills is Professor and the Director of the Centre for Teachers and Teaching Research at UCL Institute of Education, University College London, UK. He is a Fellow of the Academy of Social Sciences Australia and a former President of the Australian Association for Research in Education. He researches in areas related to social justice and education, with a particular focus on leadership, teachers' work, alternative education, school systems and gender. Recent books include *Autonomy, accountability and social justice: stories of English schooling* (with Amanda Keddie, 2019) and *Alternative education: international perspectives on policy and practice* (with Gillean McCluskey, 2018).

Jorunn Møller is Professor Emerita in the Department of Teacher Education and School Research at University of Oslo, Norway. Her professional interests are in the areas of educational leadership and governance, reform policies and school accountability. She has been a manager of several research projects examining the enactment of school reform and accountability, the interplay of legal standards and professional discretion in schools, successful school leadership and leadership identities in a Norwegian context and across countries.

Pontso Moorosi is Associate Professor of Educational Leadership and Management in the Centre for Education Studies at the University of Warwick, UK. She is also a research associate at the University of Johannesburg, South Africa, and a rated researcher by the National Research Foundation of South Africa. Her research interests include: gender in educational leadership, school leadership preparation and development, and leader identity development, with a specific focus on the African continent. Her most recent book is: *Preparation and development of school leaders in Africa* (2020), co-edited with Tony Bush.

Richard Niesche is Associate Professor in the School of Education at the University of New South Wales, Australia. His research interests include educational leadership, the principalship and social justice. His research focus is on the use of critical perspectives in educational leadership. In particular, he examines the work of school principals in disadvantaged schools and how they can work towards achieving more socially just outcomes. He has published his research in a number of books and peer-reviewed journals and he is also the founding co-editor of the 'Educational Leadership Theory' book series. His latest book is *Social, critical and political theories for educational leadership* (2019).

Anar Purvee has recently completed her doctoral study at Monash University, Australia, examining women and academic leadership in Mongolian public and private universities. She is a former lecturer of business management in Mongolia. She is the recipient of the National Taiwan University of Science and Technology's International Graduate Student Scholarship, and Monash University's Monash Graduate Scholarship and a Monash International Postgraduate Research Scholarship. Her research interests include leadership, innovation, marketing communications, green marketing, educational leadership and gender studies.

Augusto (Gus) Riveros is Associate Professor of Education Policy in the Faculty of Education at Western University in Ontario, Canada. His current research, supported by the Social Sciences and Humanities Research Council of Canada (SSHRC), examines the provision, availability and access to public education in the context of urban development. Prior to this work, he investigated theoretical issues in educational administration and leadership, and researched the adoption of education leadership standards by school administrators. His work has appeared in edited books and journals, including, the *International Journal of Leadership in Education, Educational Philosophy and Theory* and the *Journal of Educational Administration.*

Linda Rönnberg is Professor at the Department of Applied Educational Science at Umeå University, Sweden. She is also a Senior Research Fellow in the Department of Education at the University of Turku, Finland. With a disciplinary background in Political Science (PhD and Docent) she researches education governance and politics, with a particular focus on evaluation, privatization and internationalization in compulsory and higher education. Recent books include the co-edited volume *The governing-evaluation-knowledge nexus: Swedish higher education as a case* (2019) and the co-authored Swedish book *Skolpolitik (Politics of education)* (2019).

Robin Roscigno is a PhD candidate in the department of Education Theory, Policy and Organization at Rutgers Graduate School of Education, United States Her dissertation project uses a historical-sociological approach to study early behaviourism and the subsequent rise of behaviourism as a technology of social control, particularly as it relates to schooling for disabled children.

Zulfa Sakhiyya is Assistant Professor and Director of the Literacy Research Centre at Universitas Negeri Semarang (State University of Semarang), Indonesia. She is a

Fellow at the Centre for Innovation, Policy and Governance, assessing the Indonesian social-science research system funded by the Global Development Network. She was a Research Fellow at Universities in Knowledge Economy, investigating the relationship between universities and knowledge economies (European Commission funding). Zulfa is a discourse analyst with a particular interest in educational policy, women's leadership and the cultural economy of knowledge. Her work has been published in journals such as *Gender and Education, Globalisation, Societies and Education* and *Pedagogy, Culture & Society*.

Kenneth Saltman is Professor of Educational Policy Studies at University of Illinois at Chicago. He is the author most recently of *The swindle of innovative educational finance* (2018), *The politics of education* (2nd edn, 2018), *Scripted bodies: corporate power, smart technologies, and the undoing of public education* (2016) and co-editor with Alexander Means of *The Wiley handbook of global education reform* (2018).

Victoria Showunmi is Lecturer at UCL Institute of Education, University College London, UK. Her research interests are gender, class, identity and race, through which she interrupts educational leadership and gender politics. She is an associate editor for *Equality, Diversity and Inclusion* journal, Conference Chair for BELMAS and one of two International Scholars to be elected to the Special Interest Groups (SIG) Executive Committee as Member-at-Large for the American Educational Research Association (AERA). She is Programme Chair for the International Studies SIG, on the Executive Council for GEA (Gender Education Association), and the deputy convener for the ECER GENDER Network.

John Smyth is Visiting Professor of Education and Social Justice in the Huddersfield Centre for Research in Education and Society (HUDCRES) at the University of Huddersfield, UK. He is Emeritus Research Professor of Education at the Federation University, Australia, Emeritus Professor of Education at Flinders University, Australia, author of thirty-five books, a former Senior Fulbright Research Scholar, the recipient of two research awards from the American Educational Research Association, and an elected Fellow of the Academy of the Social Sciences in Australia. His most recent book is *The toxic university: zombie leadership, academic rock stars and neoliberal ideology* (2017). His research interests are in critical policy sociology.

Pat Thomson is Professor of Education in the School of Education at the University of Nottingham, UK. She is a Fellow of the Academy of Social Sciences (UK) and the Royal Society for the Arts (UK) and was awarded the Australian Public Service Medal in 1990 for outstanding services to education. She researches creativity and the arts, and school and community change. She has published twenty-five scholarly monographs and edited books: the latest is *Schooling scandals: blowing the whistle on the corruption of the education system* (2020). Her academic writing and *research blog, patter*, is patthomson.net.

Tina Trujillo is Associate Professor at University of California, Berkeley's Graduate School of Education, United States, where she has taught doctoral students in educational policy and politics and prepared school principals and superintendents for equity-oriented leadership. Tina uses tools from political science and critical policy studies to study federal and state education policy, the politics of school reform, and democratic education. Her work is published in a range of journals, and she is the co-editor of *Learning from the federal market-based reforms: lessons for the every student succeeds act (ESSA)* (2016, with Mathis).

Ting Wang is Professor of Educational Leadership and Associate Dean of the Faculty of Education at the University of Canberra, Australia. She is a member of the Board of the Australian Capital Territory Teacher Quality Institute. She is affiliated with Beijing Normal University as a Distinguished Adjunct Professor and High-End Foreign Expert awarded by the State Administration of Foreign Experts Affairs, China. Her work focuses on educational leadership development in cross-cultural settings, school leadership and professional learning communities, international education and comparative education. Her most recent book is: *Global perspectives on developing professional learning communities* (2018).

Andrew Wilkins is Reader in Education at Goldsmiths, University of London, UK. He writes about education policy and governance with a focus on risk, experts, networks, citizenship and statecraft. His recent books include *Modernising school governance* (2016) and *Education governance and social theory* (2018).

Jane Wilkinson is Professor of Educational Leadership in the Faculty of Education at Monash University, Australia. She is Victorian Fellow of the Australian Council for Educational Leaders. Her work examines issues of social justice and diversity through an educational leadership lens. Her most recent books are: *Educational leadership as a culturally-constructed practice: new directions and possibilities* (with Bristol, 2018); *Refugee background students transitioning into higher education: navigating complex spaces* (with Naidoo, Adoniou and Langat, 2018); and *Challenges for public education: reconceptualising educational leadership, policy and social justice as resources for hope* (with Niesche and Eacott, 2019).

Howard Youngs is Senior Lecturer and Director of International Development in the School of Education at Auckland University of Technology, New Zealand. He works at the junction of leadership practice, research, learning and thinking with students he supervises and educational leadership courses he teaches at and in places outside of the university. These outside places include a group of Auckland schools he has been working with since 2015, as well as managers and teachers in Asian countries such as Thailand and Vietnam. He has published in the major field journals, where he specializes in distributed leadership.

Kai Yu is Professor of Education and Public Policy in the Faculty of Education at Beijing Normal University, China. At present he serves as Vice-Chairman of China Educational Administration Society. Among other works, he is the author of *Implementation of inclusive education in Beijing: exorcizing the haunting specter of meritocracy* (2014) and *School culture development in China: perceptions of teachers and principals* (2014), as well as numerous articles, book chapters and monographs on education and public policy, school improvement and evaluation studies.

Foreword

Understanding educational leadership and conceiving of methods, models and approaches that adopt *critical perspectives and approaches* to a taken-for-granted topic like 'leadership' is something that necessarily involves a deal of courage and a willingness to endure discomfort. As Mary Beard, professor of classics and fellow of Newnham College, Cambridge University put it – this is really the central role of an academic – to 'make issues more complicated' and 'make everything less simple' (Williams, 2016). We might add to this the notion that the kind of 'searching mind' necessary for this criticalist disposition requires a proclivity towards such epithets as being 'outspoken, subversive, controversial, [and being] dangerous' (Williams, 2016). That is what this textbook is all about!

It is important to say at the outset that the qualities of being critical are not ones that are normally encapsulated in the common understanding of educational leadership. The overwhelming problem with prevailing mainstream views of educational leadership is that they are basically spineless – that is to say, they are more concerned with conformity to the dominant (i.e. 'marketized') ideology of the way educational organizations are increasingly being constituted, and lack the courage to 'stay apart from the crowd', as ecologist Joseph Fail, Jr., so delightfully put it (Fail, 2016) and challenge entrenched orthodoxies. This notion of 'standing apart' points to the very essence of what it means to adopt a critical perspective, as Robert Cox put it:

> It is critical in the sense that it stands apart from the prevailing order of the world and asks how that order came to be . . . [U]nlike problem-solving [approaches, it] does not take institutions and social power relations for granted but calls them into question by concerning itself with their origins and whether they might be in the process of changing.
> *(Cox, 1981: 129)*

To carry Cox's idea forward in how it might be applied to educational leadership, I have argued (Smyth, 2016) that critical educational leadership required stepping out in four distinctly important and interrelated ways. First, it requires adopting a highly sceptical view of the current fetish that would have us construct educational organizations as if they are unfettered marketplaces for educational consumption and choice. Reality is that talents, structures, opportunities and so-called 'choice' are not distributed in ways that enable equity of access in educational institutions – and leadership needs to have the courage to admit this and act accordingly. Second, and emerging from this, is a preparedness to openly challenge and confront the notion that educational institutions, as they exist, overwhelmingly act to advantage the already advantaged. In other words, critical leadership requires the cultivation of a disposition to stand up for something, in the sense of not accepting inequities as if they were natural, but rather seeing them as being constructed, sustained and maintained. Third, critical leadership envisages and works within local circumstances – meaning, young people, their families, culture, backgrounds and communities and their aspirations for meaningful futures – but within a frame that is highly cognizant of and attentive to the workings of larger social, economic and political forces, and the way they produce distortions and deformities. Fourth, and finally, critical educational leadership is committed to confronting all forms of authoritarianism, and supplanting them with more democratic educational experiences. In this sense, critical educational leadership sees its project as being deeply moral as well a democratic and political project. It does this in the way it fires the imagination of young people (Smyth, 2005: 101) around the 'big' issues and questions that affect their lives and futures. After all, education is fundamentally about relationships, and critical educational leadership is passionate about the way it creates and reshapes educative relationships.

All of this is by way of saying that we have some significant issues that have to be struggled against. In reviewing the agenda confronting the field of educational administration and leadership, Gunter and Fitzgerald put it most aptly when they said that both of these constitute 'a site of struggle over major issues of our time, particularly the tensions between agency of individuals and the structuring contexts in which we engage in professional practice' (2017: 192). So, what are some of the troublesome issues that have to be confronted in educational leadership?

In a piece I wrote recently, I identified five candidates, in respect of educational leadership, that are in desperate need of treatment from a critical perspective – namely:

- a pervasive detachment of leadership from an understanding of the work;
- an unhealthy pre-occupation with deliverability, targets and outcomes;
- a heroic belief that educational productivity can be 'managed' into existence;
- the ruthless pursuit of competitive individualism, at all costs;
- the blatant and dishonest disregard for authenticity that comes with the focus on securing 'market share' through organizational deception, image, brand and impression management. *(Smyth, 2018a: 33)*

All of these represent pathologies and distortions that have been allowed to infiltrate and infect educational institutions under the rubric of the neoliberal tendencies of 'the market'. In the first of my instances, there has been a violent rendering of the work of educational leaders from Indigenous understandings of the educational contexts they are supposed to be leading. To put this another way, there has been a complete detachment of what leaders are required to do, that has severed them from making professional judgements about what is in the best interests of those they purportedly lead (see for example, Smyth, 2017). This can be seen most glaringly, as I put it in my second instance above, in the substitution of authentic leadership by facsimiles such as meeting imposed performance targets, outcomes and deliverables – all in the supposed interest of enhancing international economic competitiveness. It hardly needs to be said, but none of these are features that are indigenous to educational organizations – on the contrary, they are alien, hostile imposters that run counter to the relational norms of educational places. Coupled with these unhelpful, and indeed unhealthy, preoccupations, is my third example – the leadership fantasy – some might call it a 'heroic belief' – that by some magical means, so-called 'educational productivity' can be 'managed' into existence. Quite how this hands-off process of levitation is to occur within a context of such massive leadership detachment is truly mind-boggling! The fourth, and equally fanciful but frequently proclaimed leadership fantasy, is the constantly uttered refrain that everything will fall neatly into place if only we abandon our educational instincts and engage in some form of educational Olympic Games that involves out-competing each other. What we are being urged to do here is to abandon the *raison d'être* of educational organizations – pursuing forms of democratic collaboration and collegiality – and replace these with synthetic forms that constitute an ungainly scramble in a race to the top. Finally, as if all this unreality is not enough, this entire fake edifice is to be artificially held in place by marketing hype about out-competing others through deploying deceptive tactics that have even been eschewed by used car dealers. I mean, really. . .!

The take-up message in all of this, as Gunter and Fitzgerald put it, lies in the imperative 'to relentlessly confront how and why criticality matters' (2017: 194). In other words, we need to be continually interrupting and disrupting 'ideas and evidence that enable totalitarian tendencies', so they become 'disputed, resisted and replaced' (2017: 194).

Critical leadership, therefore, derives its potency from what Paulo Freire referred to as 'the pedagogy of the question' (Bruss and Macedo, 1985: 7) or problem posing – something qualitatively different from problem-solving. The kind of questions that need to be posed to unmask how power works in order to puncture the social structures that support it lie in the kind of manifesto I proposed recently for educational leaders in schools (Smyth, 2018b) – but these might easily be reworked for any other kind of educational institution. They were questions designed to cast educational leaders as activist players in their institutions rather than passive and compliant recipients of other people's directives – questions like:

- Whose interests are being served by schooling?
- Who says schools need to be organized in this way, and what is their agenda?
- Who is being advantaged by the way schools are currently being structured and organized, and who is being excluded or left behind?
- How might this school be organized in a way to ensure that those who are the least welcome (generally taken to mean the 'most disadvantaged'), are made to feel the most welcome? What would have to occur for that to happen? What would be the obstacles and impediments? What would be the benefits?
- Who gets to speak in this school and whose voices are silenced? Whose voices are dominant, and whose are drowned out?
- Who exercises leadership in this school? When, and in respect of what? Is leadership solely invested in those who have status and high office in the school, or can it genuinely come from anywhere? Is this important? Why? And under what conditions?

- How meaningful are community relationships in this school? Are they mutually beneficial? How does the school regard its community as a resource? What does the community in turn gain from this relationship?

- How is this school positively fostering qualities like honesty, directness, authenticity, dignity, practicality, immediacy, attachment, solidarity and sense of history, while seeking to minimize the amount of self-blaming?

- How is this school connecting its students, teachers and parents with global issues? How are these global issues being worked out locally?

- How are democratic ideals being worked out and lived in an exemplary way in this school?

- How does this school take a courageous stand? On what? With what effect?

These are indicative of the genre of questions likely to animate the contributors to this volume, as they seek to position educational leadership in ways that reveal and explain the power structures and relations immanent in educational leadership and leading.

John Smyth

References

Bruss, N. and Macedo, D. (1985) Toward a pedagogy of the question: conversations with Paulo Freire. *Journal of Education*, 167(2), 7–21.

Cox, R.W. (1981) Social forces, states and world orders: Beyond international relations theory. *Millennium: Journal of International Studies*, 10(2), 126–155.

Fail, J. (2016) *Joseph Fail, Jr.* The Ecological Society of America's history and records. Available online: https://esa.org/history/fail-joseph/ (accessed 30 January 2018).

Gunter, H.M. and Fitzgerald, T. (2017) Educational administration and history part 1: reviewing the agenda. *Journal of Educational Administration and History*, 49(3), 187–195.

Smyth, J. (2005) Standards for critical inquiry. In: S.P. Gordon (ed.), *Standards for instructional supervision: enhancing teaching and learning* (pp. 91–105). Larchmont, NY: Eye on Education Publishers.

Smyth, J. (2016) Critical perspectives on educational leadership in the context of the march of neoliberalism. In: E.A. Samier (ed.), *Ideologies in educational administration and leadership* (pp. 147–158). Abingdon: Routledge.

Smyth, J. (2017) *The toxic university: zombie leadership, academic rock stars, and neoliberal ideology*. London: Palgrave Macmillan.

Smyth, J. (2018a) A critical theory analysis of the production of toxic and zombie leadership in the context of neoliberalism. In: E.A. Samier and P. Milley (eds), *Maladministration in education: theories, research and critiques* (pp. 33–47). Abingdon: Routledge.

Smyth, J. (2018b) A socially critical approach to community engagement: a matter of professional ethics. In: R.S. Webster and J.D. Whelen (eds), *Rethinking reflection and ethics for professional educators* (pp. 179–191). Singapore: Springer.

Williams, Z. (2016) Mary Beard: 'The role of the academic is to make everything less simple'. *The Guardian*. 23 April 2016. Available online: https://www.theguardian.com/books/2016/apr/23/mary-beard-the-role-of-the-academic-is-to-make-everything-less-simple (accessed 12 December 2017).

Introduction

Taking critical perspectives and using critical approaches in educational leadership

Steven J. Courtney, Helen M. Gunter,
Richard Niesche and Tina Trujillo

Welcome to our textbook!	2
Functionalist approaches to educational leadership	2
Taking a critical approach to educational leadership	4
Introducing the editors	6
References	10

Welcome to our textbook!

This is not just another textbook about educational leadership. This one is different because it presents and encourages thinking and analyses that are located in the critical part of the field. But what do we mean by this? Critical has many meanings that you may have come across in academic writing: for instance, when you engage critically with your sources, you evaluate and question them; when you are critical of someone's argument or approach, then it means that you have identified problems with it. We are using the word critical to mean a particular way of thinking about, and undertaking research activities connected to, concepts and practices such as 'educational leadership'. In this introductory chapter, we will explain what we mean by this 'particular way', as well as why we think that using critical approaches is vital to understanding and explaining educational leadership. In order to do that, we need to characterize scholarship within the field that is not from a critical perspective, in other words *functionalist* scholarship, so that you can be clear about why this textbook is different and necessary.

In this chapter we also want to tell you a little about who we are, because as we'll point out in more detail later on, *taking a critical perspective* means recognizing that we – our histories, dispositions and motives as authors and researchers – are integral to the analysis and arguments that we want to make. Knowing more about who we are enables you as a reader to understand why we think as we do, and so make a judgement about how credible our arguments are.

Functionalist approaches to educational leadership

Most research and writing that is done on and about educational leadership is in the school effectiveness and school improvement tradition, and can be called functionalist. This research has a number of characteristics, which we will sketch out immediately below. For a more detailed description and analysis, please read Chapter 10 of this textbook.

Functionalist research and writing is often normative: it not only describes, but often also endorses particular leadership models, practices or concepts. It is rarely overtly theoretical or theorized: it gains its legitimacy instead from its explicitly atheoretical framing that is based on a what-works approach (see Trujillo, 2013). More nuanced questions of what works when, for whom and at whose expense are rarely addressed. There is seldom any explicit theorization of power. Functionalist research tends to assume that leadership exists and that increasing, enhancing or expanding it would constitute an educational, organizational, or even societal, good. However, functionalist conceptualizations of educational leadership mostly equate it with normalized positional authority, where in most cases, the principal or headteacher (of a school) or the vice-chancellor or president (of a university) is the object of analysis and constructed as the key agent in institutional functioning and improvement. The mechanism for such improvement is presently compulsorily through the leader's vision. This concept is invoked in order to conjure a mechanism whereby the leader influences motivated followers to agentically buy into his or her compelling and unique vision, but this invocation disguises the true mechanism of high-accountability authority, in which subordinates are compelled to obey for fear of hierarchically enabled sanctions (Courtney and Gunter, 2015).

Functionalist research largely relies on a positivist framing of reality, where there exists an objective reality even to abstract concepts such as leadership, and that a reasonable and feasible goal of research is to quantify and measure this leadership. Key concerns in the functionalist literature are therefore effective and efficient educational leadership, both of which require measurement. These concerns position educational leadership as a policy science, where the main approach is to establish causal links as well as any slippage between intention and the reality of practice. Identifying effectiveness involves the measurement of what are agreed or assumed to be the outcomes and/or outputs of leadership, and identifying efficiency means measuring what are deemed to be constituent features, or inputs. In this functionalist framing of inputs and outputs, educational leadership is instrumentalized: it is intended to achieve specific goals – in schools, these are largely assumed to concern raising children's attainment in national examinations. In universities, these goals may concern notions such as employability or graduate economic status.

As critical researchers, we argue that this quantifiable-output-based conceptualization of education is not primarily concerned with education, which is a much richer suite of cultural practices with diverse potential outcomes, not all of which are measurable. Functionalist research is therefore susceptible to capture by other framings that share its instrumentalism, notably corporatization and privatization (see Courtney, McGinity and Gunter, 2017). Functionalist research is also often universalized: what is effective in England is promoted as being potentially effective in China. This may be achieved through the construction, commodification and international consumption of decontextualized models such as Transformational or Distributed Leadership.

Finally, functionalist research depicts reality as being potentially ideal, but with present dysfunctions: the purpose of functionalist research is to identify and address these dysfunctions (Gunter, 2016). Consequently, functionalist researchers may ask what the barriers are to, for example, inclusive leadership or to more women gaining leadership roles. These questions illuminate some of the reasons why functionalist research dominates the field: they are, on the face of it, important questions that many societies struggle with, and the normative, decontextualized functionalist framing means that the solutions offered through such research are often seen as being amenable to being turned into policy.

Our contention, and the reason for this book, is that functionalist research does not and cannot address educational purposes and practices, and the relationship with leadership, in educational contexts and in society more widely. Following Whitty, we note the importance of Grace's call for critical scholarship in order to generate 'complex hope' rather accept 'the "simple hope" of the school improvement lobby' (2002: 16). The solutions that such functionalism offers are based on inaccurate assumptions about how the world works, and so they are not as useful as they might at first appear (Thrupp, 2001). Indeed, as Gharabaghi and Anderson-Nathe note, 'as much as one tries to expand the conversation, the research keeps reinforcing existing ideas, so much so that before long, these ideas become "truths" of their own' (2017: 95).

This collection of contributions from authors around the world provides an alternative, critical way of looking not only at educational leadership, but also at how social actors in educational settings actually interact, communicate, get others to act on their behalf, put power relations to work and embody these in power-laden identities. As thinkers and practitioners in educational leadership, we need critical tools to help us think about and work in this field, tools including theories and conceptual frameworks – and in this book there is lots of guidance to help here (see, for example, Chapter 10).

But more than this, we intend through this textbook to present a variety of critical perspectives of the social world that prompt you to think about how it both has produced and reflects diverse conditions or features, understood as problems, that apparently require educational leaders to solve them. We use critical approaches to help you understand what it means to be called an educational leader, to accept that label, to undertake professional practice that is understood to align with that label, and for all that to differ depending on geographical, historical, political and social context. But what exactly do we mean by taking a critical perspective? What is a critical approach?

Taking a critical approach to educational leadership

There is no single interpretation of what it means to take a critical approach. Indeed, our primary motivation for locating Part One of this book in different parts of the world is precisely to demonstrate the range of interpretations possible. Nevertheless, there are some common themes and principles that we can bring to your attention.

We undertake this task partly in the context of what critical approaches are *not*. There is a common misunderstanding that being critical is analogous to engaging in critique, that the aim of critical research is to criticize the status quo, or to criticize proposed arrangements or policies. In other words, the goal is the critique itself. This is not the case. Over the next few paragraphs, we will show how we follow Smyth's (1989) definition of critical scholarship, drawing on it both to structure and establish what we mean by being critical and to argue for the impossibility of its reduction to mere critique.

Smyth set out three constituent elements of critical scholarship in the introduction to his landmark 1989 edited collection, *Critical perspectives on educational leadership*. First, critical approaches *take context seriously*. Knowledge about how humans engage with one another can never produce or be synthesized into universal, immutable laws, and neither can a straight line between social cause and its distal effect on other humans or their institutions ever be drawn, much less extrapolated to other social circumstances and used for prediction in individual cases. This means that all social knowledge is located in particular historical moments and geographical places with particular ideological, cultural and political features. Some forms of knowledge may travel more easily than others, drawing perhaps on common histories or dispositions (Whitty, 2016) or shared dominant ideologies or discursive resources, or influenced by supranational organizations (Verger, 2016; Saltman and Means, 2019). This situatedness is not a limitation in knowledge production to be overcome, but a core feature to be fully recognized and engaged with. Critical scholarship is therefore assiduous in making clear both what the context of the research is and in explaining and/or theorizing what it means for the analysis. The context may be political and ideological, as is the case for a range of outputs whose authors locate them in neoliberal times (e.g. Baldridge, 2014; Niesche and Thomson, 2017; Gunter et al., 2019), or new dark times (Hughes, Courtney and Gunter, 2020). Or the context may be geographical (see e.g. Chapters 2 to 9 in this collection), where a case for wider relevance must be made and cannot be assumed.

Second, for Smyth (1989) and for us, critical approaches deal fundamentally with *power*. Critical research is therefore concerned with how power might be described, explained and theorized, and so critical researchers use a range of thinking tools to help achieve that (e.g. Niesche, 2011; Niesche and Keddie, 2016). Such thinking tools are located in the social sciences, where the approach of educational leadership as a field is to draw on disciplinary resources from history (e.g. Gunter, 2016); sociology (e.g. Grace, 1995); and politics (e.g. Gunter, 2018) in order to provide understanding and explanations. This interplay with the social sciences distinguishes critical from functionalist research. The critical focus on power comes from a recognition that human beings, including teachers, students and leaders, cannot do as they please, but are enabled or constrained by the matrix of power relations within which they live and work, and in which they are positioned by others and position themselves. In other words, what we do, think, believe, value and embody is the result of a complex interplay of agency – crudely, our actions – and of structure – or the social constraints or enablers of our actions. Crucially, agency and structure cannot be thought about without an explicit theorization of power. To do so is to reduce agency to behaviours, traits or sometimes qualities – a reasonably common feature of functionalist research on educational leadership (structure is largely absent in any form). This focus of much critical research on structure and agency is not reducible to a critique of functionalist approaches, but is evidence of its alternative grounding in post-positive epistemologies (including social constructionism and critical realism) and its willingness to engage in social theory to address important issues (Niesche, 2018; Courtney, McGinity and Gunter, 2017; Niesche and Gowlett, 2019).

Taking a critical perspective, the very use of the word or concept of leadership has a power function and does ideological work. A professional is granted enhanced agency through accepting the label of leader, and so has more power or, more likely, more *authority* within an organizational hierarchy to have his or her will enacted (see Heffernan, 2018). There are therefore good grounds not only to question how such terms are deployed and taken up to organize social actors in institutions (and importantly, to convince 'followers' that their subordinated position is normal), but to question the very existence of 'leadership' as an ontological reality (Eacott, 2015). This work goes beyond critique, however: critical scholars build on productively disrupted notions of leader, leading and leadership to suggest new forms (for example, Blackmore's 2011 elucidation of transformative leadership) and new conceptualizations of educational leader identities (e.g. Courtney and McGinity, 2020).

Functionalist research does not have the tools to do this work of fundamental, productive disruption and, indeed, has been charged with maintaining and reinforcing a harmful status quo, or enabling new forms of harm in education provision and practice (Gunter, 2014, 2018). Its sustained focus on effective and efficient forms of professional practice certainly did nothing to prevent the rise of first, managerialism, devoid of educational values (see Gunter, 2008; Trujillo, 2014), and second, of totalitarianism masquerading as leadership (Courtney and Gunter, 2015).

Smyth's (1989) third definitional feature of critical scholarship and research is *empowerment*. Here, the focus extends beyond the description and theorization of power to centre on how critical scholars and practitioners might mitigate the effects of inequitable power relations. Power works to marginalize and oppress, but also to superordinate individuals and groups of people. These effects of power will be experienced by professionals going about their work, as well as by the various groups of people involved in and/ or affected by education arrangements internationally, including parents and children. They might be located in or around, for example, schools, kindergartens or nurseries, and universities. Critical scholarship exceeds the caricature of critique by maintaining a powerful focus on improving the lot of the oppressed. There is a worked example of this in Chapter 23 of this textbook, which draws on Apple's (2013) nine key tasks for critical educators to create a plan for a specific educational dilemma in the interplay between the new turn to genetics-informed policy and the ways in which educational leaders might respond.

We have shown through our explanation of critical approaches both what they are and how they are vital in making sense of educational leadership in a way that goes beyond the superficial. This goes for practitioners of educational leadership, whether that be in a formal role in an educational institution or government department, or in a professional role that has ostensibly nothing to do with leadership. We intend this book also to be vital reading for those studying educational leadership at master's or doctoral level, and for those teaching it.

Introducing the editors

We want to introduce ourselves to you as thinkers, writers and researchers in this field, so that you can understand a little more about how our backgrounds and dispositions might have influenced our interest in and approaches to researching educational leadership. As we've written earlier in this Introduction, and following the critical tradition, we think this is important for how you engage with our arguments. We want also to establish our credentials with you, following the example of Carroll, Ford and Taylor (2019), who rightly argue that, as editors, we have a duty to set out why you should trust us to be authoritative in your study or practice of educational leadership.

Steven J. Courtney

I became deputy head of year 8 after a year of teaching in London, and head of Modern Foreign Languages after three. My school then signed me up for what was talked about there as a groundbreaking professional-development programme, called *Leading from the Middle*. It was a product of the National College for School Leadership, which I subsequently learned was intended to be the conduit for 'official' knowledge about school leadership (see Thrupp, 2005; Gunter, 2012; Courtney and Gunter, 2020). Still, at the time I drank eagerly from this cup of knowledge and finished the course well on my way to becoming a *believer*. After a year, I had been promoted to assistant headteacher elsewhere in London.

Moving to Manchester gave me an opportunity to study for an MA in educational leadership. I had anticipated returning to school senior leadership afterwards, but was utterly gripped by the intellectual challenge of the MA, particularly the new critical theories and approaches that I was engaging with and which were so strong at Manchester. For the first time, I was encouraged to grapple with fundamental ontological questions concerning educational leadership and leaders, rather than focusing on *delivery*, and what any answers might mean for the interplay between policy landscape, professional practice and identity. I couldn't resist applying for PhD funding. My doctorate was supervised by Helen Gunter, and focused on school leadership at a time of system diversity, competition and flux. I took up a lectureship at the University of Manchester three-quarters of the way through my doctorate, which won three best-dissertation awards from the United States and the UK. I am now a senior lecturer in Management and Leadership, and research coordinator at the Manchester Institute of Education, University of Manchester, have published widely and presented internationally, and am more fascinated than ever by educational leadership and leaders, as well as by leadership contexts and structural influences. In my research, I have explored privatization, sexual identity, inspection regimes and distinctive forms of provision as examples of these, and used theoretical tools drawn from Foucault, Bourdieu and Arendt. I am involved in this book because I have wanted to use something like this in my teaching, but it hasn't existed.

Helen M. Gunter

I was appointed as a probationary history and humanities teacher and head of A' level British Government and Politics in a comprehensive school in the north of England in 1980, and between 1987 and 1990 I undertook a part-time MSc in Educational Management. After the first lecture I was asking myself where the knowledge had come from, and why it did not seem to come from political studies or take a historical approach (my first degree is in modern history and politics), and did not seem to have anything to say about education – teaching, learning and assessment. We learned about the technologies of budgets and strategic planning, and to adopt the behaviourism of teams and human resource management, but we did not connect it to pedagogy. I moved into higher education where I lectured in educational management, and was not able to pursue my questions about field history until I moved to a research-based university where I was able to do a PhD. My doctoral project was an intellectual history of the field of educational management, and so I researched field outputs and I undertook narrative interviews with field leaders who had brought the field into higher education. I was awarded my PhD in 1999, and I became a professor at the University of Manchester in 2004 where I continued to research field development with a range of funded projects, books and journal articles.

My research continues to take a critical approach to researching and mapping the development of the field where I remain interested in knowledge production, and what it means to read, think and practise in ways that are critical. I am involved in this book because in the midst of my PhD I wrote my first peer-reviewed article (Gunter, 1995) that was then developed for a book (Gunter, 1997), where I asked questions about the research and conceptual resources available for the profession to use at a time of rapid reforms. Based on the *Jurassic Park* novel by Michael Crichton I coined the phrase 'Jurassic Management' to characterize how schools and universities were being turned into school-improvement-and-effectiveness theme parks based on functional approaches that would not work in their own terms.

However, it seems that 'Jurassic Management' is a resilient feature of popular approaches to leaders, leading and leadership, and I am involved in this book as we need to bring to the fore the critical approaches that allow educational professionals and researchers to think and practise differently. The field of educational leaders, leading and leadership is plural, and educational professionals should have access to the full range of ideas and projects that can support the intellectual practices necessary for decision-making.

Richard Niesche

After my first year of teaching music in 2001 in New South Wales, Australia, I moved with my wife to Brisbane, Queensland where she took up a position at the University of Queensland. I subsequently began teaching in Brisbane and also undertook a MEd (Leadership) part time I was teaching. During this study, I first became familiar with a range of critical scholarship in education and was increasingly disillusioned with a lot of the mainstream educational leadership writing and research. After encouragement from one of my lecturers I enrolled in a PhD, upon which I immersed myself in the work of Michel Foucault to explore educational leadership from a more critical perspective into the work of two white, female principals of Indigenous schools in Queensland, Australia.

Upon completing my PhD in 2008, I took up a position at Griffith University as Research Fellow working on two Australian Research Council Linkage Grants looking at mathematics education in remote Indigenous schools and communities. This then led to me working up to a University of Queensland Postdoctoral Research Fellowship examining socially just leadership in disadvantaged schools and contexts. At the end of this three-year fellowship I was fortunate to gain a position as senior lecturer in educational leadership at the University of New South Wales, Sydney where I have then held roles such as postgraduate coursework programme director and more recently deputy head of school (research). I have recently been promoted to associate professor and am continuing my research into critical perspectives in educational leadership, post-structuralism and social justice. During this time, I have published a range of journal articles, book chapters and books on these topics and issues. In 2016 and 2017 I designed and taught a master's course on critical perspectives in educational leadership that was very well received by students and always scored very highly on student satisfaction surveys. However, due to university course rationalization in 2018, any course that had fewer than twenty students was considered unsustainable and this course has been on hiatus ever since (neoliberalism at work in the academy!). Nevertheless, I do continue to include this critical research in the other courses I teach.

This book is extremely important to a field that has continued to marginalize and perceive critical scholarship as less relevant and important than instrumentalist accounts and I believe the edited collection will serve as a foundational text for many postgraduate course work and higher degree research programmes around the world. I feel incredibly privileged to be working with such esteemed colleagues on this exciting and valuable project.

Tina Trujillo

I started contemplating school leadership as an urban elementary school teacher in California, USA, and, later, as a principal coach. During each experience I observed school leaders navigate increasingly high-pressure policy environments when the state and then the federal government rolled out high-stakes testing and accountability regimes. Surveilling teachers' attention to 'the test', curriculum narrowing, public shaming of teachers whose students scored low, and subtle ways to game the test were commonplace in some schools, but not others. I was both disillusioned by what I witnessed and intrigued by it. Graduate studies helped me make sense of these phenomena.

When I earned a MA in Educational Foundations, Policy and Practice at the University of Colorado at Boulder, and a PhD in Urban Schooling at the University of California, Los Angeles, I felt I'd hit the scholarly jackpot. Brilliant mentors like Drs Margaret LeCompte, Kevin Welner, Jeannie Oakes, Robert Cooper and Heinrich Mintrop exposed to me theoretical frameworks and empirical explanations of how and why schools function as they do. I was absolutely captivated by matters of epistemology, paradigms, methodology and policy. Critical and interpretive frameworks and research helped answer many of my burning questions. They also helped me ask new ones.

In 2008 I joined the faculty of the University of California, Berkeley's Graduate School of Education. Since then, I've been researching, writing and teaching about the politics of urban educational reform, federal and state policy, and democratic education. I've taught PhD students in policy and politics, as well as EdD and MA students in educational leadership. Having both taught in UC Berkeley's Principal Leadership Institute and served as its Faculty Director, I had the privilege of thinking about which questions, theories and fields of research future school leaders must grapple with if they are committed to the profession and to the communities for whom they work. I continually found that connecting the scholarly dots among leadership, power, politics and ideology required sifting through countless sources of literature to piece together a coherent collection of critical, rigorous scholarship that I wanted for our students. This book solves that problem. I hope it will serve the field of critical leadership studies as a chief resource for intellectual and practical knowledge for years to come.

We wish you well in your critical journey, and hope that you have fun learning about educational leadership with this book.

References

Apple, M.W. (2013) *Can education change society?* New York: Routledge.

Baldridge, B.J. (2014) Relocating the deficit: reimagining Black youth in neoliberal times. *American Educational Research Journal*, 51(3), 440–472.

Blackmore, J. (2011) Leadership in pursuit of purpose: social, economic and political transformation. *Counterpoints*, 409, 21–36.

Carroll, B., Ford, J. and Taylor, S. (eds) (2019) *Leadership: contemporary critical perspectives 2.* London: Sage.

Courtney, S.J. and Gunter, H.M. (2015) 'Get off my bus!' School leaders, vision work and the elimination of teachers. *International Journal of Leadership in Education*, 18(4), 395–417.

Courtney, S.J. and Gunter, H.M. (2020) Corporatised fabrications: The methodological challenges of professional biographies at a time of neoliberalisation. In: J. Lynch, J. Rowlands, T. Gale and S. Parker (eds), *Practice methodologies in education research* (pp. 27–47). Abingdon: Routledge.

Courtney, S.J. and McGinity, R. (2020) Conceptualising constructions of educational-leader identity. In: A. Heffernan and R. Niesche (eds), *Theorising identity and subjectivity in educational leadership research* (pp. 8–23). Abingdon: Routledge.

Courtney, S.J., McGinity, R. and Gunter, H.M. (eds) (2017) *Educational leadership: theorising professional practice in neoliberal times.* Abingdon: Routledge.

Eacott, S. (2015) The (im)possibility of 'leadership'. In: *Educational leadership relationally: a theory and methodology for educational leadership, management and administration* (pp. 33–47). Rotterdam: Sense Publishers.

Gharabaghi, K. and Anderson-Nathe, B. (2017) The need for critical scholarship, *Child & Youth Services*, 38(2), 95–97.

Grace, G. (1995) *School leadership: beyond educational management, an essay in policy scholarship.* Abingdon: RoutledgeFalmer.

Gunter, H.M. (1995) Jurassic management: chaos theory and management development in educational institutions. *Journal of Educational Administration*, 33(4), 5–20.

Gunter, H.M. (1997) *Rethinking education: the consequences of Jurassic management.* London: Cassell.

Gunter, H.M. (2008) Policy and workforce reform in England. *Educational Management, Administration & Leadership*, 36(2), 253–270.

Gunter, H.M. (2012) *Leadership and the reform of education.* Bristol: Policy Press.

Gunter, H.M. (2014) *Educational leadership and Hannah Arendt.* Abingdon: Routledge.

Gunter, H.M. (2016) *An intellectual history of school leadership practice and research.* London: Bloomsbury.

Gunter, H.M. (2018) *The politics of public education: reform ideas and issues*. Bristol: Policy Press.

Gunter, H.M., Courtney, S.J., McGinity, R. and Hall, D. (2019) School principals in neoliberal times: a case of luxury leadership? In: K.J. Saltman, and A.J. Means (eds), *The Wiley handbook of global education reform* (pp. 103–130). Hoboken, NJ: Wiley.

Heffernan, A. (2018) *The principal and school improvement: theorising discourse, policy and practice*. Singapore: Springer.

Hughes, B.C., Courtney, S.J. and Gunter, H.M. (2020) Researching professional biographies of educational professionals in new dark times. *British Journal of Educational Studies*, 68(3), 275–293.

Niesche, R. (2011) *Foucault and educational leadership: disciplining the principal*. Abingdon: Routledge.

Niesche, R. (2018) Critical perspectives in educational leadership: a new theory turn? *Journal of Educational Administration and History*, 50(3), 145–158.

Niesche, R. and Gowlett, C. (2019) *Social, critical and political theories for educational leadership*. Singapore: Springer.

Niesche, R. and Keddie, A. (2016) *Leadership, ethics and schooling for social justice*. Abingdon: Routledge.

Niesche, R. and Thomson, P. (2017) Freedom to what ends? School autonomy in neoliberal times. In: D. Waite and I. Bogotch (eds), *The Wiley international handbook of educational leadership* (pp. 193–206). Hoboken, NJ: Wiley.

Saltman, K.J. and Means, A.J. (2018) Introduction: toward a transformational agenda for global education reform. In: K.J. Saltman and A.J. Means (eds), *The Wiley handbook of global educational reform* (pp. 1–10). Hoboken, NJ: Wiley.

Smyth, J. (ed.) (1989) *Critical perspectives on educational leadership*. Lewes: Falmer Press.

Thrupp, M. (2001) Sociological and political concerns about school effectiveness research: time for a new research agenda. *School Effectiveness and School Improvement*, 12(1), 7–40.

Thrupp, M. (2005) The National College for School Leadership: a critique. *Management in Education*, 19(2), 13–19.

Trujillo, T. (2013) The reincarnation of the effective schools research: rethinking the literature on district effectiveness. *Journal of Educational Administration*, 51(4), 426–452.

Trujillo, T. (2014) The modern cult of efficiency: intermediary organizations and the new scientific management. *Educational Policy*, 28(2), 207–232.

Verger, A. (2016) The global diffusion of education privatization: unpacking and theorizing policy adoption. In: K. Mundy, A. Green, B. Lingard and A. Verger (eds), *The handbook of global education policy* (pp. 64–80). Chichester: Wiley.

Whitty, G. (2002) *Making sense of education policy*. London: Paul Chapman.

Whitty, G. (2016) *Research and policy in education: evidence, ideology and impact*. London: UCL IOE Press.

Part one

Critical perspectives and approaches across the world

1 Critical perspectives in and approaches to
educational leadership in the United States
Tina Trujillo and Sonya Douglass Horsford   15

2 Critical perspectives in and approaches to
educational leadership in England
Ruth McGinity and Kay Fuller   29

3 Critical perspectives in and approaches to
educational leadership in Australia
Martin Mills and Glenda McGregor   45

4 Critical perspectives in and approaches to
educational leadership in South Africa
Pontso Moorosi and Jan Heystek   59

5 Critical perspectives in and approaches to
educational leadership in China
Ting Wang and Kai Yu   75

6 Critical perspectives in and approaches to
   educational leadership in Indonesia
   Zulfa Sakhiyya and Tanya Fitzgerald   91

7 Critical perspectives in and approaches to
   educational leadership in two Nordic countries
   Jorunn Møller and Linda Rönnberg   105

8 Critical perspectives in and approaches to
   educational leadership in Chile
   Alejandro Carrasco and Germán Fromm,
   with Helen M. Gunter   121

Critical perspectives in and approaches to educational leadership in the United States

Tina Trujillo and Sonya Douglass Horsford

1

What this chapter is about   16

Key questions that this chapter addresses   16

Introduction   16

Enduring legacies of effectiveness and efficiency in American educational leadership   18

Accountability, neoliberalism and the modern cult of efficiency: contemporary models of educational leadership in the United States   19

The emergence of critical thought in American educational leadership   21

Persistent methodological constraints in American educational leadership studies   23

Educational leadership programmes in the United States today: the predominance of 'what works' rhetoric and training   24

Foregrounding the multiple purposes of schools in critical educational leadership   26

Conclusion   27

Further reading   28

References   28

What this chapter is about

In this chapter, we begin by discussing the historical roots of educational leadership and administration in the United States, namely, the origins of the Scientific Management movement and its application to educational settings. We show how principles of efficiency and effectiveness have persisted as major drivers of American educational leadership, as well as the research conducted on it. We explain how the high-stakes testing and accountability movement, situated within larger neoliberal trends, has intensified school leaders' roles as managerial, market-oriented actors. We describe how critical research approaches have problematized the assumptions behind dominant models of educational leadership, as well as helped surface the theoretical and methodological limitations of studies that concentrate narrowly on effectiveness and efficiency. We also detail the evolution of critical scholarship and how it has unpacked the ways in which leaders' practices reproduce or challenge dominant power structures and ideologies. Finally, we scrutinize the assumptions about the purposes of education implicit in various leadership models by contrasting the dominant managerial model with democratic, social justice-oriented leadership.

Key questions that this chapter addresses

1 What are the historical and political roots of current educational leadership models in the United States?

2 How have managerial principles and practices that focus on efficiency and effectiveness persisted as major drivers of American educational leadership for more than a century?

3 How do critical research approaches to educational leadership in the United States complement and challenge the dominant approaches in the field?

4 How do critical research approaches contribute to understandings about school leaders' roles in reproducing or challenging oppressive power structures and ideologies?

5 What do critical perspectives reveal about the purposes of schooling that are implied by different educational leadership models?

Introduction

To assume a critical perspective on educational leadership in the United States requires scholars, students and practitioners to acknowledge the powerful influence that the business sector has had on educational administrators for more than a century. Indeed, the study of educational leadership in the United States has long been a highly technical, managerial one, aside from a recent, rapidly growing collection of critical inquiries about power, politics and ideology. These critical studies have expanded the knowledge base about school leaders' roles as political actors, their school contexts and the multiple, contested assumptions about leadership that have dominated the field for over a century.

American school leaders have been asked to avail themselves of capitalistic practices and values since at least the Scientific Management era, when in 1899 the Bethlehem Steel Company hired Frederick Winslow Taylor, a mechanical engineer, to evaluate the factory's performance and make recommendations for minimizing inefficiencies through frequent measurement, worker surveillance and presumably scientific data-based procedures. Taylor's approach, dubbed 'Scientific Management', was characterized largely by methods for reducing complex work into discrete, quantifiable tasks; regularly measuring outputs; exercising heavy-handed managerial control over employees; and appealing to workers' perceived economic self-interest through extrinsic forms of motivation.

Scientific Management was not relegated just to factories, however. Several societal conditions at the time of its inception created a conducive context for Scientific Management as a model for both private and public sectors. First, the Industrial Revolution was flourishing at the time, which meant that much of the public looked to the titans of commerce and industry as capitalist role models to be emulated. Second, America's muckraking journalists' accounts of political corruption, graft and other unethical practices in government and elsewhere precipitated widespread intolerance for inefficiency and great enthusiasm for seemingly fair, objective institutional reforms. Finally, growing xenophobic fears over how best to Americanize racially and ethnically diverse communities amid an influx of immigration spurred many reformers to turn to the schools as sites for preserving the social and economic order.

For school principals, superintendents and other educational administrators, Scientific Management's business principles and methods offered seemingly effective solutions to their perceived crises. From that point on, school leadership in the United States was framed largely as a managerial endeavour, and many of its researchers

Scientific Management: an organizational approach intended to maximize worker efficiency and productivity, minimize worker autonomy, simplify work tasks, control workers through extrinsic forms of motivation and clearly separate management from line workers.

Managerialism: an ideology that embraces a generic set of private-sector practices, values and goals, and that emphasizes accountability for measurable results. See Fitzgerald and Hall, Chapter 21, in this volume.

Positivist Research Approach: inquiry that focuses on measurable, observable behaviours, and that assumes researchers can accurately verify one single truth about a situation.

Critical Research Approach: inquiry that focuses on concepts of power, oppression and social contexts, and that aims to generate knowledge in the service of social, political or economic transformation.

Neoliberalism: a system of political, economic and cultural beliefs, norms and practices that favour free-market capitalism and a deregulated state role in the provision of public goods, like education.

Social Justice Leadership: a model of leadership that focuses on disrupting beliefs and structures that perpetuate inequity, that redistributes power in just ways, and that protects and promotes equal opportunity for underserved and minoritized populations.

Democratic Leadership: a model of leadership that emphasizes the common good, which frames education as a public, not private good, which prioritizes the needs of the collective, not just individuals, and that prepares citizens for civic participation and decision-making.

still follow suit. For the next several decades, educational leadership studies drew primarily on concepts from management theory. Today, some educational researchers continue to frame educational leadership studies with managerial concepts. Indeed, until recently, to study educational leadership in the United States has largely been to study management 'science'. Much of this research has tended to investigate the best ways for administrators to control, monitor and measure teachers' performance to maximize bureaucratic efficiency and effectiveness.

In summary, corporate influences on public education in the United States have existed for more than a century, and the legacies of Scientific Management are still pronounced in schools today. Until recently, research has largely reflected and often reinforced a managerial model of educational leadership.

Enduring legacies of effectiveness and efficiency in American educational leadership

By the late 1960s, national conversations about schools and leaders were shifting. America's civil rights movement was in full swing. The federal government had begun funding educational programmes intended to remedy the effects of poverty for low-income students. Issues of racial and socio-economic inequality were forefront in many policy-makers' and activists' minds. Then, in 1966, American sociologist James Coleman released his groundbreaking report, 'Equality of Educational Opportunity'. Using large-scale social-science survey data, the report demonstrated that schools did not account for students' outcomes nearly as much as was previously believed. Rather, students' family background, as well as the degree of racial and socio-economic integration of their school, was found to be the largest predictor of student performance.

The report set off a series of contentious national and local debates about whether and how the federal government should best support schools in socio-economically disad-vantaged communities. From a scholarly perspective, Coleman's analysis turned much of the research on educational administration on its head. If principals and other leaders did not influence student outcomes nearly as much as the public, policymakers or practitioners had thought, where did researchers go from there?

By the late 1970s, some researchers decided to react to Coleman's findings by investig-ating the correlates of effective schools for minoritized students and students from high-poverty backgrounds. Convinced that schools and their leaders could actually make a difference, these researchers conducted a series of studies that culminated in lists of the school features that were consistently associated with higher student performance. Top among these lists was usually 'strong instructional leadership'. Soon thereafter, the discourse about school improvement in the United States became, essentially, a discourse about the imperative of strong, effective instructional leadership (e.g. Hallinger and Heck, 1996; see Eacott and Niesche, Chapter 14 of this textbook, for a deeper exploration of instructional leadership).

Theoretically, however, these studies were eventually critiqued for their atheoretical nature. Scholars pointed to the lack of theory in their designs, and their overly simplified catalogues of leadership actions that were seen more as managerial checklists for school leaders than as rigorous, comprehensive explanations of how schools and their leaders functioned.

When these effectiveness studies did actually employ theory in their design, most of them relied on very technical-rational, positivist research approaches. Concepts from management theory and organizational theory drove the majority of these studies. While such approaches contributed partial knowledge about the technical dimensions of educational leadership, they did not yield more complex understandings about the political and ideological dimensions of educational leadership, despite its nature as a complex social phenomenon.

Although educational leadership studies in the United States eventually included the role of schools' contexts in their analyses, several critical scholars still found their examination of these social contexts to be fairly superficial. Many of the studies treated schools' contextual conditions as one mere variable in their equations. Much less common were inquiries that included in-depth, qualitative explorations of schools' racial, socio-economic, political or ideological contexts.

In this section, we have shown how effectiveness studies have continued as mainstream approaches to researching educational leadership. These effectiveness studies have been critiqued for their inadequate use of theory, simplistic description of how school leadership functions and insufficient inattention to schools' social contexts.

Accountability, neoliberalism and the modern cult of efficiency: contemporary models of educational leadership in the United States

In 1983, US President Reagan's Commission on Educational Excellence released its landmark report, *A Nation at Risk*. The report decried the alleged failings of America's public schools and the threats they posed to the country's global competitiveness. It claimed American civil rights programmes and policies were financially inefficient and ineffective, called for a shift in the nation's focus on equity to excellence, and insisted that policymakers deregulate public schools in exchange for holding them accountable for test results. While some states had already been experimenting with such testing and accountability policies, the report marked the beginning of a nationwide trend toward strict accountability for schools and, once again, an increased focus on educational efficiency and effectiveness. School leaders found themselves stuck squarely in the middle of this next phase of heightened business logic.

By the early 1990s, influential American school reformers could frequently be heard calling for the development of quantitative metrics to measure schools' outcomes. References to results-based accountability, a laser-like focus on outcomes and demands for excellence in achievement were regular refrains. Without such managerial approaches, the political messaging went, our schools would fail to adequately prop up the nation's economy. Schools, according to the rhetoric of the time, existed to promote individual students' success (as measured by test scores), which would equip them to freely compete in the workplace and maximize their individual capital accumulation. Public education was like business; it became framed as a scarce private good over which families should compete. Its leaders were framed as entrepreneurial agents responsible for marketing their schools, winning students, and maximizing students' productivity and individual gain. The era of neoliberalism had arrived.

Free-market, capitalist values and practices permeated schools, along with their administrators' and many Americans' notions of good leadership. These trends were and still are pronounced most in America's urban centres, where contextual challenges are most evident. In these spaces, schools tend to serve higher proportions of immigrant students, English Learners, children of colour and children from high-poverty backgrounds.

Thus, over a century after Scientific Management entered the American educational scene, managerialist approaches to the principalship and other educational leaders still predominate. Yet now they are part of the American cultural common sense. In fact, as others in this volume show (see Saltman and Means, Chapter 22, for example), the past four decades of neoliberal reforms, marked by high-stakes, punitive consequences for low test performance, and educational restructurings designed to maximize individual, national and global economic productivity, show that the legacies of Scientific Management for educational leaders are alive and well. But today they are fortified by widespread ideological support for free-market enterprise. Today's American public schools exist in a modern cult of efficiency (Trujillo, 2014).

In the contemporary American discourse about educational leadership, administrators are often praised for their charismatic, yet scientific approaches. They set ambitious performance goals and demand nothing short of excellence. They use data to measure their success. They use language from business and industry to describe their work and to communicate with their staff and families. Good leaders in this neoliberal age are expected to take their cues from successful business leaders and to view their responsibilities in similar economic terms. Social justice, for these leaders, equates to individual gain, not collective well-being.

Activity 1.1

The history of schooling in the United States, as in many national contexts, shows that in times of perceived crises, political elites and business leaders have repeatedly turned to schools to solve social or economic problems. In these times, we often heard calls for school leaders to act more like business executives than civic leaders.

1 What assumptions are these leaders making about the relationship between schools and the economy? Between schools and society?
2 How does business logic differ from educational logic? Where might the logics be similar?

Think about the school in which you currently work, or in which you last worked. Make a list of the most notable priorities, qualities, activities and practices of your school's leader(s).

3 Where do you see business logic reflected in your school's leadership?
4 Where do you not see business logics reflected? When these logics are absent, what are the driving ideological values, beliefs and practices?

The emergence of critical thought in American educational leadership

Although mainstream conversations about educational leadership in the United States retain heavily managerialist and neoliberal assumptions about the appropriate roles and aims for administrators and their schools, critical dialogues about leadership have steadily grown over the past four decades. Beginning in the late 1970s and much more so during the 1980s and 1990s, critical scholars began to question other researchers' narrow, technical-rational focus on measuring educational leaders' effects on student outcomes. These critical scholars have continued to challenge the theoretical limitations of educational leadership effectiveness studies in multiple and varied ways.

Anderson (1991), for example, called for studies that employed critical, constructivist approaches that surfaced assumptions about educational leadership related to ideological control, power and truth. He and others generated multiple studies that looked at the ways school administrative structures and behaviours reproduce certain values and norms about teaching, learning, power and the purposes of schooling.

In 2005, Young and López argued that the field of educational leadership had been theoretically reductionist because the vast majority of its scholars had relied on narrow, positivist approaches to guide their inquiries. Positivist research approaches assume that readily observable, measurable factors can be used to verify a single truth about a phenomenon. These mainstream approaches to designing studies and analysing data were seen by many critical researchers as distorting the field's understandings about the complex ways in which schools worked and the powerful role of values, ideologies and positionalities in determining principals', teachers' and students' experiences.

The dominance of positivist research approaches, Young and López contended, had limited researchers' abilities to generate more elaborate, valid explanations of educational leadership dynamics because these approaches assume that questions about concepts that are not easily measurable or quantifiable, such as power distributions or the cumulative effects of long-standing structural inequalities, were un-empirical, or unscientific. To remedy these conceptual shortcomings, they recommended the use of critical research approaches that draw on theories like Critical Race Theory, which places the social construct of race at the centre of researchers' analyses, and enables them to more fully describe how and why educational leaders may challenge or reinforce issues of marginalization and the structural roots of inequality.

Today, after more than three decades of growing critical analyses in American educational leadership, the field includes a range of theoretical frameworks and designs that allow for deeper engagement with concepts about power and the political dimensions of schools.

Horsford (2011; Horsford, Grosland and Gunn, 2011), for example, has drawn on theories of culturally relevant pedagogy and cultural historical contexts to analyse how school leaders become racially literate, that is, how they understand what race and racism are, how they can be used to reproduce inequality and oppression, and how they can act on this knowledge to reconcile the harms done by schools and the larger society. Work in this field has furthered scholars' and practitioners' understandings about the pivotal role that race consciousness plays in determining school leaders' abilities to disrupt patterns of oppression, particularly for African American students.

Other scholars have generated both empirical and practitioner-oriented literature in the area of social justice leadership. This subfield of educational leadership tends to use theories of social justice, Critical Race Theory, identity formation and sociocultural learning theory, to understand how school leaders can advance educational equity for their schools' marginalized populations (Khalifa, Gooden and Davis, 2016). Theoharis and Brooks (2012), as well as several others, have contributed multiple practitioner resources that detail what helps and hinders leaders, and what challenges they can anticipate when they engage in redistributive resource allocation and other concrete steps for making their schools fair and safe spaces for minoritized students.

Studies of educational leadership that are framed with queer and queer legal theory, for instance, have contributed rich understandings of how heteronormativity, homophobia and other issues related to LGBTQ populations and women in the workplace function to reinforce gender roles (see Lugg and Roscigno, Chapter 17, in this textbook). In a field long characterized by men in the administrative positions, and women in teaching positions, these studies have gone a long way toward explaining how school leaders' practices, and the policies that guide them, can reproduce power asymmetries for women and members of LGBTQ communities. They also demonstrate how a leader can transmit a destructive hidden curriculum to students about the socially tolerable ways of enacting sexual orientations and gender identities.

These studies are part of a broader collection of research that examines various questions about how educational leaders' practices promote certain values and beliefs, and how they function to reproduce or disrupt marginalization in schools. Critical disability studies, English Learner studies, and studies of poverty and educational leadership have also become much more common since the 2010s. These studies often interrogate the social construction of students' and teachers' positionalities and school leaders' roles and responsibilities in creating more inclusive schools for all learners.

Finally, another strand of American critical education leadership scholarship takes up questions of democratic educational leadership. These scholars draw on theories of democracy and democratic education to frame leaders' responsibilities for safeguarding education as a public good. Anderson and Cohen (2018: Chapters 1 and 2) elaborate on the characteristics of such 'new democratic professionals' amid current neoliberal trends. Whereas contemporary, mainstream models frame principals' roles as entrepreneurs or marketers, and support deregulated administrative and teaching professions that are evaluated primarily in terms of test scores, Anderson and Cohen show how new democratic professionalism views principals as advocates for diverse, equitable schools, promotes public regulation and shared governance of principals and teachers, and relies on multiple, authentic forms of evaluation. They also maintain that managerialist models of school leadership tend to promote administrative classes that are largely white and middle class, while new democratic professional models provide for school leaders who reflect the communities in which they teach.

In essence, democratic leadership models stand in direct contrast to traditional notions of American school leadership. Democratic leaders cultivate schools in which students develop values and skills for civic participation, and in which teachers promote an appreciation for the well-being of the collective community. Individual forms of achievement and preparation for economic workplace competitiveness are secondary considerations for these civic-minded leaders who work in the service of the public interest.

Taking a critical approach to research helps scholars not only challenge the dominant approaches that have characterized the field of American educational leadership, it also helps scholars define the limitations of this field and the necessary directions for future research.

To summarize this section, educational leadership research has long been critiqued for its lack of theoretical rigour. Advances in the use of critical theories to frame studies of school leaders in the United States have strengthened the theoretical basis for the knowledge base on educational leadership. Critical research approaches can contribute more comprehensive, valid knowledge about educational leadership than positivistic research approaches can alone.

Persistent methodological constraints in American educational leadership studies

Although research on educational leadership in the United States has certainly evolved methodologically over time, the majority of the growth in tools and data sources that researchers use to investigate these phenomena have developed in the recent past.

Studying educational leadership has been, like many areas of education, a rather messy pursuit. As an applied field, its literature is often intended to inform practice. Thus, a major portion of the research on educational leadership has been practical in nature, not abstract or purely theoretical. Yet in retaining such a practical dimension, many of these studies have provided highly particularistic, experiential accounts of school leaders, not universal or analytical ones.

Moreover, cases for study have often been selected based on anecdotal evidence, reputation or convenience, rather than more systematic sampling from a particular universe of leaders or schools. And few of these designs have included long-term data generation. Additionally, researchers have tended to rely on data from schools' elite populations – administrators and, to a lesser extent, teachers. The voices of students, minoritized families and other non-dominant community members have only recently been used as regular sources of evidence. Finally, standardized test scores have usually served as the customary metric for measuring school leaders' success. Alternative outcomes, such as student engagement, perceptions of safety, or opportunities for community or teacher participation in leadership decision-making, are much less frequently included.

That said, solid progress has been made, mostly since the turn of the century, in increasing the methodological rigour of educational leadership studies. More mixed methods designs have been utilized, which have yielded both quantitative and qualitative sources of evidence from which researchers can draw their conclusions. Data-generation techniques like counternarratives, or accounts of experiences from disempowered individuals, have become more common instruments for constructing richer, fuller analyses. Ethnographic studies, which focus on questions of schools' culture, rather than just their readily measurable features, have also helped round out the field of educational leadership as it relates to issues of social justice and equity.

So, here we have argued that educational leadership research has long been critiqued for its lack of methodological sophistication and overly practical nature. However, critical scholars have made significant strides since the very early 2000s in the diversification of data-generation tools and sources of evidence used to investigate educational leadership.

Educational leadership programmes in the United States today: the predominance of 'what works' rhetoric and training

While a large share of leadership preparation programmes in the United States are rooted in dominant managerialist, neoliberal perspectives on what counts as a good leader, variation among leadership preparation programmes does exist. Increasing numbers of university-based preparation programmes are developing school and system leaders to advance social justice-oriented agendas by teaching future administrators about the socio-economic, political, racial and cultural roots of inequality; national and local histories of civil rights violations and protections; and research-based strategies for advocating for educational equity.

Nonetheless, the managerial model of school leadership in America's preparation programmes continues to thrive. Conversations about the need for stronger, bolder, entrepreneurial and innovative leaders who can shake up the system, are common messages from leadership preparation programmes, particularly alternative, sometimes for-profit preparation programmes.

In fact, several high-profile, non-university-based preparation programmes in the United States market their training by explicitly promoting highly managerial approaches to leading schools (e.g. New Leaders for New Schools, Teach For America, and the Relay Graduate School of Education). Often backed by the corporate community, marketing for such programmes can include references to preparing leaders who deliver breakthrough results, who are skilled in performance measurement and data-driven decision-making, who hold teachers and students responsible for achieving excellent outcomes, or who earn a high return on their investments. Several of these programmes also emphasize that their leadership training focuses on practical, experiential learning (rather than research-oriented, theoretical) learning.

Notably, these alternative programmes often frame their missions in terms of education representing the current generation's civil rights struggle. Yet they also often stress individual success and empowerment, rather than the collective empowerment of minoritized communities, the latter of which advocates sought during America's civil rights movement. For these programmes, notions of social justice are framed primarily in individual, not collective terms.

Case Study 1.1 Teach For America's models of educational leadership

1990 marked the beginning of Teach For America (TFA), a programme that began in the United States as an alternative teacher preparation and placement programme for hard-to-staff schools. Over the years, TFA's mission shifted to building a movement to eliminate educational inequity by selecting and preparing educational, social and political leaders. Today, TFA has seeded leaders in several high-profile school districts, prominent school-reform consultant organizations and even the US Congress. The programme is often referred to as a professional stepping stone to leadership and rapid career advancement.

Over the course of three years, Trujillo and Scott (2014) studied TFA 'corps members' ' career trajectories, as well as their beliefs about the most effective ways to equalize educational opportunity, particularly for low-income students and children of colour. Analysing interviews with more than 117 alumni and 47 current TFA members, they inquired about corps members' views on what made good educational leaders, as well as the likelihood that such leaders will promote socially just, equitable schooling in the United States. At the time of the study, their research departed from the largest share of the research on TFA, most of which consisted of effectiveness studies that tried to ascertain corps members' effects on test scores. Unlike most of the conventional research, Trujillo and Scott's research was designed to investigate questions related to how the programme may function to reproduce societal power structures and/or reduce inequalities in schools and communities.

Their findings illuminated the types of educational leadership models that TFA corps members came to value as a consequence of their programme experiences. First, they found that TFA corps members reasoned that most educational inequalities in the United States resulted from leaders' poor management of financial resources and an inability to effectively create stronger instructional capacity in teachers. If principals, superintendents and other leaders could more cleverly allocate scant dollars, then teachers would become better at their craft and students would learn more, they concluded. The majority of the study participants shared that they believed low-test-scoring schools suffered from a lack of strict accountability for results. A small minority of TFA members pointed to broader educational policies, such as inequitable school finance laws, as structural sources of inequality. By and large, these current and future leaders saw the enduring problems of education as managerial ones that required managerial fixes.

When asked what they saw as the most promising responses to educational inequality, the vast majority of these TFA recruits reported that they wanted to see stronger, more charismatic leaders who were not afraid to shake up the so-called status quo, who demonstrated a passion for measuring results and striving for excellence, and who could manage people to 'get results'.

The participants also cited role models that exemplified the current neoliberal model of leadership. They often named high-profile educational leaders who were supported by the corporate community, which often backed policies for weakening collective bargaining and expanding competitive, test-driven educational reform initiatives, such as merit pay for teachers based on test scores, closing low-performing public schools and replacing them with 'charter' schools, increasing school choice or laying off large numbers of teachers and principals in order to rapidly turn around student test performance.

Ironically, however, decades of research on school improvement have consistently documented the ineffectiveness of such punitive, market-based initiatives in improving teacher and student performance. This research has also shown how most of these policies have the consequence of destabilizing schools and their communities.

In the end, these researchers found that the programme was preparing future leaders who saw themselves more as heroic individuals than as civic-minded actors working in the public interest.

Activity 1.2

1   In what ways do TFA's leadership models reflect the principles and practices of Scientific Management? Of neoliberalism?
2   Where do you see leaders in your own workplace who resemble TFA's leadership model? Where do you see counter examples? How do these models differ from one another?
3   What do TFA's leadership models suggest about leaders' roles in a democracy?

Foregrounding the multiple purposes of schools in critical educational leadership

Implicit in all models of educational leadership are ideological assumptions about why we send our youth to school. Every model is values-based, though some are more explicitly values-oriented than others. There is no single purpose of schooling. Public schools in the United States have always served multiple purposes (Cuban, 1988).

Economic purposes have always played a role in our conceptions of good schools and good leadership practices because education has always been viewed by many as one source for developing workplace readiness. Civic purposes of schools have always existed, too, as education has historically been seen as a public good that helps prepare citizens for democratic participation, although this purpose is less to the fore in many Americans' imaginations today. Education has also always been considered to serve moral aims, where students can cultivate ethics and values that reflect their communities' or their own consciousness. Cultural concerns have also always been a part of Americans' assumptions about the purposes of schools, for better or for worse. Some have viewed schools as sites for developing a shared American identity and assimilating diverse groups; others have conceived of schools in terms of their responsibility for cultivating pluralistic values for diversity and difference.

American schools also serve socio-emotional, physical and intellectual goals, among others. At different points in the country's history, each of these purposes have played more or less prominent roles in the public's perceptions about schools' ultimate responsibilities and their leaders' obligations to their students and communities.

The prevailing model of educational leadership in the United States, the managerial model and, more recently, the neoliberal model, assumes a primarily economic purpose of schooling. Under this model, Americans send their children to school to prepare them to get a job, to maximize individual economic gain. Good school leaders are seen as working toward these aims by imparting the skills graduates are perceived to need to compete in the twenty-first-century workplace, by measuring students' mastery of these skills (usually in terms of test scores), and by endorsing individual measures of success, not collective ones. Less-common models of educational leadership, such as democratic leadership or social justice leadership, prioritize the civic purpose of schools. These less-common models of leadership are centred on goals for developing citizens' value and have the skills to participate in a democratic society, and who value and protect the common good.

Activity 1.3

1 Make a list of all of the reasons that you believe families send their children to school.
2 Which purposes do schools in your community prioritize? How do you know? What do you observe that suggests that these are the primary purposes of schooling in your context?
3 Name three educational leaders you know of who explicitly aim to advance multiple purposes of schooling (e.g. political, social, cultural, intellectual, socio-emotional, physical, economic, etc.). How do they spend their time? What messages do they communicate to their teachers, students and families? What do they prioritize and what do they do they de-emphasize in their day-to-day practices and language?

Conclusion

Without a doubt, critical perspectives on and approaches to American educational leadership have expanded over the past century. Critical inquiries that challenge dominant logic about what makes a good leader and good schools, particularly for minoritized communities, have contributed fuller explanations not just about leaders' effects on students' outcomes, but why these effects look the way they do. More varied theoretical approaches have pushed the field to look beyond purely managerial aspects of school leaders' roles and responsibilities. Questions of ideology, power and oppression are no longer relegated to the margins of this research. Nonetheless, the field still has a long way to go. More rigorous methodological designs are still needed. Research that surfaces the assumptions implicit in various models of leadership about the purposes of schooling are still in short supply. But these critical studies are growing, and as they do, so will scholars', practitioners' and the general public's understandings about the multifaceted roles of schools in a socially just, democratic society, and the complex positions that their leaders occupy as stewards of the common good.

Further reading

Hernández, L.E. (2016) Complicating the rhetoric: how racial construction confounds market-based reformers' civil rights invocations. *Education Policy Analysis Archives*, 24, art. 103. Available online: https://epaa.asu.edu/ojs/article/view/2321 (accessed 16 July 2020).

Horsford, S.D., Scott, J.T. and Anderson, G.L. (2019) *The politics of education policy in an era of inequality: possibilities for democratic schooling*. New York: Routledge.

Labaree, D. (1997) Public goods, private goods: the American struggle over educational goals. *American Educational Research Journal*, 34(1), 39–81.

Mathis, W.J. and Trujillo, T.M. (eds) (2016) *Learning from the federal market-based reforms: lessons for the Every Student Succeeds Act (ESSA)*. Charlotte, NC: Information Age Publishing.

References

Anderson, G.L. (1991) Cognitive politics of principals and teachers: ideological control in an elementary school. In: J. Blase (ed), *The politics of life in schools: power, conflict, and cooperation* (pp. 120–138). Newbury Park, CA: Sage.

Anderson, G.L. and Cohen, M.I. (2018) *The new democratic professional in education: confronting markets, metrics, and managerialism*. New York: Teachers College Press.

Cuban, L. (1988) *The managerial imperative and the practice of leadership in schools*. Albany, NY: State University of New York Press.

Hallinger, P. and Heck, R. (1996) Re-assessing the principal's role in school effectiveness: A review of the empirical research, 1980–95. *Educational Administration Quarterly*, 32(1), 5–44.

Horsford, S.D. (2011) *Learning in a burning house: educational inequality, ideology, and (dis) integration*. New York: Teachers College Press.

Horsford, S.D., Grosland, T. and Gunn, K.M. (2011) Pedagogy of the personal and professional: toward a framework for culturally relevant leadership. *Journal of School Leadership*, 21(4), 582–606.

Khalifa, M.A., Gooden, M.A. and Davis, J.E. (2016) Culturally responsive school leadership: a synthesis of the literature. *Review of Educational Research*, 86(4), 1271–1311.

Theoharis, G. and Brooks, J.S. (eds) (2012) *What every principal needs to know to create equitable and excellent schools*. New York: Teachers College Press.

Trujillo, T. (2014) The modern cult of efficiency: intermediary organizations and the new scientific management. *Educational Policy*, 28(2), 207–232.

Trujillo, T. and Scott, J. (2014) Superheroes and transformers: rethinking Teach For America's leadership models. *Phi Delta Kappan*, 95(8), 57–61.

Young, M.D. and López, G.R. (2005) The nature of inquiry in educational leadership. In: F.W. English (ed.), *The Sage handbook of educational leadership: advances in theory, research, and practice* (pp. 337–361). Thousands Oaks, CA: Sage.

Critical perspectives in and approaches to educational leadership in England

Ruth McGinity and Kay Fuller

2

What this chapter is about 30

Key questions that this chapter addresses 30

Introduction 30

Key structural and discursive policy frames 31

The Education Reform Act 1988 32

Business sponsorship of schools 33

School-type diversification 33

High-stakes accountability and performativity 33

The National College for School Leadership 36

Why does this matter? 36

The importance of theory for advocacy and resistance 38

What does all this mean for critical perspectives of educational leadership in England? 41

The importance of resistance 42

Conclusion 43

Further reading 43

References 44

What this chapter is about

In this chapter, we provide an account of the field from a critical perspective that will enable you to undertake an analysis of power which is relational and situated within the English context. In undertaking this analysis, we take seriously the notion that 'knowledge production is located in specific spaces, bodies, times and assumptive practices' (Courtney, McGinity and Gunter, 2018: 153). We will first address some of the key structural and discursive policy frames that have developed in England over the last forty years as contrivances for understanding and theorizing professional practice using critical perspectives and approaches. We will show how the field makes use of conceptual and theoretical tools and methodological approaches which produce analyses rooted in the peculiarities of the English system, whilst they simultaneously speak to global phenomena (in both policy and practice). This phenomenon is the political, ideological and social project of the nebulous set of practices and forms conceptualized as **neoliberalism**.

Key questions that this chapter addresses

1 What are the key discursive and policy frames that have emerged out of the neoliberal logic in England?

2 How have these shaped the ways in which professional practice has been:

   a enacted in the field of practice, and

   b conceptualized in the critical field?

3 In what ways are these accounts rooted in traditions of knowledge production (what is known and worth knowing) that centre social justice as an organizing principle?

Introduction

The story of educational leadership in England requires you to understand that there are multiple, competing or aligned versions of what it means to both be a leader and 'do' leadership as a form of professional practice, as well as perspectives of it as a field of study. This distinction between being, doing and conceptualizing is integral to the way you might understand the field through thinking with, and drawing on, critical perspectives and approaches. In addition, to make sense of how critical perspectives construct professional practice within England specifically, you need to understand how such analyses are located in the context of localized policy enactments. Here, critical scholarship has a strong tradition in developing analyses of the relationship between **structure** and **agency** to consider how power operates to privilege or marginalize, advantage or disadvantage. Particular identities and practices are produced to be theorized through a framework of equity.

Throughout this chapter, you will be asked to actively engage with and reflect on the issues we raise through our examples to help develop understanding and awareness of critical approaches to understanding education leadership in England.

Key structural and discursive policy frames

In order to unpack the way professional practice is conceptualized using critical perspectives and approaches, we need to identify the key structural and discursive policy frames that provide the contextual environment through which leading and leadership are practised in England.

Within the critical tradition, structural features must be considered and analysed when investigating professional practices and identities (agency). A crucial aim of critical education scholarship is to illuminate how policy processes (structure) and professional practice (agency) might intersect to either reproduce or limit the effects of educational inequalities. Focusing upon equity in this way establishes social justice as a foundation for critical approaches and perspectives.

Critical scholars understand social justice in research as maintaining a focus on (in)equality. But so do function-alist scholars (for an analysis of this, see Raffo and Gunter, 2008), whose often-normative work is tightly coupled with reform movements, particularly those from

Critical perspectives: require you to analyse the way in which a context might impact upon what is happening and how power is enacted and experienced as a result.

Critical approaches: are methods and tools that might help you to do this type of work: they can help you methodologically to undertake this type of analysis.

Structure: is the way in which society is organized to influence, facilitate or limit the choices and opportunities available to individuals. For example, these can be cultural, political and/or institutional.

Agency: the capacity of an individual to engage in practices and act within a particular environment.

Neoliberalism: a set of economic and ideological practices and processes that at the forefront of the growth of markets combined with deregulations of the state's role in the development and provision of public services, such as education.

Knowledge production: the theoretical and practical way in which ideas and understanding are developed to make sense of the world and how this relates to particular positions and identities.

the late 1990s and first decade of the new millennium. In such accounts, attention is given to what leaders do (and how they might do it more effectively) producing analyses that are theoretically superficial and that rely on prescriptive and descriptive models often divorced from context. These accounts lack theoretical engagement with analyses of how policy processes and professional practice might mitigate or perpetuate inequity within the system. Despite this, claims of social justice pervade the language of policy reform and reveal how a concept might be understood as a site of 'discursive struggle', where the allocation of value becomes diluted from its original meaning and intended use.

Critical scholars have identified this problem as a significant characteristic within functionalist knowledge production, where claims for social justice motivate normative accounts whilst lacking methodological and theoretical grounding. As such, social justice

Decentralization and autonomy: greater financial autonomy for headteachers through, for example, the dismantling of the middle tier. Examples include the Education Reform Act 1988 and the Academies Act 2010.

Diversification: peculiarly English; augmentation in range of school types as another feature of market logic and school choice – competition.

High-stakes accountability: agenda to mitigate excesses of autonomy and to facilitate market logic (through inspections, testing and league tables – all working to produce information to inform school choice).

Performativity: emphasizing the importance of system, school and (head)teacher 'effectiveness', measured through pupil performance in high-stakes tests.

as an organizing principle underpinning knowledge production in the critical field represents an important departure from functionalist modes of inquiry into leadership and policy. Using England as an example, we show how structural and discursive policy frames can work *against*, rather than *for* equity within the system. These frames are both distinctive and particular within this national context but are also part of a loose-fitting, global phenomenon of neoliberalism.

Here, we establish the significance of neoliberalism, both on policy-reform processes over the last forty years in countries such as England, and also on structural analyses of those reforms that use neoliberalism as a conceptual and ideological framework. As such, it informs critical perspectives and approaches in the field of educational leadership. For the purposes of our argument, what matters here is that neoliberal approaches in England have produced a set of policy drivers that have common features against and within which the field of educational leadership has developed. We briefly describe some key policy frames in order to reveal how critical perspectives enable analyses of how and why professionals negotiate practices and identities (agency) within a given structural context.

The Education Reform Act 1988

In England, a key date for policy reform is 1988. The Conservative government (under Prime Minister Margaret Thatcher) introduced the Education Reform Act (ERA). A major set of reforms signalled a watershed moment in embedding neoliberal logic into the policy landscape, ushering in the marketization of education in England.

In essence, policies promoted practices that enabled market mechanisms to operate within the education system. What resulted was schools being run more akin to businesses, with the competitive logic that such an approach would require. In the first instance, the ERA paved the way for greater autonomy in the system through policies aimed at decentralizing specific functions from local government control and handing school leaders new powers. This started with greater financial autonomy (what was termed Local Management of Schools) in setting budgets, and authority over areas such as recruitment and resource allocation. Successive governments from New Labour (1997–2010) to the Conservative-led coalition (2010–2015) followed suit through multiple policies designed to give greater freedom to leaders and their schools, leading to decentralization in budgets, pay and conditions, the curriculum and admissions.

Business sponsorship of schools

A key policy associated with the ERA that facilitated this ideological and material shift was the provision for schools to be sponsored by businesses, in what were named City Technology Colleges (CTCs). Although these never took off in great numbers (fifteen were established between the inception of the policy in 1986 and the end of successive Conservative administrations in 1997), the principles by which they were founded (business sponsorship, and freedom over budgets, pay and conditions, curriculum and admissions) lay the ground on which academies would be based, and would go on to redefine the landscape of schooling and its leadership in England.

School-type diversification

Diversification, thus, became another bedrock of the English school system. England already had a number of types of schools (comprehensives, grammars, secondary moderns, faith schools, and private or independent schools) but the reform strategy to increase autonomy within the system led to the Academies Act of 2010 and a huge increase in academy schools and their assorted varieties (free schools, studio schools and university technical colleges, along with stand-alone, converter and, more recently, groups of academies called multi-academy trusts). What this means, in terms of the logic of neoliberalism, is that it shores up a central component of marketized education systems – enabling competition through school-choice policies. Structurally, school choice became one of the most important policy mechanisms for embedding inequality within the system, where empirical research strongly suggests there exists a hierarchy of provision; broadly speaking, poorer children are located in less successful schools whilst richer children attend more successful schools.

High-stakes accountability and performativity

The 1988 ERA also introduced high-stakes accountability mechanisms enabling the system to run competitively as a quasi-market and holding to account the professionals working within it in a performative regime. In England, three key mechanisms produce such a regime (Ball, 2003):

1 the form and function of the inspectorate

2 high-stakes, summative testing

3 league tables.

The third of these resulted indirectly from the ERA legislation whereby the media, in particular, produce ranked tables of school performance based on the second mechanism (high-stakes, summative testing regimes). The school's inspectorate is significant structurally, because through this, schools are rated on a scale from 'inadequate' to 'outstanding' increasingly based on the same high-stakes, summative test performance. Schools might, therefore, find themselves deemed 'failing' and, as a result of the 2010 Academies Act, be subject to closure in order to reopen as an academy. This matters because there is fragility built into the system via high-stakes accountability, where parents who can vote with their feet take vital funding with them (in England, a per-pupil funding system means the money follows the child), that leaves certain types of schools with certain types of children (empirically, children from poorer homes) more or less vulnerable to the more extreme vagaries of a quasi-marketized system.

These interconnected policy frames produce a context in which there is concomitantly something quite global (neoliberal logics) and something quite situated and specific to England, that provides the environment in which critical perspectives in and approaches to educational leadership have been formed.

We want you to consider the impact of these structural features of the English system on professional practice by focusing on critical perspectives and approaches:

- **Critical perspectives** require you to look at the way in which a context might impact upon what is happening and how power is distributed and experienced within such a context. For example, how might reforms giving greater autonomy to schools affect how school leaders do their job? Why and how are some school leaders in a more advantaged position than others?

- **Critical approaches** are tools and ideas that might help you to do this type of leadership work – they can help you methodologically to undertake this type of analysis.

Drawing on Alvesson and Willmott (1992), Gunter (2001: 96–97) provides key aspirations for critical research and analysis, four of which we highlight here:

1 Emancipate those who are disciplined through objective power structures by questioning the power base of those located within privileged elite positions;

2 Problematise language, practice, beliefs and what are current and taken for granted assumptions about organizational realities and structures;

3 Reveal the existence of contradictions and dilemmas within organizations and the productive contribution of conflict;

4 Support practice through moving beyond tasks and techniques by conceptualizing action within a social and political context.

Activity 2.1

Consider the policies for greater autonomy above. Think about a school serving children from poorer homes with lower attainment levels. That school is understood as a less successful school. In turn, children from wealthier families are less likely to attend this school. Their parents exercise their right to choose another, more successful, school. Over time, the school is identified by the inspectorate, Ofsted, as failing and forced to become an academy. As a result, the headteacher loses their job, and many members of the senior leadership team resign.

Taking this example, answer the following:

1 Who has the power in this situation? Who is disadvantaged?
2 Why does this matter?
3 Are descriptors such as 'successful', 'unsuccessful' and 'failing' useful terms by which to understand what happened? If so, why? If not, why not? What alternative ways are there to describe and explain what is happening?
4 Does autonomy in this scenario mean the new academy is likely to do better than the failing school it replaced? If so, why? If not, why not?
5 What does this mean for school leaders and how we study them, their identities and their actions?

Making sense of professional practice requires us to conceptualize it as a set of relational processes situated within specific contexts at particular times. Professional practice can be made sense of, in the critical scholarship part of the field, only in relation to the structural (cultural, institutional, political) features in and through which practice is mediated. As such, a typology of leadership characteristics is unnecessary. Instead, using the framework of structure and agency reveals the complex, contingent and subjective nature of professional practice. The critical scholar can undertake detailed, theoretical and often qualitative inquiry as a means of considering the ways in which educational leaders respond to and make sense of their work and professional identities.

Much functionalist research is designed to produce models for educational leadership actions and behaviours. They are described as more or less 'effective'. These models include different conceptualizations of leadership as variously **distributed**, **transformational** and/or **instructional**. Professional practice is presented as a means of assigning labels to behaviours drawn from empirical studies. These descriptive interpretations facilitate further studies that produce similar lists of types and behaviours favoured by governmental and reform strategists. As such, accounts of professional practice will differ depending on where you look. What you are likely to find are multiple sources using normative descriptors, like distributed leadership, with little attention paid to the contextual and structural features that produce practices and actions in the first place.

This is because the normative position is to identify how leaders might lead in ways that make them capable of delivering centrally designed reforms. Within such accounts of professional practice, social justice often takes on more than it can conceptually bear; it becomes a discursive catch-all for the effective work of leaders and leadership, without the necessary engagement of what it means to undertake socially just leadership as a means of challenging inequitable processes and practices.

Professionals are constrained in what they may think and do because of the structural conditions we have described. A high-stakes accountability system might produce professional practice that lacks critical reflexivity and instead privileges the delivery of quantifiable educational outcomes, squeezing out the spaces for thinking as well as doing things differently. Professional practice is not so performative that meaningful agency is reduced, but rather, in England, the intense policy-reform agenda that privileges functionalist analyses of practice means that agency and identity have been presented in scholarly accounts and outputs tied to purposes and outcomes of the reform agenda in unproblematic ways. The following section exemplifies how this occurs.

The National College for School Leadership

The now-defunct National College for School Leadership was established by New Labour in 2000 as a training ground for school leaders to undertake professional qualifications related to their practice. Gunter (2012) shows how the National College became a powerful government-sanctioned institution that performed statecraft in the re-culturing of school leaders' professional practice as deliverers of New Labour policy. As a result, preferred leadership practices (types) and actions (tools) developed alongside the literature that described leadership as variously *distributed*, *transformational* and *instructional*. Practices were described and identified in terms of being successful at the job. These descriptive types were embedded within both government-produced literature on successful school leadership as well as in functionalist accounts and research on effective leadership practices.

The National College of School Leadership provides an example specific to England. However, it is an illustration of the power inherent in (re)packaging leadership development ideas and research as marketable products to cultivate practice for effective, efficient and measurable outcomes. In doing so, it delivered school leadership agendas derived from neoliberal logics. Whilst the College itself now no longer exists, arguably many of the conditions that produced it persist, and so it offers a useful lens through which to explore these conditions, in which the National College minimized spaces for resistance, emancipatory activism and producing exemplars of what leading, and leadership, might contribute to and achieve.

Why does this matter?

Critical approaches produce accounts that centre contextual and structural features and utilize power as a lens through which to theorize professional practice. In doing so, the field has developed analyses that use methodological and conceptual tools that move beyond normative and prescriptive typologies. Instead, they provide ways of sense-making regarding what it means to be a leader, doing leadership, under particular and often historical sets of circumstances. This is important for three reasons.

First, critical approaches bring with them (as with normative and functionalist approaches) conceptual frameworks for making sense of practice that are located within the scholarly tradition of knowledge production within the field. This means that research conducted with (and on) participants produces data that is subjected to the field's own analytical traditions where, for example, theory is used to make sense of why an educational leader might say or do something in relation to questions about their practices and identities. These theorized accounts might be used as a means of making sense of how, for example, intersecting oppressions operate to privilege and marginalize different leaders in different ways (Fuller, 2019). To push further, they might be used to make sense of how these intersecting oppressions are interpreted by participants as more or less structural, and what this might say about the possibilities and limitations available to act or think differently.

Second, spaces and critical dispositions for thinking and acting differently are not common within the field. The restrictive structural conditions that have been discussed in this chapter have to a large extent produced scholarship which reveals the totalizing nature of educational reform processes on professional practice. However, accounts demonstrate how different groups within the system (teachers, leaders, governors, for example) are not critically–reflexively engaged with their work in ways that would realize the emancipatory potential of critical dispositions. So, third, whilst attempting to address the limitations of this for professional practice, such analyses expose the liminal space that exists between research and practice – where accounts of thinking and doing things differently are partial but the theorizing and analysis that are produced as a result is both useful and productive for researching professionals.

Some accounts reveal critical dispositions to act and think differently, and their approaches focus upon (1) theorizing the relationship between structure and agency (Gewirtz, 2002) as (2) an acknowledgement that identity is integral to professional practice (Courtney, McGinity and Gunter, 2018) to (3) accounts centring social justice perspectives as mechanisms for emancipatory action (Thomson, 2010) which (4) reveal the way power operates to produce privileged and/or marginalized experiences of policies and practices in highly situated and contextualized ways (Ball, 2003).

Activity 2.2

In 'The teacher's soul and the terrors of performativity', Stephen Ball argues that:

> Performativity . . . is a new mode of state regulation . . . It requires individual practitioners to organize themselves as a response to targets, indicators and evaluations. To set aside personal beliefs and commitments and live an existence of calculation. The new performative worker is a promiscuous self, an enterprising self, with a passion for excellence. For some, this is an opportunity to make a success of themselves, for others it portends inner conflicts, inauthenticity and resistance
> *(2003: 215)*

Consider the relationship between *structure* and *agency* and how *power* operates to privilege or marginalize, advantage or disadvantage professionals and others in the school population.

1 What are the structural features that might contribute to the 'performative regime' described by Ball?
2 How might you negotiate the tensions between external policy-driven activity and professional identity?
3 In your current context, what might be your 'red lines', the limits of policy compliance?

The importance of theory for advocacy and resistance

The field is constructed through analytical interpretations of both the limitations of and possibilities for professional practice. As a result, intellectual resources are deployed to develop perspectives and approaches that enable theorization to take place. The use of theory in developing critical perspectives of professional practice in the field of educational leadership is well-established (Courtney, McGinity and Gunter, 2018). Theoretical work reveals key questions that underpin critical perspectives: who benefits from and who loses out as a result of how practices and processes play out in the professional field? In this sense, one of the main features of critical scholarship is the repoliticizing of practice within a deeply normative and depoliticized space. By deploying theoretical work, spaces of resistance can be identified and supported by critical scholars as a means of pushing back against the highly compliant agency expected as a result of the structured policy context. As such, analyses of power and identity are enabled and developed despite the many and varied limitations born from normative privileging of practice as outlined throughout this chapter.

Case Study 2.1 Worth Less? Headteachers' engaging in critical practitioner reflexivity taking collective action in England

In this case study, we recount a case of headteachers' engagement in critical practitioner reflexivity in their collective acts of resistance of education policy. Figure 2.1 shows a timeline of headteachers' collective actions in the context of national and global events.

Over four years (2015–2019), headteachers questioned systemic inequalities in school funding. In 2015, Jules White, headteacher of local-authority-maintained Tanbridge House School for pupils aged eleven to sixteen, founded the Worth Less? Campaign for fairer funding in West Sussex. He was subsequently both feted and intimidated for this achievement.

Selected reports from the regional, national and professional press are presented as a timeline in the context of political and educational reforms in England (Figure 2.1). They reveal how headteachers (local-authority-maintained schools and academies), head teacher unions, parents and pupils were united in the protest. Social media platforms were used to inform the public, mobilize supporters and publicize the campaign.

Headteachers wrote to politicians (from 2015) and parents (2016 and 2019) to describe the impact real-terms funding cuts had on schools. Their actions included resignation (2017), invoicing the government for the funding shortfall (2018), open criticism of government (2018) and a march (2018). Headteachers carried out menial tasks to save money (2019). Parents and pupils supported the protest (2018) and in more affluent areas supplemented school funding (2019).

An e-petition, started by St Joseph's Catholic Primary School, Blaydon headteacher, Andrew Ramanandi, with 113,825 signatories, secured a House of Commons debate between politicians recounting headteachers', teachers', support staff, parents', school governors' and pupils' experiences of real-terms spending cuts (Hansard, 2019). Some attributed them to education reforms from 2010; others to reforms during the New Labour government (1997–2010). Members of Parliament spoke against the funding cuts as former teachers, school governors or board members of multi-academy trusts as well as across political party elected representatives of their constituents.

The effects of the inadequate funding of schools in England included geographical disparity in funding; deficit school budgets; loss of staff through restructuring and redundancy (teaching and support staff); replacement of staff including school leaders with less experienced, less expensive personnel; reduced resources for provision for children with special educational needs and disabilities (SEND); supplementing provision for impoverished children out of headteachers' own resources i.e. paying for uniforms and food; and reducing costs by personally paying for or doing school cleaning (Hansard, 2019).

In the context of other welfare cuts connected with an austerity budget from 2010, headteachers had backfilled provision. Headteachers were 'crossing red lines' (Thelma Walker MP in Hansard, 2019). This was a 'crisis largely in disguise' precisely because of headteachers' reluctance to take collective action. They were 'loth to get involved in what they consider to be politics, or in any way to use the children they serve and teach as pawns in a political debate . . . headteachers do not want to speak about the situation quite so much, simply because, understandably, they fear competitive disadvantage' (Tim Farron MP in Hansard, 2019).

The headteachers' protest has been reported as polite and unprecedented, though some saw them as hypocritical. Ministerial responses were seen as inadequate, offensive in suggesting schools should receive funding for the 'little extras' (Hansard, 2019) and invalidated headteachers' concerns. The campaign continues.

**Figure
2.1** Timeline of
headteachers'
Worth Less?
campaign
activities.

2008	Global financial crisis
May 2010	Conservative–Liberal Democrat coalition government formed
June 2010	Austerity budget
July 2010	Academies Act – funding from central instead of local government
April 2015	Worth Less? headteachers launch campaign in West Sussex – a traditional Conservative-led local authority
May 2015	Conservative government elected
September 2016	All West Sussex headteachers write to parents/carers about funding cuts
February 2017	Head teacher resigns over cuts in Berkshire
January 2018	Headteachers invoice government for funding shortage (local authority schools *and* academies)
July 2018	Founder of the Worth Less? campaign, Jules White, intimidated by MPs
6 September 2018	Government issues advice to schools about teacher conduct not being party political
25 September 2018	Headteachers criticize government
27 September 2018	Headteachers march to Downing Street
October 2018	Parents support protest for fair funding
4 November 2018	School staff at centre of BBC2 *School* documentary respond to 'little extras' budget
6 November 2018	Jules White attends the Education Select Committee on schools and colleges funding
3 December 2018	Funding awarded to grammar schools to expand
21 December 2018	Jules White receives award
January 2019	E-petition, started by Andrew Ramanandi in a Labour-led local authority, attracts 113,825 signatures
4 March 2019	Debate about school funding in Parliament
8 March 2019	Headteachers write to parents
8 March 2019	Headteachers carry out menial tasks to save money
April 2019	School children protest against cuts
May 2019	Parents protest against schools closing early as a result of cuts
June 2019	Institute of Fiscal Studies says £3.8 billion is needed to reverse cuts
Spring 2019	Association of School and College Leaders publish research on school funding
13 July 2019	Middle-class parents supplement funding in state schools
22 July 2019	Schools have to find 2 per cent of teachers' pay award

---

Activity 2.3

Social, economic and educational policies simultaneously influence and contextualize educational-leader identities and practices as they and others construct them. Use the timeline in Figure 2.1 to consider being, doing and conceptualizing educational leadership.

1 What does it mean to be a headteacher?
2 What did headteachers do?
3 How did headteachers' actions influence their identities and vice versa?
4 How might we draw on critical perspectives to conceptualize what is happening in the English education system?

Consider the following:

5 *Structure and agency* – what examples of headteacher agency and policy structure can you identify? How do these interrelate and interplay?
6 *Critical practitioner reflexivity* – what pushed headteachers to take collective action?
7 *Power* – to what extent did headteachers subvert existing power relations in their collective resistance against economic and educational policy that produced real-terms budget cuts in their schools?
8 *Social justice* – who benefited from the economic and educational policies? Who lost?
9 *Emancipatory activism* – in what ways might their collective action be interpreted as such?

What does all this mean for critical perspectives of educational leadership in England?

The field of educational leadership, like most academic fields, does not easily lend itself to notions of the nation state when considering the processes of knowledge production. The imposition of borders seems obstructive where the unfettered flow of intellectual resources and ideas is required to sustain high-quality scholarship and debate. What follows must be read with this caveat. The productiveness of using a national lens to think about the field is tied to implications for understanding professional practice in particular context, histories, cultures and politics. In addition, internationally recognizable conceptualizations of economic, political and ideological practices and processes feature within and across multiple national contexts. Here these are defined as the logics of neoliberalism. Although highly influential in the development of reform strategies, its global effects are not felt identically, or indeed at the nation-state level. How such a nebulous set of ideas and practices play out in localized contexts is integral to analyses offered by critical approaches to educational leadership.

In England, this means the two key structural and discursive policy frames identified in the chapter as first, decentralization and autonomy; and second, diversification and high-stakes accountability have produced a set of contextually specific analyses. These simultaneously instantiate global trends playing out in localized circumstances and enable analyses that theorize why this might matter to professional practice locally, nationally and internationally.

The importance of resistance

The field has been historically and contemporaneously marginalized by normative agendas in policy, research and practice. There is a tendency to eclipse instances of resistance that exist within accounts offered through research produced by the field as well as the documentation of activism occurring in real time and reported through media channels. We have demonstrated that in our case study of the headteacher protests against funding cuts. Here, we witnessed professionals making public and high-profile statements about the conditions in which they were doing their jobs. Budget-holding becomes even starker in the day-to-day business of running a school. The protest was impactful, not least because, as a group, headteachers are not well known to protest, despite the existence of a highly unionized teaching profession. In addition, reports exist, such as those described by Hatcher and Jones (2006), of acts of resistance to other aspects of the performative regime, particularly where schools are forced into academization.

These campaigns indicate that professional practice is not immune to the critical disposition to think and act differently. When ordinary professionals are pushed to respond in extraordinary circumstances, the notion that professional practice in England is highly compliant must be contested. This matters because it is possible to forget. The structural conditions described in this chapter, and how agency might manifest as a result, demonstrate the way knowledge is produced and how concepts (such as social justice) gain purchase to become functions of policy in normative and unintended ways. As such, it is productive to look to the scholarship of Michael Apple, who implores researchers, within their own professional practice, to become 'critical secretaries' (Apple, 2013: 15). Accounts of compliance and resistance are important in making sense of conflicting and complex experiences in professional practice. They can be used to challenge the ways in which social justice has been appropriated by and for normative purposes. In offering critical approaches and perspectives, scholars in England speak to their counterparts globally, in support of professionals engaging with the ways knowledge production operates and understanding how such processes might be useful for them in making sense of their own practices and lives within a highly prescriptive, performative and fragmented system.

Conclusion

This chapter has demonstrated the multiple ways in which structure and agency intersect to prompt critical analyses of professional practice in neoliberal times. Such analyses, which draw on strong traditions of knowledge production in theorization, conceptualization and methodological approach, are essential to critical scholarship. What distinguishes critical scholarship is a commitment to making sense of such processes through a framework of equity, unpinned by an examination of how power operates within and across the system. This is useful because it offers a means to understand and make sense of the different ways in which professional practice is described, experienced and collectively deployed to support or challenge the way inequality is (re)produced through the system. This focus upon social justice is essential to critical approaches and perspectives, and whilst these frameworks of inquiry are similar for critical scholars in field work across the globe, there are contextually specific aspects to the conditions in which professional practice is enacted and understood in England that make it worthy of its own, singular contribution in this book.

What remains important is that this account is read alongside the other contributions as a means of further developing an understanding of both the general and specific nature of critical scholarship and how this can be used to strengthen analyses across the field as a means of addressing Apple's (2013: 15) call to 'bear witness to negativity and point to contradictions and to spaces for possible action'. It is through these spaces that greater understanding and ultimately change, might follow.

Further reading

Ball, S.J. (2013) *The education debate*, 2nd edn. Bristol: Policy Press.

Courtney, S.J. and McGinity, R. (2020) Conceptualising constructions of educational-leader identity. In: R. Niesche and A. Heffernan (eds), *Theorising identity and subjectivity in educational leadership research* (pp. 8–23). Abingdon: Routledge.

Gunter, H.M., Hall, D. and Bragg, J. (2013) Distributed leadership: a study in knowledge production. *Educational Management Administration & Leadership*, 41(5), 555–580.

Stevenson, H.P. (2007) A case study in leading schools for social justice: when morals and markets collide. *Journal of Educational Administration*, 45(6), 769–781.

Maguire, M., Braun, A. and Ball, S. (2018) Discomforts, opposition and resistance in schools: the perspectives of union representatives. *British Journal of Sociology of Education*, 39(7), 1060–1073.

References

Alvesson, M. and Willmott, H. (1992) *Critical Management Studies*. London: Sage.

Apple, M.W. (2013) *Can education change society?* New York: Routledge.

Ball, S.J. (2003) The teacher's soul and the terrors of performativity. *Journal of Education Policy*, 18(2), 215–228.

Courtney, S.J., McGinity, R. and Gunter, H.M. (eds) (2018) *Educational leadership: theorising professional practice in neoliberal times*. Abingdon: Routledge.

Fuller, K. (2019) 'That would be my red line': an analysis of headteachers' resistance of neoliberal education reforms. *Educational Review*, 71(1), 31–50.

Gewirtz, S. (2002) *The managerial school: post-welfarism and social justice in education*. London: Routledge.

Gunter, H.M. (2001) Critical approaches to leadership in education. *The Journal of Educational Enquiry*, 2(2), 94–108.

Gunter, H.M. (2012) *Leadership and the reform of education*. Bristol: Policy Press.

Hansard (2019) School funding. UK Parliament, House of Commons 4 March 2019, Volume 655. Available online: https://hansard.parliament.uk/commons/2019-03-04/debates/2EB33517-190D-4882-8682-4953D09C5CB0/SchoolFunding (accessed 22 July 2019).

Hatcher, R. and Jones, K. (2006) Researching resistance: campaigns against academies in England. *British Journal of Educational Studies*, 54(3), 329–351.

Raffo, C. and Gunter, H.M. (2008) Leading schools to promote social inclusion: developing a conceptual framework for analysing research, policy and practice. *Journal of Education Policy*, 23(4), 397–414.

Thomson, P. (2010) Headteacher autonomy: a sketch of a Bourdieuian field analysis of position and practice. *Critical Studies in Education*, 51(1), 5–20.

Critical perspectives in and approaches to educational leadership in Australia

Martin Mills and Glenda McGregor

3

What this chapter is about	46
Key questions that this chapter addresses	46
Introduction	46
Becoming and being a principal in Australia	47
Social justice	51

Critical educational leadership	55
Conclusion	56
Further reading	57
References	58

What this chapter is about

In this chapter, we provide an overview of important leadership attributes for principals in Australia in light of the performative pressures facing them, and of an examination of the Australian Institute for Teaching and School Leadership's (AITSL) *Australian Professional Standard for Principals* [hereafter referred to as 'the Standard'] *and the Leadership Profiles* (AITSL, 2019). We present a case study in which a school principal, 'Robert' (pseudonym), adopted a critical approach in establishing an award-winning programme for pregnant schoolgirls and young parents. We argue that a commitment to high academic outcomes in a school does not prevent an equally robust commitment to meeting the needs of highly marginalized young people. In our view, our case study demonstrates the critical leadership required to enhance a more socially just education system. We outline our view of a socially just construction of school leadership, drawing on Nancy Fraser (2009).

Key questions that this chapter addresses

1 What are the challenges for principals in Australia?
2 How does this play out in schools?
3 How is principalship constructed in Australian education policy?
4 What are the educational leadership practices that enhance social justice?

Introduction

School principals carry significant responsibilities, particularly in respect of the well-being of staff and students. They are held to account for the quality of teaching and learning, the curriculum and assessment practices and ultimately students' academic outcomes. The quality of a school's relationships with the local community is often dependent on the ability of a principal to build those relationships. Buildings, fire and safety, and managing a budget all fall into the remit of the principal. Schools are also unpredictable places where, for example, tragedies can strike students, staff and their families, where parents make sudden demands, where an excursion can go wrong, or where a school suddenly finds itself the focus of media attention, often for negative reasons, and it is the school principal who must take the final decision about how to respond to such challenges. Addressing these unpredictable events involves significant emotional and intellectual labour, a great deal of tact and flexibility. Leading a school is not a simple process.

Schools in Australia are also amazingly diverse. One only has to think of a primary school in a remote Indigenous community in, say, Western Australia and a large government urban high school in a major city such as Sydney, to see the contrast between different Australian schools. And this is before considering the differences between and within the government, independent and Catholic school sectors. As such, it is difficult to construct idealized models of the school principal for Australian schools. However, there are, in our view, important principles that principals need to adhere to in order to improve the lives of the young people in their schools and to enhance the well-being of the broader Australian community. These characteristics are underpinned by a critical approach to school leadership shaped by a commitment to social justice.

In this chapter, then, we do not explore a range of critical approaches to leadership; instead we foreground what we refer to as a socially just approach to school leadership. In the chapter, we focus on the work of principals, but recognize that 'leadership' is not restricted to principals (Lingard et al., 2003). Successful schools require leadership to be dispersed across all areas of the schools' operations. This is referred to as 'distributed leadership', 'parallel leadership' and 'density of leadership' (see Niesche, 2011: 52). In our case study later in the chapter, the principal, Robert, is quite explicit in recognizing the leadership of other staff in setting up an innovative programme. He acts as a facilitator and an advocate for the programme rather than as its instigator. The model of the lone, change-driven charismatic principal (the type who often make the central character in movies) rarely exists and such an idealized model does not sit comfortably with understandings of a socially just or critical principalship.

Becoming and being a principal in Australia

In Australia, school principals do not require any formal qualifications beyond mandatory teacher registration and 'suitability to work with children' checks, in their state or territory of employment. Some sectors have non-educational requirements for appointment to senior positions in schools (for example, religious affiliations). Learning to become a principal in Australia can be said to follow an 'apprenticeship model' whereby teachers, in working alongside senior colleagues, develop an understanding of different management positions and, depending on the school type (primary or secondary), work their way 'up' through heads of department / curriculum leader and deputy principal until obtaining a principalship.

While many universities offer masters' qualifications in education leadership, these are not mandatory to become a principal. It is often in these courses that principals (or aspiring principals) are exposed to discourses related to critical leadership and social justice. Those principals who come to the position solely through an apprenticeship model without any engagement with the research literature, may lack the critical perspectives necessary to challenge 'conventional wisdoms' about school leadership. However, in the wake of the development of professional standards for teachers, AITSL has pursued a similar account-ability framework for school principals that aim to address weaknesses in the apprenticeship model.

AITSL: the Australian Institute for Teaching and School Leadership was formed in 2010 to finalize and validate the Australian Professional Standards for Teachers (the Standards; AITSL, 2018) in order to promote excellence in the profession of teaching and school leadership across all Australian schools. 'Since 2011, the *Australian Professional Standard for Principals* (the Standard) has provided a public statement setting out what school principals are expected to know, understand and do to succeed in their work. The Standard is an integrated model that recognizes three Leadership Requirements that a principal draws upon, within five areas of Professional Practice' (AITSL, 2019: 3).

The Standard emphasizes the important 'contribution' principals make to 'raising student achievement at all levels and all stages', to 'promoting equity and excellence' and 'contributing to the development of a 21st century education system at local, national and international levels'. It argues that 'leadership must be contextualised, learning-centred and responsive to the diverse nature of Australian schools' and 'effective leadership is distributed and collaborative' (AITSL, 2019: 4). The Standard sets up a suite of integrated 'leadership lenses' to achieve these goals (AITSL, 2019: 11).

The **Leadership Requirements** lens provides a focus on:

● Vision and values
● Knowledge and understanding
● Personal qualities, social and interpersonal skills

These leadership attributes are enacted through the **Professional Practices** lens:

● Leading teaching and learning
● Developing self and others
● Leading improvement, innovation and change
● Leading the management of the school
● Engaging and working with the community

The final lens through which principals are asked to appraise their work is **Leadership Emphasis**:

● Operational
● Relational
● Strategic
● Systemic *(AITSL, 2019: 11)*

These lenses are used to develop **Leadership Profiles** that indicate levels of leadership proficiency within these integrated and developmental areas. As explained in the AITSL guidelines: '[Leadership Profile] statements are arranged for principals to view through three leadership lenses – the Professional Practices lens (linked to the Standard's five Professional Practices) the Leadership Requirements lens (linked to the Standard's three Leadership Requirements) and a third lens, the Leadership Emphasis lens (which focuses on broader leadership contexts that principals deal with)' (AITSL, 2019: 11).

Figure 3.1 AITSL's three lenses of proficient school leadership.

Activity 3.1

Select one of AITSL's professional practices from this list:

1 Leading teaching and learning
2 Developing self and others
3 Leading improvement, innovation and change
4 Leading the management of the school
5 Engaging and working with the community

Consider how you would apply this practice to improving the educational experience of a specific group within your school, paying particular attention to issues of social justice. Use some of these questions to guide your plan: Where would you start the process? Who would you involve? What knowledge do you need to acquire? Do you have access to research that can inform your strategy? How will you secure commitment of staff to any innovations?

We do not unpack these practices and requirements in depth here. However, we note that whilst many of these objectives can be read benevolently, they have can have other effects. For example, while, in our view, it is essential that principals have a good grasp of what constitutes excellent teaching and learning, placing the emphasis of responsibility for its quality on the principal in a school can have the effect of de-professionalizing teachers. We strongly support the aims expressed in the Standard but presenting it to principals / aspiring principals as little more than a guide, without substantive inducements to engage with the research that has shaped it, may simply lead to tokenistic compliance.

It has been widely recognized that there is a problem with senior teachers not wanting to be a principal or with principals leaving the position early in many countries

Neoliberalism: characterized by free-market trade, deregulation of financial markets, individualization and the shift away from state welfare provision.

(Ärlestig et al., 2016). This has been attributed to workloads, disillusionment with the ability to effect change, stress and accountability pressures. Australia has been no exception.

Whilst not meant as a mechanism for assessment, without a doubt the Leadership Profiles contained within the Standard can be used in performative ways and thus as a mechanism for 'managing' principals. A key feature of this form of governing – inscribed by **neoliberalism** – is the individualization of the principal.

The quality of a person's education in a school is not down to one person although, without a doubt, the principal has a significant influence over a school. However, the implication that this is possible places enormous pressures on principals. This is particularly the case with the unrelenting focus that governments have on results from standardized tests.

There is a wealth of literature that has looked at the ways in which current concerns about academic outcomes and associated accountability pressures have increased the demands and stresses on principals. These stresses have played themselves out in diverse ways. One concern that has been shared by many concerned with social justice is how some school principals have sought to 'rid' their schools of students who 'damage' the reputation of their school either by their behaviours or their perceived lack of academic endeavours. As systemic data indicates, those who are most severely affected by these decisions are students from poor and marginalized race and ethnic backgrounds, and in particular those from an Indigenous background. While we are not suggesting that principals directly target marginalized groups, the consequences of current pressures can bring this about. For example, if we take one of the focuses from the Professional Practice lens, 'Leading teaching and learning':

> Principals create a positive culture of challenge and support, enabling effective teaching that promotes enthusiastic, independent learners, committed to lifelong learning. Principals have a key responsibility for developing a culture of effective teaching, for leading, designing and managing the quality of teaching and learning and for students' achievement in all aspects of their development. They set high expectations for the whole school through careful collaborative planning, monitoring and reviewing the effectiveness of learning. Principals set high standards of behaviour and attendance, encouraging active engagement and a strong student voice. *(AITSL, 2019: 14)*

This description is then followed by a further four descriptors that indicate increasing proficiency in this field. However, there is a complete absence of links or references to the complexities involved in putting these words into action. There is no recognition given to social context and the diverse needs of differing school populations. These descriptions of leadership proficiency exist in a theoretical vacuum leaving them open to the possibly uninformed, erroneous interpretations of individuals who have never engaged with the theory that explores the relationship between student behaviour and poverty, for example. Indeed, we believe there is a 'lens' missing from AITSL's school leadership framework: the social justice lens.

The Standard presents a behavioural model for change for principals without interrogating the core problem of how many different types of leadership behaviour might achieve the goals described (for example), Leading management of the school: 'Principals align management procedures and processes to the educational goals and the vision and values of the school' (AITSL, 2019: 17). There are many leadership styles discussed in the education literature and we agree with Niesche and Gowlett that '"who leaders are" should not be prescribed through various forms of adjectival leadership, or from fixed categories . . . Instead, leaders are performatively constituted though various discourses and practices' (2015: 373). In accomplishing the *Australian Professional Standard for Principals*, individuals might select from a variety of differing leadership paradigms. For example, authoritarian and/or managerial, both of which imply domination of others; transactional, which involves levels of negotiation and/or influence over others; or visionary, sometimes referred to as 'charismatic' whereby there is great organizational reliance on the individual characteristics of one person for the successful running of the school. It is not our intention to explore the many possible manifestations of school leadership in this chapter, but to argue that an understanding of, and a commitment to, social justice must reside at the heart of a critical approach to school leadership.

> **Social justice:** concerned with justice in terms of the distribution of wealth, opportunities and privileges within a society and with recognizing and valuing difference. In terms of education, it means ensuring equitable and quality educational opportunities and experiences for all students, regardless of race, ethnicity, class, socio-economic status, gender, ableness, sexual identity or any other factors that might contribute to their marginalization.

Social justice

The importance of principals having a strong sense of social justice has been articulated by many working with the educational leadership field. Like many of these, we have been drawn to the work of Nancy Fraser (2009). For Fraser, social justice: 'requires social arrangements that permit all to participate as peers in social life. Overcoming injustice means dismantling institutionalised obstacles that prevent some people from participating on a par with others, as full partners in social interaction' (2009: 16).

For Fraser, three forms of injustice prevent this participation: economic injustice characterized by maldistribution; cultural injustice characterized by misrecognition; and political injustice characterized by misrepresentation. Maldistribution occurs when resources, economic goods and other material benefits from a society are shared in such a way that 'parity of participation' is prevented due to poverty. The remedy for this, she argues, is redistribution. Misrecognition comes about through various forms of discrimination, such as racism, homophobia, misogyny and ageism, which inhibit people's access to equal status in social interactions. The remedy in this case is recognition and valuing of difference. Misrepresentation occurs when people are denied a voice in key decisions affecting them. To address this form of injustice, the remedy is seen as representation. These forms of injustice and their remedies, Fraser recognizes, intersect and are at times

Terms used by Nancy Fraser

Parity of participation: more than an absence of legal discrimination. There are no institutionalized obstacles that prevent anyone from being an equal participant in social life.

Cultural justice: cultural recognition frees individuals or groups from the subordinate status of social culture as well as endowing all social members with equal cultural status and identity.

Economic justice: equal distribution of material resources.

Political justice: this concerns the nature of power and democracy within either the state or institutions. Individuals have rights to a 'voice' and to representation.

Affective justice: affective (relating to feelings and attitudes) equality as a key issue of justice seeks to make visible the affective domain of life as a site of social practice distinct from the economic, cultural and political.

difficult to untangle. She also warns about various remedies that she calls as 'affirmative' rather than 'transformative' (see Keddie, 2012, for fuller exploration). This framework provides a useful lens for exploring the ways in which critical forms of leadership can promote social justice. We also address what some have seen lacking in her framework, for example, notions of affective justice (see Mills et al., 2016, for more on this).

Kathleen Lynch (2012) has drawn attention to the ways in which 'care' has often been ignored in discussions of social justice and argues for an acknowledgement of the ways in which 'affective justice' impact upon people's well-being, participation and value within the community. For her, there are questions about who is doing the caring work and who is cared about. For her there are three levels of affective justice: love, care and solidarity. In short, love relations relate to those one is most close to (family, close friends etc.), care is evident in the relationships with known people (for example, work colleagues and students in a class) and solidarity is with groups of people that one may not know (for example, refugees).

Much has been written about the ways in which new accountabilities tied to test scores and school reputation have often worked against the interests of highly marginalized young people who are seen to be damaging to a school's reputation and academic profile. One such group is pregnant young women. There is a body of literature that indicates that girls who become pregnant whilst still at school risk not finishing their education. Education systems in Australia have policy frameworks that prohibit discrimination against such students. However, the reality is that for many of these young women, their schools may not be overly supportive (McGregor et al., 2017). Whilst for some schools the presence of pregnant girls is seen as damaging to their reputation, the programme at Banksia College (see case study) welcomes not only pregnant young women from a variety of other schools, but also their children. Many of the young women in this programme indicate if it was not for its existence they would not be in a school.

Case Study 3.1 Banksia College's social justice for young parents

Banksia College, a school we have written about previously (see McGregor et al., 2017), has a reputation in its jurisdiction as a highly academic school with diverse social justice programmes. It is also known for being LGBTQ-friendly, for enrolling refugee students and for taking young people whom other local schools do not want. In this case study we focus on an award-winning programme Banksia College has developed for young parents. We examine the school principal's involvement in the creation of the programme and the ways in which he supported others' initiatives and leadership in the area. The case study draws only on interview data generated with the principal. However, in the larger study, we also interviewed teachers and students in the programme. For a much fuller description and analysis of the school's social justice efforts see McGregor et al. (2017).

At the time of writing this case study, this programme was in the process of moving from an off-site building into a multi-million purpose-built on-site facility. The programme has acquired a high profile and has often received ministerial backing. It has received a national award; a key teacher in the programme was awarded a public-service medal; and it has become the focus of several academic studies and media stories. At the time of our site visits to the school, it had approximately 100 enrolled students.

The programme does not offer a watered-down curriculum to the participants; all have access to the national senior curriculum. However, recognizing the needs of the students to combine their studies with parenting responsibilities and the needs of their children or matters related to their pregnancy, there is no timetable and the students engage with their learning flexibly. Recent developments in information technologies have also facilitated working from home. As the principal noted: 'So the intention was always to deliver a quality year 11/12 experience that was – well, it was never going to be exactly the same experience as someone in a mainstream situation, but on par with it, a different mode of delivery. You can't just keep using the same structures.'

As with many programmes for marginalized young people, attendance was often low. The principal, Robert, spoke about how this was, early on, seen as a negative for the programme. He often disagreed with his director and had to point out that prior to the programme, the students were receiving *no* education – he noted that, 'It took me about three years to win that one'. Another issue that often surfaced was that many of the young people were at the time not completing a formal certificate in education. However, whilst in his view it would be good for the students to receive formal certification, 'it wasn't the beall and endall'. He argued that: 'What these programmes are doing is drawing students who haven't had access to education back into education but not only back into education, back into mainstream society, back into developing a trust with adults that lots of them had lost; and those things were for me way more valuable than their year 10/12 certificate.'

Robert also noted that there were other non-educational benefits to the programme. For example, he highlighted the ways in which the health of the students and their children were also addressed through involving the local health authority right from the start. He argued that: 'Young parents who wouldn't have taken the trouble to go to the local clinic were very happy to go and chat to the nurse.'

He also noted how the programme benefited enormously from a major award received as part of a banking promotion involving schools. He spoke about how an email had gone out to all principals about these awards and:

> [O]ne of the things I was thinking you have got to do as a principal is: these things come across your desk quite often and it's so easy just to delete them from your email. There are opportunities that arise and sometimes you have just got to have a sense that maybe this is worth having a second look at. I did look at that and think, 'Well, this is interesting. They are going to be in (the local area) in February. No harm in going along and listening.'

He took several staff with him, including those involved in setting up the parents' programme. With very few other principals in the audience he felt that there was a good chance of securing one of the awards so they submitted an entry. In the end they won two awards: $50,000 and $100,000.

Whilst the money was important, more significantly the award gave the programme prominence in the local jurisdiction. There was also the appointment of a new Director-General (D-G) of Education who was extremely supportive of what the school was trying to do. He spoke of how the new D-G came to visit the school and:

> I was there, with him, when we walked in the door, into that beautiful, big, open-plan learning area; and there were mummies and there were a few dads, not so many dads, and babies; and he walked and he said, 'This is great. We need to be doing more of this. In fact, we need to make this better.' And that was a big turning point because the few people who were left in the Department, who doubted that such programme should exist – well, once the directorgeneral starts saying things, people are only too happy to climb on board.

The school then became involved in a national network supporting young women who were pregnant or were new parents. He noted that 'That was another one that arose from one of these many emails that's come across the principal's desk.' The email related to a women's symposium to be held in another state and he organized for himself and two staff to go to deliver a presentation on their programme and to network with others working across Australia. In terms of the issue of supporting young women in school who were pregnant or parents, he saw their involvement as 'trying to get some national movement on it'. They hosted the symposium in a following year and managed to attract up to 200 participants from education, health and welfare agencies and some ministers of education to it. The reputation of the programme was further enhanced through a key teacher being awarded a public-service medal (after nomination by the principal and support from the D-G) for her work in the programme.

Robert also noted that their work was aligning with a variety of new policy initiatives designed to support single and teenage parents, which also meant they were attracting attention from the policy sector and managed to secure extra funding for a suite of vocational programmes. These programmes were to be delivered by an off-site provider. This meant that the funds did not go directly to the school. However this: 'didn't really matter because the students were getting access to some high-level training; training in care, beauty, business, childcare, all of those things'. One consequence of their success was that the government overseeing education in their jurisdiction awarded them $1.5 million in the budget to design 'a custombuilt facility' for the programme. This also meant that there was likely to be later government funding for a new building 'because you don't throw $1.5 million into design work' unless that was the case. And as expected this occurred. At the time of collecting our last set of interview data, the multi-million-dollar building, which had been designed by architects in conjunction with the students in the programme, was being constructed on the school site. Robert had hopes that the new building would facilitate greater integration of students into other programmes offered by the school whilst also allowing them to retain the benefits of the off-site programme.

Robert always spoke highly of the ways in which the teachers in the programme worked with the students. He saw himself as the facilitator of the work that was being done by the teachers: 'In terms of individual involvement with students, for me that's been very limited. I would go over and visit maybe once a fortnight, chat to a few people; but I didn't ever see it as my role to get heavily involved on the ground.'

He went on to say how he and the teachers in the programme all had 'different strengths' which complemented each other. He was strongly of the view that the programme was only successful because of the efforts, vison and commitments of others.

Critical educational leadership

We use this short case study to illustrate the aspects of what we see as critical educational leadership and then link this to the AITSL Standard. We begin with an illustration of how the programme was shaped by a commitment to social justice.

Those who come to the principalship with a critical perspective invariably have a vison that is shaped in consultation with others, but is often framed within a commitment to social justice. For example, in the case study, the principal spoke of the need for adults to regain the trust of those young people who had lost faith in 'mainstream society' and that that was 'more valuable than their year 10/12 certificate'. Implicit in his arguments was the need to ensure 'parity of participation' in 'social interactions with others' for these (mainly) young women. This commitment was also evident in his view that the new building's location on the main campus would facilitate the students' access to the mainstream school activities and curricula, whilst retaining the benefits of their own space.

In Nancy Fraser's terms, young women who become pregnant or who have children while at school are a 'despised' group in that they experience injustices based on *recognition*. We have interviewed many young women at this and other schools who have told us of being stared at on buses, of overhearing derogatory comments, of being told by their former schools 'to hide the bump' or to wear baggier clothing. Many of these young women also experience economic hardship, some have the help of families, but some are in families already lacking economic resources, some 'go it alone' or move in with their usually young boyfriends and struggle to meet commitments like rent, food and other necessities, never mind coping with the financial demands of attending school.

The principal of Banksia was very well aware of the issues facing the young women who attended the programme. In relation to school, he acknowledged that it was illegal for schools to 'expel' pregnant students, but noted that whilst, 'There are certainly policies that say that shouldn't happen, the reality is very different to the good intentions that might be enshrined in policies'. Such students could be discouraged from attending a school by being told 'there's no way that we can really cater for you easily, or it's going to be really hard for you if you are coming here. Just think of what the other students will be saying.' He also noted that many suffered financially and some had no support from their immediate family. In many of his comments there was a clear commitment on his part to social justice and addressing the discrimination, or 'stigmatization', that these young women experienced.

In terms of *distribution*, he was not prepared to see these young women offered a curriculum that was of a lesser standard than that offered in a mainstream. He explained that the student body in the programme was varied and was reflective of the mainstream school population. He stated that 'They are not any more or any less talented than any other young person'. As such he was of the view that they should be provided with the same opportunities. This is important as restricting these young women to a lesser or 'dead-end' curriculum will restrict their life chances and opportunities to secure economic security in the future. This is a view that is widely shared by many school principals and couched in terms of 'high expectations'. However, contained within this view there is often the expectation that the young mothers will also meet all of the same curriculum requirements under the same conditions. This is often impractical. Again, this was recognized by the principal. Recognition was also implicit in the ways in which the school developed flexible approaches to, for example, attendance and submission of assignments.

There was also an acknowledgement that *representation* was critical for parity of participation. This was evident in the ways in which the students were heavily involved in the construction of the new building. On one of our visits to the school prior to the building being completed, a small group of young women showed us the plans that they had been developing in consultation with the architects; they had a real sense of ownership of the building. This demonstrated that their voices mattered to the principal, that in a socially just world they would be able to contribute to key decisions that affected them.

We also want to highlight the presence of affective justice within the discourses being articulated by the principal. His connection to the programme could be framed in Kathleen Lynch's terms as an act of '*solidarity*'. He did not have close relationships with the people in the programme, but saw that as a matter of social justice these young women required more opportunities than were currently being provided by the education system. He also *cared* about the staff with whom he worked, as exemplified by his efforts to ensure that one of the key teachers in the programme was nominated and secured a public-service medal. We have highlighted the role of the principal in this chapter, not to perpetuate a hero narrative, but to illustrate the possibility of expanding AITSL's Standard to include a social justice 'lens' so as to embed critical perspectives within paradigms of school leadership.

Conclusion

In this chapter, we have argued that the Standard used in Australia to construct notions of educational leadership is missing a 'fourth lens' of social justice. Through our case study, we have exemplified what leadership might look like with this lens added, by exploring the professional practices of a school principal committed to providing an education for *all* young people through attempts to dismantle 'institutionalized obstacles that prevent some (young) people from participating on a par with others'. This commitment to young people is evidence of an approach to education that sees its purpose as including but going beyond academic achievement. As such it reflects a view of schooling that assists young people in making sense of their world, of being able to live a meaningful life in that world, and to make changes to that world in order to make it a better place. The actions of this principal and those of the associated staff are clearly aligned (without any explicit reference to it) with the expectations of the Standard.

Critical leadership often involves speaking back to powerful people and systems, especially when it comes to matters of social justice. There is sometimes an assumption that school leaders are the implementers of policy mandated by 'central office' and/or government. However, as the case study principal stated, 'it took me three years to win that one'. In our view the Standard can be employed to facilitate this speaking back. For example, it indicates that leaders must support all young people in their right to access an education. We would like to see the addition of the 'fourth lens' of social justice to remove some of the ambiguity of the current framework. However, in the meantime, this ambiguity facilitates its use as a critically reflective tool.

Activity 3.2

1 What kind of school leadership styles have you observed?
2 What are the key qualities you would look for in a school principal?
3 Construct your own visual representation of what the 'socially just school' might look like.

Further reading

Blackmore, J. (2016) *Educational leadership and Nancy Fraser*. New York: Routledge.

Connell, R. (2009) Good teachers on dangerous ground: towards a new view of teacher quality and professionalism. *Critical Studies in Education*, 50(3), 213–229.

Dinham, S., Collarbone, P., Evans, M. and Mackay, A. (2013) The development, endorsement and adoption of a National Standard for Principals in Australia. *Educational Management Administration & Leadership*, 41(4), 467–483.

O'Brien, P.C. (2015) Performance government: activating and regulating the self-governing capacities of teachers and school leaders. *Educational Philosophy and Theory*, 47(8), 833–847.

Thomson, P. (2009) *School leadership: heads on the block?* Abingdon: Routledge.

References

Ärlestig, H., Day, C. and Johansson, O. (eds) (2016) *A decade of research on school principals: cases from 24 countries*. Cham: Springer.

Australian Institute for Teaching and School Leadership (AITSL) (2018) *Australian Professional Standard for Teachers*. Melbourne: AITSL. Available online: https://www.aitsl.edu.au/teach/standards (accessed 17 July 2020).

Australian Institute for Teaching and School Leadership (AITSL) (2019) *Australian Professional Standard for Principals and the Leadership Profiles*. Melbourne: AITSL. Available online: https://www.aitsl.edu.au/tools-resources/resource/australian-professional-standard-for-principals (accessed 17 July 2020).

Fraser, N. (2009) *Scales of justice: reimagining political space in a globalizing world*. New York: Columbia University Press.

Keddie, A. (2012) Schooling and social justice through the lenses of Nancy Fraser. *Critical Studies in Education*, 53(3), 263–279.

Lingard, B., Hayes, D., Mills, M. and Christie, P. (2003) *Leading learning: making hope practical in schools*. Buckingham: Open University Press.

Lynch, K. (2012) Affective equality as a key issue of justice: a comment on Fraser's 3-dimensional framework. *Social Justice Series*, 12(3), 45–64. Dublin: University College Dublin.

McGregor, G., Mills, M., te Riele, K., Baroutsis, A. and Hayes, D. (2017) *Re-imagining schooling for education*. Basingstoke: Palgrave Macmillan.

Mills, M., McGregor, G., Baroutsis, A., te Riele, K. and Hayes, D. (2016) Alternative education and social justice: Considering issues of affective and contributive justice. *Critical Studies in Education*, 57(1), 100–115.

Niesche, R. (2011) *Foucault and educational leadership: disciplining the principal*. Abingdon: Routledge.

Niesche, R. and Gowlett, C. (2015) Advocating a post-structuralist for educational leadership. *Educational Philosophy and Theory*, 47(4), 372–386.

Critical perspectives in educational leadership in South Africa

Pontso Moorosi and Jan Heystek

4

What this chapter is about 60

Key questions that this chapter addresses 60

Introduction 60

Policies contributing to contemporary practice 62

What educational leadership looks like in South Africa 63

Understanding social justice in the context of South Africa 64

A critical perspective on leadership for quality education using social justice 67

Critical perspectives of the field of educational leadership 68

Social justice as Ubuntu 69

Transformative leadership for social justice 69

Conclusion 71

Further reading 72

References 72

What this chapter is about

In this chapter, we adopt a social-justice approach to examine critical perspectives in and approaches to educational leadership in South Africa. The background for our analysis is the apartheid regime, whose laws, policies and practices divided education privilege and economic opportunities along racial lines, reserving the most lucrative jobs and opportunities for the white population, leaving Black women most disadvantaged. This created lasting systemic inequalities within society, mainly between Black and white, prompting the democratic government to adopt a corrective approach to create a more balanced society. In bringing a critical perspective to bear, we elucidate Ubuntu leadership, which is a traditional Indigenous construct focusing on communality and interdependence, and which we argue has considerable significance as a resource for thinking about and doing educational leadership. We draw mainly from school-based experiences, and yet our discussion has relevance for educational leadership across different levels, including higher education.

Key questions that this chapter addresses

1 What are current professional practices of educational leadership in South Africa?
2 What is the historical background underpinning these practices in South Africa?
3 What are the meanings of social justice as it relates to the South African educational leadership context?
4 How might we use critical perspectives in and critical approaches to educational leadership as underpinned by the social-justice framework in the South African context?

Introduction

Before 1994, South Africa was governed for over four decades by a system of apartheid that propagated racial segregation, preceded by white colonial rule that had dispossessed Black native communities from their land. The post-apartheid laws and policies driven by the Constitution of South Africa (1996) were therefore underpinned by a social-justice agenda to eliminate social and economic gaps. Since education policy had been used as an instrument of control to protect power and segregation, the effects of the past are deep-rooted and still felt more than two decades after the demise of apartheid. Current educational leaders are therefore expected to play a significant role in facilitating dialogue and action through which more democratic processes and socially just ways of learning and leading can be enacted.

While South Africa has been (and still is) a patriarchal society, the oppression of women was exacerbated by apartheid laws that reserved more senior jobs for white men, confining women, particularly Black women to domestic responsibilities and teaching at lower levels. Indeed, in one of the most famous speeches in 1953, the former apartheid minister of Native Affairs, later prime minister, H.F. Verwoerd, said:

> As a woman is by nature so much better fitted for handling young children, and as the great majority of Bantu children are to be found in lower classes of primary school, it follows that there should be far more female teachers than male teachers . . . Quota will be laid down at training colleges as regards numbers of male and female candidates respectively which may be allowed to enter for the courses *(Truscott, 1994: 22)*

This entrenched the feminization of teaching, particularly at lower levels, pushing men into higher-paying positions with better chances of promotion. However, Black men's educational preparation was still the poorest compared to racial counterparts, given the unequal provision for education.

Under apartheid, education was divided into racially and ethnically determined multiple departments that provided different qualities of education, unequally funded. Thus, the ideology of segregation and an inferior type of education amongst Black people was deliberately entrenched. Although the Apartheid system of education has been legally eradicated in the new dispensation, and a unified non-racist system of education created, the legacy of unequal quality education is still prevalent, whereby most Black people are still at the very bottom educationally, economically and socially. Some deeply held cultures, values and practices within schools and universities remain unchanged, leading to a continuing imbalance and an increasing economic gap within society. It is in this sense that the education system is seen as the chief

> **Apartheid:** a legislated system of racial discrimination that officially divided the South African society along racial and ethnic lines from 1948 to 1994. Under apartheid, people were classified into four racial groups (white, Indian, Coloured and Black) that were prohibited by law from interacting with one another; for example, interracial marriages were prohibited and separate living areas were created. In 1994 apartheid was abolished and a new democratic government was elected.

'culprit in the reproduction of historic patterns of inequality in South Africa today' (Chipkin and Meny-Gibert, 2013: 8); where quality education remains inaccessible to most children and poor results are reproduced for poor Black South Africans. Against this backdrop, the role of educational leadership is deemed critical in advancing fairness, equality and inclusion within the broader frame of social justice.

As a direct legacy of apartheid, only about 25 per cent of schools in South Africa today provide functional quality education with regard to international tests comparisons, local examination results, standardized testing programmes and general transition from school to the higher-education system (see Spaull, 2013). Schools in this category are mostly at state-of-the-art, world-class standard with regard to facilities, resources, learning inputs and outcomes. They include independent schools, historically white schools with some former Indian and Coloured schools. The rest of the schools (approximately 75 per cent) are on a continuum from a few schools built of mud to those closer to the state-of-the-art schools physically but largely characterized by poor performance, leadership, governance and resources. Most of these schools are former Black-only schools, engineered to provide a poor quality of education, deemed to be dysfunctional in the apartheid era and still regarded mostly ineffective in the present era (Spaull, 2013). While the current disparity is a direct result of the apartheid system, it endures twenty-five years after the first democratically elected government.

Policies contributing to contemporary practice

Post-1994, a plethora of education policies in South Africa informed by its highly progressive Constitution, and founded on social-justice principles, have advanced democratic participation, inclusivity, equity and gender equality. The South African Constitution, Article 9(3), prohibits discrimination on any grounds, including race, gender, language, disability and others. Education is driven primarily by the South African Schools Act (SASA) of 1996 that stipulates that all schools must be inclusive to all learners regardless of their background, and regards any form of discrimination based on grounds of diversity an offence punishable by law. From the legal perspective, equal and quality education is guaranteed for all learners, hence the mandate for open access and inclusion. However, it may be argued that these ideals remain highly normative, lacking operative commitment.

The SASA also makes provisions to increase democratic participation for school management (through school management teams: SMT) and governance (through school governing bodies (SGB) and learner representative councils (LRC)) in recognition of required democratic representation and inclusive participation in the running of schools. Supplementing the Act, the three most important documents that explain the roles and responsibilities of principals, promotional posts and teachers as well as the assessment of all these posts are the Personnel Administrative Measures (PAM), the Integrated Quality Management Systems (IQMS) and the Standards for Principalship, all available on the Department website education.gov.za. Although these three documents are managerial and functionalist and do not explicitly refer to social justice, they do make reference to social-justice values linking to socio-economic conditions in schools.

As a result of the new anti-racist policies, significant progress has been made in some areas with regard to redressing the inequalities inherited from the past. In particular, the SASA mandates open access and free education into schools that were previously not accessible to all learners. Open-access education has resulted in more diverse demographic profiles of learners in historically white schools that Black learners were previously not allowed to attend (although the profiles of teachers and leaders are still lagging behind). Additionally, affirmative-action policies, driven by the Employment Equity Act (1998) have also had significant impact improving the chances of women getting promoted into leadership position and improving economic opportunities for Black people, although significant improvements are yet to be seen in educational leadership.

What educational leadership looks like in South Africa

Three key aspects currently characterize the landscape of educational leadership in South Africa that we will focus on for the purposes of this chapter. First, due to the constitutional principle of democratic participation in South Africa, there is a demand for schools to practise democratic governance and an expectation on school leaders to adopt more democratic practices of leadership that encourage wider participation. However, under the historical structural constraints, research shows that school leadership is often equated to principalship, which tends to exclude other members of the SMT and teachers from decision-making. School principals are also held accountable for the quality of education in their schools and the performance of teachers, which is likely to influence the autocratic style of leadership they operationalize, since 'the buck stops' with them. This shows that old models of controlling autocratic power inherent from the old autocratic system (Grant, 2014) remain resistant to change despite some rhetoric to more democratic forms, thereby making educational leadership socially exclusive.

Second, educational leadership is also characterized by unequal representation on both gender and racial terms respectively: more men than women are still seen as principals and chairs of governing bodies. Leadership is thus constructed in male terms, wherein quality and effective leadership are attributed to dominant notions of leadership that favour men through masculine cultures of work and traits such as assertiveness, strength and decisiveness. As women have historically been confined to primary teaching and within a dominant culture of patriarchy, they do not ordinarily benefit from such discourses and are often excluded from positions of leadership. Another issue is that of racial representation where the demographic profiles of the majority of teachers and school leaders and in some SGBs in historically white schools do not reflect the diversity of the student profiles (Wray, Hellenberg and Jansen, 2019). Thus, despite the policy rhetoric of democratic participation and equal representation, issues of gender and racial representation remain a significant social-justice challenge that is likely to perpetuate social exclusion inherent from the past.

Third is the effectiveness of educational leadership in ensuring that equity and inclusion of all learners are upheld and that all learners are offered quality education regardless of their socio-economic background. There are two ways in which achieving social justice is a challenge in this regard:

1 Despite the legal provision of free education, learners from poor backgrounds are not exempt from school fees in the higher-quintile schools which are the independent and historically white schools that mostly provide good-quality education. In these schools, decisions on whom to include are primarily driven by individual learners' socio-economic conditions, which leads to perpetual exclusion of learners from poor backgrounds, denying them access to quality education.

2 Some of these schools remain culturally inaccessible; learners who have overcome the socio-economic barrier experience an ethos of cultural exclusion, wherein they are expected simply to assimilate into the prevailing ethos of the existing schools

(Brown, 2006; Wray, Hellenberg and Jansen, 2019). In these schools, educational leadership values and practices remain 'unambiguously chauvinistic and deeply authoritarian' (Brown, 2006: 514). While most of these principals were trained in the old system, a younger generation of school principals is gradually getting into the system, and change remains to be seen.

Understanding social justice in the context of South Africa

Social justice is now a commonly used concept in many educational contexts as a way to recognize the need to support students from diverse backgrounds to equally enjoy the best benefits of a learning environment.

Social justice: the meaning of social justice is widely acknowledged to be complex and evolving given the varying nature of the sources of injustice in different contexts and the circumstances within which is it expected to operate. Despite the different adaptations, however, social justice recognizes unjustifiable inequalities and starts from the premise of commitment to anti-oppressive laws, policies and practices that create a society in which everybody, regardless of their backgrounds, stands to benefit. For the purposes of this chapter, social justice is understood as a philosophical standpoint founded on the principles of fairness, equity and equality of human rights, distribution of services, resources and opportunities to all people.

In the South African context, where social and racial injustices were legislated against a group of people, it follows that social-justice principles are equally legislated in response to uprooting all forms of discrimination, redressing the imbalances of the past and establishing a new set of values. Chipkin and Meny-Gibert (2013) state that the concept of fairness, which is central to social justice, only arrived in South African discourse in the 1990s when the fight against racism and white capitalism became a legislative affair. It therefore follows that the significance of the social-justice agenda is established by the Constitution, which serves as the cornerstone of South African democracy. Although social-justice principles underpinned the Constitution by prohibiting all forms of discrimination, educational leadership and management policies subsequent to the Constitution do not explicitly provide for the implementation of social justice. It might therefore be difficult for some school leaders to apply social justice in their decision-making and general enactment of leadership without clear guidance.

Let us consider Figure 4.1. It illustrates the three pillars of social justice, namely equality, equity and fairness. We define each of these pillars in turn and attempt to apply them to educational leadership in the South African context in the sections following. **Equality**, being equal or being treated equally, for example, before the law is taken to mean that everyone has equal rights and same status and that everyone receives the same treatment; but it does not mean that everybody is the same. For school leaders, equality implies that learners must be treated equally and not be discriminated against because of their backgrounds. However, the reality is that not everybody starts from the same equal level, and this is where equity comes in to level the playing field.

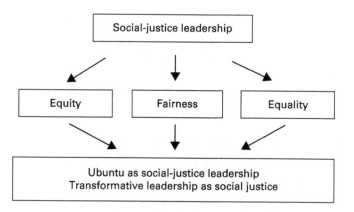

Figure 4.1 Social-justice leadership.

Rawls (1999) posits that societies have traditionally been characterized by inequalities whether of poverty, gender or ability/disability. More poignantly, the South African reality is such that the unlevel playing field between Black and white people and between men and women was legally orchestrated. **Equity** is thus about ensuring that people get access to the same opportunities and resources, which may mean differential treatment in view of the different opportunities created by the previous regime. Equity implies that school leaders may exempt some learners from paying school fees if the parents are not able to pay. This would allow the learners to have equal access to quality education even though the exemption may mean that schools would have less funding, which may have some influence on the quality of education in the longer term.

Equity is much more linked to, and difficult to separate from, the concept of fairness. **Fairness** denotes operating in a more egalitarian society where everyone holds basic equal rights. For school leaders, the legislation provides for exemption from school fees, which makes it possible for learners from all backgrounds to access quality education. Fairness may also mean that a qualifying member of the previously marginalized group is selected for promotion over a member of the previously privileged in order to achieve full gender or racial parity. While equality and equity can both be used to produce fairness, fairness is more of a challenge for educational leaders since it can be contextual and subject to interpretation.

In Figure 4.1, the three pillars of social justice are divided for conceptual clarity but end up converging into Ubuntu and transformative leadership (defined in more detail later) which has direct implications for leadership practice in what we propose. It is arguably more difficult (if not unhelpful) to separate the pillars of social justice in actual practice as they are inextricably entwined. In Rawls's (1999) concept of 'justice as fairness', these three concepts are interlinked and are all necessary for a just society based on what we understand as social justice in this chapter. What is important is that all practices of educational leadership must be underpinned by an understanding of what marginalization means and the disposition to act appropriately so that meaningful social change can be achieved. The implementation of this may therefore be a challenge to school leaders who are not attuned to prejudice, and whose understanding of inequities is limited within the school environment.

Our case study will explain the challenges of applying the principles of social justice at different levels of educational leadership practice, especially in a demanding social-justice environment. For example, there may be competing interests between the principal at the school and leaders at other levels, even though they would all be driven by the desire to provide quality education for all learners.

Case Study 4.1 Overvaal School vs Gauteng Ministry of Basic Education

Overvaal is a high school in the Gauteng province, classified as a former white Afrikaans school; Afrikaans still serves as the official medium of instruction as allowed by the Constitution. Since 1994, schools may not discriminate against learners with regard to language, religion, gender and others and learners are allowed access to any school where it is *reasonably practical*. The challenge in this case is for education leaders across the system to provide equal access for all learners to quality education. Overvaal is perceived as one of the 'best' schools by the broader community in the area where the school is located. Although the school was filled to capacity (according to the school's report), at the beginning of the 2018 academic year, the provincial Department of Basic Education, responsible for allocation of learners to schools, attempted to placed fifty-five learners who did not speak Afrikaans in Overvaal which would force the school to adopt a dual or parallel medium of instruction. The school did not want to accept the children in the school and rejected the learners on the grounds of lack of capacity. This led to violent protests from the community of Black parents whose learners were rejected by the school. The school's governing body (which is responsible for the policies) took the Department to court and won the case on the grounds that the Department did not consider the fact that there were other English medium schools within a practical and realistic distance from Overvaal, which had capacity to accommodate the fifty-five learners, although the community does not perceive the other schools to be the same level of educational quality as Overvaal. Although the school felt the court's judgment was fair, the outcome of the case was not acceptable to the parents of the learners and the wider community, which felt the school was using language to maintain the status quo.

Activity 4.1

1 What do you consider to be fair and unfair in this case? To whom?
2 How would you balance the needs of the larger group versus the needs of the individual with regard to social justice?

A critical perspective on leadership for quality education using social justice

In putting forward a disposition to act differently, we view social justice not as an alternative style of leadership, but as a principle underpinning all educational leadership practice. We align our argument with discourses emerging in the context of South Africa advocating ways which foreground democracy and social justice in enacting leadership.

How then, can we use a social-justice framing to argue for alternative practices of educational leadership? What might such practices look like? What might they contribute to the overall provision of quality education and social change?

Against the backdrop of the structural limitations already described, the ideal is to provide quality education for all South Africa's children regardless of racial or socio-economic background. The SASA stipulates the provision of an education of progressively high quality for all learners, which we would argue aligns with Rawls's conception of virtue of quality life and liberty. In this sense, leadership has a moral responsibility to facilitate dialogue aimed towards the achievement of high-quality educational outcomes. Currently, quality education is associated with, amongst other things: high-quality facilities which include the proper school infrastructure (buildings, classrooms, sanitation, water), high-quality teaching (shaped by motivated, well-trained and qualified teachers with positive attitudes) and the provision of learning materials and support, as well as efficient leadership and management of instruction. It is specifically schools in the lower socio-economic communities that are challenged to provide better instructional leadership; schools and communities living under the most difficult circumstances struggle to attain such quality. We acknowledge that, although the school infrastructure is an important factor in providing high-quality education, it is not the most important factor. Some schools in low socio-economic areas do not possess state-of-the-art facilities but consistently perform highly, producing good academic results against the odds (e.g. Naicker, Grant and Pillay, 2016). This suggests the need to critically examine what constitutes quality education in different contexts in South Africa. In redefining quality, school outcomes do not have to be limited to high academic performance, but can be defined differently by school communities in view of their own circumstances, and linked to children's holistic development, guided by social-justice values. This perspective arguably presents educational leaders with a dual challenge of (re)defining quality education and achieving it within the means of their school environment. Within this framing, in order for schools to provide holistic quality education for all learners, the whole education system would need to change and measures of success be redefined.

There are two strands to our argument:

1 Current research provides evidence of resilient schools that perform well nationally despite adverse socio-economic conditions. Such schools show that effective leadership, shared beyond the principal and the SMT, can enable change. In such cases, teachers possess high professional capital including leadership, which makes them agentic social actors (Naicker, Grant and Pillay, 2016). This is often linked with dedication and commitment to teaching and leadership which facilitate a good

learning experience, including attendance and time on task, willingness to walk the extra mile not necessarily driven by external rewards (e.g. salary and extra funds), but driven by deep intrinsic motivation based on values to serve and support the learners and staff to achieve their best. Schools are therefore not isolated from the environment, context and collective nature of the communities in which most of them are located. In fact, research on resilient schools shows higher levels of community interdependence, an aspect deeply rooted in Indigenous ways of living.

2 Creating autonomy for school leaders (and arguably for teachers as well) requires professional recognition. As we have argued, the social-justice perspective considers school leaders to possess a moral imperative to act in socially just ways, ensuring dialogue that facilitates social change. Leaders could also act as agents facilitating change, active participants in policymaking rather than passive recipients of policy or 'policy implementers'. Research often shows school principals lamenting their role as mere policy implementers who are not even consulted for policy decisions (e.g. Bantwini and Moorosi, 2018). By being more active in the policy process, school leaders and teachers would play a more active and responsible role in representation (e.g. in unions) and would arguably have more agency in influencing meaningful change. We recognize the need for capacity-building through leadership preparation and continuing leadership development programmes in order for educational leaders to achieve this level of political activism, which Blackmore (2011) argues is essential for sustainable change and transformation, but would also ensure a restored sense of professionalism in educational leadership and teaching.

Critical perspectives of the field of educational leadership

The foregoing discussion foregrounds some critical points. First, current practice suggests that school leadership is constructed in autocratic rather than democratic terms. There is a limitation to this practice, based on the nature of schools within the South African context and the policy and law governing education from the perspectives of social justice and democratic participation. Autocratic forms of leadership are more likely to exclude rather than include, perpetuating marginalization of peripheral voices. Second, we realize that if we are to contribute to how leadership practitioners in South Africa and indeed across the world are to develop socially just ways of leading, we ought to provide some theoretical perspectives to be drawn upon. We recognize that some school leaders may be willing to enact social justice in their leadership but may lack the know-how. Equally, students may want to interrogate the concept further, but lack the tools of investigation and theories of analysis. We acknowledge that there may be other ways and we therefore do not proclaim we have all the answers. But we attempt to provide some of the ways in which practices of social-justice leadership can be thought about, enacted and investigated in the South African context.

Social justice as Ubuntu

An undeniable strength of Indigenous African communities is their ability to work together for the benefit of the community. This is rooted in communal and interdependent ways in which members of the community live – an understanding that is deeply rooted in African-ness, known as Ubuntu (humaneness), meaning, 'a person is a person through others'. This philosophy denotes a way of life that instils the spirit of unity within a community that benefits all.

> **Ubuntu**: in its traditional sense, a construct explaining a way of life indigenous to most African societies, where there is communality and interdependence. Ubuntu is premised on the common good, communal solidarity emphasizing the idea of interdependence rather than independence (Nkondo, 2007).

Our understanding of social justice is communitarian and assumes that human beings are interdependent. This interdependence is central to the Ubuntu philosophy and we find social justice as a sociopolitical agenda within which Ubuntu would thrive. Thus, for the principle of Ubuntu to be actualized, school leaders would operate in collective and collaborative ways that recognize strengths and weaknesses and provide solidarity and upliftment within members of the school community. In the philosophical framing of Ubuntu, social justice is inevitably a way of life where people exercise compassion and fairness, embodying notions of communal justice (see Letseka, 2014). This way, communities pull resources together, forming communities of practice with improved chances to deal with contending interests.

Ubuntu therefore implies that educational leaders will function on the principles of justice and fairness, since doing what is morally right and fair is demanded by humanness within the community. This encourages open communication that gives educational leaders an opportunity to be more consultative in taking decisions that are for the good of those involved. Traditional African communities had existing groups and groupings through which they engaged issues that concern the public. Similarly, schools have different stakeholder groups (learners, teachers, parents, etc.), which could be drawn upon and be engaged to tackle problems, understanding their root cause and working collaboratively with the wider community to find solutions. As Nkondo (2007) suggests, educational leaders can use their popular mandate to discourage and disrupt old cultures and practices inherent from the past, to create new ones that are informed by Ubuntu social-justice principles.

Transformative leadership for social justice

Transformative leadership is closely linked to Ubuntu through its emphasis on interdependence and interconnectedness. It is also closely linked to and in some instances used interchangeably with social-justice leadership. However, transformative leadership goes a step further by emphasizing a shared vision and activism in challenging the status quo. Shields (2010) reminds us that transformative leadership starts by asking questions about equity and justice; principles that are central to what we advocate in this chapter. Transformative educational leadership is particularly relevant in the South African context, where transformation is already linked to the political agenda of transforming society from exclusion to a more inclusive one. For educational leaders to be transformative and take the necessary action, they would have to be conscientized to issues of marginalization and be able to recognize injustice as and when it happens and take action. Perhaps this suggests the need to build sensitization into training programmes so that educational leaders learn how to develop sensitivity to injustice as part of building a repertoire of skills to tackle prejudice and injustice.

Consciousness-raising is arguably a significant step towards a more transformative and socially just way of leading, driven by values that have a strong foundation in humanity and are also shared across different societies and religions. Madimbo (2016) sees transformative and engaging leadership as an approach of African spirituality and resilience to bring about change within different spheres of influence. This would require a more systemic and systematic change that builds more capacity and capability among different generations of leaders and teachers, giving school leaders more autonomy. We believe that with autonomy comes responsibility and accountability; and thus, educational leaders across the different levels can be made as accountable for social justice as they are or should be for instructional leadership and overall management of education.

An alternative role for education may be needed to refocus schools, making them more holistic and values-driven, and working towards developing morally responsible citizens rather than just focusing on high pass-rates in examinations. Heystek (2014) argued for a culture of a deep moral accountability to children, their parents and the broader community that may also facilitate a wider political and social function through engagement of stakeholders, working with existing community groups in serving for the public good. This means involvement of different stakeholder groups such as learners, parents and government: after all, social justice is about hearing the different voices. Developing alternative goals for education would arguably curb high dropout rates of learners and address other social challenges in the system, improving children's life chances overall. This means enacting leadership that transforms rather than maintains the status quo and requires moral courage to make change happen. So our case-study school leadership and community may need to think more critically about ways in which more inclusion can be encouraged rather than maintaining the way things have always been. Transformative leadership practices promote emancipatory pedagogies that arise from social and political movements (Blackmore, 2011). In the post-apartheid era, leaders need to be given capacity and autonomy to decide, so that they can initiate dialogues that deconstruct discourses that are taken for granted and transform the education system to be more inclusive, more equitable and more socially just.

Activity 4.2

Social justice is not just a legal expectation or a policy ideal. Social justice is contextual and is a process of fairness that can be applied in real situations facing educational institutions on a daily basis. This means that people will have different perspectives on and interpretations of social justice, hence the notion of competing interests. We acknowledge the challenge of encouraging educational leaders to act in transformative and socially just ways given the depth of the injustices inherent from the apartheid past and beyond. This in itself may mean different interpretations for different people. In fact, as authors from different backgrounds we had to negotiate our own differences and how they inform our understanding and interpretation of social justice.

What has influenced your own understanding and practice of social justice?

When there are high levels of dialogue, issues such as those raised in the case study for this chapter would not end up in a court where a judgment is made, but may still not be acceptable to different interest groups in the situation. Therefore it is important to understand that social justice has a much more human face and not only a legal face, and this is what is expected of school leaders: to work according to social-justice principles and to satisfy the needs of different and contesting role players.

The Constitution even makes provision for fair discrimination where needed to comply with the principles of social justice (Bill of Rights section 9).

Conclusion

Educational leaders have a strong, although indirect, influence on the quality of education as currently understood and measured by examination results. The social-justice approach to educational leadership we advocate provides an alternative challenge and call for principals – one that asks them to dig deep, act humanely and challenge the status quo. Achieving equal opportunity, equity and fairness for all learners is not only the responsibility of the principal at every local school, but the local community is needed as part of the school environment to provide equity of opportunities for all children. This social-justice perspective therefore calls for shared collaboration and collective action between schools and local communities, as well as with district, provincial and national resources. Bridging the gap between schools is a significant challenge and we appreciate that our suggestions for the achievement of socially just leadership made in this chapter have implications for leadership development and making educational leaders accountable for social justice, something that may be difficult to enforce.

Social justice with regard to equal and fair access to schools is still an issue of authority for schools. This aspect of social justice involves sufficient political involvement at provincial and national level, for example, the case Overvaal versus the Member of

Executive Council in Gauteng should not only be viewed as a school problem, but as a system problem that needs concerted effort to deal with. Principals in such schools may find it challenging on their own, but it may be easier to work within a collective effort, involving stakeholders of a school community that goes beyond the school for the common good. Schools and principals that are known to prevent learners entry into their school based on language are normally located in high socio-economic areas, and are already exclusive due to high fees which can only be afforded by learners from affluent backgrounds. These issues are complex and need a joint effort in providing solutions. But the status quo certainly cannot be allowed to prevail as business as usual.

Further reading

Grant, C. (2011) Distributing school leadership for social justice: finding the courage to lead inclusively and transformatively. In: J.A Ramírez (ed.), *Public leadership* (pp. 141–152). New York: Nova Science.

Ncube, L.B. (2010) Ubuntu: a transformative leadership philosophy. *Journal of Leadership Studies*, 4(3), 77–82.

Ndlovu, P.M. (2016) *Discovering the spirit of Ubuntu leadership: compassion, community, and respect*. Basingstoke: Palgrave Macmillan.

Ngunjiri, F.W. (2016) 'I am because we are': exploring women's leadership under Ubuntu worldview. *Advances in Developing Human Resources*, 18(2), 223–242.

Shields, C.M. (2018) *Transformative leadership in education: equitable and socially just change in an uncertain and complex world*, 2nd edn. New York: Routledge.

Subreenduth, S. (2013) Theorizing social justice ambiguities in an era of neoliberalism: the case of post-apartheid South Africa. *Educational Theory*, 63(6), 581–600.

References

Bantwini, B.D. and Moorosi, P. (2018) The Circuit Managers as the weakest link in the school district leadership chain! Perspectives from a province in South Africa. *South African Journal of Education*, 38(3), art. 1577.

Blackmore, J. (2011) Leadership in pursuit of purpose: social, economic and political transformation. In: C.M. Shields (ed.), *Transformative leadership: a reader* (pp. 21–36). New York: Peter Lang.

Brown, K. (2006) 'New' educational injustices in the 'new' South Africa: a call for justice in the form of vertical equity. *Journal of Educational Administration*, 44(5), 509–519.

Chipkin, I. and Meny-Gibert, S. (2013) *Understanding the social justice sector in South Africa: a report to the RAITH Foundation and Atlantic Philanthropies*, February. Houghton, South Africa: RAITH Foundation. Available online: http://www.raith.org.za/index.php/files/59/RAITH-Commissioned---Funded-Research/311/ (accessed 25 January 2020).

Grant, C.C. (2014) Leading for social justice in South African schools: where have all the activists gone? In: I. Bogotch and C.M. Shields (eds), *International handbook of educational leadership and social (in)justice* (pp. 521–539). New York: Springer.

Heystek, J. (2014) Principals' perceptions about performance agreement as motivational action: evidence from South Africa. *Educational Management Administration & Leadership*, 42(6), 889–902.

Letseka, M. (2014) Ubuntu and justice as fairness. *Mediterranean Journal of Social Sciences*, 5(9), 544–551.

Madimbo, M. (2016) *Transformative and engaging leadership: lessons from Indigenous African women*. Basingstoke: Palgrave Macmillan.

Naicker, I., Grant, C. and Pillay, S. (2016) Schools performing against the odds: enablements and constraints to school leadership practice. *South African Journal of Education*, 36(4), art. 1321. Available online: https://files.eric.ed.gov/fulltext/EJ1133784.pdf (accessed 17 July 2020).

Nkondo, G.M. (2007) Ubuntu as public policy in South Africa: a conceptual framework. *International Journal of African Renaissance Studies*, 2(1), 88–100.

Rawls, J. (1999) *A theory of justice*, revised edn. Cambridge, MA: Harvard University Press.

Shields, C. (2010) Transformative leadership: working for equity in diverse contexts. *Educational Administration Quarterly*, 46(4), 558–589.

Spaull, N. (2013) *South Africa's education crisis: the quality of education in South Africa 1994–2011*. Johannesburg: Centre for Development and Enterprise. Available online: https://nicspaull.files.wordpress.com/2011/04/spaull-2013-cde-report-south-africas-educa (accessed 17 July 2020).

Truscott, K. (1994) *Gender in education*. Johannesburg: University of Witwatersrand, Education Policy Unit.

Wray, D., Hellenberg, R. and Jansen, J. (2019) *A school where I belong: creating transformed and inclusive South African schools*. Johannesburg: Bookstorm.

Critical perspectives in and approaches to educational leadership in China

Ting Wang and Kai Yu

5

What this chapter is about	76
Key questions that this chapter addresses	76
Introduction	76
Educational transformation policies and ideologies	79
Shanghai's education system	79
Framework of critical approaches to educational leadership in China	81
Implications	87
Conclusion	88
Acknowledgement	88
Further reading	89
References	89

What this chapter is about

In this chapter, we examine educational leadership in the context of China, and specifically of Shanghai. We take a critical approach by focusing on system strategic leadership, principal instructional leadership and teacher pedagogical leadership. This will allow you to understand the modernizing trends based on globalized and travelling leadership models interplayed with traditional values and practices in China. By examining the research evidence and debates on critical perspectives in educational leadership in China, we enable exploration of Chinese leadership traditions and contextual analysis at multiple layers. Our chapter explains key aspects of culture and values in China that make educational leaders, leading and leadership distinctive. It examines education policies and ideological and organizational factors that are contributing to contemporary educational-leadership practices. Using the Shanghai education system as a lens, we critically assess the roles and approaches of leadership in terms of system strategic leadership, principal instructional leadership and teacher pedagogical leadership.

Key questions that this chapter addresses

1 What does educational leadership look like in China?
2 What reforms have taken place to education in China?
3 What roles and approaches to educational leadership are evident in China?
4 How can the case study of the Shanghai education system provide insights into educational leadership?
5 What are the implications of the reform trends for educational leadership in China?

Introduction

In China, strong administrative leadership at the system level emphasizes strategic decision-making, alignment and harmony. School principals are moral leaders and focus on quality teaching and learning by promoting a collaborative culture. The cultural values of relationship-building and collectivism support dispersed teacher pedagogical leadership. A strategic approach to policymaking and implementation intermingled with the collectivist culture significantly influences school leadership strategies and actions in China.

Leadership is acknowledged in China as a value-laden concept. It is constructed within a social milieu comprising multiple and constantly shifting contextual factors, such as cultural, political, historical and economic influences. Societal culture exerts a significant influence on educational leaders beyond that of the specific organization's culture (Wang,

2011). Walker and Hallinger (2007: 259) recognize the enduring nature of culture and argue that this is 'because they are reinforced continually through social as well as institutional interactions'.

Chinese culture and values have been consistent over long years. There are certain historical-social influences on the development of leadership and management practice in China, such as Taoism, Confucianism, the strategic thinking of Sun Tzu, leadership as a practical moral art, face and collectivism (Wang, 2008). These six aspects of culture and values in China make educational leaders, leading and leadership distinctive.

1 **Taoism:** a holistic philosophy that emphasizes the interrelationship and interaction of everything in the world. Every entity comprises varying (or opposing) internal elements, *Yin* and *Yang*. Harmony must be maintained between these elements to secure the wholeness and the integrity of that entity. Nothing is immutable; change is natural and inevitable. This is similar in spirit to the Western 'Gaia hypothesis', popular in the ecological/environmental movement.

2 **Confucianism:** Confucius (b. 551 BCE) was a Chinese sage, whose doctrines became known as Confucianism. Confucianism became a structure of ethical precepts for the management of society based upon the achievement of social harmony and social order within a hierarchically arranged society. It also involved the concept of *ren*, which entails benevolence, humaneness and patronage in the treatment of others. Confucius defined five basic human relations (*Wu lun*) and principles for each person. Relationships are structured to deliver optimum benefits for both parties. These five principles emphasize hierarchical structure and social harmony.

3 **The strategic thinking of Sun Tzu:** Sun Tzu's (500 BCE) book, *The Art of War*, describes effective and ineffective strategies by which to fight wars or defeat the opponent. Since Chinese tend to perceive the marketplace and politics as a *battlefield*, strategies for waging war have therefore been applied to strategies for waging business and management. An analogue in the West would be Machiavelli's *The Prince*, an Italian Renaissance text that has since been applied to success in business, war and politics.

4 **Leadership as a practical moral art:** morality is emphasized by traditional Chinese culture, and leadership is regarded as a moral art in action (Wong, 2001). China, since Confucius' time, has valued leadership and prepared leaders on moral grounds. The Chinese are known for their pragmatic approaches towards life. Although Chinese philosophers spend time on the meaning of moral value, they are more interested in the practical aspects of morality and develop ways to do good.

5 **Personal relationship (*guan xi*) and face:** *guan xi* means cultivating, developing and maintaining personal relationships on the basis of the continuing exchange of favours. Friendship and empathy between the two parties are of secondary importance, though they are useful in reinforcing the relationship. Achieving harmony requires the maintenance of an individual's face. Face is a person's

dignity, self-respect, status and prestige. Social interaction or negotiation should be conducted so that nobody loses face.

6 **Collectivism:** Chinese societies are more collectivist than individualist. In group-oriented societies, ties between people are tight, relationships are firmly structured and individual needs are subservient to collective needs. Goals and the means for their attainment are decided by leaders and may be carefully and humanely imposed. There is conformity to the 'natural' order of power relations. Leadership legitimacy is often contingent on leaders' non-utilitarian qualities. The role of the principal may focus on developing and ensuring harmony among staff, and enforcing common, standard approaches to governance, organization, curriculum and instruction.

A major responsibility of the educational leader in China is maintaining harmony, a core value of Confucianism. The influences are evident in society and schools. The Chinese perceive disturbance to group or interpersonal harmony as shameful. Collectivism and 'shame' are important features of social control in China. Conformity is linked strongly to socially functional notions of interpersonal harmony and collectivism. The disturbance of interpersonal relations and group harmony by conflict can cause lasting animosity in Chinese cultures. As a result, the Chinese tend to avoid open confrontation and assertiveness. In the school context, this may be manifested through teachers and principals avoiding open disagreement by a tacit acceptance that it is always the leader's view which prevails (Wang, 2008).

In Chinese culture, there is a high level of collectivism, high-power distance relations and an overriding concern with the maintenance of harmonious relationships at work. Respect for and maintenance of hierarchy, conflict avoidance, collectivism, face, social networks, moral leadership, and conformity are the key values that have affected leadership traditions in China. The traditional conceptions of leadership are mostly associated with a directive, hierarchical and authoritarian 'headship', together with an emphasis on moral leadership, self-cultivation and artistry in leading (Wang, 2011).

Bush and Qiang (2000) have argued that the diversity and complexity of culture is reflected in the following aspects in the Chinese education system. Contemporary Chinese culture is a mixture of traditional, socialist, enterprise and patriarchal cultures. Consequently, leadership traditions and conceptions have been influenced by different elements of culture and forces. Leadership is regarded as culturally complex and context-dependent. These major elements of contemporary Chinese culture continue to shape educational leadership, which is overwhelmingly male, with a balance between hierarchy and collectivism. Although the emergence of enterprise culture and market socialism seems to be slowly changing Chinese contemporary culture and social values, such cultural change is unlikely to be radical and transformational. A slow and incremental cultural change is expected in Chinese school education. The next section examines education policies and ideologies which are contributing to contemporary educational-leadership practices.

Educational transformation policies and ideologies

This section explicates three ways in which change is undertaken in education in China. Huang, Wang and Li (2016) recognize that it is challenging to identify particular factors that led to educational transformation in the past decades in China. They are in fact intertwined and present as a paradox. First, there are two prominent threads of the global–local and decentralized–centralized continuum throughout the process of educational changes. Educational reform has been characterized by decentralized centralism. During the process of restructuring, some governmental powers are decentralized, while others are recentralized. The government remains powerful in leading educational changes and takes an active role in meeting the challenges. Educational transformation is thus government-dominated within the context of rebuilding the state and globalization. Incremental, rather than radical changes, take place.

Second, educational changes in China follow the incremental-coherent change path, epitomized in the process of **plan–pilot–implement–reflect–revise**. The transformation concentrates not only on certain unique aspects of education, but also on the systematic and coherent promotion of mutual reinforcement and interaction within the government and between governments and communities. The ultimate purpose of the educational changes is to contribute to economic development, social cohesion and the holistic development of students.

Third, Chinese education policymakers have adopted a balanced and 'moderate' approach, aiming to maintain a balance between globalization and localization, centralization and decentralization, top-down and bottom-up, equity-oriented and quality-oriented approaches. They tend to choose a balanced position along the dynamic continuum, which reveals the Chinese philosophy of the golden mean and the traditional culture of *Yin–Yang*. It reflects China's ambition in addressing education quality, equality and social justice, reducing urban/rural and regional disparities. Educational change is not an event, but a process involving complex political dynamics of numerous systems, institutions, levels and activities. These educational policies and overarching ideological structural factors are inevitably contributing to contemporary educational-leadership practices in China.

Shanghai's education system

This section assesses leadership roles and approaches, utilizing Shanghai's education system as a lens and exemplar. China has the world's largest education system, serving 20 per cent of the world's students (200 million in elementary and secondary education) with less than 2 per cent of the world's education resources. It is a challenge to address the rural–urban and regional disparities in educational and economic development in a nation with 1.4 billion people. Shanghai is a prosperous and competitive business centre and a global city. It leads economic and educational transformation in China and showcases phenomenal economic growth and education-reform success. Shanghai enjoys a higher level of autonomy than other jurisdictions. Its innovations and best practices are often emulated nationwide. In the Organisation for Economic Co-operation and Development's (OECD) 2009 and 2012 Programme for International Student Assessment (PISA) assessments, fifteen-year-old students in Shanghai topped every league table by a clear margin.

Shanghai is an important lens for showing critical approaches to educational leadership in China. Shanghai has pioneered reforms in curriculum, assessment, teacher professional development and equity. Curriculum reforms have brought about significant improvement in student learning and teaching practices since 1989. The vision of enhancing the learning outcomes and holistic development of every child is widely shared by school educators in Shanghai. Many teachers' traditional ideas and pedagogical practices have been transformed in response to the priorities of curriculum reforms. A strategic and consistent approach in education policymaking and implementation is a salient feature in Shanghai. A coherent process is created at the municipal, district and school levels, which ensures strategic alignment, implementation of policies and compliance with standards. This works well in a primarily centralized system and strong collectivist culture. Another distinctive feature is decentralized centralism. Decentralization, centralization and recentralization often coexist in Shanghai, as elsewhere in China (Huang, Wang and Li, 2016).

Over the past thirty years, increasing the rigour of initial qualification and enhancing the quality of Shanghai's teachers have been consistently prioritized in education reforms. Every reform to education and teaching has been closely connected with action research conducted by teachers and principals. The teacher-development system has three essential components: the teacher career ladder, in-service training and development, and performance appraisal (Zhang, Ding and Xu, 2016). Shanghai tends to be prescriptive about what constitutes effective professional learning in schools. Strategic reforms aim to build professional learning into daily practice and teachers' professional identities, generating a culture in which teachers share responsibility for their own and others' professional learning and creating structures for recognizing teaching expertise (Jensen et al., 2016).

Shanghai has created a career ladder system that spans entry level to senior classroom teachers and school principals. There are thirteen levels on the ladder for teachers; the principals' career ladder has five. All principals must first have been successful teachers and they are required to continue teaching during their principalship (Zhang, Ding and Xu, 2016). There is approximately one master teacher for every 1,000 teachers. About 30 per cent of principals are senior-level principals and about 5 per cent are masters. Teaching in Shanghai is promoted as a desirable lifelong career, an occupation that requires professionals who continuously hone their skills. Effective in-service teacher development is the glue that holds the system together. Teachers enter the profession as apprentices with a full-year induction before they are certified as teachers. They participate in 120 hours of professional development and are assigned a mentor who is a senior-rank teacher with mentoring expertise. All teachers must undergo at least 360 hours of in-service development every five years to upgrade their educational philosophy and capacities. For secondary-school senior teachers, the amount of professional development required rises to 540 hours every five years. New school principals complete an additional 60 hours of training after taking on their leadership roles (Zhang, Ding and Xu, 2016).

Ting, the first author of this chapter, spent three months in Shanghai in 2015 and conducted a study on Shanghai school reform and leadership. Qualitative data were generated through face-to-face, semi-structured interviews and observations in six case-study schools in Shanghai. The twenty-five interviewees included three senior officials from municipal education authorities and twenty-two participants from six public schools comprising four primary schools, one Year 1–9 Primary to Junior Secondary School and one Senior Secondary school. The framework of critical approaches to educational leadership presented in the next sections has emerged from the interview data analysis and observations.

Framework of critical approaches to educational leadership in China

Figure 5.1 presents the framework of critical approaches to educational leadership in China, drawing upon the research evidence about Shanghai system improvement and leadership. The framework has three key leadership elements at the system, school and teacher levels respectively. Strategic leadership consistently exerted by policymakers and administrators in a centralized system, instructional school leadership enacted by principals, and teacher pedagogical leadership form the cornerstones of critical approaches to leadership. A critical disposition to act differently in changing contexts highlights the importance of strategic thinking and maintaining harmony of varying elements. The ultimate goal of leadership actions and strategies is to improve teachers' professional learning and quality teaching in order to enhance learning and the holistic development of all students.

System strategic leadership: in China, refers to a policymaker or administrator's potential and ability to express a strategic vision for a system, to motivate and persuade others to acquire that vision, and to achieve harmony and alignment of policymaking and implementation. Strategic leadership or a systems approach is not a Western concept. The holistic philosophy of Taoism and Sun Tzu's strategic thinking have inspired Chinese people for over two thousand years. A strategic approach to policymaking and implementation intermingled with the collectivist culture deeply influences leadership decisions and practices.

Principal instructional leadership: in China, is focused on leadership for quality learning of both learners and teachers. It includes developing and communicating the school vision, supervising and participating in teacher development, leading curriculum development and promoting a culture of learning and collaboration. Principals are expected to be moral leaders and balance conformity and innovation in schools.

Teacher pedagogical leadership: in China, recognizes that multiple teacher leaders, both formal and informal, interact with others to support peers and share responsibilities. Teacher leaders collaborate with other teachers and motivate colleagues with ideas, knowledge and passion, and collectively improve pedagogical practices and student learning. They play an important role in leading innovation and disseminating best pedagogical practices in schools and across the system.

System strategic leadership

The history of Chinese strategic thinking can be traced back to Sun Tzu's *The Art of War* in 500 BCE. Chinese philosophical tradition also highlights Taoism's holistic philosophy

Figure 5.1 Critical approaches to educational leadership.

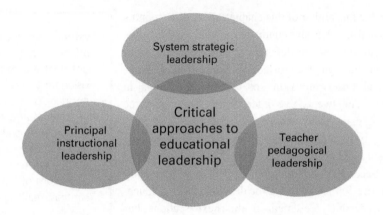

and 'the harmony of heaven and humanity'. The criticality in Shanghai is the strong administrative leadership and a balanced approach in policymaking and implementation. Strong system leadership is evidenced in a coherent approach in curricula, learning and teaching, teacher development and performance appraisal. This approach determines the common standards, the way educational resources are deployed and how curricula are taught in schools. The mission statement is that 'every school is a good school, every student is a good student, and every teacher is a good teacher'. Fundamental structural change must be supported by profound cultural change and sustained capacity-building of all teachers. Accountability is built into the system as a social expectation and becomes an essential part of school leadership and teachers' professionalism (Wang and Pang, 2019).

Teaching is a respected profession as well as an increasingly demanding job in China. The turnover rate of teachers in Shanghai is low. It is achievable for the system to recruit the top graduates from initial teacher education programmes and provide them with mandated induction programmes and continuous professional learning opportunities. Systematic teacher professional learning and recognition of teacher pedagogical and curriculum leadership are evident in the schools and across the system. Effective class-teaching and engaged student learning are prioritized in the schools, supported by a well-designed and well-implemented teacher professional learning framework, as well as Teaching and Research Group arrangements. It is widely acknowledged that teachers should be moral role-models for students: every teacher has a duty to be a good teacher with a well-defined professional identity. Strong work ethics of professionalism and dedication are highlighted in the induction programmes and continuous professional learning activities across the system.

School priorities and leadership practices are driven by system priorities and mandated policies. School leaders are required to satisfy the mandated requirements about prescribed curriculum delivery and teacher professional learning. Teachers are exposed to various profound professional learning experiences ranging from district and system-mandated training programmes to network-based, across-school and school-based professional learning activities. Some teachers even have opportunities to undertake overseas study and short visits / study tours. The study suggests that teachers in Shanghai have ample exposure to different education ideas and perspectives, such as from overseas and local education experts, university professors and exemplary teachers, personal involvement in hands-on workshops and teaching skills competitions. The pressures and incentives for their quick professional growth and progression are paramount. The Teaching and Research officers in the district education bureaus and Municipal Education Commission play an important role in standardizing teaching requirements and disseminating the best practices across the districts. A distinctive feature of the system is to establish high expectations and benchmarks and achieve system-wide improvement with concerted efforts and high support.

Case Study 5.1 System leader A

System leader A was the Deputy Director of Shanghai Municipal Education Commission and key facilitator of Shanghai's participation in 2009 PISA and 2013 Teaching and Learning International Survey (TALIS) studies. He described the tri-level leadership mechanism – at municipal, district and school levels – in Shanghai. He highlighted four factors contributing to educational quality and equity: consistent public education policies and a focus on student learning; a teaching-development system and Teaching and Research Groups practices; teacher commitment and professionalism; and parents' high expectations and support. He reported that both hard and soft approaches in leadership and management were utilized. A high value on being moderate, not radical or capricious, is embedded in the mindsets of policymakers and educators. On the one hand, absolute compliance with the explicit rules and regulations and core values is required. On the other hand, a soft approach of engaging teachers with emotional bonds is adopted in schools, and a sense of a caring family and community spirit is shared in the system. The open mindset and exposure to progressive education perspectives and global practices have equipped policymakers and educators in Shanghai with the necessary skills and alternative perspectives to examine their current practices and project future-oriented initiatives.

A sense of urgency in an increasingly competitive world and dedication to high-quality education for the holistic development of children have driven the Shanghai education system to strive for continuous improvement and excellence. What makes the underlying leadership approach distinctive is the leaders' deep understanding of Chinese cultural values, political system and social norms. They mediate the influences from Chinese traditional values, socialist values and market values. The ultimate compromise of different forces leads to a pragmatic approach to education policymaking and its implementation with Chinese characteristics.

Principal instructional leadership

The key elements of principal instructional leadership in Shanghai include developing and communicating the school vision, supervising and participating in teacher development, leading curriculum development and promoting a culture of learning and collaboration. Principals lead the implementation of the prescribed curriculum and the development of school-based curricula. They work with teachers in a purposeful manner and develop teacher collective efficacy that supports student improvement and achievement of system agenda and school goals. Principal leadership is also influenced by Chinese cultural values of achieving social harmony and social order within a hierarchical structure. Principals are expected to be moral leaders and balance conformity and innovation in schools.

Principal leadership practices are not fragmented, piecemeal approaches nor individual idiosyncratic actions. System thinking and a clear focus on alignment, cohesiveness and collective capacity-building guide principals' actions and leadership practices. Thanks to a shared understanding of school contexts and missions, common standards required at the system level do not seem to dampen the enthusiasm for diverse, innovative practices in schools. More importantly, the systems approach offers a strong scaffolding structure and coherent message. Collective capacity-building and collaborations within the school as well as partnerships and engagement with the wider school community hold all these seemingly discrete elements together in a glue characterized by shared commitment and dedication.

In this study, most principals' responses revealed that they implemented the system policies and mediated external forces to ensure a supportive environment for teachers and students. All schools were required to design a five-year plan in line with the system mandate on strategic planning. A striking similarity in their approaches towards shaping the school strategic plan was a deliberate consideration of the school's contexts, and a recognition of current needs and the system agenda.

Successful principal instructional leadership is particularly focused on quality teaching and learning by cultivating a culture of spontaneous and seamless collaborations among teachers, and thus embedding professionalism in daily activities of teachers. Principal B, seen in Case Study 5.2, was a moral leader and achieved a balance of maintaining harmony and striving for innovation.

Case Study 5.2 Principal B

Principal B led an exemplary primary school located in a central area in Shanghai. As an experienced administrator in a district education bureau for many years, she was not a visionary leader who put forward the grand vision for the school when she took over the principal position. Rather, she immersed herself in getting to know the pulse of the school, its uniqueness, its trajectories and internal contradictions. She highlighted the importance of considering the school's cultural roots and history, and then re-energizing the core values and mission of the school. Her critical approaches towards developing and shaping the school's strategic plan and vision included deliberate consideration of the school's contexts, extensive consultations with internal and external stakeholders, and several rounds of consultation, revisions and iterations. According to her, it was no use to present her vision and impose it on the staff. It was critical to be a role model, get all teachers on board and have shared expectations, understandings of the purpose and goals of the school. The synergy of collective power in shaping the school goals was acknowledged by teachers. Her strong leadership was evidenced by the way she nurtured a culture of learning, innovation and collaboration. The presence of the mascot 'Little Ants' of this school was strikingly visible in every corner of campus while the sprit was keenly felt in student character development, relationship-building and school-based curriculum development. The school promoted and lived a shared vision of 'connecting with the world and a culture of little bright ants in terms of cultivating confident, hard-working and collaborative kids'. She believed that leadership was a moral art in action.

Teacher pedagogical leadership

Pedagogical leadership in Shanghai represents forms of practice that shape and form teaching and learning. Teacher leaders collaborate with other teachers and motivate colleagues with ideas, knowledge and passion, and collectively improve pedagogical practices and student learning. Teacher leadership encourages teacher empowerment and engagement in a dynamic leadership process in schools. Dispersed teacher leadership recognizes that multiple teacher leaders, both formal and informal, interact with others throughout the school to support decision-making and action steps.

In Chinese schools, harmony and relationship / *guan xi* are part of the glue that binds people together. The cultural values of relationship-building and collectivism support dispersed teacher pedagogical leadership. Contrary to the belief that Chinese principals tend to have control-and-command approaches, the principals in this study demonstrated efforts in establishing a distributive leadership structure and shared power and authority. High-performing teachers were encouraged to be mentors and apply for promotion to senior teachers or high-calibre subject leaders at the district level. They were required to demonstrate evidence of mentoring and supporting junior teachers. They played an important role in leading innovation and disseminating best pedagogical practices in schools and across the system. Peer support and shared responsibility for collective learning were evident in these schools. A sense of trust and community was considered fundamental to school improvement. The underpinning philosophy was that continuous development was an indispensable duty of a teacher.

Professional learning in schools under study is much broader than the Teaching and Research Groups activities. The forms of professional learning include differentiated activities that work in different schools. Despite the unified mandate of 360/540 hours across the system, each school has identified and developed appropriate school-based professional learning structure and strategies to cater to teachers' specific needs. Achieving unity and common standards does not mean devaluing the school-based professional learning activities and best practices. There is a repertoire of school-based, network-based and district-based professional learning activities. There are abundant new ideas, innovative approaches and alternative programmes to promote schools' innovations. As commented by Principal D in a suburban primary school, principals should be selective in their engagement in various innovative new projects and prioritize their resources and staff capacity in pursuing new initiatives. There was a consensus among principals that each school should be careful about system-driven initiatives. It was not desirable to put more agenda items on an already overcrowded plate of curriculum and school development. They balanced the system demands and local needs, and hence acted as the buffer to safeguard the smooth running of the schools and routines.

Case Study 5.3 Primary school C

In primary school C, with more than 4,200 students and three campuses, empowering teachers and sharing responsibility provide a solution to the complexity of managing a large school. Principal C delegated the responsibility for managing projects and coordinating events to classroom teachers so that they can develop their self-efficacy and a sense of empowerment. As a designated M District base school for new teachers, School C offered an annual induction programme for twenty new teachers from different schools. Mentor teachers demonstrated strong pedagogical leadership by setting up a high standard of teaching practices and mentoring relationships. The District-supported induction programme helped to break down the barriers of schools, effectively utilize the expertise of exemplary teachers in the base school, facilitate professional dialogue and hone the skills of new teachers, and support experienced teachers to be more reflective and effective mentors.

Moreover, 'Famous Teachers Workshops' play an important role in drawing interested aspiring teachers and helping them become high-calibre teachers within a short time. Connections, dialogue and change catalysts are encouraged and acknowledged in the system and schools. The exemplary teachers are visible teacher leaders and acknowledged by various honorary titles and monetary remuneration.

Activity 5.1

We invite you to reflect on the case-study stories about System Leader A, Principal B and Principal C.

1 What practices and beliefs have Chinese principals and teachers inherited from Chinese leadership traditions?
2 How do Chinese principals interpret, mediate and implement educational reform initiatives?
3 What leader, leading and leadership actions and strategies contribute to system improvement and quality teaching in Shanghai?

The centralized system highlights the alignment of priorities and core values across the system, yet it may leave limited autonomy for schools and teachers to innovate and pursue diversified approaches. Therefore, principals and teachers value the space and flexibility they can get to innovate their practices (e.g. 15 per cent school-based curriculum and project-based learning). The professional learning activities are centred on the improvement of teaching practices, and how to improve the effectiveness and efficiency of delivery and thus enhance student learning. Although cultivating students' creative thinking, independent learning and problem-solving skills have been increasingly promoted in recent years, the pervasive examination culture in Confucius-heritage cultures and emphasis on high-stakes exams can hardly release pressures on principals, teachers and students.

Implications

Leaders, leading and leadership are contextualized and culturally dependent. Social, cultural, economic and political factors inevitably shape and impact on the design and enactment of leaders, leading and leadership. A strategic approach to policymaking and implementation intermingled with the collectivist culture deeply influences school leadership decisions and actions in Shanghai. A primarily centralized political system characterized by decentralized centralism in recent years drives strong system leadership and a coherent approach to policy implementation (Huang, Wang and Li, 2016). Leadership for system-wide educational improvement in Shanghai thus relies on a coordinated systems approach and strategic alignment at the municipal, district and school levels. The primary focus of leadership within the schools is principal instructional leadership and teacher pedagogical leadership. Collaboration and shared responsibility are built into the daily lives of teachers and school leaders. Collective capacity-building within the schools and engagement with the wider communities can act as the glue to hold the system together (Wang and Pang, 2019).

In Shanghai, deliberately designed structures undoubtedly provide alignment, common standards and benchmarks. It also allows for certain flexibility and innovative practices within the system so long as the schools follow the rules and do not deviate too much from benchmarks or touch the redlines. It should be noted that the rigid top-down, control-and-demand approaches will not guarantee the success of a dynamic, vibrant education system.

It is evident that many education-reform policies and initiatives are implemented in education systems across the world. It is important to assess the impacts of historical, cultural and social factors and system priorities in the design and implementation of these reform initiatives. The power of cultural change and collective teacher capacity-building are drivers for system continuous improvement. One key lesson learned from the success of the Shanghai educational system is the relentless efforts of the system leaders, principals and teachers in achieving the alignment of the reform agenda at the system, school and team levels, and getting the teachers on board and engaged in the change initiatives. The message from the system must be clear and consistent. The alignment of policies and initiatives must consider the unique features of different schools and individual teachers. As one principal in the study commented, 'The easiest part of change is to reshuffle the furniture and clean up the room, yet the hardest work is to get the staff engaged and committed to a shared vision'. Various influencing factors in a school are like 'the tentacles of an octopus, intertwined to impact the core business of the school, that is teaching and learning'.

Conclusion

In Shanghai, centralized system imperatives, socialist ideologies and core values are mediated by a fluid, contemporary modern culture in a globalized, cosmopolitan megacity. The fluidity, complexity and vitality in a vibrant education system are intriguing. The cultural expectations and aspiration of affluent middle-class parents have put additional pressure on principals and teachers. High expectations for school education quality, teachers and student learning outcomes are evident in schools and across the system. It should be noted that mainstream core values and ideologies are highlighted in teacher professional ethics and student moral education. Chinese principals need to achieve a balance between change and stability, between innovation and conformity.

Leadership approaches must be adapted to fit the needs and expectations of the specific cultural and school context. Adapting leadership to context requires applying leadership approaches carefully and critically rather than adopting an undifferentiated approach. What is considered an innovation in one education system may be well-established practice in another system. What is appreciated as an improvement may be rejected elsewhere. What is counted an effective leadership approach in Shanghai may end up in failure in a very different context. Leadership is contextualized, and therefore, culturally sensitive and contextually specific perspectives in educational leadership are essential. There is a growing agreement that there exists a generic set of leadership practices that must be adapted to meet the needs and constraints that describe different school contexts. Several different contexts (e.g. institutional, community, sociocultural, political, economic, school improvement) can influence leadership practice (Hallinger, 2018). The next generation of scholarship in educational leadership should turn away from describing 'what successful school leaders do' and towards 'how they do it differently' in a specific context.

Acknowledgement

This work was supported by the Fundamental Research Funds for Central Universities of China.

Further reading

Law, W.-W. (2012) Educational leadership and culture in China: dichotomies between Chinese and Anglo-American leadership traditions? *International Journal of Educational Development*, 32(2), 273–282.

Tucker, M.S. (ed.) (2011) *Surpassing Shanghai: an agenda for American education built on the world's leading systems*. Cambridge, MA: Harvard Education Press.

Walker, A. and Qian, H. (2015) Review of research on school principal leadership in mainland China, 1998–2013: continuity and change. *Journal of Educational Administration*, 53(4), 467–491.

Walker, A., Hu, R. and Qian, H. (2012) Principal leadership in China: an initial review. *School Effectiveness and School Improvement: An International Journal of Research, Policy and Practice*, 23(4), 369–399.

Wang, T. (2015) Contrived collegiality versus genuine collegiality: demystifying professional learning communities in Chinese schools. *Compare: A Journal of Comparative and International Education*, 45(6), 908–930.

References

Bush, T. and Qiang, H. (2000) Leadership and culture in Chinese education. *Asia Pacific Journal of Education*, 20(2), 58–67.

Hallinger, P. (2018) Bringing context out of the shadows of leadership. *Educational Management Administration & Leadership*, 46(1), 5–24.

Huang, Z.J., Wang, T. and Li, X.J. (2016) The political dynamics of educational changes in China. *Policy Futures in Education*, 14(1), 24–41.

Jensen, B., Sonnemann, J., Roberts-Hull, K. and Hunter, A. (2016) *Beyond PD: teacher professional learning in high-performing systems*. Washington, DC: National Center on Education and the Economy. Available online: https://ncee.org/beyondpd/ (accessed 20 July 2020).

Walker, A. and Hallinger, P. (2007) Navigating culture and context: the principalship in East and South-East Asia. In: R. Maclean (ed.), *Learning and teaching for the twenty-first century: festschrift for Professor Phillip Hughes* (pp. 255–273). New York: Springer.

Wang, T. (2008) *Chinese educational leaders' conceptions of learning and leadership: an interpretative study in an international education context*. Saarbrücken: VDM Verlag Dr. Müller e.K.

Wang, T. (2011) Critical perspectives on changes in educational leadership practice. *Frontiers of Education in China*, 6(3), 404–425.

Wang, T. and. Pang, N.S.K. (2019) System-wide educational reform agenda in Shanghai: supporting leadership for learning. In: S. Hairon and J.W.P. Goh (eds), *Perspectives on school leadership in Asia Pacific contexts* (pp. 61–77). New York: Springer.

Wong, K.-C. (2001) Chinese culture and leadership. *International Journal of Leadership in Education*, 4(4), 309–319.

Zhang, M., Ding, X. and Xu, J. (2016) *Developing Shanghai's teachers*. Washington, DC: National Center on Education and the Economy. Available online: https://ncee.org/developing-shanghais-teachers/ (accessed 20 July 2020).

Critical perspectives in and approaches to educational leadership in Indonesia

Zulfa Sakhiyya and Tanya Fitzgerald

6

What this chapter is about 92

Key questions that this chapter addresses 92

Introduction 92

The context of Indonesia: history, policies and contemporary practice 94

A critical feminist perspective 96

Implications for educational leadership in Indonesia 97

Introducing the case studies: women leading in Indonesian higher education 99

Conclusion 103

Further reading 103

References 104

What this chapter is about

Drawing on Indonesian higher education as an analytical site, in this chapter we undertake a critical approach to analysing educational leadership by interrogating the gender dynamics in three specific educational institutions. We begin with a set of organizing questions that are intended to assist and enhance both theoretical and contextual understandings. We offer a broad interpretation of the key terms used as they are applied to the narrative and analysis. We then present three illustrative case studies that highlight the significance of women's entrée into leadership in Indonesian higher education as well as the myriad challenges faced as the first generation of female leaders. Finally, we propose a number of concluding questions to assist you with your own critical reflection on current practices and organizational culture.

Key questions that this chapter addresses

1 Why should there be a concern about, or attention to, gender?

2 What is the historical, cultural, social and political framework of Indonesia?

3 How might the gender dynamics of leadership in Indonesian higher education be understood?

4 What is a feminist critical perspective and in what ways can this illuminate professional practices in Indonesia?

5 What does it take to resist and contest the current neoliberal model of university?

Introduction

This section is an overview of ways in which gender and leadership interconnect. We do not offer an exhaustive analysis, as a more comprehensive overview can be found in Chapter 16 of this textbook. Rather, we introduce key ideas to further assist you with your interpretation of the illustrative case studies presented at a later point in this chapter. Our core purpose is to introduce the key aspects of debates and explore issues of gender that continue to impact on professional work and identities.

Globally, leadership in higher education is predominantly a masculine domain (Fitzgerald, 2012, 2014; Morley, 2013; O'Connor, 2015). In the main institutions of higher education numerically dominated by men, masculinity and power are intertwined in such a way that institutional norms recognize and reward male ways of working. Based on their numbers, women are the institutional 'other' and the disruptors of institutional and gendered norms. Hierarchical institutional structures and modes of governance limit their attendance and participation. Leadership that is constructed as rational and objective alongside leadership skills and attributes that are described as visionary, goal oriented, entrepreneurial and competitive place emphasis on male ways of working. Blackmore (2006) argues that the prominence afforded these physical, intellectual and psychological characteristics construct leadership as a male domain.

Terms such as 'caring', 'sensitive', 'intuitive', 'collegial', 'collaborative' and 'cooperative' are used at times to simultaneously describe and define feminine ways of working. These discourses are inherently problematic as the underpinning assumption is that feminine leadership qualities exist and that women in leadership inevitably have to develop more masculine ways of interacting in order to be seen as authentic in their roles. Qualities traditionally associated with femininity produce a normative femininity that presupposes women 'naturally' possess certain characteristics and 'naturally' lead in predetermined ways. Unlike their male colleagues, women must visibly and overtly demonstrate that they possess credible leadership skills, knowledge and dispositions; skills, knowledge and dispositions linked with masculinity and men (Collinson and Hearn, 1996). Consequently, women who are seen to display masculine behaviours no longer 'fit' into prevailing stereotypes or conform to expectations held by either men or women. In many ways, women senior leaders can be viewed as interlopers in this predominantly male world, intruders in the masculine terrain of leadership (Fitzgerald, 2018). We are not suggesting here that there is a distinctive gender 'style' but rather highlighting that those women who do take up leadership roles are subject to a number of normative practices and beliefs about leadership and what it means to lead and be a leader (Blackmore, 2013, 2017; Fitzgerald, 2014).

Leadership in universities has become both definable and measurable. It is definable against adjectival criteria such as visionary, entrepreneurial and transformative, and it is measured against indicators such as research and teaching metrics, global institutional rankings, profitability and student outcomes. One of the consequences in the drive to be 'world class' has been a focus on leadership to alleviate and remedy any institutional shortcomings through restructuring and repurposing the workforce. A consequence has been the intensification as well as casualization of work. And it is women who are disproportionately located in casual and part-time employment as well as in the lower academic ranks (Fitzgerald, 2014; Morley, 2013).

Curiously, universities trumpet their roles as critics and conscience of society, yet institutional logics continue to reinforce visible masculinist practices and beliefs. For women, the more senior their role in an institution, the greater the potential exists to pressure for change. Yet, the more senior the role, there is a corresponding intensity of pressure to conform to institutional norms and practices. Perhaps as Blackmore (2013) suggests, what is required is a reorientation of leadership and serious questions to be raised – not about the numerical absence of women but about the masculinity of power. Thus, despite the changes across institutions of higher education, it is crucial that attention continues to be paid to the continuing consequences of these neoliberal changes from a gender perspective.

A key task of a feminist leader is to build more transparent, accountable and democratic ways of addressing organizational behaviours and the institutionalization of hierarchies of power. Feminist leaders work collectively and collaboratively to better understand these power dynamics in a bid to create opportunities for all individuals to contribute to a shared transformative agenda (Blackmore, 2006; Morley, 2013). Feminist leadership is therefore a collective social practice that is grounded in a commitment to inclusive principles in order to build coalitions and bring about institutional change. It is the recognition of regimes of both visible and invisible power that marginalize and oppress women that provide a focus for feminist leaders. **Visible power** refers to hierarchical structures and authority whereby those in power are known due to the labels formally linked with their roles and organizational position (such as Vice Chancellor). **Invisible power** is less tangible. It is the informal power generally linked with the dominant ideologies, values and characteristics of a dominant group; usually white and male. It is this group that can shape and define an organizational culture and exclude, or limit, access by the less powerful to decision-making structures and resources. It is the working of both visible and invisible power that feminists pay particular attention to and challenge in a bid to identify and contest those barriers that restrict women's full participation in social, political, economic, cultural and institutional settings. Broadly speaking, feminism is a lens through which to view unequal relationships of power and to search for alternative conceptualizations of leadership.

Activity 6.1

1 How do you understand critical feminist perspectives?
2 What leadership principles can be drawn from feminist perspectives?
3 How has the gender dynamic and its relation to educational leadership been played out in your country/institution and to what effect?
4 How would you apply feminist perspectives at your institution as a leader and a practitioner and in what ways can it illuminate professional practices in your institution/country?

Having helped you reflect upon the key ideas and principles of critical feminist perspectives in educational leadership, in the next section we will substantiate the key ideas and apply them to the Indonesian context.

The context of Indonesia: history, policies and contemporary practice

Historical records demonstrate that during the struggle for Indonesian independence from Dutch and Japanese colonization, women emerged as leaders. Indonesian traditional customs and ethnic groups are patriarchal to varying degrees, despite one that is highly matriarchal (Blackburn, 2004). These traditional gender relations have been magnified by the oppressive New Order regime (1966–1998) that has socially and politically engineered the construction of womanhood. **State Ibuism** (literally translated State Motherism), as explained by Suryakusuma (1988), is the New Order's ideology in defining and disciplining women to be 'good wives' and 'good mothers'. It was seen as the new way to refer to women, from *perempuan* to *wanita*. *Perempuan* is constituted from *empu*, which means someone with competence, while *wanita*, short for *wani-ditata*, refers to women with the willingness (*wani*) to submit (*ditata*) (Budiman, 2002). In essence, what this means is that the state has defined and prescribed what it means to be a woman and those duties that a woman ought to 'naturally' undertake. It is this underpinning ideology that has permeated social, economic, political and cultural life. Despite a number of additional reforms, this has remained a powerful ideology.

The collapse of the New Order administration in 1998 marked the birth of democracy in Indonesia, as well as the empowerment of women. The country had signed up to constitutional, political and institutional reforms in order to give women a greater place in public life. To ensure the success of gender mainstreaming, a ministry on women's empowerment was established. Also introduced was a 30 per cent gender quota for women running for legislative candidacy. However, while this may have been the political rhetoric, the reality remains that women continue to encounter systems, structures and beliefs that run counter to these prevailing discourses.

Despite the rise of women's representation in the political arena, women remain underrepresented in senior leadership positions in the education sector. In secondary schools, for example, and despite the fact that women constitute the majority of classroom teachers, the Indonesian Ministry of Education and Culture data indicates that there were only 14 per cent junior secondary and 12 per cent senior secondary female school principals by 2010 (Directorate of Higher Education, 2016). This represents a pyramid where women are located at the bottom of the structure which is also reflected at higher-education level. According to the database of the Directorate of Higher Education (2016), the lower academic positions (teaching assistant and lecturer) show a balanced distribution between male and female academics. However, the top academic positions (senior lecturer and professor) demonstrate a notable gap (see Table 6.1 for the statistics of academic positions by gender). This feminization of labour is evident in the preponderance of women occupying the 'basement' rather than the 'tower' of university structures (Fitzgerald, 2012).

A similar pattern can be found in the university senior management. There are only five women rectors in public universities in Indonesia, compared with 115 men who occupy this position (Directorate General of Higher Education, 2016). Despite the advancement women have made in terms of their participation rate as undergraduates, this has not translated into success in breaking the academic glass ceiling. Masculinity and power are intertwined in such a way that men represent the standard. That is, men represent the norm against which the presence and performance of women are scrutinized and measured.

This academic pattern is a familiar one. In Australia, for example, as well as in many other Western countries, although numbers of women in academic positions are steadily rising, women continue to be under-represented at senior levels in university leadership (Bagilhole and White, 2011; Fitzgerald, 2014; O'Connor, 2015). One of the consequences is that women are frequently exposed to gendered expectations that serve to

Table 6.1 Statistics of academic positions in Indonesian higher education by gender in 2016

Academic position	Women	Men
Professor	905	3,864
Senior lecturer	10,451	20,038
Lecturer	19,835	29,523
Teaching assistant	20,930	25,908

Source: Directorate General of Higher Education, 2016.

limit opportunities for leadership. The significant absence of women in senior posts is a recurrent theme across public policy debates, and despite sustained attention to these issues, there is a remarkable persistence of inequities (Morley, 2013). Those women who do succeed are lone figures in senior roles and therefore rarely able to shatter the male enclaves of power.

Women in senior leadership roles can find themselves in an ambiguous position. On the one hand they are expected to adopt and adapt their ways of working and align with the dominant managerial culture yet on the other, their very presence signals a disruption to this order and culture. Paradoxically, women in senior roles are reluctant to openly discuss discriminatory practices as they may well be labelled 'troublemakers' or 'dangerous' (O'Connor, 2015; Fitzgerald, 2018).

It is important to recognize that there are situated institutional, cultural and geographic practices that both contribute to and dominate Indonesian higher education. Traditional values and traditions temper contemporary sociocultural practices, yet at the same time reveal the universal persistence of gender inequalities, both overt and covert, as well as the workings of formal and informal power. That is, women differentially and disproportionately experience unequal dominant regimes of power that continue to impact on their professional lives and work.

A critical feminist perspective

Feminist theories do not focus merely on gender, but more importantly they challenge dominant categories and constructs as well as interrogate who is marginalized and silenced via prevailing discourses, subjectivities and practices. Feminists seek to deconstruct leadership because it is concerned with whose values and interests get represented (Blackmore, 2006). It enables us to ask: who benefits from particular arrangements, how and why; who dominates and who is being marginalized? Feminist leaders work towards shattering and ameliorating disadvantages and silences as well as uncovering underlying and existing inequalities and identifying ways in which visible and invisible power operate. Access to leadership opens up both space and possibilities for women and marginalized groups to collectively change structures and influence organizational cultures.

However, this is not an easy task as both formal and informal power work to ensure the continuance of the organizational status quo. What is primarily needed, we suggest, is a dismantling of social relations of gender that brings about a reduction of male advantage.

In addition, feminist perspectives have the potential to test dominant metanarratives of educational leadership by using women leaders' life histories. Their stories potentially challenge the dominant masculine narratives of educational leadership – of doing leadership differently. As the three case studies demonstrate, the emergence of women leaders in Indonesian higher education signifies this changing nature of gendered leadership in traditionally masculine, and masculinized space (Collinson and Hearn, 1996) of the public universities (Sakhiyya and Locke, 2019). Their emergence is a productive indication that women *can* take parts in various arenas of critical decision-making where values around educational institutions are negotiated, decided and implemented. These new ways of working offer the possibility of a softening of hierarchy and structure, and subsequent opportunities to confront prevailing modes of domination and subordination. And while women play a crucial role in social and familial spheres, their entrée to senior leadership in higher education prompt a reconfiguration of this public sphere of work. What is further needed then is an examination of how women leaders are both perceived and received and a broader understanding of ways in which gendered perceptions of leadership work to constrain and limit women leaders. One of the ways in which these questions can be surfaced is through a feminist critique of leading and leadership. It is through critique that alternative ways of thinking and practising educational leadership can emerge.

In the dynamic global landscape, what remains imperative is a commitment to critical feminist work.

Undertaking this work requires a recognition and contestation of mainstream (or malestream) literatures that almost universally feature academics from the global north and west and to contribute to a critical trajectory that simultaneously works within/against dominant knowledge regimes.

> **Critical feminism:** focuses on the critique of regimes of power and a commitment to social change that leads to just outcomes.

Implications for educational leadership in Indonesia

From a feminist perspective, gender is a central element in the organization and division of labour. The conceptual implication of considering gender as one significant 'structuring structure' in understanding the practice of educational leadership in higher education means that leadership is a conceptual lens to problematize the university's nature, purpose and capacities in a bid to transform practices in more socially just ways (Blackmore, 2017). The contemporary shift of universities from being publicly oriented to being market driven has brought about a level of organizational restructuring in order to align with corporate objectives and to 'deliver' on outcomes (Sakhiyya and Rata, 2019). The rapid increase of demand in productivity and accountability has contributed to a reconfiguration of masculinities and femininities in the division of labour. That is, there has been a regendering of work in the academy whereby work that is valued is predominantly undertaken by men, and work that is vital to the ongoing maintenance of the organization is undertaken by women (Fitzgerald, 2014). It is this administrative and relational work that is undertaken in the ivory basement; those spaces in universities that women mainly occupy (Fitzgerald, 2012). On the contrary, men dominate the apex of the structure where the concentration of power and symbolic control is located. In both historical and contemporary settings, men exercise both formal and informal power. Their work is usually associated with 'hard' management tasks such as finances, resources, entrepreneurial activities and executive power whereas women frequently take up institutional housekeeping roles such as student and staff well-being, quality assurance and those tasks that require emotional intelligence (Fitzgerald, 2012).

Even if women occupy leadership positions, they are usually in less prestigious roles and, as the case studies highlight, their professional work and lives remain dominated by cultural and social belief systems that define and frame institutionalized relations of gender. Only through a critical reading of the contemporary environment can the issues of leadership and social justice be adequately discussed.

Feminist theories challenge this taken-for-granted feminization of labour in higher education and ask a fundamental question: is the issue of women's under-representation in leadership the problem of, and for, women if there are not enough 'eligible' women in the field? If it is so, then how might leadership practices be transformed in more socially just ways? For those women who do aspire to and take up leadership roles they encounter significant challenges and obstacles (Bagilhole and White, 2011; Blackmore, 2013; Fitzgerald, 2018; Sakhiyya and Locke, 2019). In Indonesia in particular, women are confronted with and constantly reminded of an essentially patriarchal culture that treats as the 'norm' male leaders and masculine characteristics. In order for Indonesian women to take that step into leadership, they must act as transgressors within this culture. The hurdles are threefold: home, society and institutional. Or put another way, familial, social and societal.

Metaphors such as 'glass ceiling', 'glass cliff', 'glass staircase' and 'leaky pipelines' have been used to denote that gendered obstacles and barriers exist, many of which are both invisible and misrecognized (Fitzgerald, 2012). The rise in the numbers of women in leadership positions does not break the 'glass'; rather, this potentially works to place women in an ambiguous position where antithetical and contradictory discourses intersect, namely empowerment and meritocracy (Sakhiyya and Locke, 2019). Women are located in between the individualistic discourse of meritocracy and the collective and progressive empowerment discourses that promote gender equity and women's participation in decision-making processes (Bagilhole and White, 2011). This paradox invites a more critical stance on the representation of women leaders.

A shift from women's under-representation in formal leadership to more substantive issues of leadership (power relations, university hierarchies and regimes of power, access to and participation in decision-making) is required to address the issues of equity. In other words, it is only through refocusing the gaze away from the numerical representation of women leaders to the social relations of gender and power that enables women to act differently. If leadership is understood as a democratic process and practice, it embraces alternative models of shared leadership. But let us be mindful here of the distinction between democratic leadership and shared leadership (Blackmore, 2006). While the former views educational institutions as sites of democratic processes that accommodate stakeholders' voices, the latter places emphasis on more technical strategies to achieve certain outcomes. If the focus remains on 'counting' women in, what continues to be ignored are the power inequalities that both create and institutionalize unequal conditions of work in universities. There is no straightforward solution. As the case studies show, while women are slowly breaking the academic glass ceiling, as lone interlopers into the corridors of male power they are in a risky situation. Risky because their gender can be used as a reason to highlight their presence or indeed their absence (i.e. 'glorify' or 'blame' women), to provoke a backlash because women may not possess normative leadership characteristics and ways of working (and normative practices remain unchallenged), and for those women who may not succeed, their gender is viewed as the reason for their failure, without recourse to the institutional and the workings of visible and invisible regimes of power.

Activity 6.2

1 What are the different roles men and women have in your institution and how might these be categorized?
2 Who undertakes the majority of work around staff support and pastoral care and what patterns can you see emerging?
3 At meetings, who speaks for the majority of the time? Whose agenda dominates and why? Whose voice might not be heard? How might this data be understood and interpreted?
4 How might work practices be more inclusive?

Introducing the case studies: women leading in Indonesian higher education

Three case studies of women's experiences as senior leaders in Indonesian higher education are presented next. In each of the cases, the women appointed to these roles were breaking new ground; that is, each was the first woman to hold this post in her university. The research data, drawn from a project that investigated the tension between meritocracy and empowerment discourses in Indonesian public universities (Sakhiyya and Locke, 2019), illustrates the challenges women encountered. Responses from four women at three different universities are extracted from in-depth interviews. The respective institutions are given pseudonyms: Nusantara, a first-cluster public university, Atlas, a second-cluster public university and Pahlawan, a second-cluster private university. These categories used to describe institutional status are derived from the Indonesian Ministry of Research,

Technology and Higher Education. Together these three cases provide instances of how historical organizational, cultural, social, political, economic and geographical legacies are mediated through practice by localized gender regimes and orders. We move away from problematizing a range of female/male binaries to focus on the slow progress of women in Indonesia gaining access to senior leadership in higher education. We document the experiences and perceptions of four women who have been appointed to these formal and senior roles and while the micro-practices reveal the culturally specific sites in which these women work, live and operate, the case studies further expose that despite being in powerful roles, women do not necessarily feel powerful.

Case Study 6.1 Nusantara University

Nusantara University is one of the oldest and largest public higher-education institutions in the country catering for around 50,000 students. It is ranked in the first cluster due to its high-profile research standing. The female Rector provided an overview of the institutional vision and her own research contributions:

> Our university should be locally rooted and globally recognized. This means the presence of our university should impact on the nation's social, economic and cultural development, so that we could contribute to Indonesia's civilization. Internationalization should be based on our local strengths. Our local strength is diversity. For example, to handle disaster response in Papua, we cannot simply apply a disaster method that has been implemented in Java. We have tried this, and it did not work out. This difference demands creativity and innovation to generate the appropriate disaster approach and method. If we advance this thinking to a global level, Indonesian diversity makes us learn to innovate that can be globally implemented.

Since its establishment post-independence (1949), the university rectors have solely been men and the highest position a woman could reach was Vice Rector. In 2014 the first female Rector was elected. In effect, this new female senior leader occupied a space and institutional culture historically dominated by men and masculinity. Her comments reflect these dynamics and inherent challenges: 'Culture might have its effect [on this leadership matter]. Our culture is patriarchal, except in West Sumatra where it is matriarchal. Other than culture . . . I think opportunities [to lead] are there [for women].'

She highlighted several leadership traits women should possess that are generally understood as masculine characteristics:

> As far as I am concerned, we need to be resilient and tough. If we are too soft and [easily touched – feeling], it's going to be hard. We have to be firm and able to take risks. We have to be able to say yes or no firmly. This is not easy, isn't it? But actually, women can do that. Perhaps because we are perceived as soft, thus we are not expected to be bold. That's the hardest part. To establish rules, we have to be bold. Also, women are more meticulous, attend to detail, and easily moved. Sometimes leadership traits are not like that. If I go into too much detail, I will be reminded [by my staff] that leaders do not do details.

In addition to possessing the necessary leadership traits, the importance of empowerment and encouragement for women was emphasized. Her former (male) Rector had sponsored and supported her candidacy for this senior position: 'The previous Rector had a concern that one of the Vice-Rectors should be female. This concern was then taken up by the senate and the University Board of Trustees . . . there were only two women in the Board of Trustees . . . Then to run for the Rector's election, gender did not matter. It was all about competence.'

Optimistically she predicted that changing demographics might slowly impact opportunities for women:

> But I think slowly this will change. According to the data I got, female students in our university outnumber male students. The number of female lecturers whose age is under forty years old are the same with men. There is a trend for this. In terms of professors, we still have more men, because lecturers above fifty years old are dominated by men.

Perhaps serendipitously, at the point at which she was promoted, change was occurring in other universities: 'It happens to other universities too. The Rector of UPN [a state middle-tier university in the same town] is a woman. Others like Unhas, Sam Ratulangi, and the Open University. Women are in charge now.'

Case Study 6.2 Atlas University

Atlas University is a state university, and was previously a teacher-training college established in 1965. In 2000, it was given a wider mandate to develop a stronger research capacity. With this added research component, it was upgraded to be a state university. Compared to Nusantara University, Atlas University is relatively smaller having a student cohort of around 35,000 and a mixed orientation of research and teaching.

Like Nusantara University, top leadership positions were traditionally held by men and it was not until 2015 that the first female Dean was elected. Previously the highest academic rank a woman had held was that of Vice-Dean. In 2019, across the eight faculties there were three female Deans. Notably, this first female Dean was adamant that it was her competence that had secured the role, not her gender: 'For me, the main challenge is achievement, not gender. I challenge myself to achieve better, not to defeat men . . . I do not think in simple gender binaries.'

The male Rector of Atlas University commented too on her communications skills, networks and scholarship: 'First, because the new Dean speaks English very well. Secondly, the person has a bold commitment to knowledge and scholarship. Thirdly, habitat recognition. We can be a centre of excellence if we have an international community that recognizes us. She is internationally recognized and affiliated to international professional associations.'

It would seem, in this case, that gender was largely absent from the conversation. The interview with the second elected female Dean who led the Faculty of Law offered insight into her own career trajectory: 'I was the head for the office of intellectual property rights and legal aid at the university. It was the university's asset. In the middle of doing this job, the Rector asked me to apply for candidacy in the Dean election. On 7 December 2015, I was appointed.'

In taking up the new leadership position as a Dean, she emphasized that the position was underpinned with a performance mandate: 'This position is a mandate that brings about consequences, i.e. commitment and integrity. So it is not easy to say yes to a mandate. As the consequence is self-esteem. So when I say yes, there are a lot of things to do.'

Case Study 6.3 Pahlawan University

Pahlawan University is a private university established in 1968. Similar to Atlas University, Pahlawan University is classified in the second cluster. It has a student cohort of around 12,000 and a mixed orientation of research and teaching. Compared with Atlas, Pahlawan University has a better track record in appointing women to strategic senior leadership positions. Although it has male Rector, in 2019, out of four Vice-Rectors, three of them are women. In addition, out of eight Deans, half of them are women. One of the female Deans from Psychology described her preliminary misgivings taking up the role and the perceptions held of her: 'When I was asked to lead for the first time, I did not feel like I had the competence of a leader. Maybe because I am a woman, as in our culture, most leaders are men. But other people believe that I have the leadership competence.'

The female Dean acknowledged that women encounter more challenges in their aspiration to senior leaders and the advancement of their career. In addition to that, family support and understanding is, she believed, the key to women's success.

> I do think that female lecturers encounter more challenges [than men] to advance in the career ladder. Many of my colleagues are not as lucky as I am who have more domestic problems. My colleagues will laugh [in disbelief] if I tell them that my husband forbids me from being active outside the house. I realize that I am lucky. Other people might have spouses who are unsupportive, or children with disabilities with more demanding attention.

Activity 6.3

Reflect upon the three cases of women senior leaders described in the case studies in relation to the critical feminist perspectives raised in this chapter and analyse the extent to which the themes of feminist perspectives emerge in the account of the three women leaders. Then, evaluate the extent to which the accounts of the three women resonate with your own experience of working (or studying) in educational institutions.

Conclusion

Women remain the numerical minority in senior leadership roles in higher education: this is an *institutional* problem, and institutional cultures, hierarchies and ways of working reinforce skills, knowledge and dispositions usually linked with men and masculinity. The professional practice challenges of ensuring a more gender diverse workforce are numerous and challenging and, in the first instance require the dismantling of normative and discriminatory practices. Women in senior roles are frequently the organizational 'other' and negotiate and navigate expectations placed on them as 'women' and as 'leaders'. For those women who do take up senior leadership roles, although they may pave the way for their female colleagues, there is a disproportionate expectation placed on them as 'women' and as 'women leaders'.

We suggest that the focus on numbers of women taking up positions is misplaced. Rather than situate women as the 'problem', the focus ought to be on the way leadership is both constructed and enacted. More sophisticated tools and methods are required to better understand the complexities women leaders face with regard to exigencies of gender, race, class, ethnicity, religious and cultural beliefs and spatial location. What is further required is a more nuanced understanding of the social relations of gender and how different femininities and masculinities are constructed in relation to each other and in specific contexts. Without this integrated focus, the stories that are told will always be incomplete. The critical questions to ask are: which women and which men are advantaged/ disadvantaged within specific contexts? And which women and which men get to be leaders and why?

Further reading

Aiston, S.J. (2014) Leading the academy or being led? Hong Kong women academics. *Higher Education Research & Development*, 33(1), 59–72.

Burkinshaw, P. (2015) *Higher education, leadership and women vice chancellors: fitting into communities of practice of masculinities*. Basingstoke: Palgrave.

Leathwood, C. and Read, B. (2009) *Gender and the changing face of higher education: a feminised future?* Maidenhead: McGraw-Hill, Open University Press.

White, K., Bagilhole, B. and Riordan, S. (2012) The gendered shaping of university leadership in Australia, South Africa and the United Kingdom. *Higher Education Quarterly*, 66(3), 293–307.

Wijaya Mulya, T. and Sakhiyya, Z. (2020) 'Leadership is a sacred matter': women leaders contesting and contextualising neoliberal meritocracy in the Indonesian academia. *Gender and Education*.

References

Bagilhole, B and White, K. (eds) (2011) *Gender, power and management: a cross-cultural analysis of higher education*. New York: Palgrave Macmillan.

Blackburn, S. (2004) *Women and the state in modern Indonesia*. Cambridge: Cambridge University Press.

Blackmore, J. (2006) Social justice and the study and practice of leadership in education: a feminist history. *Journal of Educational Administration and History*, 38(2), 185–200.

Blackmore, J. (2013) A feminist critical perspective on educational leadership. *International Journal of Leadership in Education: Theory and Practice*, 16(2), 139–154.

Blackmore, J. (2017) Leadership in higher education: a critical feminist perspective on global restructuring. In: S. Wright and C. Shore (eds), *Death of the public university: uncertain futures for higher education in the knowledge economy* (pp. 90–113). Oxford: Berghahn Books.

Budiman, M. (2002) Courage and submission: rereading the Dharma Wanita and its legacy on today's women. In: D. Elsara (ed.), *Wani Ditata Project: women construction through state bureaucracy* (pp. 180–198). Jakarta: Risnam Antartika.

Collinson, D.L. and Hearn, J. (1996) *Managers as men: critical perspectives on men, masculinities and managements*. London: Sage.

Directorate of Higher Education (2016) Database of lecturers and university students. Indonesian Ministry of Education and Culture. Available online: https://forlap.ristekdikti.go.id/ (accessed 28 July 2020).

Fitzgerald, T. (2012) Ivory basements and ivory towers. In: T. Fitzgerald, J. White and H.M. Gunter (eds), *Hard labour? Academic work and the changing landscape of higher education* (pp. 113–135). Bingley: Emerald.

Fitzgerald, T. (2014) *Women leaders in higher education: shattering the myths*. Abingdon: Routledge.

Fitzgerald, T. (2018) Looking good and being good: women leaders in Australian universities. *Education Sciences*, 8(2). Available online: https://www.mdpi.com/2227-7102/8/2/54 (accessed 20 July 2020).

Morley, L. (2013) The rules of the game: women and the leaderist turn in higher education. *Gender and Education*, 25(1), 116–131.

O'Connor, P. (2015) Good jobs – but places for women? *Gender and Education*, 27(3), 304–319.

Sakhiyya, Z. and Locke, K. (2019) Empowerment vs meritocracy discourses in Indonesian public universities: the case of female leaders. *Asian Journal of Women's Studies*, 25(2), 198–216.

Sakhiyya, Z. and Rata, E. (2019) From 'priceless' to 'priced': the value of knowledge in higher education. *Globalisation, Societies and Education*, 17(3), 285–295.

Suryakusuma, J. (1988) State Ibuism: the social construction of womanhood in the Indonesian New Order. Master's thesis. The Hague: Institute of Social Studies.

Critical perspectives in and approaches to educational leadership in two Nordic countries

Jorunn Møller and Linda Rönnberg

7

What this chapter is about 106

Key questions that this chapter addresses 106

Introduction 106

Welfare trajectories and contemporary transformations in Sweden and Norway 107

The framing of school leadership in Scandinavia 111

Distributed and heroic framing of school leadership 112

Business-management approaches gaining terrain 114

A closer look at the Swedish transformation 115

From a public to private good? Critical reflections and spaces for action 116

Creating spaces to think differently 117

Conclusion 118

Further reading 118

References 119

What this chapter is about

In this chapter, we situate educational leadership in the Nordic countries in relation to political-ideological transformations that have taken place during in recent decades. We do this by exploring the comparatively divergent development of neoliberal reform in Sweden and Norway and critically discussing implications for education as a public good and for educational leadership.

Our aim is to situate educational leadership within the broader political environments that often go unaccounted for in studies of school leadership. We show how school principals as political agents may enact their roles in ways that are defined not just by their local contextual conditions, but also by their macro-level political structures. By connecting policy and leadership scholarship, we contextualize the field of educational leadership to include an explicit consideration of the broader policy forces and political contexts that act on educational leaders' work. This approach promotes critical reflection on the implications of the reciprocal relationship between school leadership and education policy.

Key questions that this chapter addresses

1 Which changes in the political economy have influenced and challenged the idea of public education in Sweden and Norway?

2 What characterizes patterns of and responses to marketization and privatization and the language of public education and educational leadership in the two national settings?

3 How do school principals cope with marketization and privatization, how are they trained, and what knowledge are they expected to use?

Introduction

In this chapter, we explore the social-democratic welfarist historical legacy in Norway and Sweden, followed by the growth of neoliberal reforms, and point to important commonalities and differences. We then trace the images of school leadership in Scandinavia by analysing both their historical distinctions and forces caused by the spread of political expectations and the impact of transnationalism. Against this background, we then critically discuss how the role of schools, the positioning of school principals in these transformations and the notion of education as a public good has been challenged.

The definitions (see box) are central to the structure of the chapter and its key learning points.

We begin by setting out the two national contexts of Sweden and Norway, which will serve as case studies.

Welfare trajectories and contemporary transformations in Sweden and Norway

The social-democratic welfarist legacy

Sweden and Norway are geographically, historically, linguistically and culturally very close. Both countries have a strong ideological tradition of emphasizing the role of educational institutions in the making of civic society, which has been built on ideas of comprehensiveness and egalitarian values. In addition to preparing children to become able employees, schools should also prepare children to play constructive roles in a democratic society. School access for children from all socio-economic groups, free of charge and with little streaming or tracking has been considered important (Møller, 2009).

However, over the last twenty years, neoliberal reforms of education have been gradually adopted in the Nordic countries, albeit to varying degrees. In fact, Sweden and Norway represent marked contrasts in in this respect and this makes them interesting cases to compare in this chapter. While Norway has remained more reluctant and has defended the comprehensive and public organization of education, Sweden has allowed private providers to play a much more significant role in delivering education services.

There is no straightforward explanation as to why these countries have embarked on different routes when it comes to marketization and privatization in education. Even so, factors such as varying macroeconomic conditions and different parties in government have been highlighted as parts of the answer. The role of the Social Democratic parties has also differed, and this party has been more willing to enable market reforms on education in Sweden (Wiborg, 2013).

Educational leadership: an emergent relational accomplishment politically positioned within the administrative field in education. It is based on a mandate, but the mandate is a living social process of power and trust that the leaders both are given and must take. It implies a reciprocal interplay as leadership both shapes and is shaped by the conditions where it takes place, in both time and space (Crow, Day and Møller, 2017).

Social-democratic welfarism: a commitment to reducing social and political inequality through a generous universal welfare system along with redistributive measures based on need and sustained investment in public education. It encompasses a view that education is integral to democratic development (Møller, 2009).

Education as 'public good': emphasizes 'a common school for all' with the aim of securing equality in terms of equal opportunities. It is a perspective of education as a social right of citizenship (Englund, 1994).

Education as 'private good': implies a possessive individualism where it is possible to differentiate schooling in relation to the specific needs or wants from students and/ or families. It means developing a school system based on parents' and their children's priorities and judgements about their future (Englund, 1994).

Neoliberalism: a theory of political economic practices that proposes that human well-being can best be advanced by liberating individual entrepreneurial freedoms and skills within an institutional framework characterized by strong private property rights, free markets and free trade (Wiborg, 2013).

Marketization: processes in which market-oriented values, and principles from the private sector are introduced and transferred to the education sphere, often under the umbrella of New Public Management (NPM) (Rönnberg, Lindgren and Lundahl, 2019).

Privatization: the transfer of responsibilities from the state and/or public domain to private actors and/or organizations regarding the provision of education (Rönnberg, Lindgren and Lundahl, 2019).

The period from 1945 until about 1970 is often referred to as the golden era of social-democratic welfarism. The cornerstones were citizens' equal rights; state responsibility for welfare of all citizens; narrowing income gaps; and promoting social justice. This model has been supported by the labour-market model, with collective bargaining in cooperation between governments and labour organizations (Telhaug, Mediås and Aasen, 2006).

Additionally, the development of the comprehensive school system in Scandinavia must be seen in connection with the unique tradition of consensus-seeking politics in education. Both the right- and left-wing parties have sought compromises and agreements on educational reforms. This joint effort has its historical roots in the political mobilization of, and alliance between, the farmers and the workers. It does not mean absence of conflicts, but there has traditionally been a political striving for consensus. The Social Democratic parties were not rooted in radical socialism, and after the Second World War the workers were able to ally themselves with the growing white-collar middle class (Møller, 2009).

A supplementary dimension to understand the history of education in Scandinavia is the very special form of popular resistance that was constituted by anti-elitist lay religious movements in the nineteenth century. Particularly in Norway, which, unlike Sweden, did not have traditional aristocracy and economic elites in the late nineteenth century, these movements grew strong. They implied a broad public involvement in both economic and educational developments. In both countries, local teachers became important agents of civic society and played a crucial role in the processes of shaping national identities. They had the cultural and social capital to act on a trans-local level and to mobilize people to fight for their rights (Ahonen and Rantala, 2001).

The growth of neoliberal reforms in education

At the beginning of the 1990s, a neoliberal reform gained ground internationally. In the Scandinavian countries, it was argued that the welfare-state project had turned national and local authorities into unresponsive, bureaucratic organizations (Uljens et al., 2013). By promoting NPM-related features such as local autonomy, devolution, horizontal specialization and flattened municipal hierarchies, the aim was to have more individualized and efficient public-service delivery. During the next fifteen years, Norwegian and Swedish governments responded quite differently to these new transnational NPM approaches to educational reforms.

Case Study 7.1 Norway

In Norway, during the 1990s, the NPM agenda did not directly challenge the established tradition of schooling, but it had consequences for the restructuring of the local school administration in terms of deregulation, horizontal specialization and management by objectives. However, the launch of the first Programme for International Student Assessment (PISA) report in 2001 accelerated a move to a policy influenced by neoliberalism and a shift from more input-oriented policy instruments towards a more output-oriented policy. It became a turning point in the Norwegian public debates about educational quality. In White Paper No. 30, 'Culture for Learning, 2003–2004', it was argued that teachers and school leaders needed to do better than before and be more able and willing. This directly suggested that schools had previously failed in raising students' academic achievements. Each school would need ambitious school leaders with positive attitudes towards change and improvement. Leadership and accountability became the new panacea for school improvement.

The PISA results have been used to legitimate new forms of bureaucracy in continuous documentation, monitoring of work and a shift in how trust in education is communicated. New assessment policies with an emphasis on performance measurement and emerging accountability practices characterize the transition processes of the 2010s. Prior to these new policies, the public and parents had trust in professionals above all, but now attention was increasingly directed towards trusting what can be measured by results (Møller and Skedsmo, 2013).

To some extent, a market approach to educational reforms has been adopted, but marketization as a principle has been less embraced in the Norwegian context, probably because a market of school choice for students and parents is only possible in larger cities, and private providers are by law not allowed to operate as 'for-profit' entities. In Norway in 2018, only 3.8 per cent of students attended a private elementary school, and 8 per cent of students attended a private upper-secondary school. There is a huge regional variety. While 16 per cent of the upper-secondary students in Oslo and Hordaland (including Bergen) attend a private school, in Finnmark, less than 1 per cent did so (Statistics Norway, 2018). The population in Norway is widely dispersed, and decentralized settlement is still a desirable aim for most political parties. Moreover, there has also been cross-party consensus to defend the traditional welfare state and a comprehensive school (Wiborg, 2013).

Even so, the language of education at a policy level has increasingly been replaced by the international discourse of learning, which implies an economic way of thinking about education as a commodity to be delivered. This new language may erode a broader discussion about education for citizenship over the long term (Biesta, 2004).

Case Study 7.2 Sweden

In Sweden, a market approach to educational reform has been pushed much more strongly by, for example, permitting publicly funded but privately owned providers of schooling, which are even allowed to operate as for-profit organizations. Within a short time during the 1990s, Sweden went from a strictly state-regulated and state-delivered system to one inviting and encouraging private interests in the provision of education (Alexiadou, Lundahl and Rönnberg, 2019). The introduction of parental school choice, liberal regulations to open private schools, and the introduction of managerialism into the running of the schools became distinguishing features. In the Nordic and European perspective, Sweden constitutes somewhat of an extreme.

The transformation has undermined the notion of a common school for all. As an illustration, the notion of equity in education has been a key term in Swedish education policy, but to accommodate the policy changes, the notion has increasingly come to signify equal access to choice of education, rather than the social-equality dimension it used to encompass (Alexiadou, Lundahl and Rönnberg, 2019). When parents are choosing a school for their child, they require 'value for money', and the language is rephrased into understanding the teacher as a provider and education as a commodity to be delivered (Biesta, 2004).

It is worth reiterating that the Swedish Social Democrats went much further with marketization and privatization than the Norwegian Social Democratic Party. Leading Swedish Social Democrats adopted an NPM-oriented agenda and this policy direction became evident in the implementation of decentralization and school-choice reforms. While in office, this party has not abolished regulations permitting providers to operate private independent so-called free schools, nor policies allowing these providers to operate for profit from revenues from a tax-funded voucher (school fees are not allowed).

Swedish politicians attached high hopes to the school choice and privatization reforms, but there is little evidence that the reforms have lived up to these intentions. Even if parents have been offered far more choice and autonomy, at least in the urban regions, the costs in the form of, for instance, increasing segregation are high. In the 2010s, public bankruptcies and misconduct of school companies, as well as the steep Swedish PISA decline in 2013, put pressure on education policymakers. But these pressures have not yet resulted in any strong measures to change the overall policy direction (Alexiadou, Lundahl and Rönnberg, 2019).

In the early 1990s, there was a very slow expansion in terms of providers and share of students attending free schools. At the turn of the millennium, however, it became evident that businesses operated as private limited companies were gaining ground. Increasingly, national and international venture and equity firms emerged as actors, and over time, there has been an ownership concentration; a handful of large companies host the majority of the free-school students. In urban areas, about 50 per cent of the students at the upper-secondary level are attending free schools, and the corresponding figure nationally is 25 per cent – a fivefold increase since the early 2000s (Rönnberg, Lindgren and Lundahl, 2019).

These transformations, even if unfolding differently in Sweden and in Norway, have put pressure on school leaders and shaped expectations in particular directions. Next, we turn to these issues, initially by looking back at how school leadership traditionally has been conceptualized.

The framing of school leadership in Scandinavia

From *primus inter pares* . . .

Both Sweden and Norway have a long history of framing school leadership as *primus inter pares* or 'first among equals'. This has resulted not only in a flat hierarchy in schools, but also in uniform teacher training until recently, with little or no formal distinction among members of the teaching staff. Also, trust in teachers' work has long been a tacit dimension of principals' approach to leadership.

In **Norway**, there was, for many years, no specific formal training for school principals, only non-obligatory in-service education provided at the regional level. The choice of candidates for leading positions in the educational system was in general adjusted towards formal assessable criteria, such as number of years in professional service. As a consequence, school principals regarded their administrative functions mostly as applying to rules and regulations. Many principals continued to look upon themselves as teachers with some administrative duties in addition to teaching.

During the 1990s, however, established zones of control were challenged, as some parents and other people outside schools questioned the individual autonomy each teacher had in his or her classroom. This focus shifted the power relationship between the parents and the school, and more emphasis was given to the control of the educational processes. This shift essentially moved the principal from being 'first among equals' to a manager, at least in the dominant discourses and in national policy documents.

In **Sweden**, state involvement in the training of school leaders has occurred since the late 1960s, with the provision of short-term courses in a number of educational and administrative areas. Starting in 1986, a national training programme for principals was delivered by the National Agency for Education. Since 1992, programmes have been carried out by different universities, while the Agency has kept the overall responsibility. As we will elaborate more later in his chapter, the current training on management and legislation issues has solidified the shift of principals' work from pedagogic to managerial.

. . . to trained managers

In **Norway**, the interest in principals as managers began to gather momentum in the 1990s, influenced by the NPM discourse, with its focus on strong leaders and entrepreneurs as a vehicle for the modernization project in education. New titles were created for managers at the municipal level, and these people were trained and accredited as managers using business models. Master's programmes in educational leadership and management at the university level were first launched at the beginning of the new millennium, and a national programme for newly appointed principals that contains key elements of NPM was introduced in 2009, mainly as a consequence of the country's participation in the Organisation for Economic Co-operation and Development's (OECD) 'improving school leadership' initiative.

A major assumption was that successful leadership was a key to large-scale education reform and to improving academic achievement, and models of best practice served as a celebration of the hard work of school principals. Based on the education agenda set by the OECD, we argue that some research knowledge (e.g. knowledge about school effectiveness – how to ensure effective learning strategies and increase excellence in literacy and numeracy) has been emphasized by policymakers and administrators in designing these programmes in both Sweden and Norway, while research that problematizes power structures has often been marginalized (Møller, 2017).

In **Sweden**, the National Agency for Education defines the goals, content and coverage of training for school principals. As in Norway, the overall direction has been to situate principals as managers and administrators. The current programme includes three courses – laws and legal knowledge; management by objectives; and leadership – indicating the types of knowledge principals are expected to turn to and use, in which more critical scholarship has had a marginal role. For principals, competition to attract students and the public display of performance measurements have created new tasks. Information, public relations and marketing strategies, as well as development of school profiles and school programmes, are time-consuming parts of principals' everyday work. This is the case for leadership in both public and private free schools, both of which need to compete for students to keep the schools running and their teachers employed.

Later in the chapter, we will listen to the voices of some Swedish principals and how they express how marketization and privatization affect them (Figure 7.1). But before we do that, we move on to situate national and international discourses on leadership in relation to our national cases.

Distributed and heroic framing of school leadership

Today, an overall tension can be discerned in both Norway and Sweden between those who argue for top-down conceptions of 'strong' leadership and those who argue for a participative approach and the need for distributive leadership. Overall, the changing social environment in Europe in general has led to new governance structures that provide a particular context for educational reforms, and both the European Union and the OECD seem to play powerful roles in driving and attenuating policy across nation states. These structures also affect the roles and responsibilities of school leaders and the approach to leadership development.

But even if the international dimension is both important and constitutive, there are national and historical particularities, as well as more overall ideologies (and research) on what constitutes 'successful' education, that contribute to the framing of educational leadership. We will use findings from the International Successful School Principalship Project (ISSPP) to illustrate this point (see Day and Gurr, 2014; Møller, 2017).

The ISSPP study, which mainly included case studies of successful principals constructed by the researchers based on interviews with principals, teachers, students and parents, provided a window into the lived experience of successful principals across more than twenty countries. The goal was to understand under which cultural, social and political conditions leadership was considered successful.

The Swedish and Norwegian cases in this project emphasized furthermore how the construction of leadership identity was grounded in the view that education should promote democracy as a fundamental social value and an ethical guide to citizenship. Mutual trust and respect between school leaders and teachers were at the core of what they thought should count as a successful school. Simultaneously, the Scandinavian studies recorded a stronger focus on managerial practice and external accountability. Understanding leadership as *primus inter pares* was often recognized by the principals as a romanticized, old-fashioned view of leadership in schools. Today, Scandinavian school leaders have, like their colleagues in other countries, taken on many more administrative and managerial tasks. Their superiors, the teachers and the parents all expect far more of our school leaders than ever before. Evident in all stories of the participating principals across countries is an ethic of care, and an important claim is that successful leadership is distributed. However, how principals' work is embedded in social structures of power is obscured.

Thus, although models of distributed leadership have gained terrain both in research like ISSPP and in Scandinavian policy documents, we argue that such models rarely address political and normative dimensions of this type of work (Møller, 2017). Let us take a few moments to think a bit about leadership as a context-sensitive, moral and political enterprise.

Activity 7.1

In current policy documents, both strong and distributed leadership are emphasized. While it is argued that strong leadership (often equated with the traits and actions of a heroic principal) is needed to transform schools into learning organizations, distributive leadership recognizes that there are multiple leaders in a school and focuses on the complex interactions and micropolitical activities. However, none of these perspectives challenge the wider power structures in which the school is embedded and they do not pay attention to the processes that create and sustain social justice.

Different lenses on leadership present an opportunity for reflecting upon leadership practice in your school. Therefore, we ask you to reflect on what is considered a successful school and successful leadership in your context.

- Success in what and for whom?
- Success under what conditions?
- Who is included/excluded?

How is your understanding of successful educational leadership aligned with our definition?

Activity 7.2

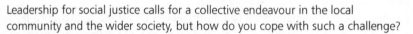

Leadership for social justice calls for a collective endeavour in the local community and the wider society, but how do you cope with such a challenge?

1 How can you include stakeholders at the local level in the work for a more democratic and just society?
2 Whose voices are allowed to be heard?
3 How is it possible to facilitate arenas for the many voices?

Business-management approaches gaining terrain

So far, we have concluded that school leaders in Sweden and in Norway are increasingly influenced by business-management approaches. How such approaches are gaining terrain is further developed next, using the case of Norway as the focal point of the discussion.

A recent feature in Norway, as a consequence of the restructuring of municipal governance of schools, is the fact that many principals today coordinate various functions that earlier were handled at the municipal level.

This new arrangement, recommended by the OECD and coined 'system leadership', has both pros and cons. The advantage is that the principals distribute their leadership energies, experiences and knowledge between their own schools and others. Everyone finds himself or herself in a new space of more intensive communication with colleagues from other schools, and this interaction across schools may open up mutual learning. In the absence of the principal, the staff members have to take responsibility for internal affairs. This creates a potential for the building of deputies' and teachers' capacities, but it also burdens them with greater workloads. Often, this move has taken the shape of increased responsibility combined with decreased authority in a context of often insufficient resources. In particular, the implementation of NPM at municipal level has resulted in less time and attention for providing leadership for improved teaching and learning.

The use of new evaluation technologies by both managers at the municipal level and principals to monitor student outcomes can be read as a shift towards what has been termed 'organizational professionalism', which incorporates standardized work procedures and relies on external regulation and accountability measures (Evetts, 2011). It echoes the management discourse promoted by the OECD, where a performance orientation is one of the main pillars, closely connected to output control. New expectations of public reporting and external accountability create both challenges and possibilities for school leaders, but how these affect the work of school leaders very much depends on the local organizational work contexts.

In some of the larger cities, merit pay for both teachers and principals has been introduced, but so far it has been tricky to measure any effect. Policymakers argue that competition among schools will promote school improvement and that parental choice is a guarantor of democracy. The line of reasoning is, as in Sweden, that vouchers and choice will give 'everyone' a right to choose the school that best serves his or her interests, regardless of social class, gender and ethnicity. However, others argue that a market model will work only for some parents and schools, to the disadvantage of others and hampering equality of educational opportunity. In Sweden, this debate is more silenced.

A closer look at the Swedish transformation

Bringing a language of education for private good into play has allowed for a reinterpretation of the educational process in terms of an economic transaction. It is not only principals who become positioned in particular ways. In the overall policy rhetoric, parents and students also become situated as not making the 'right' choices, positioned as not acting 'rationally enough' and as being in 'need' of certain nudging measures to help them to choose 'better' and 'more actively'. Such positioning becomes constitutive for how blame is attributed and for how solutions are legitimized. Indeed, it also works to leave the overall policy direction favouring choice and competition unchallenged and even reinforced (Alexiadou, Lundahl and Rönnberg, 2019).

In the Swedish case, there are few attempts to politically change or alter these developments towards both extensive marketization *and* privatization. This is a bit peculiar, as this shift surely comes with a 'price' in terms of, for instance, segregation and a declining emphasis on social justice. Teachers and principals remain largely silent on these issues as well, which also is a bit peculiar, since their daily work and working conditions are affected to a considerable extent by these shifts.

We said we would return to the Swedish principals and listen to how they describe their work in times of extensive marketization and privatization. As Figure 7.1 exemplifies, their talk describes significant changes, including schools being businesslike, segregated and the task of leadership as an entrepreneurial manager, requiring knowledge and skills that reach far beyond the traditional pedagogical domain. The changes have affected principals in both public and private free schools.

The quotations in Figure 7.1, along with other evidence, point to the quite remarkable transformation that was made possible in the Swedish case, in which education and the work of school professionals have been significantly altered. Very few policymakers, or even researchers, predicted that these realities would be the result of school choice and the introduction of private (for-profit) school operators in combination with tax-funded vouchers.

The quotations in Figure 7.1 also illustrate that neoliberal reforms do more than shape policy and curriculum. They also influence how school principals (and teachers) understand themselves as professionals. An ethos of public service is challenged by the discipline of the market and outcomes-based accountability.

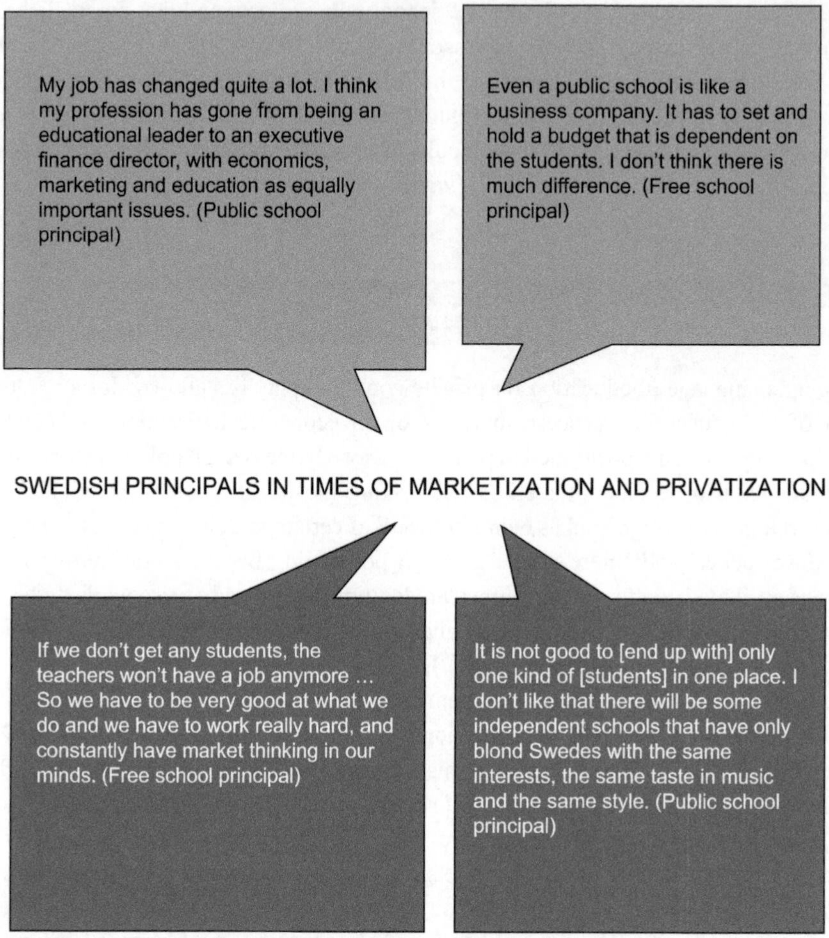

Figure 7.1 Voices from Swedish principals.
Note: Figure created by the authors. The quotes are from Holm and Lundström (2011).

My job has changed quite a lot. I think my profession has gone from being an educational leader to an executive finance director, with economics, marketing and education as equally important issues. (Public school principal)

Even a public school is like a business company. It has to set and hold a budget that is dependent on the students. I don't think there is much difference. (Free school principal)

SWEDISH PRINCIPALS IN TIMES OF MARKETIZATION AND PRIVATIZATION

If we don't get any students, the teachers won't have a job anymore … So we have to be very good at what we do and we have to work really hard, and constantly have market thinking in our minds. (Free school principal)

It is not good to [end up with] only one kind of [students] in one place. I don't like that there will be some independent schools that have only blond Swedes with the same interests, the same taste in music and the same style. (Public school principal)

From a public to private good? Critical reflections and spaces for action

So, what do these national cases tell us? Let us go back to our key concepts presented at the beginning of the chapter and Englund's (1994) notions of education as a public and/or private good. We think this conceptual distinction is useful as a way to promote discussion on the aims and overall drivers of education in relation to its political context, and consequently also to critically discuss how the roles and functions of school principals and their agency are being repositioned. This is an urgent discussion in times of marketization and privatization and the transformations that have taken place in the 'social democratic welfare states' we have studied in this chapter. Education as a public good has more or less been taken for granted in the policy rhetoric, but the overall policy direction has clearly promoted the idea of education as a private good in both countries, even if Sweden has taken further steps in this direction than Norway – so far, at least.

In current policy documents from both countries, it is argued that education policy should simultaneously be driven by values of social justice and inclusive education as well as the market. Politicians do not see themselves as tearing down the welfare state. On the contrary, as it is argued that marketization reforms can mobilize teachers and school principals to do better than before. There is, however, an uneasy tension between public and private good embedded in such arguments. It is difficult to see how a mixed public/private education system relying on a possessive individualism could prepare citizens better for the communicative society than a public education that provides the right of the child to encounter the pluralist society within the school (Englund, 1994).

Creating spaces to think differently

Schools are sites of struggle, and politics is the essential mechanism of that struggle. Certain interests are threatened by change, both within the school and in the wider political community. Professional development for both teachers and principals should pay attention to the ethical challenges principals and teachers are facing within a society dominated by economic rationales. It should include reflective analysis of how broader political and economic policies are affecting education for public good. As researchers, scholars and educators, we should reclaim a language of education based on trust and risk, subjectivity and agency, challenge and responsibility.

Future educational leaders will inevitably have to deal with the realities of marketization and privatization and their different national and local manifestations. We argue that these leaders also need to be provided with conceptual tools, perspectives and agency that enable them to unmask the corporate myths that the business community and the associated market-based discourses promote. We need critical leaders (and scholarship) to take these discussions further, learn from them and to find ways of strengthening and defending education as a public good.

In the light of the concepts and ideas related to the critical perspectives and approaches to educational leadership that have been discussed so far in this chapter, and before summing up our main argument, we would now like to invite you to engage in two activities.

Activity 7.3

A reflective policy designer promoting education as a public good

Answer the following questions:

1 Is there a tension between education as a 'public good' and 'private good' in your national and/or organizational context? Why? Why not?

2 When it comes to formal and informal expectations on educational leadership and educational leaders, are there particular features linked to education as a public or private good that are embedded in these expectations?

Be a 'policy designer'

You have been commissioned to develop national or local policy that will aim to strengthen the public dimension in education and promoting education as a public good. What policy would you design and what measures and strategies for implementation would you suggest for its success? Why? Unlike reality (and luckily), there are no budget restrictions attached to your hypothetical policy design experiment.

Conclusion

We have highlighted changes in the political economy that have challenged the idea of public education in both Norway and Sweden, but to different degrees. We have illustrated how policy and expectations on school leadership have been transformed as a response to marketization and privatization as well as to international trends and actors. We have also discussed how the languages and ways of talking about public education and educational leadership have been affected in the wake of these transformations. In this context, the Swedish far-reaching marketization and privatization of education may serve as a cautionary tale to learn from.

Marketization has put principals in a position in which they have to cope with demanding challenges, and to do so they need both training and different forms of support. But principals can also, importantly enough, critically reflect upon their own agency and what spaces there are for action, in terms of, for instance, defending social justice and democratic values in times when they are challenged. In particular, and as a key learning point, we have wanted to highlight the importance of finding room for acting differently in relation to defending education as a public rather than a private good (Englund, 1994).

Further reading

Antikainen, A. (2010) The capitalist state and education: the case of restructuring the Nordic model. *Current Sociology*, 58(4), 530–550.

Dovemark, M., Kosunen, S., Kauko, J., Magnúsdóttir, B., Hansen, P. and Rasmussen, P. (2018) Deregulation, privatisation and marketisation of Nordic comprehensive education: social changes reflected in schooling. *Education Inquiry*, 9(1), 122–141.

Hall, J.B. (2018) The performative shift: middle leadership 'in the line of fire'. *Journal of Educational Administration and History*, 50(4), 364–378.

Lundahl, L. (2016) Equality, inclusion and marketization of Nordic education: introductory notes. *Research in Comparative and International Education*, 11(1), 3–12.

Møller, J. (2012) The construction of a public face as a school principal. *International Journal of Educational Management*, 26(5), 452–460.

References

Ahonen, S. and Rantala, R. (2001) *Nordic lights: education for nation and civic society in the Nordic countries, 1850–2000*. Helsinki: Studia Fennica, Historica 1.

Alexiadou, N., Lundahl, L. and Rönnberg, L. (2019) Shifting logics: education and privatization the Swedish way. In: J. Wilkinson, R. Niesche and S. Eacott (eds), *Challenges for public education: reconceptualising educational leadership, policy and social justice as resources for hope* (pp. 116–132). Abingdon: Routledge.

Biesta, G. (2004) Against learning: reclaiming a language for education in an age of learning. *Nordisk Pedagogik*, 24(1), 54–66.

Crow, G., Day, C. and Møller, J. (2016) Framing research on school principals' identities. *International Journal of Leadership in Education*, 20(3), 265–277.

Day, C. and Gurr, D. (eds) (2014) *Leading schools successfully: stories from the field*. Abingdon: Routledge.

Englund, T. (1994) Education as a citizenship right – a concept in transition: Sweden related to other Western democracies and political philosophy. *Journal of Curriculum Studies*, 26(4), 383–399.

Evetts, J. (2009) New professionalism and New Public Management: changes, continuities and consequences. *Comparative Sociology*, 8(2), 247–266.

Holm, A.-S. and Lundström, U. (2011) 'Living with market forces': principals' perceptions of market competition in Swedish upper secondary school education. *Education Inquiry*, 2(4), 601–617.

Møller, J. (2009) Approaches to school leadership in Scandinavia. *Journal of Educational Administration and History*, 41(2), 165–177.

Møller, J. (2017) Leading education beyond what works. *European Educational Research Journal*, 16(4), 375–385.

Møller, J. and Skedsmo, G. (2013) Modernizing education: NPM reform in the Norwegian education system. *Journal of Educational Administration and History*, 45(4), 336–353.

Rönnberg, L., Lindgren, J. and Lundahl, L. (2019) Education governance in times of marketization: the quiet Swedish revolution. In: R. Langer and T. Brüsemeister (eds), *Handbuch Educational Governance Theorien: Educational Governance, vol. 43* (pp. 711–727). Wiesbaden: Springer.

Statistics Norway (2018) *Facts about education in Norway*. Oslo: Statistics Norway. Available online: https://www.ssb.no/en/utdanning/artikler-og-publikasjoner/facts-about-education-in-norway-2018 (accessed 21 July 2020).

Telhaug, A.O., Mediås, O.A. and Aasen, P. (2006) The Nordic model in education: education as part of the political system in the last 50 years. *Scandinavian Journal of Educational Research*, 50(3), 245–283.

Uljens, M., Møller, J., Ärlestig, H. and Frederiksen, L.F. (2013) The professionalisation of Nordic school leadership. In: L. Moos (ed.), *Transnational influences on values and practices in Nordic educational leadership: is there a Nordic model?* (pp. 133–158). Dordrecht: Springer.

Wiborg, S. (2013) Neo-liberalism and universal state education: the cases of Denmark, Norway and Sweden 1980–2011. *Comparative Education*, 49(4), 407–423.

Critical perspectives in and approaches to educational leadership in Chile

*Alejandro Carrasco and Germán Fromm,
with Helen M. Gunter*

8

What this chapter is about	122
Key questions that this chapter addresses	122
Introduction	122
A critical approach to GERM: the Chilean case	123
Educational leadership in Chile	125
Conclusion	133
Further reading	134
References	134

What this chapter is about

In this chapter, we help you to take a critical approach to the relationship between the Global Education Reform Movement (GERM) and headteachers as leaders of schools in Chile. Chile is a site where GERM has had impact and is also where many of those reforms were tested out before being adopted by other national systems. We examine the structure, context and consequences of Chilean educational leadership development policies, which have installed the standardization of school administration, with a narrow testing culture, accountability through regulation, and steering rationales. Through adopting two case studies of headteachers in Chile, we show how and why headteachers have become a highly regulated but 'unwilling taskforce' who are required to implement centralized school test scores.

Key questions that this chapter addresses

1 What is GERM and how does it impact on school leaders?
2 What impact has GERM had on the provision of education in Chile?
3 What have been the consequences of this impact on headteachers and their work?
4 What is the way forward for education in Chile?

Introduction

Chile is not only a site where the reforms known as the Global Education Reform Movement (GERM) have had impact, but also is regarded as a laboratory where many of those reforms were tested out before being adopted by other national systems (see Carrasco and Gunter, 2018). We examine in particular the focus on standardization, and the impact this has had on the selection and evaluation of headteachers, and on professional in-service training in order to illuminate how the education system imposes regulation techniques and steering rationales through framing and judging the identities and practices of educational leaders. We undertake a critical approach by using two case studies of headteachers in Chile, where we provide evidence that they are immersed in a system that pushes them into standards compliance and implementing centralized decisions. The advantage is held by the political hierarchy that can administer, incentivize, control and punish headteachers, making them accountable for their school's test scores.

A critical approach to GERM: the Chilean case

The current Chilean education system implemented major neoliberal reforms, as Ball (2014) would describe them, following the civic-military regime in the 1980s. As such, Chile became a testing ground for implementing policies without public deliberation. These reforms were not created by Chile, but were part of GERM promoted by supranational agencies.

GERM has a number of common features:

- *Competition* among schools.
- *Standardization* through output performance measures such as test results.
- Focus on *core subjects* in the curriculum.
- *Test-based accountability* for children and teachers.
- *School choice* where parents can access school places. (Sahlberg, 2015: 144–147)

GERM has crossed borders and impacted on national and local educational systems in a range of ways. There is lots of evidence of the same ideas travelling around the world but impacting differently. For example, school autonomy is very popular with different versions of school types, from charter schools in the United States, through to academies in England and free schools in Sweden. There can be major contrasts: in Chile, the provision of school places is privatized and accessed by parents as consumers, yet this has been rejected in Finland, where all schools are public schools, local and universal (see Seppänen et al., 2015).

> **GERM:**
>
> The idea of the Global Education Reform Movement, or simply GERM, evolves from the increased international exchange of policies and practices. It is not a formal global policy program, but rather an unofficial educational agenda that relies on a certain set of assumptions to improve education systems . . . GERM has emerged since the 1980s and is one concrete offspring of globalization in education. It has become accepted as 'a new educational orthodoxy' within many recent educational reforms throughout the world, including reforms in the United States, many parts of Australia, Canada, the United Kingdom, some Scandinavian countries, and an increasing number of countries in the developing world. *(Sahlberg, 2015: 143)*

> **Activity 8.1**
>
> Consider how GERM has impacted on an education system known to you. Is that system closer to Chile or to Finland? What evidence and reasons can you provide in support of your characterization?

GERM impacts on the identities and practices of educational professionals. This is particularly through transforming headteachers into entrepreneurial charismatic leaders, and through re-culturing teachers as subordinate followers in order to deliver high-quality student test data, enabling the school to compete in the marketplace and attract parental support.

Activity 8.2

Think about GERM and the impact of competition, standardization, core subjects, test-based accountability and school choice on professional identities and practices in a system known to you.

For example, one change has been from *educational* leadership (which is open to teachers and students to participate in decisions about teaching and learning) to *organization* and *performance* leadership (where teachers and students have to produce data to demonstrate organizational success).

To what extent is this the case in your system? What does this reveal of the purposes of education in your system?

The Chilean educational system has been described as the juxtaposition of four coherent modes of regulation: privatization, standardization, testing and accountability (PSTA) (Carrasco, 2013; Seppänen et al., 2015). This impacts differently on headteachers, depending on whether they are in the public or private provision. The Chilean education system operates through various educational suppliers: the public system known as 'municipal'; the subsidized private system, which means that parents have vouchers to 'pay' for a place; and private schools, where parents pay fees. Changes continue to take place, but overall about 6 per cent of children attend private schools, and the major shift has been in municipal schooling, which in 1981 educated 81 per cent of children but now it is 37 per cent. The change has been due to the deregulation of school places, resulting in 'subsidized private schools', which educate 57 per cent of children (Carrasco et al., 2015).

In the public system, the job of a headteacher is highly regulated and affected by policies designed by the Ministry of Education; in the subsidized and private schools the job is completely deregulated.

One change has been to introduce standardization. This is evident in the curriculum, student and teacher performance, headteacher objectives, and school outcomes. Consequently, the Ministry of Education controls educational purposes and quality assessments, and as such it discredits the professional judgements of educators and imposes 'one size fits all' solutions to highly complex schools and their students (Carrasco, 2013). The interplay between standardization and competition means that headteachers operate according to endemic accountability pressures, particularly as they are held responsible for a school's success. Improvement is data-determined: a testing regime is operationalized through a centrally driven and yearly examination comparing all schools. This is proposed as guidance for educational policy and constitutes an informal school-performance ranking. Standardization refers to the degree of imposition, regulation and prescription that the state places upon headteachers (among other actors) for the professional practice of school administration (or pedagogy and learning among other functions). It is important to note that the problem is not the existence of standards per se, but using them in a rigid fashion, where divergence and localized practices are penalized. Such an approach is directly related to competition that is driven by parents as consumers, whereby school data can be used to inform parents' decisions to change from one school to another, directly affecting its funding. The voucher for each student is paid directly to the chosen school's stakeholder (owner or municipality), and this means that headteachers are obliged to make the schools appear as successful as possible in the yearly assessment (Carrasco and Fromm, 2016). Schools can open and close depending on voucher income and its relationship with student enrolment. This has implications for educational leadership in Chile, and we now turn to this as a case study.

Educational leadership in Chile

As we have noted, headteachers in Chile now work in a highly privatized system, where the majority of schools are subsidized private schools. After reinstalling democracy, three governmental pilot programmes (P-900, Montegrande and MECE-Media) were developed during the late 1990s and included the importance of principals for school improvement. However, despite reforms to school administration regulations, Chile had no public policies for recruitment, selection, training, capacity-building and professional career designs, beyond the general regulations for teachers called 'Estatuto Docente [teaching statute]' (Donoso et al., 2012). Change took place in 2000 when the Ministry established a unit tasked with setting standards for educational leadership practice, seen in the 'Framework for Good Principalship and School Leadership' (Ministerio de Educación de Chile, 2015). While the unit was intermittently closed and reopened in 2008/2009, it remains the case that the Framework outlines the requirements for defining functions, responsibilities and standards. We will present and discuss two case studies comprising aspects of the law in regard to (1) headteacher selection and evaluation; and (2) in-service leadership training. We present in Table 8.1 an overview of the key points to be made regarding leadership as performance by the headteacher in relation to the municipality and the staff of the school.

Table 8.1 Case study overview of educational leadership in Chile

Cases	Performance technology	Performance commitment	Performance regulation	Performance tensions
8.1: Selection and evaluation	Performance plans presented when applying for post	Delivery on plans, with early exit from the job if the plans are not on track	Centralized steering of educational purposes by using test results to judge school performance	Headteachers accountable for test results, with support from the municipality that also evaluates heads
8.2: Professional development	Performance training programmes at universities and specialized centres	Delivery operationalized by fear of losing job, combined with micropolitical oversight by the municipality	Centralized training controlled through funding	Training to undertake problem-solving, but over-optimism that problems can be solved

Case Study 8.1 Headteacher selection and evaluation

Headteachers of municipal schools are appointed for five-year periods, when they can reapply to the same school or another. A Qualification Committee is in charge of evaluating these applications: they review a 'work plan' that each applicant formulates for the school they are applying to. Until 2016, 3,893 principal applications had been adjudicated through this system (Servicio Civil, 2016). These nominations indicate that seven of ten people did not have previous principal jobs and 45 per cent are women.

The process consists of a series of steps:

1 The municipality establishes a requirement and profile for the required principal in a given school. The requirements are nationally established, but locally implemented. This means that the system design gives parameters that have to be respected in the whole country, but are put into practice by every municipality in accordance with local needs.

2 The requirement is passed on to an External Advice business that recruits and evaluates possible candidates. The applicants need to be professionals, but not necessarily with pedagogical backgrounds, despite the fact that 97 per cent are teachers. The requirement is an eight-semester long title or licence (Law 20.501, 2011). They also require at least three years of classroom teaching (in Chile, non-teacher professionals can teach classes during a given period before being required to get a professional teaching degree). They do not require past experience as principals, but it is strongly recommended, or at least in other school-administrative jobs.

3 The candidates' evaluations are revised by a Qualification Committee constituted of a designated professional of the municipality, a principal in service from the municipality, and a representative of the centralized 'high director positioning system'. This accountability mechanism is often problematic for applicants, because it is negotiated

with the political authorities in the municipality, related to standardized test results, and carries consequences such as removal from the job.

4 The applicants are selected, can be interviewed if needed, and their proposed work plan is negotiated and formalized as a 'performance commitment' (Laws 19.979, 2004 and 19.070, 2011). This is the only device that requires legal responsibility from the headteacher. Headteachers are held accountable for the goals they 'offer', but there may be no clear (or transparent) interpretation or associated consequences if part of the commitment is not achieved (or indicators are partially achieved). Therefore, some degree of negotiation with the municipality remains on a personal and informal level, urging the principals to avoid the final evaluation (see next) or to remain in a favourable position with the supervisors.

5 Every year the 'performance commitment' is evaluated by the municipality in order to check for its achievement. If the negotiated indicators are not met satisfactorily, the headteacher can be evaluated negatively or even fired. This has generated a loophole in the system, where many do not end their period in their appointed school and instead from the third year on, they take up posts in other schools. This way, they avoid the uncertainty of not being elected after the fifth year for the same school due to better competing candidates or bad results with their 'performance commitments'. This has increased principal turnover in schools (Valenzuela, Allende and Vanni, 2018).

Thinking about Case Study 8.1

While the system reported in Case Study 8.1 is only fifteen years old at the time of writing, it has signified a movement from deregulated public office work to accountable professionals that are associated with good and bad results (Montt, 2012). This movement can be considered positive, in the sense of spurring quality, but focusing only on standardized tests has detrimental effects, too. Indeed, there is consensus among policymakers and academics in regard to the usefulness, advantages and convenience of basing decisions upon test scores, leading to their institutionalization and multiple uses (Carrasco, 2013). The headteachers evaluation is not exempted from this belief, operating under the idea that *good school leaders are able to raise testing scores in their schools*. However, because of the power that politicians exert over headteacher applications in Chile, the job is not attractive and many five-year terms are unfinished. Turnover is high (Valenzuela, Allende and Vanni, 2018), because in order to avoid uncertainty about the performance requirements, serving headteachers apply for new posts in other schools long before finishing their five-year period. This is a consequence of the evaluation system, where the principal is not autonomous, is overloaded with work, and is held highly accountable with high-stakes consequences and remunerated only marginally above teachers (Cancino and Monrroy, 2017). It seems that it is not actually used as an authentic management tool, but instead it is perceived as a bureaucratic task (Waissbluth and Pizarro, 2014).

A study of the Centre for Educational Policy and Practice Studies of the Catholic University of Chile examined in 2012 some characteristics of the newly appointed principals. The results showed that the system had been implemented at municipal level much more in municipalities that were urban, bigger and closer to the capital. In regard to school level, it was better implemented in primary schools, with more enrolment (and corresponding funding), coming from higher socio-economic status backgrounds (Ministerio de Hacienda, 2014). This profile tends to respond to more availability of applicants, faster policy implementation and economies of scale in the selection processes in bigger municipalities (Ministerio de Hacienda, 2014).

The individuals were younger (average age 53.3 vs 56.5) and more women (44 per cent vs 42 per cent) than the ones not selected by the system. Other characteristics are longer (8.5 vs 8.3 semesters in average) and more specialized (57 per cent with speciality vs 41 per cent without) studies in their professional trajectories, but with less working experience (in average five years less). They also have more teachers with a background in secondary as opposed to primary (32 per cent vs 22 per cent) and studied in face-to-face programmes (97 per cent vs 94 per cent) instead of online courses (Ministerio de Hacienda, 2014).

Some of the benefits of the implemented system are that users in general have a positive impression of the new system compared to the former one (Waissbluth and Pizarro, 2014). This is attributed to more transparent decision-making, more specialized professionals working in the system, and to the interruption of political appointments for undetermined periods. However, the system faces difficulties in regard to political appointments in the superior or supervising municipalities, problems with accountability regarding implement-ation, and a lack of funding. In addition, there is a lack of good applicants and little control over exceptional situations (for example, 'surrogate' principals acting for many years in the post) that limit effective functioning (Waissbluth and Pizarro, 2014).

In addition, the power to remove headteachers from their job when they do not achieve the goals included in the performance commitments belongs to the Chief of Education from the municipality, designated directly by the Mayor (Law 20.501, 2011). Moreover, the power to not remove them is held by the same person. This makes the process susceptible to micropolitical dynamics that the principals need to navigate. An external way of removal is the direct order from the Quality Agency to close or intervene the school, but this seldom occurs.

Judgements about performance are based on a calculation for each school and their headteacher and constitute a basis to apply penalties and/or shared responsibility and support. Through an extensive testing culture and regulation, measured performance determines public and institutional responsibility. It seems that testing is not centred on the students and their learning, but on the comparison of schools in the marketplace. Therefore, how municipalities evaluate and select headteachers is shaped by the *judgements* more than local and contextualized need assessments of the schools.

What is emerging from this regulation by testing are new subjectivities and social relationships between the state and schools. Carrasco (2013) has explained that this testing regulation technique 'flourished with such unusual vigour in Chile' because of expert knowledge legitimizing its institutional use without investigating the consequences. It becomes a *constitutive* dimension of educational practice as the results provide inputs for multiple operations, including evaluating the compliance of headteachers to the centrally steered school-improvement fantasy. Municipal authorities evaluating headteachers think first and foremost about accountability, making improvement goals both explicit and binding in the performance commitments; second, making headteachers responsible for it; and third, penalizing them for the lack of compliance.

There are a number of consequences emerging from this process. The arbitrary manner in which school leaders are evaluated and made permanent means that headteachers need to constantly estimate the external and the internal; municipal and personal pressures in order to develop their professional agendas. They require these competencies to operate in a tight standardized and centralized framework that downplays the importance of contextualization and internal trust dynamics.

Moreover, many standards that even take the form of legal prescriptions like 'supervise teachers in classrooms' are not explained and not included in the evaluation system. Many principals are forced to rely on non-educational (and even anti-pedagogical) practices in order to optimize the perception their employers will have about them (Carrasco and Fromm, 2016). This means reducing the principalship to instrumental practices that might impact on immediate school results, and overstating indirect associations with their effective influence.

Another crucial aspect of any evaluation system is the relationship between (1) what the national law requires in regard to appointments and evaluations of headteachers, and (2) further data-driven decision-making by supervisors and the municipalities. This has not been implemented or addressed through policy design, and so it relies on local initiatives, like training, mentoring, learning communities and external support. Consequently, support for headteachers from the evaluators and stakeholders is voluntary, as the standards requirements do not compel them to collaborate with the school. This does not mean that stakeholders are unwilling to collaborate as an intrinsic professional motivation, but what it does do is to locate school improvement and professional development into negotiations and the dynamics of a political arena.

Activity 8.3

1 What has *taking a critical approach to educational leadership* achieved in regard to understanding the appointment and evaluation of headteachers in Chile?

2 What recommendations would you make to reform the processes? What do you think would help or hinder whether these recommendations are adopted?

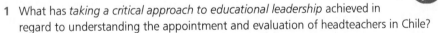

Case Study 8.2 Headteacher in-service training

A major change in the development of educational leadership is the 'Centre for Training, Experimentation, and Research in Pedagogy' from the Ministry of Education (CPEIP: Centro de Perfeccionamiento, Experimentación e Investigaciones Pedagógicas del Ministerio de Educación). In 2011, the Centre started a policy called: 'Training of Top-Level School Principals Plan', starting with more than 150 participants each year in eight universities.

Estimates obtained from the CPEIP website's data show that about 2,700 professionals have been trained. Considering that a little more than 8,000 headteachers are in post, this means that about one in three have been trained in these programmes. However, many of the participants were not appointed headteachers at the time of training, and it cannot be confirmed if they assumed leadership positions during or after their training.

The plan has gradually expanded to established agreements with fourteen Chilean universities reaching more than 750 professionals each year, in order to constitute a nationwide network that provides centrally steered training programmes. This means that almost every master's programme given by universities in regard to school leadership and administration is aligned with the CPEIP. The alignment covers mostly content design in regard to the aforementioned national Framework for Good Principalship and Leadership (Ministerio de Educación, 2015).

Recognition of localized interpretations has generated innovation in the training curriculum, and universities demonstrate pragmatism in regard to their provision and how they decide what to include or exclude. Since 2016, in parallel to the centrally steered curricula, two specialist centres for Educational Leadership were founded, which took the task of experimenting with different training models and measuring their respective effects.

One of the centres, CEDLE (Centro de Desarrollo de Liderazgo Educativo: Educational Leadership Development Centre) follows an indirect approach to training, making alliances with regionally distant universities in Chile, particularly in teaching the trainers how to train headteachers. Their programmes undertake ongoing review and development, where the main strategy relies on including an experienced headteacher to mentor and accompany participants during training. This has been a widely recognized as effective strategy in regard to learning outcomes. The effects measurement of this centre is still under development at the current date.

The other centre, Lideres Educativos [Educational Leaders], has made local alliances with municipalities, headteachers and senior leadership teams in order to undertake a four-year training programme. This uses distributed leadership by empowering teams through long continuous reflections over practice. The effects of the centre showed increased evaluation of leadership practice as perceived by the teachers in the schools where the teams work (Fromm et al., 2018).

Thinking about Case Study 8.2

The alignment of university master's programmes with CPEIP provides the highest percentage of principals specializing in school leadership and administration in the Latin American region: however, research on the training effects is still required. There are a number of features that need to be given recognition. For example, holding a specialized master's degree is not a prerequisite for selection tenure. Such an inconsistency is part of what is perceived as a general lack of coherence between the educational leadership regulations (Weinstein et al., 2019). Furthermore, the training has not been taken only by headteachers, but also (and intentionally) by other school leaders, supervisors, and teachers that have and seek leadership careers. Therefore, the master's degree in a specialized programme is not a formal requirement, and gives recognition to the importance of a distributed approach to school leadership. This impacts on the five-year applications for the renewal of head-teacher tenure, as the post is dependent on data that is a product of a team effort, but in reality, the headteacher is the winner or loser.

While, resources, efforts and expectations for the training and teaching of school leaders about how to improve their practice are determined at national level, the selection and evaluation is still influenced by political alliances in the municipalities' Qualification Committee and befriending the Mayor. This reveals misalignment between what is declared good leadership training and informal micropoliticking in the municipalities. Educational agents will not take a critical stance for or against what programmes offer. In fact, the only thing that really matters is the relationship that the headteacher has built with the municipalities' supervisor. As long as they are recognized reciprocally as 'doing good leadership' it really doesn't matter what is put into practice. Furthermore, in order to avoid critical questions about underperformance and bad practice, educational leaders tend to be hard working and educationally engaged professionals, clearly showing intrinsic motivation.

The two centres described in case two (CEDLE and Lideres Educativos) have produced valuable knowledge in regard to training effectiveness and practical knowledge for school leaders to apply daily. What seems to be emerging is a decentralized curriculum that is generating two different models. The mentoring approach is highly person-oriented and directly uses the work experience of mentors and learners. The local-alliances model develops work teams in the contextualized and local communities that constitutes the schools and emphasizes reinterpretation of what usually are rigid standards. This means that Chile is developing on what Hargreaves and Shirley (2009) could consider 'fourth way' reforms. However, the low scale and lack of long-term funding of both centres put the initiative in jeopardy, despite the positive results.

What is also important is that these two centres examples show that the national training curriculum needs to be revised in regard to content, methods and transference to the schools. This acknowledgement is a heartfelt problem among leadership trainers and students. For instance, there is a need to consider what work experience implies for practitioners. On the one hand, the training programmes are still at introductory level after eight years of training, and on the other hand the performance system means that the same head teachers have to reapply every five years for the job they already have.

The training programmes overemphasize the optimism that underpin leadership-theory narratives of 'positive influence', 'do real changes', 'make it happen in the classroom' that are mistaken as standards. The curricular focus is on quality-management models, resource-management orientation, technical planning and data-driven decision-making as management discourses. This is allegedly helping headteachers to meet the standards but, in reality, it is inauthentic problem-solving for schools. The vicious use of performance commitments creates a lot of work that does not actually connect with teaching and learning.

Activity 8.4

1 How does adopting a critical approach to reviewing leadership training in Chile help you to understand what is happening and what needs to happen?
2 What recommendations would you make to improve leadership training? How would you link your agenda with Case Study 8.1?

In summary, a critical approach to researching educational leadership in Chile has identified a multilevel but discordant approach to head-teacher recruitment, evaluation and in-service training. First, at the national policy-design level, there are clear PSTA regulations; second, at the training level, the approach is to both instruct and produce performance-driven instructional leaders; and third, at the accountability level, what matters is whether the municipalities' supervisor decides to 'overlook' the head-teacher performance data or fire the headteacher. In other words, PSTA sets rules for practice that every agent in the system is meant to follow, and the accountability measures ensure compliance. The training may be inspiring but it is over-optimistic because it does not help with transference, contextualization, development and deeply rooted improvement processes. What is really important for the head-teacher's job and career is not what they actually put into practice, not what they are trained in, but maintaining good terms with the municipality.

Activity 8.5

Review the case of Chile and undertake a comparison with a system known to you. To what extent do you see the same features regarding head-teacher tenure, training and performance? Why? What is different and why? What does this say about the reality and impact of GERM?

Conclusion

The GERM reforms that have travelled the world have their origins in the Chilean system: leadership training for headteachers emerged in Chile, was taken up globally and has travelled back to Chile. Critical approaches to research have revealed how and why the Chilean implementation of PSTA regulation techniques are having no inherent positive effects for the discussed processes of head-teacher selection and evaluation nor in-service training. The reformed policies are ideologically aligned with the underlying assumptions of the educational system, but as such only make evident the problems for practice and quality. Various studies from other countries that implemented such reforms during the 1990s or 2000s tend to conclude that these contributed greatly to de-professionalization, segregation, mechanical learning, school demoralization, simplification of the curriculum, academic and civic disaffection, short-term achievements, relocation of pedagogically sound purposes and illusory autonomy in schools (Carrasco, 2013; Seppänen, et al., 2015). However, Chilean policymakers and educational authorities seem to be still in thrall to the assumptions of testing-centred performance for headteachers, steering rationales and compliance to standards of the 'unwilling taskforce'.

The two cases have deepened this understanding and expanded the conceptual framework through the politicization of the agents that happens informally, but are also institutionalized in the policy designs. In this sense, politicization, understood as constant politicking and overshadowing of professionalism through informal relations in the micro-political arenas, could be understood as another regulation technique of the system. This happens not unintentionally, as already explained, but because of the hierarchy that sets politicians with political interests on top of the educational units. This is rather an intentional part of the system conforming to a new acronym: PSTAP – privatization, standardization, testing and accountability, and politicization too.

Moreover, the fundamental assumption of the GERM-driven educational reforms in Chile is that education does not develop well because of the professionalism and motivation of teachers and directors, but through central steering strategies. As education must function through incentives, competition and punishment, schools lack intrinsic reasons for action. Therefore, everyday practice must be standardized and headteachers, as an 'unwilling taskforce', execute the masterplan to implement improvement of indicators for standards. This is exemplified by the way in which evaluation and training use policy devices of performance commitments centred on school test scores, where the only flexibility that these devices show is politicized. The selection, evaluation and in-service training are shaped by informal good-term relations with the municipal authorities that collude with overlooking non-compliance with standards. This might lead to the conclusion that standardization and accountability are actually well designed, but badly implemented because of politicization. However, the system was and is inherently political and therefore cannot be understood as 'parts' that work and do not work. The tendency to implement radical GERM orientations can only be understood if a lack of public deliberation in its origin is taken into consideration. More so, if the international experience and recommendations tend to orient reforms otherwise.

The scope of this research was to consider two cases, where the intention is to serve the international audience by showing problematic attempts through critical lenses that contribute to informing worldwide GERM-oriented reforms. The Chilean audience is invited to engage in the same fashion with all other reforms to its educational system, affecting practitioners, trainers, academics and, foremost, headteachers. This requires a Chilean approach to understanding how schools do national policy in relation to the power and role of the municipality (Ball et al., 2012). As long as professionals and the wider public are not engaged in collective criticism of the profession, of how training is performed, of how jobs are appointed and evaluated, then the system will stay as it is. Therefore, this international engagement with the Chilean case helps to exert the criticism apparently needed to support authentic development and change.

Further reading

Beyer, H., Eyzaguirre, B. and Fontaine, L. (2000) *La reforma educacional chilena: una apreciación crítica*. Santiago de Chile: Centro de Estudios Públicos.

Campos-Martínez, J., Pössel, F.C. and Inzunza, J. (2015) Mapping neoliberal reform in Chile: following the development and legitimation of the Chilean system of school quality measurement (SIMCE). In: W. Au and J.J. Ferrare (eds), *Mapping corporate education reform: power and policy networks in the neoliberal state* (pp. 106–125). New York: Routledge.

Carrasco, A., Gutiérrez, G. and Flores, C. (2017) Failed regulations and school composition: selective admission practices in Chilean primary schools. *Journal of Education Policy*, 32(5), 642–672.

Castro-Hidalgo, A. and Gómez-Álvarez, L. (2016) Chile: a long-term neoliberal experiment and its impact on the quality and equity of education. In: F. Adamson, B. Åstrand and L. Darling-Hammond (eds), *Global education reform: how privatization and public investment influence education outcomes* (pp. 16–49). New York: Routledge.

Valenzuela, J., Bellei, C. and de los Ríos, D. (2013) Socioeconomic school segregation in a market-oriented educational system: the case of Chile. *Journal of Education Policy*, 29(2), 217–241.

References

Ball, S.J. (2014) Globalised, commodified and privatised: current international trends in education and education policy. *Education Policy Analysis Archives*, 22(41). Available online: https://doi.org/10.14507/epaa.v22n41.2014 (accessed 21 July 2020). [In Spanish.]

Ball, S.J., Maguire, M. and Braun, A. (2012) *How schools do policy: policy enactments in secondary schools*. Abingdon: Routledge.

Cancino, V.C. and Monrroy, L.V. (2017) Políticas educativas de fortalecimiento del liderazgo directivo: desafíos para Chile en un análisis comparado con países OCDE. *Ensaio: Avaliação e Políticas Públicas Em Educação*, 25(94), 26–58.

Carrasco, A. (2013) Mecanismos performativos de la institucionalidad educativa en Chile: pasos hacia un nuevo sujeto cultural. *Observatorio Cultural*, 15, art. 1. Available online: https://www.researchgate.net/profile/Alejandro_Carrasco6/publication/318471663_Mecanism (accessed 21 July 2020).

Carrasco, A. and Fromm, G. (2016) How local market pressures shape leadership practices: evidence from Chile. *Journal of Educational Administration and History*, 48(4), 290–308.

Carrasco, A. and Gunter, H.M. (2019) The 'private' in the privatization of schools: the case of Chile. *Educational Review*, 71(1), 67–80.

Carrasco, A., Seppänen, P., Rinne, R. and Falabella, A. (2015) Educational accountability policy schemes in Chile and Finland. In: P. Seppänen, A. Carrasco, M. Kalalahti, R. Rinne and H. Simola (eds), *Contrasting dynamics in education politics of extremes: school choice in Chile and Finland* (pp. 53–80). Rotterdam: Sense.

Donoso, S., Benavides, N., Cancino, V., Castro, M. and López, L. (2012) Análisis crítico de las políticas de formación de directivos escolares en Chile: 1980–2010. *Revista Brasileira de Educação*, 17(49), 133–158.

Fromm, G., Valenzuela, J.P., Vanni, X. and Herrera, J. (2018) Evaluación longitudinal de las acciones formativas del Centro de Liderazgo para la Mejora Escolar en establecimientos públicos. Informe Técnico No. 3. Universidad de Chile.

Hargreaves, A.P. and Shirley, D.L. (2009) *The fourth way: the inspiring future for educational change*. Thousand Oaks, CA: Corwin Press.

Ministerio de Educación de Chile (2015) Marco para la buena dirección y el liderazgo escolar. Santiago de Chile: Centro de Perfeccionamiento, Experimentación e Investigaciones Pedagógicas, CPEIP.

Ministerio de Hacienda (2014) Informe Final de Estudio: Caracterización de Directores/as electos por el Sistema de Selección establecido por la Ley No. 20.501. Santiago de Chile.

Montt, P. (2012) Políticas educativas y liderazgo pedagógico en Chile: una lectura de dos décadas de desarrollo (1990 a 2011). *¿Qué Sabemos Sobre Los Directores de Escuela En Chile?* pp. 397–426. Santiago de Chile: Fundación Chile y CEPPE.

Sahlberg, P. (2015) *Finnish lessons 2.0: what can the world learn from educational change in Finland?* New York: Teachers College Press.

Seppänen, P., Carrasco, A., Kalalahti, M., Rinne, R. and Simola, H. (2015) *Contrasting dynamics in education politics of extremes: school choice in Chile and Finland*. Rotterdam: Sense.

Servicio Civil (2016) *Estado del Sistema de Alta Dirección Pública*, May. Santiago de Chile. Available online: https://www.serviciocivil.cl/wp-content/uploads/2017/05/Informe-Final-CADP_04.05.2017.pdf (accessed 21 July 2020).

Valenzuela, J.P., Allende, C. and Vanni, X. (2018) *Trayectoria de los directores chilenos durante la última década: primeros hallazgos para políticas públicas*. Nota técnica No. 8. Líderes Educativos, Centro de Liderazgo para la Mejora Escolar, Chile.

Waissbluth, M. and Pizarro, X. (2014) Diagnóstico y propuestas para el Sistema de Selección de Directivos Escolares. *Serie Sistemas Públicos*, No. 10. Centro de Sistemas Públicos (CSP) del Departamento de Ingeniería Industrial, Universidad de Chile.

Weinstein, J., Muñoz, G., Sembler, M. and Rivero, R. (2019) La opinión sobre las políticas educativas de directores de centros públicos y privados subvencionados en Chile. *Professorado*, 23(2), 13–39.

Part two

Critical perspectives on models and methods in educational leadership

9   Leading and managing in educational organizations
Helen M. Gunter and Emiliano Grimaldi   139

10   Using theory in educational leadership, management and administration research
Pat Thomson and Amanda Heffernan   155

11   Research methods in educational leadership
Scott Eacott and Gus Riveros   171

12   A historical deconstruction of leadership style
Fenwick W. English and Lisa Catherine Ehrich   187

13   Distributed leadership
Howard Youngs and Linda Evans   203

14 Educational and instructional leadership
Scott Eacott and Richard Niesche   **221**

15 Educational reform and leading school change
Jill Blackmore and Rachel McNae   **237**

Leading and managing in educational organizations

Helen M. Gunter and Emiliano Grimaldi

9

What this chapter is about	140
Key questions that this chapter addresses	140
Introduction	140
Three approaches to leaders, leading and leadership in education	145
Power and educational services	150
Conclusion	152
Further reading	153
References	153

What this chapter is about

In this chapter, we argue that leaders, leading and leadership of educational organizations generates three main approaches: **functional**, **critical** and **socially critical**. We present three case studies from research in Naples to illustrate each one, and we examine the way that power works, particularly through micropolitical activities in organizations.

We focus directly on formal organizations for educational services, that is, kindergarten or nursery, school, college and university. In doing this we are directly concerned with first, the leader: whom this is; second, leading: what a leader does and why; and third, leadership: or how power operates and is exercised. To make our argument that educational leadership has functional, critical and socially critical approaches, we begin with the dynamics of the organization to develop a conceptual framework. We ask you to reflect on three case studies based on empirical research, and to think about emotional intelligence and micropolitical processes.

Key questions that this chapter addresses

1   What is an educational organization?

2   What are the dynamics of educational organizations, and how have they been studied in the field?

3   What issues for organizational design do these dynamics generate for professionals and researchers?

4   What approaches can be taken to understanding educational leaders, leading and leadership in this dynamic context?

5   What are the implications of theories of emotional intelligence and micropolitics for organizational control?

Introduction

The kindergarten, school, college or university as an organization is a core feature of the field of educational leadership. What the organization means now is historically located, as well as part of the everyday activities of professionals and students. When we think about the kindergarten, school, college or university as an organization, we tend to consider structures, systems, cultures and people. Read the definitions in the box.

These organizational dynamics tend to be focused on ensuring the educational services provided actually happen; crises are appropriately dealt with; and that change is planned and enacted. Historically this has been called educational administration, and in some parts of the world it still is labelled as such. However, from the 1960s onwards, administration was mainly used to describe clerical work, and the 'top job' was framed as a 'managing director' with a wider claim to be a field of educational management. More recently, management has been downgraded as a form of localized delivery with the growth in educational leader, leading and leadership taking over as the label for strategic direction and change. We intend focusing in this chapter on leadership as encompassing management.

The meaning of leader, leading and leadership is historically rooted. We begin with the Theory Movement from the 1950s in North America where the main aim was to identify and deploy a scientific and unified approach to the organization based on an objective and reliable theory, where facts and values are separated. Halpin characterizes the organization as having 'four components' of 'the task', 'the formal organization', 'the work group' and 'the leader' (1966: 28–29). The purpose of the organization is secured through formalized structures where humans are controlled by leader behaviours: 'if a leader – whether he be a school superintendent, an aircraft commander, or a business executive – is to be successful, he must contribute to both major group objectives of *goal achievement* and *group maintenance*' (1966: 87, original emphasis). The case is made that delivering outcomes through people therefore requires a focus on identifying, measuring and evaluating the leader by followers through a 'Leader Behavior Description Questionnaire' (1966: 87) with scores about the frequency with which 'he speaks in a manner not to be questioned', 'he sees to it that staff members know what is expected of them', 'he finds time to listen to staff members', 'he is slow to accept new ideas' (1966: 89).

In summary: the leader is a role within rational structures, systems and cultures that enable control and planned delegation; the person appointed to that role does leading by demonstrating the correct type of behaviours necessary to make the structures, systems and cultures work efficiently and effectively, and leadership is the identification and deployment of behaviours in relation to others as staff and students as followers.

During the 1960s, this approach was questioned from within the research community: Griffiths argued that: 'the search for one encompassing theory . . . should be abandoned' (1969: 166). In 1974, Greenfield gave a paper at the Bristol session of the International Intervisitation Programme conference, where he challenged the reality, values-free status and independence of the organization from the people located within it. Greenfield argued that organizations exist in the subjective phenomenology of the individual and are a constructed social reality: 'organisations come into existence when we talk and act with

Structures: the 'division of labour' that tends to be hierarchical with vertical and horizontal roles, job descriptions and pay differentials. Tends to be drawn as a pyramid, with spans of control from the top person (headteacher, principal, director, president, vice-chancellor, rector) downwards from senior roles to middle roles to classroom/lecturer roles.

Systems: the policies that are used to determine how the structures work regarding the type and location of decision-making and action, e.g. student recruitment, line management, performance review, timetables and rooming, budget, appointments and promotion.

Cultures: the espoused 'values', 'mission' and 'purposes' of the organization that facilitate accepted good practice, habits and ways of working, e.g. 'this is how we do things here'.

People: those who are appointed to the staff as professional educators (e.g. teachers, lecturers) and as professional support staff (e.g. bursar, clerical assistant), and who are promoted to particular roles (e.g. school business manager, deputy head, dean); and those who are students and who have a place to study either within the compulsory (e.g. school) or non-compulsory (e.g. university) sectors.

others . . . concrete specific action is the stuff organisations are made of' and so he goes on to say 'in both their doing and their not doing, people make themselves and they make the social realities we call organisations' (Greenfield and Ribbins, 1993: 53). Rejecting leader behaviours, Greenfield argued for values as a philosophical engagement with moral responsibility rather than a science of cause and effect: 'I think the most valuable form of training begins in a setting of practice, where one has to balance values against constraints – in which one has to take action within a political context' (Greenfield and Ribbins, 1993: 257).

In summary: the scientific claims were built on through a critical approach that shifts from behaviours to values underpinning relationality. The leader needs to reflect; leading is about questioning and making decisions about fundamental issues such as the purposes of the organization in regard to the curriculum, pedagogy and assessment; and leadership is about confronting with others the tough moral questions about education.

From the 1960s onwards, the 'science' approach to educational organizations was challenged by those who focused on the exercise of power, and how the kindergarten, school, college or university are sites where wider injustices are in evidence and make a difference to professionals and students. While 'values' matter, it was argued that there is a need to go further and address how class, gender, race and sexuality operate in schools to 'sort people' according to hierarchies of advantage and disadvantage, and how this is enabled through the behaviourism of 'science' and is not fully addressed through the philosophy of 'values'. As Smyth argues, there are two matters that need addressing in the science and values traditions: first, that professionals and students are constrained by 'discussions about traits, personalities and styles' (1989: 5) because the aim is to control through a focus on structure, behaviours and technical problem solving; second, that there is a need to rethink, where 'the agenda becomes one of empowering school participants by helping *them* to unmask the unquestioned and oppressive managerialist modes that have come to constrain them' (1989: 5, original emphasis). Consequently, leadership is not 'a property inherent to individuals' but instead is 'an act performed within a social context' and so it is communal and shared through exchange relationships (Foster, 1986: 181).

In summary: structures, cultures and systems are in operation, but leader, leading and leadership are disconnected from hierarchy and especial people. Organizational members can be recognized relationally as a leader, and so the plural 'leaders' is important, all can do leading in the form of decision-making and enactment, and leadership is a power process that all can access and deploy in order to work with students who are resourceful through recognizing their contribution and community.

Purposes and practices: the *discursive politics* of educational services. Is the focus on the delivery of the mission of the unitary organization and/or on the negotiated and agreed activities of those within the organization?

Structure and agency: the *logic of control* of educational services. Is the focus on the objective and rational organizational structures, and/or on the subjectivity and co-construction within the working of structures in order to enable agency?

Hierarchy and participation: the *regulation* within and connected to educational services. Is the focus on a structural division of labour with command and control roles, pay grades and line management, and/or on the diverse, spontaneous, relational, cooperative contributions and involvement of those within the organization?

Internal and external: the *networks* and *boundaries* of educational services. Is the focus on the individual organization such as a school and/or on the contextual location of the school within a community, system and wider globalized world?

This brief overview of debates in the dynamics of knowledge production in the field gives recognition to the complexity of different trends that are evident in our contemporary world: there is a 'scientific' emphasis on the effectiveness of the leader and where evidence is not yet available there is a strong normative claim for such effectiveness to be implemented; through to concerns about how values play out in practice; and a need to recognize how power works in regard to education as a business to be traded or as a human right to be provided. Importantly these debates examine a range of issues regarding structures, systems, cultures and people, where there may be exclusive emphasis on one or the other, or strategies focused on understanding the complexities involved in the interplay between them. See Activity 9.1.

Activity 9.1

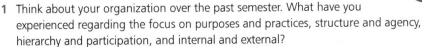

1 Think about your organization over the past semester. What have you experienced regarding the focus on purposes and practices, structure and agency, hierarchy and participation, and internal and external?
2 Why has the focus been in that way? Do you support such a dynamic? If so, why? If not, what changes do you envisage are necessary?
3 Read the text that follows. It provides two approaches to accountability, and then come back to your answers to 1 and 2, and make any necessary adjustments to your analysis.

A good way to recognize these issues is to focus on major reform strategies that are common in different educational services and across national borders. We illustrate this by examining the debates about the best form of professional and student accountability. Ranson identifies a form of 'hierarchical answerability' (2003: 461), whereby the person calculates the self and is evaluated through externally imposed objective standards. So structures are designed, policies scoped and enacted, and cultures espoused in order to technically regulate performance through data production and evaluation. Hence purposes and practices is about delivery; structure and agency is about external control through government and/or faith and/or business centralization; hierarchy and participation is about performance compliance; and internal and external is about the educational service in the consumer marketplace. This is evident in global trending ideas where the organization is objectified to deliver 'standards' and 'quality' according to consumer choice decisions, and so the organization is judged to be variously 'effective', 'intelligent' and 'empowered'. Here leader, leading and leadership is framed as requiring identified and trained behaviours sustaining efficient organizational arrangements and cultures, and where the location of power is concerned with the unitary delivery of outcomes.

Concerns have been raised about how 'managerialism' may be contrary to the *education* in educational services: Ranson challenges these developments as 'eroding public trust in the stewardship of public services because it has embodied flawed criteria of evaluation and relations of accountability' (2003: 470). He calls for structures, cultures and systems that enable 'reflexive' accountability that focus beyond performativity upon how professionals and/with students have 'obligations'. This means that we 'give and take reasons/accounts for our beliefs and actions, enable mutual understanding and agreement' and so 'accountability in these interpretations is not a summons to compliance but rather provides ... shared ways of constructing the meanings that inform our social orders' (2003: 461). Hence, purposes and practices is about inclusive communication, structure and agency is about shared control, hierarchy and participation is about relational agreement, and internal and external is about the educational services within a localized but cosmopolitan context. Such approaches are evident in research into democratizing educational services and 'where students, teachers, parents and administrators exercise and develop their capacities to communicate and work with one another and others' and the 'locus of control over cooperation does not reside solely within the school, but instead retains the capacity for spontaneity, unpredictability and ongoing rich relationships with diverse constituencies' (Gale and Densmore, 2003: 131).

In summary, this historical and contemporary view of the dynamics of educational organizations and the issues involved leads us to consider how best to frame leaders, leading and leadership for and within the organization. We intend doing that by presenting three main positions: functional, critical and socially critical (see Gunter, Hall and Bragg, 2013). Table 9.1 provides an overview of these positions.

Table 9.1 Functional, critical and socially critical approaches to leader, leading and leadership

	Functional	Critical	Socially critical
Leader	A person located in a structural role, job description and delivery remit	People who work together based on explicit values and relational systems	People who are activist in identifying inequity and work for social justice
Leading	A person who demonstrates predetermined effective behaviours	People who have valid experiences and ways of working that demonstrate creative spontaneity that enable change	People who are activist in challenging power structures through questions that bring about changes that are equitable
Leadership	A person who exercises power over followers in order to eradicate dysfunctional people, structures, systems and cultures	People who share values and experiences in order to enable the realities of their contribution to be recognized and a source of reflexivity	People as activists exercise power as a shared and communal resource that all can have access to and use relationally

Three approaches to leaders, leading and leadership in education

In this section, we use the three approaches in Table 9.1 in order to present a thematic case study based on primary research, using three case studies to support reflection opportunities regarding leaders, leading and leadership (Grimaldi and Serpieri, 2016).

Functional approaches

Functional approaches to the organization set out to characterize and define leader, leading and leadership in ways that focus on the smooth running of structures and systems in order to avoid and eliminate dysfunctions. Such dysfunctions may concern the efficient and effective recruitment of students and staff, the economical deployment of budget resources, and the technical management of change that delivers and evaluates goal achievement.

Functional approaches have their origins in the 'scientific' dynamics of organizations, and are focused on rational control and delivery through clear internal (e.g. line management) and external (e.g. brand) boundaries. Such an approach is outlined in Case Study 9.1, about St George School.

Case Study 9.1 St George School, Naples

St George is one of the best-performing secondary schools in the Naples area, according to national test results and an influential national school ranking released annually by a private foundation in Italy. In a 2016 research project on teachers' evaluation in schools, we observed how Clare, the headteacher, has worked hard to build 'a culture of evaluation', to value merit and to promote an evidence-based approach to education and pedagogy among teachers at St George. Her motto was 'at St George we are student-centred and all about educational success and excellence'. Since her arrival at St George in 2011, Clare's first area of intervention has been the use of data as evidence to reflect on educational practice and design improvement actions. 'As educators we do evaluate', she used to say, 'and we cannot be against or afraid of evaluation. I want to self-evaluate myself and be evaluated! This is essential to improve'. To reach her objective, she has worked on school organization, modelling the school middle management as a delivery chain through which the school self-evaluation committee's analyses on national tests and school students' results are brought to and discussed within each subject department and classroom board. She also nominated one of her deputies (a mathematics teacher and an external evaluator for INVALSI, the Italian school evaluation agency) as responsible for school 'self-evaluation and improvement', asking him to lead the process of data analysis, school self-evaluation and agenda-setting in relation to the annual school-improvement plan. Among the improvement actions annually implemented at St George, a major role has been played by professional development courses for teachers delivered by external experts on testing, data analysis, evaluation epistemology, project-cycle management and data-driven innovation in Italian and maths. Using as a window of opportunity the principles established in a 2015 school reform (Law 107/2015), her second area of intervention has been the promotion of a culture of merit through the introduction of an internal system for teacher evaluation and a related mechanism to reward 'deserving teachers'. Such a system functioned as follows: (1) each year the school dedicated a budget to reward the best 30 per cent of its teachers; (2) teachers were annually evaluated and positioned in a ranking, resulting from the triangulation between peer, student and parents reputational evaluation; (3) the whole process was designed and coordinated by a teachers' evaluation committee led by Clare herself and two elected teachers. The system was intended to favour a culture of 'healthy competition' and promote 'virtuous processes of imitation' among them as a key to create a dynamic and successful school.

Activity 9.2

1 What is functional about this approach to leader, leading and leadership at St George?
2 What can you recognize in this account in your own organizational context?
3 This approach to leading, leaders and leadership seems to be dominant in global reform: why do you think this is the case?

Critical approaches

Critical approaches to the organization set out to characterize and define leader, leading and leadership in ways that make the experiences of professionals and students matter in regard to structures, cultures and systems. Such experiences are concerned with the realities of doing the job with habits and relational exchanges, and the 'everyday-ness' of what it means to work and study within an educational service such as a kindergarten, school, college or university.

Critical approaches have their origins in the 'values turn' in the field, where issues we have engaged with are focused on practices that are discursively constructed through subjective meaning, developed through formal and informal communication that is both internal and external to the organization. Such an approach is outlined in Case Study 9.2, of Rainbow School.

Case Study 9.2 Rainbow School, Naples

Rose is the headteacher of Rainbow, a primary school located in a disadvantaged area of the suburbs of Naples. Rainbow is institutionally constituted as an underperforming school with an 'at-risk' school intake, through national test results, special-needs education programmes and other 'labelling' institutional practices. Every year Rose and Rainbow teachers receive, discuss and publish within their Annual Self-Evaluation Report (RAV) negative national tests results on Italian and mathematics, and this continuously reinforces the formation of a negative school identity. Teachers manifest paradoxical feelings, alternating professional pride, frustration and fatalism. Test results increasingly act as catalyst of the Rainbow internal debate and preoccupations and monopolize the 'improvement' agenda.

In a research project about the use of national test data in Italian schools run in 2014–2015, we observed Rose and her staff launching a set of initiatives to challenge the formation of such a negative identity for the school, and the establishment of its priority mission in terms of 'raising the standards'. With the objective to 'value' teachers' professional competence and practice, to recognize the school's daily effort to educate (rather than deliver learning), and call into question 'test results objectivity', Rose and her staff decided to set up an internal and parallel system to monitor students' achievements in Italian and mathematics. Over two years they studied the national tests and organized seminars with experts in the field to understand their evaluative and pedagogical underpinnings. Through collective discussions, Rose agreed with the teachers that the negative results were in part the effect of a partial misalignment between the cultural code and learning objectives inscribed into the national tests, the average cultural capital of Rainbow's intake and the educational and pedagogical choices of Rainbow's professional community. After that, they searched for different kinds of standardized test that were less culturally biased and more akin to their pedagogy (e.g. the Cornoldi AC-MT arithmetic achievement test). Once they had identified the two alternative models for Italian and mathematics, Rose and her teachers enacted their internal system to monitor students' achievements, doing the tests with all their students in September, February and May of each year. This was framed as a way to 'measure' diachronically, contextually and effectively the achievements of Rainbow students, bringing back into the picture students' background and teachers' pedagogic choices. Thanks to the statistical expertise developed within a group of teachers in charge for school self-evaluation, the internal test results were analysed and made comparable with national test results. The differences emerging from the results and the insights coming from the comparison is the point where Rose and her staff started from in order to produce the RAV and socially construct a different narrative about Rainbow, the quality of education and the achievements of its students.

Activity 9.3

1 What is critical about this approach to leader, leading and leadership in Rainbow School?
2 What can you recognize in this account in your own organizational context?
3 This approach to leading, leaders and leadership seems to be absent from much reform but evident in research accounts of and with educational professionals: why do you think this is the case?

Socially critical approaches

Socially critical approaches to the organization set out to characterize and define leader, leading and leadership as a resource that all can access, demonstrate and practise regarding structures, cultures and systems. The starting point is to recognize that educational services are located in an unjust world, where power processes simultaneously enable and deny access to education as a professional or as a student, and so the kindergarten, school, college or university can be a site where this is recognized, confronted and a different approach to power enacted.

Socially critical approaches have their origins in work that identifies the limitations of the 'scientific' and 'values' forms of leader, leading and leadership, where the impact of poverty, racism, misogyny and homophobia in the organization, community and wider society is not only recognized but also activist strategies are put in place to work for educational services that are based on social justice. Such an approach is outlined in Case Study 9.3, of Bridge School.

Case Study 9.3 Bridge School, Naples

Bridge is a 'Second Chance' secondary school established in Naples in 1999 by a group of teachers who had previous experiences in bottom-up experiments to develop progressive and inclusive pedagogies in primary and secondary schools. Its teachers had a special authorization by the Ministry to work outside the school hierarchy and organize themselves with a high degree of autonomy to tackle early school-leaving in three disadvantaged areas in the city, building a curriculum centred on care, the valuing of difference and mutual recognition within an educational community. Bridge teachers labelled themselves 'street teachers' and worked in groups with no head teachers, inside and outside schools to bring drop-out students back to school and help them to complete low secondary school. They were hosted in three ordinary schools but were autonomous in terms of enrolment, classroom organization, curricular, pedagogic and evaluative choices. To make the school work, Bridge teachers organized themselves by establishing a decentred and non-hierarchical structure. In each of the hosting schools, they established a collegial board where Bridge teachers, 'street' educators and parent-volunteers had an equal voice in the governing of the school. Each board was facilitated by an academic psychologist, who was asked to sustain collective reflexivity. Operationally, Bridge adopted the model of an activist learning community, with parents involved in educational activities, democratic assemblies with students, and collaboration with universities (psychologists, sociologists, pedagogists) to implement activities of 'care' for teachers. Over twelve years of activity, Bridge teachers, educators and parents have carried out a struggle for political power and an administrative battle, confronting themselves with diverse problems originating from the impersonality, fixity and rigid temporality of the ministerial bureaucracy, the formal requirements of a school system based on disciplines that inhibited mutual adjustment between the school and the learner, the difficulties in the coordination with their 'formal' headteachers, and the imperative to be accountable in terms of a certain kind of performance. Year after year they negotiated with the Ministry and local administrators for funding, buildings, teachers' enrolment and institutionalization (the project to make Bridge a permanent experience and not an experiment) and explored new possibilities participating to bids and calls to sustain and expand their activity. As social activists and public intellectuals, they have constantly built alliances, with academics, local communities, parents and teachers' professional associations, organizing public meetings and seminars, encouraging research of their experience and building national and international networks with educators involved in similar experiences. What has emerged is a fragile and unstable compromise, a never fully developed organizational and pedagogical model, an experience of constrained freedom and creativity. If Bridge collective leadership and management has succeeded in making of it a widely known and inspiring experience and a point of reference in the educational thought in the public debate, it has lost the struggle for its institutionalization. Due to ideological differences (local conservative government) and austerity policies of cuts in services, Bridge was closed in 2011.

Activity 9.4

1 What is socially critical about this approach to leader, leading and leadership in Bridge School?
2 What can you recognize in this account in your own organizational context?
3 This approach to leading, leaders and leadership is evident in research accounts of and with education and community activists, but can be 'short term experiments' rather than system-wide: why do you think this is the case?

These case studies facilitate thinking about different approaches to leaders, leading and leadership that are evident in the realities of educational services, and the ways in which you may have read about, witnessed and developed recommendations about and for change. We intend in the final section of this chapter to take up the issue of power because so far it has been present but we have not fully examined the meaning and implications for professionals and students.

Power and educational services

The framing of leader, leading and leadership as functional, critical and socially critical provides insights into the meaning and operationalization of power:

- **Functional:** the focus is on the location of legitimate power of a person in a post and who uses power *over* those who are structurally located as followers. The leader is *in power* and *holds power*, leading consists of the behaviours and tasks performed by the leader to 'tell' followers and leadership is focused on the impact of power upon others. Power is a technology, and power relations are hierarchical and directional.

- **Critical:** the focus is on the realities of experiential and habitual exchanges between people where power is used to both achieve and prevent outcomes. Alongside functionality there is recognition of how power is *exercised* by a leader, leading is to 'sell' by communicating and negotiating, and leadership is premised on respecting values and knowing how work gets done. Power is humane, and power relations are interrelational.

- **Socially critical:** the focus is on recognizing power *for* and *with* all organizational and community members, and their location within a wider and unjust society and economy. Power is shared within a community, where participants can take on a leader role (temporarily), can do leading through 'consent' and 'agreed' action, and where leadership power is a communal resource. Power is activist, and power relations are mutual.

In Activity 9.5, there are three activities for you to choose from in order to think about the different ways in which power is conceptualized in educational services.

Activity 9.5

1 **Think about your professional context** and try to characterize the dynamics of the educational organization you work within in terms of *structure*, *system*, *culture* and *people*. Continue this characterization focusing on the prevailing *discursive politics*, *logic of control* and *regulatory model*. Then, use the functional, critical and socially critical approaches to describe how and why leaders, leading and leadership are enacted in your organization. Taking into account the issue of power and power relations, can you think of significant situations over the past five years, and how would you characterize power?

2 **Think about the national policy context** and visit the website of the ministry or department of education in your country. Examine the key government policy documents on leaders, leading and leadership. Once you have read the policy documents, answer the following questions:

   (a) Is the approach to leader, leading and leadership functional, critical and/or socially critical?

(b) How is the relationship between leadership and power conceptualized?

(c) If you were a policymaker, a professional or an academic, would you provide a different perspective on leader, leading and leadership in educational organizations? What would you say?

3 **Think about the global policy context** and visit the OECD website: oecd.org/education/school/improvingschoolleadership-home.htm and look at the document 'Improving school leadership: the toolkit', at oecd.org/education/school/44339174.pdf

Once you have read these documents, answer the following questions:

a Is the approach to leader, leading and leadership functional, critical and/or socially critical?

b How is the relationship between leadership and power conceptualized?

c If you were a policymaker, a professional or an academic, would you provide a different perspective on leader, leading and leadership in educational organizations? What would you say?

Research shows that the current emphasis in officially mandated professional practice and training, national and global policy texts is primarily on functionality with some recognition of critical realism. It is out of the scope of this particular chapter to consider the reasons for this, but we will consider the implications.

What has become fashionable in professional training is the promotion of emotional intelligence. In other words, those who are functionally 'in charge of' and those who are followers but 'responsible for' processes and outcomes, are required to harness and use emotions in order to be enthusiastic deliverers of organizational, national and global policy, and to hold 'negative' emotions 'in check' where responses from critique through to anger are considered to be disruptive. When this is linked to empowerment as a form of licensed delivery of policy and organizational requirements then functionality is privileged and connects with preventing the potential 'answering back' from critical insights into organizational habits and processes. It is also a means through which socially critical approaches are banished as oppositional, where those who work for democratic forms of empowerment are rendered troublemakers. However, the ongoing work of critical and socially critical approaches to leaders, leading and leadership brings perspectives to educational services as organizations which not only reveal emotional intelligence as a self-control and other-control process, but also examine power micropolitically in ways that are recognized by professionals.

One of the outcomes of this analysis is how the discipline of organizational participants can misrecognize power relations. There is a need to examine the use of emotional rhetoric such as visioning, the manipulation of people through to direct command and control that is integral to delegation as empowerment. Historically the field has identified that, while functionality proceeds and can accommodate critical realities, it seems that the major concern is what is called 'micropolitics'. Here we adopt Hoyle's (1999) approach that looks at educational organizations as sites of social conflict in response to external pressures (policy micropolitics) and the strategies whereby people in educational organiz-ations pursue their interests (management micropolitics). People within organizations have shared histories that are usually professional, have career interests and ambitions, and have relationships that could be personal and intimate. The functionality of decision-making may not be rational, and it may not be possible to access or engage with why a new innov-ation is not working in the way that was planned. Complexity can be further intensified through how change strategies are more about ideological struggle than neutral delivery, where deep-seated values and political positions with coalitions formed, and are so important as to generate conflicts that may or may not be 'in the open'.

This focus on micropolitics within organizations has implications for how leaders, leading and leadership is thought about:

- Functional approaches see micropolitics as a problem to be solved, particularly through both eradicating people who are identified as the source of the problem, and disciplining people through emotional intelligence and licensed empowerment to prevent such disorder.

- Critical approaches see micropolitics as an everyday matter regarding how people get their work done, where shared values and organizational processes can prevent trouble by making 'what we stand for' as open as possible, and handling 'outbursts' as they happen.

- Socially critical approaches see micropolitics as revealing the way that power works in ways that are functionally authoritarian, and as an opportunity for those who regard themselves as powerless to speak back to the powerful, and so the focus is on respect for diversity of standpoints, and empowerment as a democratic participation.

Here, we make two recommendations: first, review your notes and consider the place of micropolitics in your thinking and research about leaders, leadership and leadership in educational services; and second, read this chapter alongside other chapters in this textbook, so that you can think creatively about organizational design and practice, and how it relates to professional knowledges and wider equity agendas.

Conclusion

Much has been studied and written about leading and managing educational organizations, and our framework of functional, critical and socially critical approaches enables meaning and an explanation for the fundamental issues that are always being debated. These approaches are not formalized categories where leader, leading and leadership are boxed into one way of thinking, but are lenses through which to view what is happening and what is advocated as in need of change. Consequently, such approaches are not intended to fit a situation but are helpful in illuminating what is happening and what is regarded as an agenda for change. As you move forward in your reading and thinking, you may find this framework helpful but you may also seek to develop or even replace it. In doing so you need to give recognition to the historical and contemporary context in which you, as a professional and as a student, are located, and so consider the meaning of power in regard to the claims about the dynamics involved in the organization of educational services.

Further reading

Ball, S.J. (1987) *The micro-politics of the school: towards a theory of school organization*. London: Routledge.

Blase, J. and Anderson, G. (1995) *The micropolitics of educational leadership: from control to empowerment*. London: Cassell.

Evers, C.W. and Lakomski, G. (eds) (1996) *Exploring educational administration: coherentist applications and critical debates*. Oxford: Elsevier Science.

Gunter, H.M. (2016) *An intellectual history of school leadership practice and research*. London: Bloomsbury Academic.

Sahlberg, P. (2015) *Finnish lessons 2.0: what can the world learn from educational change in Finland?* New York: Teachers College Press.

References

Foster, W. (1986) *Paradigms and promises: new approaches to educational administration*. Amherst, NY: Prometheus Books.

Gale, T. and Densmore, K. (2003) Democratic educational leadership in contemporary times. *International Journal of Leadership in Education*, 6(2), 119–136.

Greenfield, T. and Ribbins, P. (eds) (1993) *Greenfield on educational administration: towards a humane science*. London: Routledge.

Griffiths, D.E. (1969) Theory in educational administration: 1966. In: G. Baron, D.H. Cooper and W.G. Walker (eds), *Educational administration: international perspectives* (pp. 154–167). Chicago: Rand McNally.

Grimaldi, E. and Serpieri, R. (2016) Scuole a 'prova' di Invalsi: la valutazione tra riflessività e fabbricazione. In: P. Landri and A.M. Maccarini (eds), *Uno specchio per la valutazione della scuola: Paradossi, controversie, vie di uscita* (pp. 65–91). Milan: FrancoAngeli.

Gunter, H.M., Hall, D. and Bragg, J. (2013) Distributed leadership: a study in knowledge production. *Educational Management Administration & Leadership*, 41(5), 555–580.

Halpin, A.W. (1966) *Theory and research in administration*. New York: Macmillan.

Hoyle, E. (1999) The two faces of micropolitics. *School Leadership & Management*, 19(2), 213–222.

Ranson, S. (2003) Public accountability in the age of neo-liberal governance. *Journal of Education Policy*, 18(5), 459–480.

Smyth, J. (ed.) (1989) *Critical perspectives on educational leadership*. London: Falmer Press.

Using theory in educational leadership, management and administration research

Pat Thomson and Amanda Heffernan

10

What this chapter is about   156

Key questions that this
chapter addresses   156

Introduction   156

Educational leadership
management and adminis-
tration research and theory   159

Using theory   160

Bringing theory to your
educational leadership and
management research
project   166

Conclusion   168

Further reading   168

References   169

What this chapter is about

A question guaranteed to make almost any educational leadership scholar feel a little uncertain – if not downright nervous – is 'What is your theoretical framework?' In this chapter, we provide a framework to help provide an answer to this discomfiting question. We begin with a discussion and definition of theory, delineating it from a conceptual framework. We explain what we mean by praxis and show how this interrelates with research and practice. We then discuss the reasons for using theory, giving examples of the kinds of theoretical resources available to leadership researchers. We offer examples from our own experience to show how theory might be used, drawing on the ideas of Foucault and Bourdieu. We conclude by considering some of the risks involved in researching and writing with theory.

Key questions that this chapter addresses

1 What is theory?

2 What is praxis?

3 How has theory been used in the field of educational leadership, management and administration (ELMA)?

4 In what ways is theory a framework?

5 What approaches might be taken to using theory in your research?

Introduction

When theory is discussed, it is most often referred to as a set of organizing ideas that both explain and guide hypotheses about, and analysis of, phenomena. However, there is no agreed definition of theory. For the purposes of this chapter, we have opted for a common-sense definition that focuses on what theory does (see box).

Theory allows us to investigate and make sense of happenings, sayings and doings, beings and becomings. Theory helps to interrogate and classify things we see, hear, feel and remember. Theory helps us to design our research projects, decide what data we want to collect and why, choose how to analyse data and how to explain phenomena to ourselves and to others. Theory gives us a way to connect the immediate phenomena we are concerned with to wider patterns, associations, relationships, structures and cultures. Theory allows us to get beyond the surface of events, sayings, relationships, policies and practices. As Jean Anyon (2009: 3) puts it,

> *Theory:* an explanation, a way of saying how things relate to each other, why they are the way that they are, and how they relate to other things.

'Without theory, our data on school experience or social phenomena do not go very far, and do not tell us very much that is not already obvious. Our data do not leave the ground on which they were found, our explanations do not soar, and they may fail to inspire.'

A theory differs from a concept. A theory unites several concepts to do its explanatory work. To understand the difference between theory and concept it is helpful to take a prosaic example – a seat belt. A seat belt is simply the couple of straps that fasten around your body to stop you lurching forward when your car stops suddenly. The work energy principle and conservation laws not only explain the way the seat belt works but also why it does. This is scientific theory, which uses multiple concepts – work, energy, power and conservation – to provide a cogent explanation. The theory applies not simply to seat belts but also all other similar phenomena. A theory has broad applicability.

Theory is often seen as abstract. The word theory comes from the Greek *theoria*, which means speculation or contemplation. The origins of the term point to the ways in which theory requires deep thinking, over time. Some theories have changed the way we understand our history (the big-bang theory, or the theory of evolution). Other theories have changed the way we see ourselves and understand each other and the world around us (this is where social theory does much of its work). It is worth starting, then, with the understanding that the practice of theorizing is one that cannot be rushed and is not mechanical or technical. Working with theory is not a matter of taking something off the shelf and simply wrapping it around a set of data. Theorization requires application and space/time. However, working with theory is not simply a process of philosophizing for its own sake.

Working with theory is not a neutral activity. Just as with any other form of research practice, theoretical endeavour does particular work in the world. It acts in particular interests. We position ourselves with colleagues who use *critical* social theory directed towards exploring, documenting and critiquing relations of domination and subordination. We are interested in social theory that allows us to go beyond description in order to deconstruct but also reimagine and reconstruct inequitable social economic and political relations in education.

Practice is often separated from theory. Practice can be understood as doing, as action on and in the world, rather than being about the world. Theory on the other hand can be seen as being separate from everyday mores and problems. Many who talk about evidence-based practice suggest that theory is applied to practice – we understand and explain and then do. But in education, and in other professions, theory and practice are often brought together in the notion of praxis – making critical social theory practical.

Paolo Freire (1972) referred to praxis as reflection and action directed to political action, to structures that need transforming. Praxis (see Figure 10.1) occurs when theory is used together with action in order to change things for the better. The notion of praxis is important to educators working for social justice as it requires 'practical wisdom', moving between the grounded and particular and the general and principled. Praxis is important for educational and leadership scholars too, as it suggests that there is no a priori answer to a given situation. Rather it is in the theoretically informed deliberation about a particular situation – a school, a system, a policy – that generates productive ideas about what, as well as how, we might act. Ends and means; thought and action are in continual conversation.

Figure
10.1 Praxis.

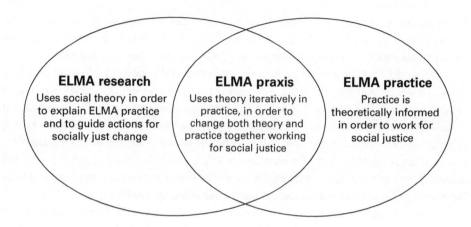

ELMA research
Uses social theory in order to explain ELMA practice and to guide actions for socially just change

ELMA praxis
Uses theory iteratively in practice, in order to change both theory and practice together working for social justice

ELMA practice
Practice is theoretically informed in order to work for social justice

For a researcher who is temporarily away from everyday action, doing postgraduate study for example, the notion of praxis suggests that it is important to always have in mind that simply coming to a plausible and defensible explanation is important but not enough. A praxis-oriented researcher will continue to seek the practical implications of, and possibilities for, their theorizing, and for the social-justice outcomes. And this suggests exercising some caution in relation to theory.

Connell suggests that a general social or cultural theory, that is, the kind likely to be applicable in educational leadership and management research, is one which develops 'a broad vision of the social, and offers concepts that apply beyond a particular society, place or time. Such texts make propositions or hypotheses that are relevant everywhere, or propose methods of analysis that will work under all conditions' (2007: 28). According to Connell, social theory is characterized by its ambition and sweep. It is a way to make sense of the way the world works, or if not the entire world, a very substantive aspect of it. A social theory works to tidy up ideas, bring them into line, codify and categorize them, establish causalities and connections. It generalizes. It offers constructs for seeing diverse phenomena and for generating sum and substance. It offers a logical and clear narrative thread that draws a rational border around that which is to be explained, eliminating mess and ill-fitting pieces.

Connell (2007) identifies three problems with the ways in which theoretical frameworks are developed and used:

1 General social theories make claims to apply everywhere, at all times and in all places – a bid for universality. Geographical, historical and cultural specificities and particularities are forgotten, as is change. General social theories ignore their own temporality.

2 Social theories mostly read the world from the centre – largely from Europe and its histories of intellectual thought. In the general social theories most in use in English-speaking universities, significant theoretical traditions from 'the periphery' of the European world are ignored. A Western perspective is assumed to be universal.

3 General social theories assume that the questions addressed and the methods used will be the same everywhere. The local, idiosyncratic and particular are excluded, although these may actually signal that the theory is limited and partial.

Connell's concerns alert us to the need for care in using social theory, to watch for the ways in which theory can make phenomena general rather than particular, situated and limited.

Educational leadership management and administration research and theory

ELMA is not a field in which 'blue sky' research is generally practised. It is unsurprising, given its origins and composition, that the ELMA field was and is dominated by questions emerging from practice. The area was always, and still is, profoundly directed to the world of schools, colleges and universities. The notion of praxis is thus as important as that of theory.

As a field, ELMA scholars have been primarily concerned with understanding what leaders do, how they do what they do, how they might do the job better and how they might be taught to do the job. Analyses of scholarship about and for school leaders (e.g. Gunter, 2016) suggest that there is a recognizable strand of ELMA scholarship that uses various psychological theories to address these questions. Psychology-based research primarily investigates motivation, personality, group behaviours and stress; this work has strong connections with industrial and human-relations scholarship in business studies. Some human-flourishing scholars have considered the question of the emotional work that leaders do (e.g. Harris, 2007). There is also some application of learning theory to educational leadership research through for example 'communities of practice' (Wenger, 1998).

To a lesser extent the field has been concerned with questions about who becomes a leader and how; how knowledge about ELMA is generated; why the job of leading is the way that it is, and how leaders might contribute to social justice. We can think, for instance, of studies of: the ways in which leaders are positioned by particular policies and how they respond to them; everyday life in disadvantaged schools and how leaders work to redress the production and reproduction of the status quo; and examinations of leadership professional development, the criteria used to design them and the ways in which they do // do not reproduce systemic and inequitable power relations. These kinds of questions benefit from the use of theory that draws from sociology, anthropology, cultural studies and politics (e.g. English, 2011). Such critical social theories might mobilize explicitly feminist, postcolonial, critical race and decolonizing, and queer scholarship.

While psychologically based studies might examine the personal life histories of leaders, and generate heuristics that show the connections between context, biography and location, these are different from sociological studies that focus on the ways in which an individual is always social. Social theory is not used to produce generalized accounts of individual behaviours/feelings, but to explain how wider patterns come to be, and why leaders act and feel as they do, and why organizations produce and reproduce power-saturated knowledges, relations and actions.

An example helps to show the difference between these two different fields. The vast majority of leadership studies include the policy context in which leaders are situated. Psychology-influenced scholars might examine the ways in which leaders respond to particular policies and/or their work is framed, enabled or constrained by policy with a focus is on the individual, their feelings and their actions. These actions and feelings can be aggregated and codified to show generalized behaviours and activities (e.g. Day et al., 2000). By contrast, social science–located researchers might investigate the relationships between individuals, groups, institutions, and larger social relations and structures. Sociologically inclined ELMA policy research often focuses on investigating the ways in which policy produces and patterns leaders' identities and their work. Researchers see an individual leader as a window to the ways in which the work of leaders more generally is constructed, and while individual idiosyncrasies of person and location must be taken into account in any study, the objects of study are the socially produced patterning of leadership actions, emotions and relations, as well as the purposes and outcomes (e.g. Morrison, 2009).

For social scientists, the social is not a contextual container, but simultaneously a complex (re)productive set of relations and practices and a 'pincushion of a million stories' (Social Science Space, 2013). In critical social sciences in particular, the 'little picture' of leader and school is always connected to a 'big picture' of the wider society and its unevenness, inequalities, histories and habituated practices. Importantly, as we have noted, what might at first appear to be abstracted critical social theory actually aims to support, via dialogue and iterative reflective action (praxis), changes in the conditions in which educational leaders, staff and students work.

Educational leadership management and administration research and theory

There are two ways to think about the purposes and use of theory. These are as (1) a framework, and (2) as a resource. We are not suggesting either of these is more important. Rather, both are necessary and neither is sufficient alone. We discuss each in turn.

Theory as a framework

In educational and leadership research, theory is most often taken to be a framework. Two metaphors are helpful to explain what this 'frame' means.

Think of a house frame, often built of wood or steel. This frame is a skeleton around which the rest of the house is built. The frame provides a basic structure – houses built using the same frame might vary a lot, but they still follow the same underpinning design and logics. A house built around a frame has been planned. The frame makes the plan solid. A planned house differs from a house where rooms are just added on higgledy-piggledy.

That's because the plan has a kind of logic about where things go – the bathroom here, the bedrooms there. The layout has been designed with a particular kind of everyday life in mind. Thus, most houses – and their frames – support multiple zones of activity and there's a pleasing flow from one area to another. The house frame also provides stability. The frame stops the house wobbling about, keeps the roof in one piece. Thinking about a house frame then prompts us to think about **structure, stability, flow** and **zones of activity**.

A picture frame is something that you put around the outside of something – the frame creates a border, differentiating what's inside the frame from what's outside. The frame gives the whole a finished appearance. The picture frame has particular component parts – a rim, and a front and back cover. So the frame is a kind of solid casing that stops the contents moving about. It also allows the whole – picture and frame – to be hung, stored or stacked, for instance – it completes the package. Thinking about the picture frame generates some additional helpful ideas – **borders, solidity, parts that fit together, portability** and **wholeness**.

These things – structure, stability, flow, zones of activity, borders, solidity, parts, portability, wholeness – are essentially what a theoretical framework does for research.

A theoretical framework is the *overall explanation* that is used to provide **coherence and focus** to a research project and the subsequent thesis/report/papers. It provides: a **structure** that is used to design a study, generate data and analyse it; **borders** that allow you to say what is included and what is not; a **basis for connecting** to other research, for example comparing the results generated by your framework with others; a linked **set of parts, ideas that guide research and the writing** and help to create the red thread of argument; and a potentially **reusable approach** which can be duplicated with other topics and/or data.

There are four common approaches to timing the development of a theoretical framework:

1 The framework *grows organically with the research* – the benefit of this approach is that the framework is bespoke to the particular topic and data. One risk with this approach is that the research ends up being more like a higgledy-piggledy house that is retro-fitted with a framework that perhaps doesn't quite work. Or the end result is a framing that is logical but there isn't the data to make the explanation hang together and flow.

2 You arrive at a framework *somewhere in the middle* of the project, when you have enough data to know what kind of explanation is needed. The benefit of this approach is that there is time to consider what might work best for the particular topic and the necessary data is generated. The risks include generating at least some data that doesn't fit and being distracted by the continued pressure to arrive at a suitable framework.

3 The theoretical framework is developed *at the outset of the project* and is used to guide problem-posing, designing the research questions and data-generation strategy as well as the subsequent analysis and writing. Two benefits of this approach are that you make sure that you have the kind of data you need, and you have a very clear approach to analysis. A risk is that the early framing eliminates important information and becomes as much a set of blinkers as it does a support.

4 The theory is developed towards or *at the end of field work*. This approach is advocated in grounded theory, although it also occurs in many others. The benefit of ending with the theory is that the theory is specific to the data that is generated. The associated downside is that the theory can be simply laid over the data rather than being used to develop and interrogate it.

The idea of a framework and its timing points to structural and technical questions – the need for a research project to be coherent. A theoretical framework provides the means through which the aims, questions, data and analysis become aligned and are able to be presented in a logically organized text.

Theory as a resource for thinking and acting

If theory is as we have suggested, an explanation, a way of saying how things relate to each other, why they are the way that they are, and how they relate to other things, then it has particular affordances. Theory offers a language, specific terms that capture concepts. Theory brings these designated and specifically named ideas into relationships; theory evidences and connects the concepts together. If you remember our earlier seat-belt example, the concepts of work, energy, power and conservation – specific terms each with their own background information and exemplification – were brought together in the work energy principle and energy conservation laws. While each concept can stand alone, together they make something particular. The whole cannot be understood, or used, by looking at or using the parts separately. The whole theory is more than the sum of its conceptual parts.

When it comes to educational leadership and administration, we think it is helpful to give you some examples to show how a holistic social theory might work as a resource for thinking. We are going to draw on our own work to show two ways in which bringing theory to ELMA questions can be used. The first is to decide on questions: this uses Bourdieu. The second is to rethink the taken-for-granted: this uses Foucault.

Case Study 10.1 Bourdieu's 'toolkit' of concepts

Bourdieu offers a complex interrelated 'toolkit' of concepts directed towards researching and explaining the production and reproduction of economic, social, cultural and political privilege and disadvantage. His key concepts of field, capitals, habitus and doxa are often used separately, something he specifically warned against. Pat (Thomson, 2017) has argued that Bourdieu's social theory offers researchers four important things:

1 **An ontological orientation:** a way of understanding the world as social and relational. Bourdieu wanted to understand the logics of inter- and intra-actions that produced societies and particular practices such as education, art, politics and economics. He can be seen as epistemologically relativist, as he maintained that knowledge was a social construction, specific to time and place; truth practices such as research are thus also socially produced.

---

2 **A commitment to rigour:** Bourdieu argued strongly that even though they and their work were socially produced, researchers must work dispassionately and ensure that their work was sufficiently 'expert' to be used to effect in the struggles for social and economic justice.

3 **Reflexivity:** Bourdieu argued that taking account of and interrogating the ways in which we as researchers are disposed to know and act must become an embodied and embedded scholarly disposition.

4 **A broad methodological approach:** Bourdieu's thinking tools were specifically designed *through* and *for* research that understands the social, institutional and individual as mutually constructed. This aim oriented the kinds of questions that were asked as well as the kinds of data that was generated. He argued, for instance, that researchers should begin by understanding the specific field, its capitals, logics and beliefs in relation to the wider field of power. They might then examine the positions in the field and the relations within them. After this, the system of dispositions constituting the positional habitus can be explored.

What does thinking with Bourdieu look like in practice?

Pat has recently been working on unethical and corrupt practices in the school system. Her research question, following Bourdieu, is to try to map and explain the proliferation of reports of schools engaged in fraud, secretive practices, fabrication of results, bullying, lack of consultation and so on.

Her research followed Bourdieu's three-step approach. She first looked at the education field and its parallels with the economic field, dominated by a particular kind of market entrepreneurialism and neoliberal governing practices. She examined the ways in which the education field in England was changing, re-hierarchizing, through academization policies and the production of new positions such as multi-academy trusts with their highly paid chief executive officers. She also looked at the logics of the field where the logic of choice and competition (re)produced advantages for middle-class families and favoured 'successful schools and leaders' as measured through institutional performance in audit and test results and satisfaction measures. This analysis allowed her to 'see' the ways in which the logics of the field diminished the ethos of the public good and failed to reward ethical practices. The third step in the research was to examine the system of 'bad behaviour' leader dispositions being produced and reproduced in the field.

As a result of the research she is able to explain what is happening in education policy and practice in England, and also make suggestions about what might need to change.

Case Study 10.2 Foucault's theoretical 'gadgets'

Foucault's theories focus on power and understanding the way power works within society. He advocated that the various ideas within his work should be adopted as 'gadgets' (Foucault, 1980) to be used in ways that work for researchers. His work contains key concepts that can be found in critical educational leadership research. Some are explained briefly here, though this is not an exhaustive list. Additionally, the ideas are explained in relation to the ELMA field of research, to provide some context for understanding.

1 **Discourse:** a cornerstone of Foucault's work and a way of describing and constructing the world. Inherent in the study of discourse is an understanding of the influence of power and 'truth'; or which discourses are accepted as truth and which are marginalized and set aside. Discourses are the implicit and explicit expectations that shape school leaders' worlds. Discourses can be complementary or competing – discourses of education for student achievement, for example, might focus on what is easily measurable, while discourses of holistic education might focus on that which cannot be easily measured. Research might explore the struggle for school leaders to understand and respond to different discourses in their work.

2 **Subjectivity:** a way for us to understand how discourses shape an individual. The 'subject', or the individual, is constructed via their interactions with people and systems, and will therefore be constructed differently depending on the situation or circumstance. Subjectivities can be influenced and shaped by discourses in the form of official and unofficial policy; external expectations placed on leaders; and social interactions and power structures (to name a few examples). Complex power relations and shifting expectations means that school leaders' subjectivities vary depending on context.

3 **Discipline:** how individuals are managed, and how their subjectivities are constructed by a range of forces including dominant and alternative discourses, and systems of power.

What does thinking with Foucault look like in practice?

Foucault's work has been taken up by ELMA researchers in various ways. Some examples of these have been to understand and problematize discourses that permeate the work of schools; power dynamics within a school, community or school system; the ways school leaders are monitored; and the ways school leaders comply with or resist externally imposed expectations and requirements.

Amanda (Heffernan, 2018) used Foucault's gadgets as part of a study that analysed school leaders' enactment of school-improvement discourses and policies. Foucault's ideas provided a set of tools with which to think through the ways school leaders responded at a micro (individual or personal) level to a macro (departmental or system-wide) school-improvement agenda. She employed notions such as discourse, subjectivity, discipline and surveillance to help understand the ways leaders' identities, practices and beliefs were being shaped by a new and urgent system-wide school-improvement agenda.

Amanda's research was guided largely by notions of discourse within participants' professional worlds – their individual thoughts, beliefs and practices about leadership; the discourses about schooling and school improvement that were found at a school, local and system-wide level, which were informed by global education discourses. These discourses existed in many forms including formal and informal policy, media and political commentary on schooling, requirements from the education department, and expectations communicated via conversations and interactions with students, staff and school communities. Being able to seek out, identify, and define the most common and influential discourses was a first step in understanding the ways those discourses were disciplining principals and helping to create their subjectivities as individual leaders. The next step was to seek to understand how principals were responding to those discourses, and the study explored the ways the work of school leaders had changed under school-improvement policy conditions.

Reflection

Amanda: I was first drawn to Foucault as a way of coming to understand individual people's responses to systematic issues of policy, politics and power. I was theorizing the wider policy landscape and the other theories I was using were insufficient in helping me to understand why people were responding and acting in the ways that they were. Understanding concepts like subjectivity and discipline were the first steps in making sense of this problem.

Pat: Bourdieu has become my default theory. His thinking toolkit is just part of the way in which I approach any kind of research. This means I always start from the position that I am looking at something where there are unequal power relations and that the logics of practice and ways of thinking about them need to be critically examined. I think of this as a kind of ontological–epistemological–methodological knot as he simultaneously points me to a view of the world, knowledge and knowledge production.

Amanda: When you use Bourdieu's thinking toolkit as a starting point, do you find yourself reaching for any other theoretical devices or frames to add to his ideas? One of the great aspects of Foucault's work for me is his own encouragement for people to take up the ideas that fit where they can, and use them in ways that work for the problem or the task at hand.

Pat: Yes, no theory does everything. And sometimes even if I start thinking with Bourdieu I end up using other theories instead. But it's sometimes tricky putting theories together when they are really different in their orientations. I'd shy away from using Bourdieu and Foucault together. Foucault gives more purchase on knowledge and subjectivity questions whereas I find Bourdieu is more useful to me in thinking about inequality and schooling as a social institution.

Activity 10.1

We ask you, now, to consider how these points so far build upon your knowledge of using social theory in educational leadership research. What ideas can you take from this conversation to help you understand your own research? How might Bourdieu or Foucault serve as a starting point for your own exploration of theory?

Bringing theory to your educational leadership and management research project

It is important to have a clear idea about why and when social theory might be useful for your research. A helpful example can be found in a paper by Jon Nixon. He recounts a particular incident that puzzled him. He wrote,

> In the course of conducting the study I interviewed a number of teachers and students, but the comment of one teacher in particular has stayed with me over the years. 'It's not just that expectations need raising' argued this teacher, 'It's that our pupils need to see that they can achieve.' Then the interviewee added: 'There's some sort of subtle difference there I think.' *(2018: 902)*

Nixon goes on to say that he has 'pondered' for a long time on what that subtle difference might be. He writes that the teacher's statement raises a 'fundamental pedagogical question: how to translate aspiration into functioning capability?' And this is the reason he turned to a social theory. He says

> I have found Martha C. Nussbaum's work particularly helpful in thinking through – and working through – that question. Her specification of what she terms the ten 'central capabilities' has in the past provided me with a very helpful framework, notwithstanding what some would see as its colonialist and/or universalist bias (criticisms that Nussbaum robustly counters). . . . Hans-Georg Gadamer's later work on 'applied hermeneutics' has also provided me with some hugely important insights into what he calls 'the primacy of the question' in the development of understanding both within the humanities and more generally. More recently I have come across Paul Gibbs's . . . work on happiness and contentment, which has helped me approach the question from some interestingly di erent angles. *(2018: 902–903)*

Nixon goes on to explain his take on Gibbs, which he then brings to the question of pedagogy, and students' ambitions. Three things are important about Nixon's introduction and his description of his thinking process. He makes very clear:

- the need for theory. Nixon wants to understand something that he hasn't been able to let go of. It's nagged at him, so he turns to theory to help make sense of it. This is not theory for its own sake. This is calling on theory for a specific reason;

- the thing that he needs to explain. The 'problem' that he wants to answer is expressed crisply, briefly and in a way that makes sense to the reader; and

- his agency. The theory Nixon is going to use isn't his only choice – he has considered others. He wants to use Gibb because, he suggests, it offers something new and interesting.

Nixon as exemplar shows that it is important for a researcher to think carefully about why theory is being used, when in the research process and to what ends. While not all researchers will have nagging problems that they want to deal with, these three points – a need to explain, an intellectual problem related to practice and a deliberate choice of theory – are important for all of us.

Making a conscious choice about what the particular theory will do is not a simple matter and the notion of choice implies that the researcher has a range of theoretical resources at their disposal. It is thus often helpful to think at the beginning of a research project about how theory might help and what theories might be helpful. For postgraduate researchers this does mean reading papers in which a range of theoretical resources have been used to make sense of educational leadership problems. Understanding the options then leads on to reading some of the theoretical options in their original form.

It can be very beneficial when formulating a research project to think about the three questions the Nixon example alerted us to – need, problem and choice. Some experimentation at the outset (see Activity 10.2) with different theories and their affordances can be important in making choices – or postponing a choice until the data is in.

Here is a short paragraph from a book by Valerie Harwood and Julie Allan. It's not about leadership but it does concern issues crucial for school leaders. It's a succinct way to pin down what theory is being used, how and for what reasons.

Theoretical perspective

In this book we draw on the work of Foucault to make our argument that psychopathology has become instrumental in schools and that schools play an instrumental role in expanding the new psychopathologies of children and young people. Foucault's emphasis on truth, power and the constitution of the subject . . . is especially useful to our analysis as it allows us to think through the ways in which psychopathology at school is produced and has productive effects. To this end Foucault's . . . conceptualization of power as productive is generative for grasping how schools can indeed be instrumental in a field that, on first glance, appears to be the province of medical and health sciences (especially psychiatry, clinical psychology and psychopharmacology). It is here also that Foucault's attention to dominant and subjugated knowledges is of value for informing how to understand how dominant knowledges of school disorders such as ADHD, direct attention from those practices that enable psychopathology to sit comfortably in contemporary schooling and educational environments. *(Harwood and Allan, 2014: 10–11)*

Activity 10.2

When you strip out the content, you can see the thinking they have done about theory, expressed as a sentence skeleton. It can be very helpful to use such a skeleton to help clarify how you might use theory in your particular project. Just put your project details into the blanks in the sentences.

Skeleton: Explaining theoretical choice

In this (thesis/paper/book/chapter) I draw on the work of (name theorist) to make my argument that _____ (this is your major argument in one or two points).

(Name of theorist)'s emphasis on _____ is especially useful to my analysis as it allows me to think through _____ (name the major purpose to which the theory is put).

To this end, (name of theorist)'s conceptualization of (name major aspect of theory) is generative for grasping how (name major application of the theory to the argument you are making).

It is here also that (name of theorist)'s attention to _____ (another aspect of the theory) _____ is of value for informing (another piece of the argument for which the theory is essential).

Conclusion

In this chapter, we have introduced you to theory, to theoretical frameworks, and to two commonly used theorists (Bourdieu and Foucault). Their work, as explored in our recommended readings, might serve as a starting point. The readings we have recommended, from critical ELMA researchers, provide an entry point into other social theory and theorists that will be of interest and of use. We hope that the idea of a theoretical framework invokes less fear after reading this chapter. We hope that you feel empowered to engage with different ideas to find what works for you and what helps you to study and understand the world around you, and ELMA as a phenomenon.

Further reading

Blackmore, J. (2016) *Educational leadership and Nancy Fraser*. Abingdon: Routledge

Dressman, M. (2008) *Using social theory in educational research: a practical guide*. New York: Routledge

Eacott, S. (2015) *Educational leadership relationally: a theory and methodology for educational leadership, management and administration*. Rotterdam: Sense.

Gillies, D. (2013) *Educational leadership and Michel Foucault*. Abingdon: Routledge.

Gunter, H.M. (2013) *Educational leadership and Hannah Arendt*. Abingdon: Routledge.

Murphy, M. (ed.) (2013) *Social theory and educational research: understanding Foucault, Habermas, Bourdieu and Derrida*. Abingdon: Routledge.

References

Anyon, J. with Dumas, M.J., Linville, D., Nolan, K., Pérez, M., Tuck, E. and Weiss, J. (2009) *Theory and educational research: toward critical social explanation*. New York: Routledge.

Connell, R. (2007) *Southern theory: the global dynamics of knowledge in social science*. Cambridge: Polity.

Day, C., Harris, A., Hadfield, M., Tolley, H. and Beresford, J. (2000) *Leading schools in times of change*. Buckingham: Open University Press.

English, F.W. (ed.) (2011) *The Sage handbook of educational leadership*, 2nd edn. Thousand Oaks, CA: Sage.

Foucault, M. (1980) *Power/knowledge: selected interviews and other writings, 1972–1977*, ed. C. Gordon, trans. C. Gordon, L. Marshall, J. Mepham and K. Soper. New York: Pantheon.

Freire, P. (1972) *Pedagogy of the oppressed*. London: Penguin.

Gunter, H.M. (2016) *An intellectual history of school leadership practice and research*. London: Bloomsbury Academic.

Harris, B. (2007) *Supporting the emotional work of school leaders*. London: Paul Chapman.

Harwood, V. and Allan, J. (2014) *Psychopathology at school: theorizing mental disorders in education*. Abingdon: Routledge.

Heffernan, A. (2018) *The principal and school improvement: theorising discourse, policy, and practice*. Singapore: Springer.

Morrison, M. (2009) *Leadership and learning: matters of social justice*. Charlotte, NC: Information Age Publishing.

Nixon, J. (2018) Becoming ourselves. *Teaching in Higher Education*, 23(7), 902–907.

Social Science Space (2013) Doreen Massey on space. *Social Science Bites*, 1 February. Available online: http://www.socialsciencespace.com/2013/02/podcastdoreen-massey-on-space/ (accessed 22 July 2020).

Thomson, P. (2017) *Educational leadership and Pierre Bourdieu*. Abingdon: Routledge.

Wenger, E. (1998) *Communities of practice: learning, meaning and identity*. Cambridge: Cambridge University Press.

Research methods in educational leadership

Scott Eacott and Gus Riveros

11

What this chapter is about   172

Key questions that this chapter addresses   172

Introduction   172

What are the ideological, historical, political and organizational contexts of research methods in educational leadership?   173

Technical details as legitimizing of research   179

The effects on professional practice of this understanding of research methods   180

What are the effects on understandings of educational leadership?   181

What needs to change to mitigate these issues?   181

Conclusion   184

Further reading   184

References   185

What this chapter is about

In this chapter, we examine the relations between theory and method and the implications these have for knowledge claims in educational leadership research. Our core argument is that educational leadership literatures tend to privilege method over methodology. This creates an artificial partition between theory, method and data. Attempts to be more scientific and apolitical are misdirected as they misrecognize the ways in which the underlying generative principles of research (e.g. ontology, epistemology, normative/ethical assumptions) play out through methods. Therefore, the frequent claim of employing a mixed-methods approach to overcome the weaknesses of quantitative and qualitative approaches confuses an empirical problem (needing multiple sources to strengthen knowledge claims) for a theoretical/methodological one (the nature of knowledge claims).

Key questions that this chapter addresses

1　Is it possible to discuss methods without theory?

2　How do the underlying principles of educational leadership speak to research traditions in the natural sciences and in the humanities?

3　What is the relationship between the selection of research methods and:

　a　ontology

　b　epistemology

　c　normative/ethical considerations?

Introduction

Educational administration and leadership research have frequently been critiqued for both a lack of scholarly quality and impact on practice. In arguing for more rigorous and robust knowledge claims, theory, method and practice are often discussed separately, as though they represent different stages of and choices about knowledge generation. The underlying generative principles of educational leadership research (also known as theory) exist in an enduring struggle between the natural sciences (seeking universal law-like generalizations for improving school outcomes) and the humanities (the particularism of schooling and communal trajectories). Matters such as ontology, epistemology, normative/ethical considerations and research traditions are discussed separately (if at all) to the selection of research methods for projects. If they are discussed, it is often limited to the somewhat artificial partitioning of quantitative, qualitative or mixed methods and then a parallel discussion of specific generation (e.g. questionnaire, interviews) or analytical (e.g. statistics) techniques.

Despite recent attention to research methods in educational leadership through books (e.g. Briggs, Coleman, and Morrison, 2012; Lochmiller, 2018), and special issues of *International Journal of Educational Management* (29(7)) and *Management in Education* (32(1)), there is a dearth of field-specific literature, with most of that work being picked up by more generic education-research texts (e.g. Green, Camilli and Elmore, 2006).

Compatibility thesis: the belief that the combination of qualitative and quantitative methods in research would provide a better understanding of social and educational phenomena.

Mixed methods: an approach to research that explicitly combines quantitative and qualitative approaches in a single study. This approach is only made possible through belief in the compatibility thesis.

Normative/ethical assumptions: in applied fields, all knowledge claims involve some form of assumption about what is fair, what is right and the moral justification of actions and beliefs.

Objectivity: the condition of being detached from any subjective influence or perception.

What are the ideological, historical, political and organizational contexts of research methods in educational leadership?

The establishment of educational administration in US universities during the early twentieth century consisted of courses taught by experienced (and often recently retired) school administrators and researchers from different disciplinary backgrounds – such as Ellwood Cubberley at Stanford who had a background in geology and physical science (Bates, 2010). In many ways, this trend met the criterion of work that had an impact on practice. However, what was missing was the establishment of a body of knowledge built on rigorous and robust knowledge generation.

This need was met by Frederick Winslow Taylor through his principles of scientific management. Taylorism was influential in early programmes in the United States, and its legacy continues. The attractiveness of Taylor's work was its focus on data generation (usually through stop watches / time and motion studies) and the pursuit of 'one best method'. Tasks were broken down into their smallest measurable units to establish the most efficient

Ontology: concerns the study of the nature, conditions and manifestations of reality and is usually discussed in terms of realism and relativism – but they are only two forms.

Research tradition: the inquiry lens of a research programme and/or study. Similar to, but more focused than a paradigm, a research tradition has an intellectual trajectory, canon and associated discourse community.

Subjectivity: the quality of including personal influences, perceptions and beliefs.

means of achieving effectiveness. Unlike trial and error or anecdotes from the field, there was a sense of credibility generated through the use of data and the perception of evidence-informed decision-making. This was still, however, very much a professional field rather than one with scholarly, or scientific, credibility within the academy.

The Theory Movement

Theory Movement: a significant, but US-centric, movement in educational administration in the mid-twentieth century that incorporated principles from logical positivism to the study of organizations.

A major development for research and research methods in educational administration and leadership occurred in the 1950s, with what became known as the Theory Movement and the pursuit of a science of educational administration built on logical empiricism.

Substituting trial and error or experience for what were perceived as objective scientific methods from the lab, the Theory Movement sought to establish credibility for the field. Jack Culbertson (1981), a key figure in advancing the Theory Movement, articulates four ideas that were fundamental to its claims: (1) effective research has its origins in theory and is guided by theory; (2) effective theory development requires the use of social and behavioural science concepts and modes of inquiry; (3) theory and research should concentrate on description, explanation, prediction; generalizations prescribing courses of action or specifying what administrators should do are beyond the purview of researchers and the capacity of science; and (4) the ideal exemplar of theory is found in hypothetico-deductive systems. However, in shaping the Theory Movement by concepts and modes of inquiry from mathematics, physics, chemistry and other well-established natural sciences, major questions were raised about the applicability for guiding study in a field of professional practice. A challenge that proved difficult to overcome for advocates of the Theory Movement was the extent to which the human element needs to be factored into the methods and methodology of the field.

Towards a proliferation of paradigms

In his famed 1974 Bristol paper for the International Inter-visitation Program, Thomas Barr Greenfield critiqued the US-centric Theory Movement and argued for a humane science of educational administration recognizing the power of subjectivity (see Greenfield and Ribbins, 1993). Although this critique was not well received by US-based scholars, it was far less controversial for those from the Commonwealth. This is not surprising, given stronger ties to the broader social sciences / humanities in countries such as the United Kingdom, Australia, Canada and New Zealand (e.g. Baron and Taylor, 1969). The divisions captured in the Theory Movement and Greenfield intervention are reflective of the paradigm or theory wars in administration and leadership research (e.g. Waite, 2002), which, while no longer as overt as during the late 1970s and early 1980s (a time when Bates was also advancing his Critical Theory of Educational Administration), continue to plague the field today through various collectives of scholars preferring particular forms of knowledge. However, despite the rise of many alternatives in recent years (e.g. postmodern/structuralist, social critical, relational, among others), there is relatively little dialogue about methods and methodology across positions in the field.

Although the paradigm wars have de-intensified, the aftermath has led to an artificial partitioning of research into quantitative (often considered interchangeable with objective) or qualitative (often linked with the subjective) categories. This simplistic separation of data form (e.g. numbers or texts) conflates generation with analysis. It also means that methods discussions are limited to an analytical dualism without serious engagement with the underlying generative principles that shape choices of methods and/or analysis. The contemporarily popular solution of using a 'mixed-methods' approach does not adequately engage with these underlying issues.

> **Epistemology:** concerns the nature of knowledge and the justification of belief.
>
> **Quantitative data:** expressed primarily through numbers, with a focus on measurement to establish causality, generalizability and replicability.
>
> **Qualitative data:** generated, primarily through words/text, with a focus on context to understand participant perspectives by valuing description and detail.
>
> **Paradigm wars:** a significant division in the education-research community during the early to mid-1980s, particularly between those advocating for quantitative and qualitative approaches.

'What works' rhetoric and research in educational leadership

Rather than attention to specific cutting-edge methods driving the agenda of educational administration and leadership research, it is the underlying generative principles of research that define the frontiers of knowledge generation. In the pursuit of intellectual credibility, the promotion of particular methods is based on alignment with what one believes to be truth(s) and quality knowledge. For those seeking law-like generalization with the potential to have greatest influence on policy and practice, there is a push for large-scale projects. While this is commonly linked to the trend towards big data and/or large data sets from national and international testing regimes, it is not necessarily limited to what are commonly labelled quantitative studies. For example, Leithwood in discussing the number of case studies that constitute the International Successful School Principals Project (ISSPP, arguably the longest running and largest study of school principals) notes: 'the number of cases being developed in some countries is beginning to appropriate sample sizes not uncommon in quantitative research. So we are nibbling at the lower edges of external validity within countries' (2005: 626).

Therefore, while the ISSPP has developed a standard protocol for generating case studies, and used methods (e.g. interviews, focus groups) traditionally aligned with qualitative data-generation strategies, it seeks to achieve legitimacy by appealing to the standards (e.g. external validity) of quantitative research. What is of paramount importance here is the underlying generative principles of research and appeals to truth. Case studies are very common in educational administration and leadership research. A scan of many journals confirms this observation. Arguably, the reason behind this frequency of case studies, and the common approaches of interviews and focus groups, is an appeal to the importance of context and participant voice (bringing in the human) in seeking to understand what works (and does not) in educational organizations.

An enduring tension for educational administration and leadership research methods is the desire to maintain a connection to practice as an applied field (the particular) and delivering insights as to what traits, behaviours, practices, conditions and so on are important for improving organizational outcomes across contexts (the universal). The perceived choice of methods is therefore not so much an interchangeable variable as it is often portrayed and instead is intimately part of the positioning of the research within broader research traditions.

What are the commonly held key features of this model?

The legacy of pursuing scientific credibility and impact on practice plays out through orthodox reporting approaches. Arguably symbolic of the systems thinking that is common in the field (without being explicitly recognized or acknowledged), methods, as with other aspects of research, are considered as malleable or interchangeable variables in project design. While relationships between the parts matter and are often the point of critique in theses/dissertations, journal submissions and funding applications, there remains a perceived distance between methods and other parts.

Artificially partitioning research into its constituent parts, reflective of Tayloristic approaches to management, leads to atomized discussions of what constitutes quality research. Aided by field writing conventions such as the 'structured abstract' used by some journals (e.g. *Educational Administration Quarterly*, *Journal of Educational Administration*, *International Journal of Educational Management*) to enhance the searchability of content through the online databases of the contemporary online academy, there is the perception that one simply chooses a method for a project. Methods, while aligned, are somewhat disconnected from the problem, theoretical resources, literature and analysis in ways that are unhelpful for researchers and audiences. The most obvious articulation of this default position is through the common structure of an academic paper:

Introduction → literature review → methodology → results→ findings → discussion → conclusion

While there is a pedagogical value in dividing research into sections both in writing and instruction, too frequently this leads to a silencing of the underlying generative principles of research – ontology, epistemology, normative/ethical assumptions. It is as if a research problem emerges outside of the lens through which the researcher (and others) view the world. This is further reinforced within training programmes, including those in doctoral programmes, often having explicit courses based on the quantitative and qualitative division and removing issues of generation and analysis from the origins of inquiry. The consequence of this model of training (and writing) is that methods are perceived as a choice, an interchangeable variable, rather than central to projects' genesis. The decoupling of theory and method is problematic. As Thomson argues:

'Choosing a method' presumes that the researcher has at their fingertips a wide range of research tools. This is not always the case. But let me assume for the sake of argument that it is. A further implication of 'just choose your methods' is that the researcher has total control of their decision. It is as if the choices that the researcher makes are free-floating, outside of disciplinary, institutional, spatial, national and discursive framings. Choice of methods is just a technical matter. There is no need for, or benefit from, a more critical interrogation of the workings of particular tools and approaches. *(2017: 216)*

The separation of theory and method has meant that appeals to rigour and robustness, and by virtue of greater scientific credibility, come through exhibitionism of data and procedure. In what is often argued for as greater transparency in the research process, the choice of method, the generation of data and its analysis are reported in fine detail in academic writing. However, minimal attention is paid to the genesis of inquiry. Not only why a question or topic is considered important, but why such a question was even possible.

Methods of data generation (e.g. questionnaire, interviews, among others) are not synonymous with methodology. The attribution of particular methods with notions of qualitative/qualitative or objectivity/subjectivity does little to explain the underlying generative principles of research. For example, while questionnaires are frequently granted the status of objective quantitative instruments, the creative enterprise that is the coding and (often many times) recoding of data in statistical software to meet analytical models is as, if not more, interpretive than reporting verbatim on interview (or other text) data and analysing it for or with themes. Similarly, textual analysis where words are counted for frequency – and arguably removed from context/meaning – is far more quantitative analysis than any form of interpretivist analysis.

Judgements about the quality of research and the appropriateness of research methods are less about the specific method and instead more concerned with coherence among the ontological, epistemological and/or normative/ethical assumptions of research and/or the person making the judgement.

The underlying generative principles of research (see Figure 11.1) are therefore of significant importance for understanding methods. In the fallout from the paradigm wars, particular methods have become synonymous with quantitative (e.g. questionnaires, large-scale data sets) or qualitative (e.g. interviews, focus groups, documents) research. Those aligned with a particular position are unlikely to engage with different perspectives.

Activity 11.1

With a critical focus on power relations, structure and agency, what are the:

1 ideological;
2 historical;
3 political; and
4 organizational functions of this model?

Figure 11.1 The
underlying gener-
ative principles of
research.

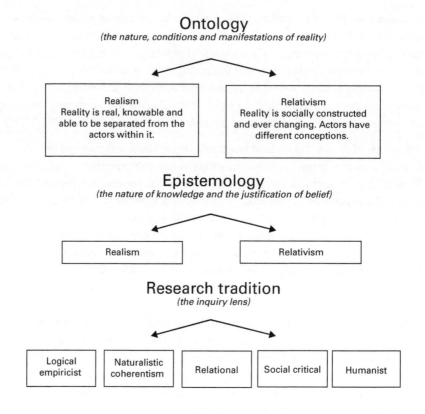

Common approaches for understanding and teaching about research traditions present them as distinct models of knowledge generation. In doing so, no particular tradition is intrinsically superior to others. Despite this, education administration and leadership research has shown a preference for some traditions over others. Such preferences are not permanent, however, because intellectual fields are sites of ongoing struggle over what is considered legitimate ways of knowing. For example, during the 1970s and 1980s, humanist approaches were more common following the critique of the Theory Movement. Currently, attempts to make practice 'evidence-based' (with evidence taken to be synonymous with objectivity) and somewhat standardized, combined with the perceived legitimacy and credibility of statistics, have resulted in privileging methods that provide generalizability over those focused on situatedness and context.

Journals exemplify this most obviously; not only through what gets published – signalling legitimation – but even in instructions to authors. For example, much like how the Theory Movement sought to establish value-free scholarship through objectivity and rigour, the *Journal of Educational Administration* (JEA) and *International Journal of Educational Management* (IJEM) – both published by Emerald – explicitly state 'Authors should avoid the use of personal pronouns within the structured abstract and body of the paper', going so far as to say that 'this paper investigates' is correct and 'I investigate' is incorrect. Their instructions establish a hierarchy of methods that privileges empiricism, noting that the category of conceptual papers is for work not based on research (narrowing what is meant by research to certain forms of empiricism), and that case studies are subjective and will not generally report on research. The empiricism implicit in such instructions grants greater value to work that involves research participants (e.g. question-naires, interviews) over other forms of data generation and analysis (e.g. document analysis).

Further legitimizing orthodox notions of scientific inquiry, many major international journals in educational administration and leadership (e.g. *International Journal of Leadership in Education, School Leadership and Management, Leadership and Policy in Schools, Journal of Educational Administration and History*) have instructions for authors that require submissions to be structured in the following order: title page, abstract, main text introduction, materials and methods, results, discussion, acknowledgements, declar-ation of interest statement, references and appendices. As with the previous example, this favours a particular type of research and, to some extent, methods. It may be possible to claim that these journals' instructions to authors are just default publisher (Taylor and Francis) statements (and a cursory scan of published papers may support this claim), as other publishers (e.g. Sage, which publishes *Educational Administration Quarterly* and *Educational Management, Administration and Leadership*) are far less prescriptive. However, *Critical Studies in Education* (another Taylor and Francis journal), explicitly states that it rejects generic headings for article sections (e.g. literature review, method-ology, findings, discussion) and instead wants articles with headings that 'reflect the substantive contribution of the section to the specific issue at hand (i.e. headings that reflect the articles' unfolding arguments)' and also a preference to see 'methodological issues discussed within an article's introduction rather than as a discrete section'.

Technical details as legitimizing of research

The separation of theory and method, combined with orthodox approaches to academic writing, means that research methods are reduced to a technical exercise. Textbooks and research training courses teach the technical skills of how to implement particular methods in ways removed from their guiding theoretical principles. The required structures from the major international journals cited earlier have no explicit reference to theoretical resources. Matters of ontology, epistemology and normative/ethical assumptions are silenced in preference for detailed technical descriptions of methods.

With policymakers desiring evidence to support their initiatives, the technical (over) reporting of research methods (as opposed to methodology) generates the appearance of sophisticated analysis – without the need for dense theoretical language. As educational leaders are viewed as a significant policy lever for activities, and with increasing fiscal pressures on governments, there is a desire to discover once and for all what works in schools. Although single-site or small-scale case studies persist in the field's journals, there is an increasing want for research that applies not a single case or small number of cases but to a large group of schools and/or individuals. Examples include Grover (Russ) Whitehurst's call for randomized controlled trials, following his term at the (US) Institute for Education Sciences, and the rise of meta-analysis (see Viviane Robinson's work on leadership and student outcomes) and mega-analysis (see John Hattie): all locate scientific credibility in the demonstration of high technical competence in executing methods.

While past attempts such as the importation of Taylorism into programmes and the Theory Movement have arguably failed to deliver on the promise, their legacy remains in how research methods are reported and legitimized (or not) in the contemporary field. Largely, significant outlets still explicitly prefer objective/value-free inquiry and empirical data generation (at scale) as a basis for quality research. Some localized small-size projects or non-empirical work is tolerated, but this is peripheral to the field's core work. Translating this knowledge generation into practice, preferably at scale, further legitimizes large-scale empirical work and cost-effective methods (e.g. questionnaires). The knowledge generated through such methods has a major influence on the impact of research on professional practice and our understanding of educational leadership.

The effects on professional practice of this understanding of research methods

The partitioning of theory, method and context leads to context-free knowledge. This is not to say that context is not considered, it often is – as a variable. Rather, technically competent execution of methods de-professionalizes the field by generating generic lists of desirables. An example is the international keynote cartel of educational leadership conferences. Putting aside whether such individuals do research (which is another issue entirely – but one important for the field), what remains as an argument is a list of traits, behaviours and practices that, at face value, are difficult to refute. Who does not believe that involving others in decisions that affect them will lead to better outcomes, or that without a vision of where you are going, it is tough to achieve it? However, such approaches rarely ask questions about what leadership is, or what others mean when they discuss leadership. What constitutes an effective, successful or improving school? Who gets to decide, and for what purposes? On what criteria are such decisions made? Are alternate perspectives valued, or even heard? Many of these issues are silenced without attention to the underlying generative principles at work. The technically competent researcher can answer a question but does not necessarily question the genesis or implications of the question. Much like narrowing research to the technical execution of methods, practitioners are reduced to problem-solvers rather than problem-generators. It reduces professional practice to getting better at what we are currently doing, rather than asking whether what we are currently doing is right. Without deliberate effort, social issues will not be resolved by simply problem-solving. Significant issues such as structural inequities, race, gender, ethnicity, sexuality and so on are limited to measurement variables and data points rather than being connected to a grounded and defensible position on what education is and can be.

What are the effects on understandings of educational leadership?

As with all professions, educational leadership research contains a sense of advocacy: some recognizes and acknowledges it and some does not. As theoretical inquiry becomes less significant in the formulation of research problems, technical skills become not only the means but also the end of research. When the problem and the focus of inquiry have been predefined through matters such as journal instructions, selective conferences, research training programmes, leadership standards and so on, the work of researchers turns from defining research problems to finding methods that validate existing ideas of legitimate knowledge-generation. If this is the case, then any sense of disciplinary knowledge becomes of secondary, if not peripheral, importance to technical skills. As a consequence, the uncritical adoption of the research object (e.g. educational leadership) and the privileging of technical methods skills have the potential to dissolve the field itself. Scholarship could be reduced to the development of measurement constructs and empirical findings that support claims for the purposes of interventions. Research becomes a servant of others, notably reproducing the social world as it is.

What needs to change to mitigate these issues?

To address the issues, we propose three recommendations: first, the need to explicitly articulate the underlying generative principles of research; the call for a greater social epistemology in the field; and finally, evaluating research on the basis of coherence.

As an initial intervention, an explicit requirement to articulate the underlying generative principles brings to the level of discourse the assumptions that shape knowledge generation. This apparent humanity is not a weakness but a strength in any pursuit of social science. Recognizing our own position makes it possible to look beyond the world as it is and contribute to different ways of understanding. Importantly, it facilitates locating claims within broader discourses and a means of explaining alternatives. This social epistemology is less concerned with the superiority of one set of claims over others, and more concerned with how knowledge claims contribute to advancing understanding. It means being willing to embrace the messiness of educational leadership and that there is no one-size-fits-all approach. The clarity of position through the explicit articulation of the underlying generative principles of research and locating work in relation to others means that research can be read accordingly. Contributions are no longer evaluated according to whether the work aligns with the audience's position, but rather according to its coherence. In other words, research should be judged on whether there is coherence between ontology, epistemology and normative/ethical assumptions into the theory of the subject, methods and claims. These are not separate parts that make a whole. Research is about coherence.

This coherence brings robustness to knowledge claims, which are then further advanced through locating claims within broader discourses (within and beyond the field). Research methods are simultaneously emergent from and constitutive of theory. We cannot think of them as separate.

Case Study 11.1 Lochmiller

As a case study of the argument we have been putting forward in this chapter, we focus on Lochmiller's (2018) *Complementary research methods for educational leadership and policy studies*. As a text, consists of eighteen chapters and totals 381 pages plus index. Published by a major international publishing house (Palgrave, an imprint of Springer), the contributors to the volume are, however, primarily US-centric (only four out of thirty-five contributors, including one ex-pat, are from outside the United States). As a contribution to the field (or discipline, as the editor refers to it), the text is described as presenting 'a variety of different qualitative and quantitative research methodologies and methods that collectively may be uniquely suited to unearthing the salient (dis)connections between policy and practice' (2018: 7). It is organized into three parts: qualitative and critical approaches; quantitative approaches; and mixed, applied and collaborative approaches. Once again, research methodologies and methods in the field are discussed in terms of generation and/or analytical processes rather than underlying theories.

Situated by the editor among recent comprehensive volumes describing research methods used in leadership, the overall intent of the text is to highlight the complementary nature of educational leadership and policy, and to illuminate possibilities for greater insights through methods. This is based on the idea that leadership and policy exist on a continuum and the pursuit of better methodologies and methods to investigate areas of mutual interest. Each chapter is intended to introduce a specific methodology or perspective, relate that to the field of leadership and policy and offer recommendations for those unfamiliar with methods discussed. As noted by the editor, the volume serves as:

> an introduction to various qualitative, quantitative, mixed, and applied research methodologies and methods, it should not be used as a substitute for an in-depth introduction to any particular methodology or method. Rather, scholars should treat this volume as a primer designed to assist them in considering which methods may be useful in conducting a study or program of research related to educational leadership and policy. *(2018: 11)*

Methods again are conceived of as a choice and technical matter rather than embedded and embodying of spatio-temporal conditions. Lochmiller goes on to suggest that reading the book might provoke some methodological questions such as 'considerations related to the design of the research study, including how the scholar will frame the study design, and the particularities of participant selection, data collection strategies, and the overarching analytical approach, as well as consideration of the potential limitations of the study relative to its questions or aims' (2018: 12). The difficulty here is that the underlying generative principles of leadership and/or policy are not explored. As a volume, there is far greater attention paid to matters of design than methodology. This is not to say they are missing. In the concluding chapter, Riehl argues that 'when researchers choose the methods they will focus on, they are usually choosing the discourse community within which they will work' (2018: 375). That said, the issue remains that methods are mostly discussed separately from the theory from which they emerge and of which they are constitutive – an issue that is enduring for texts on research methods.

A focus on research methods is difficult to sustain. Chapters are often written to develop the capacity of readers to technically execute the method. In doing so, methods become decoupled from theory. The limitation in this approach is similar to discussing educational leadership practice without context. Just as it is context that gives meaning to activities, it is theory that gives meaning to methods. Calls to expand our understanding by 'enlisting multiple, complementary methods to examine the increasingly complex context within which these issues are necessarily situated' and to 'utilize research methods in tandem to pull back the veritable "layers" of the issue, topic, or concern' (Lochmiller, 2018: vi) only make sense if coherent with the underlying generative principles or theory.

The question that we raise in this chapter is that you cannot think of methods without theory. The implications that this has for readers concern how we seek to read and evaluate research. Rather than applying a pre-existing orientation, or asking whether research aligns with our view, the explicit articulation of the underlying generative principles of research means that the most important criterion needs to be one of coherence. That is, are the methods mobilized consistent with the articulated theoretical position and the claims advanced?

Activity 11.2

Working with our argument that methods cannot be understood without theory, this activity is focused on taking notes from literature to build the basis for further research. As an analytical framework, choose articles you like (for whatever reason) from an educational leadership journal and make notes – possibly in a table or spreadsheet with each heading in a different column – on the ontological assumptions, epistemological assumptions, normative/ethical assumptions, theory of the subject, methods employed (sampling, data sources, measurement, timeframe) and causality implied. This is in addition to the usual content notes you make when reading. Constructing such a table will enable you to establish a very strong foundation from which to comment on, and contribute to, the literatures on your topic. It facilitates making comments on the methodological state of play while contributing to ongoing knowledge generation.

In addition, while thinking through the content, consider these questions:

1 What is the problem?
2 How is it conceptualized?
3 From what theoretical perspective?
4 What are the proposed solutions?
5 What is rejected?

This will further enable commentary on the state of the field or topic and on how your contribution adds to knowledge.

Conclusion

The key argument of this chapter is that you cannot discuss research methods without theory (see Chapter 10 of this textbook). Methodology at once emerges from and is constitutive of theory. In other words, theory is method and method is theory. Orthodox approaches to working with research methods centres on the notion that methods are a choice, related to but at a distance from theory and other aspects of research.

Educational leadership, management and administration (ELMA) as a field of as a field of inquiry has long sought scholarly credibility. This has resulted in an enduring tension between approaches to research that aspire to objectivity and value-free inquiry with more human-based means of understanding the work of schools and educational institutions. Discussions of research methods are therefore much more complex than quantitative, qualitative and mixed methods. Field-based practices, particularly publishing conventions, significantly shape what is and is not considered legitimate knowledge. However, embedded in all inquiry is a sense of advocacy. It is only by acknowledging our own underlying generative assumptions that we can relate to (not simply reject) alternatives and judge them on their coherence rather than their alignment with what we see as right.

Activity 11.3

We have argued for the importance of coherence among the espoused theory, methods and analysis of research in educational leadership. As a coherent piece of scholarship, the theoretical resources are at once constitutive of and emergent from the work. The key point for reflection when engaging with research centres on whether the work articulates a coherent methodology. Thinking back to a recent paper/chapter/book that you liked, or possibly even more productively, did *not* like, does it demonstrate coherence? What evidence is there for this (lack of) coherence? Furthermore, does the articulated position align with your own preferences or not?

Further reading

Eacott, S. (2013) Research as a political practice: the fallacy of data speaking for themselves. In S. Eacott and R. Niesche (eds), *Empirical leadership research: letting the data speak for themselves* (pp. 215–229). Niagara Falls, NY: Untested Ideas Center.

Evers, C.W. and Lakomski, G. (1991) *Knowing educational administration: contemporary methodological controversies in educational research*. London: Pergamon Press.

Burgess, D. and Newton, P. (eds) (2014) *Educational administration and leadership: theoretical foundations*. New York: Routledge.

Murphy, M. and Costa, C. (2016) *Theory as method in research: on Bourdieu, social theory and education*. New York: Routledge.

References

Baron, G. and Taylor, W. (eds) (1969) *Educational administration and the social sciences*. London: The Athlone Press.

Bates, R.J. (2010) History of educational leadership/management. In: P. Peterson, E. Baker and B. McGraw (eds), *International encyclopedia of education, volume 4*, 3rd edn (pp. 724–730). Oxford: Elsevier.

Briggs, A.R.J., Coleman, M. and Morrison, M. (eds) (2012) *Research methods in educational leadership and management*, 3rd edn. London: Sage.

Culbertson, J.A. (1981) Antecedents of the theory movement. *Educational Administration Quarterly*, 17(1), 25–47.

Green, J.L., Camilli, G. and Elmore, P.B. (eds) (2006) *Handbook of complementary methods in education research*. Mahwah, NJ: Lawrence Erlbaum.

Greenfield, T.B. and Ribbins, P. (eds) (1993) *Greenfield on educational administration: towards a humane science*. London: Routledge.

Leithwood, K. (2005) Understanding successful principal leadership: progress on a broken front. *Journal of Educational Administration*, 43(6), 619–629.

Lochmiller, C.R. (2018) *Complementary research methods for educational leadership and policy studies*. Cham: Palgrave Macmillan.

Thomson, P. (2017) A little more madness in our methods? A snapshot of how the educational leadership, management and administration field conducts research. *Journal of Educational Administration and History*, 49(3), 215–230.

Waite, D. (2002) 'The paradigm wars' in educational administration: an attempt at transcendence. *International Studies in Educational Administration*, 30(1), 66–81.

A historical deconstruction of leadership style

Fenwick W. English and Lisa Catherine Ehrich

12

What this chapter is about   188

Key questions that this
chapter addresses   188

Introduction   188

The research study   189

Researcher biography and
context in which research
is undertaken   195

How culture and context
shaped Lewin's social ideas   196

The long shadow of
confirmation bias in
leadership studies   198

Manipulations of results:
making the study come
out right   199

Further statistical and
rhetorical permutations   199

Conclusion   201

Further reading   201

References   201

What this chapter is about

In this chapter, we engage critically with the current popular notion of leadership style and its origins in an experimental study conducted by Lewin, Lippitt and White (1939). We argue that the research was deeply flawed in its design, the researchers held fundamental biases that they ensured were reflected in the results.

This chapter has two aims: to indicate how a deeply flawed social experiment led to a concept that was not supported by the actual results; and that all readers should learn to be critical about reading research in regard to design and recommendations regarding particular forms of leadership, and how it is transferred into educational settings. This chapter can be considered a case study of how the experiences of a researcher in growing up can lead to later scientific work that is biased toward a specific result. Lewin's life and work are thus a kind of biographical case study.

Key questions that this chapter addresses

1 What is leadership style?
2 What are the research origins of leadership style, and what critiques can be made of methodology and methods?
3 What are the implications of the flawed methodology and methods for the adoption of leadership style in education?

Introduction

One of the most common questions asked in an interview of a candidate for a leadership position is, 'What is your leadership style?' This question is most often asked with a definitive level of certitude, i.e. that such a thing as 'style' exists and is discernible, stable and independent of any situational context. The job of the interviewers is to take the stipulated 'style' and ask themselves if it is a 'good fit' to the context and situation they represent. The concept of **leadership style** is thus well established in the literature of educational leadership. Depending upon one's source there may be three, five, nine or even twelve such 'styles' today. Few practitioners or researchers know the actual history of leadership style as a concept, or the 'experimental studies of group life' conducted by famed German-American social psychologist Kurt Lewin (1890–1947) involving eleven-year-old boys engaged in 'theatrical mask-making for a period of three months' (Lewin, Lippitt and White, 1939: 271). This pioneering so-called scientific experimental study had enormous impact on educational administration as a field. Getzels, Lipham and Campbell explained that, 'We venture to say that, despite the unlikely source of the findings, no other psychological experiment so rapidly and completely captured the imagination of both students and practitioners of administration, perhaps especially of educational administration. The terms "democratic," "authoritarian," "laissez faire" became everyday words, democratic leadership being, of course, "good" and "authoritarian" leadership "bad"' (1968: 38).

This chapter re-examines the experimental study conducted by Lewin and colleagues (Lewin, Lippitt and White, 1939) and argues that it was deeply flawed in its design, was altered midcourse in its experimental conduct with no indication of such alterations when the study was reported in research journals of the time, and that the researchers held fundamental biases about how it should come out and made sure it did reinforce those biases at the study's end.

The research study

The research study which established the concept of 'style' was actually several studies conducted between 1937 and 1939, whose object was to conduct 'controlled experiments'. 'Control' meant one factor could be varied 'while holding other factors as constant as possible, it gives relatively clear evidence as to what is the cause of what' (White and Lippitt, 1960: 12). The first study was carried out by Ronald Lippitt under the supervision of Kurt Lewin (see Lewin and Lippitt, 1938). The design principle was to match two groups of experimental subjects as closely as possible so that the variance in outcome would be due to the leader's behaviour and to nothing else (see the definitions in the box).

The first experiment was set up with two groups of eleven-year-old boys and girls. The leader of the groups was Lippitt. In one group he played a 'democratic' leader and in the other group an 'autocratic' leader. There were five children in each group, and they met eleven times. There were five observers who took notes: 'The results consisted of the contrasting behavior of the two groups as recorded by these observers' (White and Lippitt, 1960: 13).

> **Leadership style:** 'the underlying need structure that motivates the leader's behavior in various interpersonal situations. In this theory of leadership style is a personality trait of the leader, a relatively enduring characteristic that is not directly observable; it is the pattern of needs that the leader seeks to fulfill interpersonal interactions' (Silver, 1983: 154).
>
> **Behaviour:** 'Every psychological event depends upon the state of the person and at the same time on the environment, although their relative importance is different in different cases. Thus we can state our formula $B = f(PE)'$ . . . . Behavior is a function of Personality in interaction with Environment' (Silver, 1983: 367).

The second experiment was modelled after the first with some variation (Lewin, Lippitt and White, 1939). One of the concerns of the first experiment was that the children's personalities were not well controlled. So in the design of the second experiment, only ten- or eleven-year-old boys (no girls) were participants. They were volunteers. To try and create equal conditions within the groups, before the clubs were organized:

the schoolroom group as a whole was studied . . . the interpersonal relations of the children, in terms of rejection, friendships, and leadership were ascertained. Teacher ratings on relevant items of social behavior (e.g. teasing, showing off, obedience, physical energy) were secured, and observations were made on the playground and in the schoolroom by investigators. The school records supplied information on intellectual status, physical status, and socio-economic background. *(Lewin, Lippitt and White, 1939: 272)*

In order to control for group behaviour, 'each group was studied in different social atmospheres so it could be compared to itself' (Lewin, Lippitt and White, 1939: 272). Another method was used 'to ensure that all of the groups had approximately equal degrees of cohesiveness, and of general social adjustment' (White and Lippitt, 1960: 18). Each group of the four groups was then subjected to 'five six-week periods of autocracy, five of democracy, and two of laissez-faire' leadership behaviours (or styles) (White and Lippitt, 1960: 22 and see Figure 12.1). The task before all of the groups was the creation of plaster masks.

Figure 12.1
Categorization of the types of behaviours in the leadership of each group. Adapted from Lewin, Lippitt and White (1939: 273).

Authoritarian	Democratic	Laissez-faire
The leader determines all aspects of policy	All policies were subject to group discussion and decision, encouraged and facilitated by the leader	No strictures on any individual or group to decide on any and all matters without leader input
The leader determined and dictated all of the steps and procedures to be performed with future steps not always indicated	Activity steps sketched out with suggestions by the leader of alternative steps where they might be required	The leader supplied materials and only provided information when prompted by the boys
The leader decided the nature of the work tasks and which boys would work with one another	Boys could work with anyone they desired and they decided the nature of the tasks of work to be undertaken	The leader avoided working directly with any specific group
The leader had a pleasant personality when rendering praise or criticism but chose to stay detached from becoming an active member of any group	The leader maintained a posture of objectivity in giving praise or criticism but did not do very much of the actual work of any group	Non-committal on group activities or choices unless directly questioned by the boys

The data gathered on the groups experiencing different leadership styles was laid out in Lewin, Lippitt and White (1939: 274):

1 a quantitative running account of the social interactions of the five children and the leader of each group, in terms of symbols for directive, compliant and objective (fact-minded) approaches and responses, including a category of purposeful refusal to respond to a social approach;

2 a minute-by-minute group structure analysis giving a record of: activity subgroupings, the activity goal of each subgroup initiated by the leader or spontaneously formed by the children and ratings on degree of unity of each subgrouping;

3 an interpretive running account of significant member actions, and changes in dynamics of the group as a whole;

4 continuous stenographic records of all conversation;

5 an interpretive running account of inter-club relationships;

6 an 'impressionistic' write-up by the leader as to what he saw and felt from within the group atmosphere during each meeting;

7 comments by guest observers; and

8 movie records of several segments of club life.

More data was produced when extra-club information was gathered, which consisted of interviews with each child during transition periods (when children went from one leadership style to another) and at the end of the experiment. Parents were also interviewed, as were teachers who were asked to comment on behaviour patterns acquired in a club. Every club member was given a Rorschach, or projective personality test. The amount of data gathered was staggering, especially in an age before computers. The experimental data was analysed and compiled. In the research journals in which the results were presented and discussed, the data displayed was fairly simple; simple graphs, bar charts and diagrams that showed the space of free movement possible in autocracy and democracy (Lewin, Lippitt and White, 1939: 292) and the rigidity of group structure as a tension factor in autocracy and democracy (Lewin, Lippitt and White, 1939: 294).

The researchers presented their results along two main themes. The first was an interpretation of sociological or group-centred data. The second was an interpretation of psychological or individual-centred data.

The researchers considered their second experiment satisfying because 'the leaders were successful in modifying their behavior to correspond to these three philosophies of leadership is clear on the basis of several quantitative indices' (Lewin, Lippitt and White, 1939: 278). They noted that 'the ratio of "directive" to "compliant" behaviour on the part of the autocratic leaders was 63 to 1; on the part of the democratic leaders it was 1.1. to 1' (Lewin, Lippitt and White, 1939: 278). Leader participation in the laissez-faire groups was less than half of those of autocratic or democratic.

The researchers noted a bimodal reaction of the boys to autocratic leadership. In some groups there were many acts of aggression. In other groups there was complete apathy. Their answer was that what looked like apathy was really 'bottled up tension' which was exhibited when the boys entered a transition from one atmosphere to another. The so-called apathetic boys in autocratic groups behaved wildly or at times when the autocratic leader stepped out of the room (White and Lippitt, 1960).

In summary, the average number of aggressive actions per meeting in the different atmospheres were given as follows (Lewin, Lippitt and White, 1939: 281):

- laissez-faire: 33
- autocracy (aggressive reaction): 30
- democracy: 20
- autocracy (apathetic reaction): 2.

Furthermore, when interviewed, the boys themselves (nineteen of twenty) preferred the democratic leaders.

When explaining the results of the matter of aggression, the researchers noted that there were two types, 'aggression within a group' or 'aggression against an outgroup' and 'Both kinds of aggression occurred in our experiments' (Lewin, Lippitt and White, 1939: 290). The researchers attributed these aggressions to a 'momentary emotional situation' (Lewin, Lippitt and White, 1939: 290). Four factors were observed to be behind these aggressions. One was tension within the group. A second was the space of free movement. A third was the rigidity of the group structure and the last was the culture of the group. When these factors interacted with one another the level of aggression was increased. It was noted that 'autocracy provided a much more rigid social group than democracy' (Lewin, Lippitt and White, 1939: 295).

The culture of a group determined how certain behavioural responses were permitted. The researchers compared such responses to 'habits'. In addition, they determined the cognitive structure within a given situation which was likely to have for any specific person was of primary importance because it 'determines under what conditions aggression will be, for the individual concerned' (Lewin, Lippitt and White, 1939: 296).

The researchers warned against any 'one-factor' theory of aggression. They claimed that 'it is the specific constellation of the field as a whole that determines whether or not aggression will occur' (Lewin, Lippitt, and White, 1939: 297).

In looking at the experiment as a whole the researchers observed that, 'The varieties of democracies, autocracies or "laissez-faire" atmospheres are, of course very numerous' (Lewin, Lippitt, and White, 1939: 297). However they balanced this admonition by saying that:

On the other hand, it would be wrong to minimize the possibility of generalization. The answer in social psychology and sociology has to be the same as in an experiment in any science. The essence of an experiment is to create a situation which shows a certain pattern . . . the generalization from an experimental situation should, therefore, go always to those life situations which show the same or sufficiently similar general patterns. *(Lewin, Lippitt and White, 1939: 287)*

The outcome of the two experiments was that in the first experiment:

hostility was 30 times as frequent in the autocratic as in the democratic group. Aggression was 8 times as frequent . . . In the second experiment, one of the five

autocracies showed the same aggressive reaction as was found in the first experiment. In the other four autocracies, the boys showed an extremely non-aggressive, 'apathetic' pattern of behavior . . . four types of evidence indicate that this lack of aggression was probably not caused by lack of frustration, but by the repressive influence of the autocrat.
(Lewin, Lippitt and White, 1939: 298)

How robust was the design of the experiments?

The first examination of the design of the 1938 and 1939 experiments warrants admiration for thoroughness and the intense effort to control all of the possible intervening factors that might provide a rival hypothesis to the principal ones being tested. Extraordinary efforts were made to match all of the groups as exactly as possible so that variations in the *leadership styles* and the reactions of the boys to them were the causative agents producing the observed patterns.

Yet by today's standards of experimental design, the experiments were deeply flawed. To determine the extent to which such flaws were present, the 1938/1939 experimental design was compared to Campbell and Stanley's (1963) work, 'Experimental and quasi-experimental designs for research on teaching' which was published in the first *Handbook of research on teaching* edited by N.L. Gage. In this work, Campbell and Stanley identified twelve common threats to valid inference from an experiment in education.

The basis of the Campbell and Stanley presentation was based on Fisher's (1925) work *Statistical methods for research workers*. In this, Fisher demonstrated that the best way to equalize groups in experiments was not by matching, but by randomization where groups were equated by chance and not by matching strategies, no matter how thorough or exquisite they might be.

Campbell and Stanley separated the design problems of experiments into those factors threatening **internal validity** and those involving **external validity.** The factors that are part of an experiment's internal validity constitute 'the basic minimum without which any experiment is uninterpretable' (1963: 175). Internal validity answers the question, 'Did the experimental treatments make a difference in this specific experimental instance?' (1963: 175). In contrast, external validity deals with generalizability and answers the question, 'To what populations, settings, treatment variables, and measurement variables can this effect be generalized?' (1963: 175)

Eight extraneous variables and the experimental design

Campbell and Stanley (1963) identified eight different types of extraneous variables that could compromise the internal validity of an experiment that might produce effects that are confounded with the experimental treatment. These are now reviewed with a commentary on the 1938/1939 leadership style experiments.

The first extraneous variable was **history**, the uncontrolled events that occurred between the first and second measurement in addition to the experimental variable. In the 1939 experimental study, the total length of time involved was three months. Each group was subjected to adult leader behaviour of autocracy, democracy and laissez-faire. Figure 12.1 shows the types of behaviours which comprised each cluster of behaviours or styles. We proffer that there was no mention by the researchers as to any specific historical events that might have impacted the children in their write-up in the research journals of the time. However, there were historical events going on in the time frame of the experiments that might have impacted the adult leaders and the oversight supervisor, Kurt Lewin. We will say more about this shortly.

The second extraneous variable that might be confounding the experimental variable was what Campbell and Stanley (1963) labelled **maturation.** This variable refers to the phenomenon that with the passage of time the respondents grow older, more tired, and perhaps wiser. This prospect is not acknowledged by the researchers. Each group of boys was subjected to the three behavioural packages (styles) but in different sequences. The research journals reported this sequential experiment as though it were freshly experienced for each group of boys. Over time between the treatments, however, the groups reacted differently and therefore they 'matured'. This possibility is actually encapsulated in the records within the patterns of responses. Patterns can only exist as a kind of repetitive response. We argue that maturation was part and parcel of the patterns which were the heart of the experiment.

The third extraneous variable was that of **testing**, meaning that the effects of testing were confounded in the boys' responses when they took tests a second time. There had to be learning from the first to the second testing. These went unreported in the research reported in the journals of the time.

The fourth variable that may impact the result of an experiment is **instrumentation.** This factor refers to 'changes in the calibration of a measuring instrument or changes in the observers or scorers used [which] may produce changes in the obtained measurements' (Campbell and Stanley, 1963: 175). This phenomenon occurred in the 1939 experiment when a new category of leadership style was created after the experiment was underway and the results did not adhere to the effects the researchers were after. It subsequently went unreported and unreferenced in the sharing of the results in the 1939 study (Billig, 2015: 455).

The other four possible inferential factors were **statistical regression, selection biases, experimental mortality** or **selection–maturation interactions**. *Selection bias* occurred because the participants were all boys, all volunteers and they were not included by randomization. Some boys did leave some of the groups and so there was *experimental mortality*. Finally, there was a strong likelihood of possible **multiple-treatment inter-ference** because all groups were subject to all of the leadership styles sequentially. The impact that these multiple treatments had on one another was unknown, whether singularly or collectively, compared to a group that experienced only one of the styles and no others (which would have been a control group).

Four factors jeopardizing external validity of the experiment

Four factors which could jeopardize the *external validity* or *representativeness* of an experimental design were: (1) **the reactive or interaction effect of testing** in which the respondents in the experiment because of their interaction with the test were less representative of the population of the universe who were not tested; (2) **the interaction effects of selection biases and the experimental variable**; (3) **the reactive effects of experimental arrangements** in which how the respondents behaved in the experimental environments would be different from persons exposed to the treatment in the absence of such arrangements; and finally (4) **multiple-treatment inferences** 'likely to occur whenever multiple treatments are applied to the same respondents, because the effects of prior treatments are not usually erasable' (Campbell and Stanley, 1963: 176).

The major design flaws in the 1939 experiment were the lack of randomization in the selection of the participants and the lack of a control group. In addition, we count at least seven possible confounding effects within factors pertaining to *internal validity* (*history, maturation, testing, instrumentation, selection biases, experimental mortality and selection–maturation interactions*) and at least two regarding *external validity* (*reactive effects of experimental arrangements, multiple-treatment interference*). These flaws and lack of controls may explain why when 'the study was subsequently replicated in other parts of the world, [they yielded] entirely different results' (Smith and Peterson, 1990: 9).

Perhaps the most glaring threat to generalization was researcher bias, i.e. the background of the researchers, particularly Kurt Lewin, and Lewin's connection to the events of the times – its *history*. Or in the words of Smith and Peterson, 'The researchers' decision to compare autocratic and democratic styles of leadership was an expression of their preoccupation with the political events of the late thirties. The impact of the study shows how widely shared were those preoccupations' (1990: 8).

Researcher biography and context in which research is undertaken

We intend examining the evidence base about leadership style by undertaking a case-study analysis of the key researcher. We do this because integral to critical research is the need to question the interplay between the agency of the researcher (e.g. status, values, education, assumptions) and the structuring context (e.g. the political and economic system in which research is designed, funded and reported on) in which projects are designed and completed. Let us briefly examine the background of the chief architect of the 1937–1939 leadership style studies, Dr Kurt Lewin.

Case Study 12.1 Biography of Kurt Lewin

Kurt Lewin was born in 1890 in Mogilno, a small village in Germany (now Poland) where his parents owned a general store. His father was well-respected in the Jewish community and for a time was head of the board of the local synagogue. Yet in the wider community and country, the family, like other Jewish families, were viewed as second-class citizens because of anti-Semitism. At that time, no Jewish person could own a farm, work in the civil service or be an officer in the military (Lewin, 1992). In a letter Kurt Lewin wrote to a colleague in 1933, he described Mogilno as a place where: '100% anti-Semitism of the coarsest sort was taken for granted, and constituted the basic stance, not only of the landed aristocracy, but also of the peasants in the surrounding area' (quoted in Lewin, 1992: 16).

In 1905, the family moved to Berlin, where Kurt and his siblings could gain a better education. After high school, Lewin started medical studies at the University of Freiburg. He then transferred to the University of Munich, and then the University of Berlin. He changed the focus of his study to psychology and philosophy. Lewin received his doctorate in 1914 and around the same time he, along with his two brothers, enlisted in the army. He served in France and Russia. He was wounded in August 1918 and spent eight months recuperating before being discharged (Lewin, 1992). While Lewin entered the war holding a strong love of his country, the war experience left him opposing militarism and German nationalism (Wheeler, 2008).

Following the war, he became an assistant at the Psychological Institute at the University of Berlin, establishing his academic career by publishing papers in the philosophy of science, and field theory (Lewin, 1992). Towards the end of the First World War, Lewin married a fellow doctoral student and they had two children. The marriage ended in divorce in 1927. His ex-wife and their two children emigrated to Israel a couple of years later owing to the impending Nazi threat. When Hitler became Chancellor in 1933, Lewin and his new wife and children left Germany and settled in the United States. His first position was at Cornell University. He spent considerable time during the war years applying for and gaining immigration papers for his relatives (Lewin, 1992). This was a challenging feat as the Immigration Act of 1924 restricted immigration for people from Eastern European countries (Wheeler, 2008). Lewin's mother and his mother's sister, along with many relatives on both sides of the family, died in the Holocaust (Lewin, 1992).

How culture and context shaped Lewin's social ideas

It is clear that Lewin's traumatic experiences in Germany as a Jew deeply influenced his life's work and in particular his 'leadership style' experiments:

> Selected aspects of his childhood, his education, his experiences as a combat soldier in World War I, and his experiences with anti-Jewish prejudice earlier in his life resulted in the unusual equalitarianism that so many people who knew him observed, as well as a

distinctive approach to psychology. The massive impact of fascism – the effect of his flight from Germany, his efforts to rescue his extended family, and the death of his mother in the Holocaust – greatly influenced his choice of and his approach to research problems. *(Lewin, 1992: 15)*

Lewin was said to have had a deep respect for democracy and democratic institutions. He believed that all nations, including Germany, would be better off if they turned to a democratic way of life (Lewin with Lewin, 1999 [1941]). Underpinning much of his work, especially that on group dynamics, organization development (OD) interventions, and action research are democratic principles of working with others and decision-making that is participatory and respectful of all individuals. Lewin said that:

> democracy is opposed to both autocracy and laissez-faire; it includes long-range planning by the group on the basis of self-responsibility; it recognizes the importance of leadership, but this leadership remains responsible to the group as a whole and does not interfere with the basic equality of rights of every member. The safeguard of this equality of status is the emphasis on reason and fairness rather than personal wilfulness. *(Lewin with Lewin, 1999 [1941]: 325)*

That Kurt Lewin chose social psychological research that enabled him to pursue fundamental human concerns and social problems is not surprising. It can be argued that most researchers choose research topics that hold personal interest for them or reflect their ideologies or values. Thus, research can have an 'autobiographical' element. Lewin's supervision of the classic studies relating to what became known as leadership style were conducted in the time period 1937–1939. It is instructive to see what *historical events* were occurring in Europe during that same time period and how these events shaped his life and work. Some of these events are shown in Activity 12.1.

Activity 12.1

1933   Adolf Hitler appointed German Chancellor
1933   Hitler granted dictatorial powers – Enabling Law
1933   First concentration camps erected by the Nazis in Germany
1933   Boycott of Jews begins in Germany
1938   Hitler appoints himself War Minister; pogroms in Germany
1938   Anti-Jewish legislation enacted in Italy
1939   Germany occupies Bohemia and Moravia, places Slovakia under 'protection' and renounces non-aggression pact with Poland
1939   Germany invades Poland
1940   German invades Norway and Denmark
1940   German troops enter Paris
1941   Germany invades Russia; Jews rounded up and killed

Kurt Lewin and his family suffered much in the rise of Nazism in Germany.

Reflect on how these events may have left him with a pervasive anti-authoritarian bias to the point where he shaped his experimental studies to reinforce those biases.

How was this historical background most likely an example of what researchers call 'confirmation bias' in conducting an experimental study?

Have you experienced this in any other reading about leaders, leading and leadership? For example, much research assumes that there are no social injustices or discrimination in educational organizations (e.g. gender, race, class, sexuality). Examine a leadership theory that interests you and consider what assumptions the researchers have made that limits the validity of the theory.

We posit that Lewin's experience with the Nazis and the rise of anti-Semitism in Germany, and his deep love and respect for democracy and the United States, created a bias in his interest in studies of autocracy and democracy and created the aura of *history* as a long-standing bias, if not inclination, towards favouring democracy. We present evidence to this effect in the next section.

The long shadow of confirmation bias in leadership studies

Billig (2015) performed a penetrating analysis of the Lewin-directed leadership studies. First, he noted that Lewin and colleagues used ordinary language that included binary opposites in framing their research. Billig observed that Lewin 'was, of course, a refugee from an anti-democratic, autocratic regime and his writings about social conflict reflected his deep concern with the dangers of fascism and the need to establish democratic principles in practice' (2015: 445).

Lewin used the words *democracy, democratic atmosphere* and *democratic style of leadership* interchangeably and according to Billig he assumed that 'the democratic atmospheres and styles, that they were observing, were actually democratic, rather than being democratic appearances that hid non-democratic realities' (2015: 445–456).

Instead of basing their key concepts on psychological theories, Lewin and colleagues used their everyday understandings and values about them in their work. They thus failed to interrogate their own ideology about what they were observing. They took their so-called 'natural' language as non-political.

Furthermore, a close examination of what the so-called democratic leader actually did in the boys' groups indicated that they did not always let the boys decide on all matters. What was discussed was determined by the leader, not the boys. Notes Billig, 'If this was a "democracy", it was a very limited democracy, for power firmly resided in the hands of the adult leaders' (2015: 447).

In order to protect the integrity of the experimental conditions, the adult leaders had to be sure they behaved in the appropriate fashion and what was 'democratic' and 'autocratic' were consistent. It seems that: 'this led to a paradox . . . sometimes democratic leaders were more controlling than authoritarian leaders when they sought to control what they considered to be undemocratic behaviour' (Billig, 2015: 447). However, 'by contrast, the autocratic leaders could not be too autocratic, because, in order to be successful experimenters, they had to permit the children to behave freely' (2015: 447). Given that democracy was 'good' and 'authoritarian' was bad, 'It was in the interests of the experimenters to let the participants behave badly in the autocratic groups' (2015: 447).

Manipulations of results: making the study come out right

In the second 1939 study (Lewin, Lippitt and White, 1939), a situation arose where in one democratic group the boys became so unruly that the situation nearly went out of control. The group was not behaving as 'a well–integrated democracy' (White and Lippitt, 1960: 110). One boy in particular treated the democratic leader as an equal. This led to an undemocratic atmosphere. The researchers considered this a threat that democracy was being erased and this prospect provoked White and Lippitt to fear 'that the behavior of this group in the democratic condition was threatening the success of the experiment, because democracy did not seem to be emerging well' (1960: 455). The possibility that democracy was not going to come out well in this instance created a problem for the researchers. According to Billig, Lewin saved the day. 'He suggested that White had been allowing the boys too much freedom and that his leadership should not be called "democratic" but "laissez-faire". The team decided to build White's style into the experimental design by running further laissez-faire groups' (2015: 450).

This singular change in the second experiment was never mentioned in the journal reports. The way the journal presented this occurrence was that the experiment involved three 'leadership styles' and subsequent narratives reported that the addition of 'laissez-faire' 'had been planned in advance' (Billig, 2015: 450). The addition of a new category saved the **democratic–autocratic binary** and it saved an anarchic democratic group from being called 'democratic' when it was clearly not democratic. 'Thus, Lewin protected the concept of "democracy" rhetorically, attributing the bad results to a form of non-democratic leadership' (Billig, 2015: 450).

Further statistical and rhetorical permutations

A further act of relabelling study results occurred in the reporting of aggressive behaviour by leadership style. The common wisdom that appears in textbooks regarding behavioural aggression indicates that there was more aggressive behaviour in the authoritarian-led groups (Stogdill, 1974).

Some manipulation of the aggression of the participants occurred to smooth out and retain the notion that aggressive reactions to authoritarian leadership were higher than anywhere else. Lewin, Lippitt and White (1939) showed that 'autocracy' had two scores. Had there been only one such score the mean would have been 7.5 which would have been lower than democracy which was 20. In order for democracy to be lower than autocracy, the aggression index was set at 30 with the apathetic reaction within autocratic groups at 2. The rationale for having two groups labelled autocracies enabled the aggressive actions to be viewed negatively instead of terms such as 'non-aggressive autocracies' or even 'peaceful autocracies' (Billig, 2015: 451). In this manner, there were no positive results within the autocratic groups. Contrary comments were made such as by Lippitt and White, who wrote that it was 'interesting to find nearly as high a level of interpersonal friendliness in the authoritarian situations as in the democratic and laissez-faire situations' (1958: 504).

There are many more questions that this historical deconstruction raises in the conduct of social-science research. Activity 12.2 raises some additional issues relative to studying a variety of leadership dimensions in work settings. You may complete this on your own, but if you are working in a class setting, select one as a group activity and report back after your conversation.

Activity 12.2

There are issues about the transferability of leadership styles from this project into a school or university context. Think about the experiments conducted by Lewin and colleagues into leadership styles which involved children in contrived situations and compare to the type of activities undertaken by educational professionals who are currently working in educational and/or other types of organizations.

1 Explain how the complexity of the work tasks and the clarity of outcomes work to create different types of leadership requirements in the experimental situation compared with the real-life working context. Even in a real-life working context there is a difference between manufacturing and a service that is based on human interactions.

2 For example, think about how the production of a car might be different from putting a person on the Moon. When contextual ambiguity is a significant factor in a work environment, what are the requirements for effective leadership versus producing a number of predesigned products per hour or per day?

3 Now develop a new formula which captures your discernment beyond that developed by Kurt Lewin in his formula B=f (PE) (that behaviour is a function of the person, including their history, personality and motivation, and their environment, which encompasses their physical and social environment).

Conclusion

The result of these early and fundamental experimental studies of what became known as 'leadership style' is that 'leadership studies have been simplified into a moral fable, in which democracy was shown to be "good" and autocracy "bad". It does not matter whether the levels of aggression are reported as being high or low under autocracy, the results are morally similar in that autocracy is found wanting' (Billig, 2015: 452).

Compared to the research of the times, the Lewin, Lippitt and White's experimental studies of the 1930s were complex and multifaceted, and appeared to have tight controls via matching that tended to support the researchers' contention that they could discern patterns by controlling extraneous sources that might invalidate or compromise those patterns. Unfortunately, matching does not result in the kind of rigorous control that is obtained via randomization of selection.

But perhaps the most pernicious outcome of the Lewin, Lippitt and White experiments was the oversimplified notion of leadership style itself. Even more, the concept of 'leadership style' was born, which encapsulated the idea that a single, coherent, stable cluster of behaviours could be identified and one such cluster could be identified as superior over all others in all situations. Only the most unsophisticated leadership advocates would hold such naive views today, though there are still managerial consultants hawking those same simplistic bromides with different names. Caveat emptor!

Further reading

Argyris, C. (1972) *The applicability of organizational sociology*. London: Cambridge University Press.

English, F.W. and Ehrich, L.C. (2016) *Leading beautifully: educational leadership as connoisseurship*. New York: Routledge.

Galbraith, J. (1973) *Designing complex organizations*. Reading MA: Addison-Wesley.

Niesche, R. (2014) *Deconstructing educational leadership: Derrida and Lyotard*. Abingdon: Routledge.

Temes, P.S. (1996) *Teaching leadership: essays in theory and practice*. New York: Peter Lang.

References

Billig, M. (2015) Kurt Lewin's leadership studies and his legacy to social psychology: is there nothing as practical as a good theory? *Journal for the Theory of Social Behaviour*, 45(4), 440–460.

Campbell, D.T. and Stanley, J.C. (1963) Experimental and quasi-experimental designs for research on teaching. In: N.L. Gage (ed.), *Handbook of research on teaching* (pp. 171–246). Chicago: Rand McNally.

Fisher, R.A. (1925) *Statistical methods for research workers*. Edinburgh: Oliver & Boyd.

Getzels, J.W., Lipham, J.M. and Campbell, R.F. (1968) *Educational administration as a social process: theory, research, practice*. New York: Harper & Row.

Lewin, K. with Lewin, G. (1999 [1941]) Understanding the child. In: M. Gold (ed.), *The complete social scientist: a Kurt Lewin reader* (pp. 321–325), Washington, DC: American Psychological Association.

Lewin, K. and Lippitt, R. (1938) An experimental approach to the study of autocracy and democracy: a preliminary note. *Sociometry*, 1(3–4), 292–300.

Lewin, K., Lippitt, R. and White, R.K. (1939) Patterns of aggressive behavior in experimentally created 'social climates'. *The Journal of Social Psychology Bulletin*, 10(2), 271–299.

Lewin, M. (1992) The impact of Kurt Lewin's life on the place of social issues in his work. *Journal of Social Issues*, 48(2), 15–29.

Lippitt, R. and White, R.K. (1958) An experimental study of leadership and group life. In E.E. Maccoby, T.M. Newcomb and E.L. Hartley (eds), *Readings in social psychology*, 3rd edn (pp. 496–511). New York: Holt Rinehart and Winston.

Silver, P. (1983) *Educational administration: theoretical perspectives on practice and research*. New York: Harper & Row.

Smith, P.B. and Peterson, M.F. (1990) *Leadership, organizations and culture: an event management model*. London: Sage.

Stogdill, R.M. (1974) *Handbook of leadership: a survey of theory and research*. New York: Free Press.

Wheeler, L. (2008) Kurt Lewin. *Social and Personality Psychology Compass*, 2(4), 1638–1650.

White, R.K. and Lippitt, R. (1960) *Autocracy and democracy: an experimental inquiry*. New York: Harper.

Distributed leadership

Howard Youngs and Linda Evans

13

What this chapter is about   204

Key questions that this chapter addresses   204

Introduction   204

The conceptual development of distributed leadership   208

Process thinking and distributed leadership   210

Applying a social critical understanding of distributed leadership   212

Researching distributed leadership   217

Conclusion   217

Further reading   218

References   218

What this chapter is about

In this chapter, we argue that leadership is a phenomenon across and between multiple people, inclusive of and beyond organizational roles labelled as managers or leaders. In this chapter, we draw from the leadership studies field and the field of educational leadership, management and administration (ELMA). We introduce you to entitative thinking, with its emphasis on individual people, process thinking and what these mean for how we make sense of leadership. These ways of thinking inform the four perspectives of distributed leadership discussed in this chapter. The four perspectives are:

- **Entitative-Formal:** leadership is role-based and distributed by managers to others
- **Entitative-Informal:** leadership is not restricted to management roles and the notion of leader and follower is interchangeable for individuals throughout an organization
- **Process-Formal:** leadership is a process emerging from the practices distributed amongst those in management roles
- **Process-Informal:** leadership is a process that emerges from the practices distributed across an organization.

Key questions that this chapter addresses

1 How do our implicit leadership theories inform our assumptions related to distributed leadership?

2 How do entitative thinking and process thinking inform different ways of understanding distributed leadership?

3 Why has distributed leadership become a dominant theoretical viewpoint in educational leadership scholarship?

4 What is a social critical understanding of distributed leadership, and how can this understanding be applied to practice and research?

Introduction

Distributed leadership is positioned alongside other post-heroic concepts in the Leadership Studies field, such as: shared leadership; collective leadership; dispersed leadership; democratic leadership; collaborative leadership; relational leadership; and team-centric leadership. Post-heroic concepts are an alternative to leader-centric theoretical viewpoints, such as transformational and charismatic leadership, behavioural and trait/style-based theories that 'personify' leadership (Evans, 2018): that is, they emphasize the study of those individuals labelled as leaders and they rely on the construction of others as 'followers' or subordinates. Post-heroic concepts represent an evolving addition to decades of leader-centrism where leadership theory and research have been restricted to focusing on those in executive and team manager roles, as well as individuals positioned by others or themselves as exceptional. In acknowledging that leadership may be enacted by people who do not necessarily hold designated management roles, post-heroic concepts partially remove restrictions on who may be considered a leader, and they also open up the possibility of understanding leadership as a process emerging in between people and non-human elements. In this chapter, we are using the definitions set out in the box.

To limit confusion between the terms leader and manager, we use 'manager' to represent someone in a formal role of organization-wide or team responsibility. This frees us up to use 'leader' to convey decoupling from formal organizational roles. For example, organizational members may position, or consider, as a leader a colleague who has no designated organizational role that carries the formal title of manager, leader, management or leadership.

Leader-centric: the focus of leadership is on individuals who usually hold a designated management role.

Post-heroic: leadership is not restricted to those in a designated management role.

Entitative thinking and leadership: leadership is assumed to have stable material existence in individuals.

Process thinking and leadership: leadership is a temporal organizing and direction-forming process.

Entitative thinking: places leadership residing in individuals as a prerequisite for practice direction, whereas **process thinking** places leadership as an emergent and consequential component of practices. This distinction between leadership as a prerequisite for practice and leadership as a consequence of practice has implications for how we think about distributed leadership.

Activity 13.1

To understand distributed leadership, you need to be clear about your own understanding of what leadership is. Only then can we consider what is actually being distributed or is already in a potentially distributed state. Over the years you have formed and reformed your own implicit leadership theory – that is, who or what you consider a leader and leadership to be. We encourage you to go beyond a surface response to the activities suggested below, and to the questions posed.

Take time to reflect on your own definition of leadership.

1 How might you best represent or convey this definition – in writing, for example, or as a drawing?
2 How and why have you come to form this understanding?

In this chapter, we refer to four perspectives of distributed leadership. One or more of these four perspectives may reflect your own implicit leadership theory. To map these four perspectives of distributed leadership, we discuss different ways of thinking about leadership. This will help you locate your implicit leadership theory in relation to these differing perspectives of distributed leadership. Distributed leadership has become a dominant theoretical viewpoint in education, and in the following section we identify factors that have contributed to its popularization. These factors, in addition to the four perspectives, illustrate the complexity and diversity of distributed leadership as a concept. In the final sections we develop a critical understanding of distributed leadership, engage you with a case study, and conclude with recommendations for socially critical practice and research.

Activity 13.2

At the mention of 'leadership', what initially comes into your head? Do you think of a person or people – real or imaginary – whom you categorize as a leader or leaders? In other words, do you assume leadership has material existence in individuals? Such thinking represents what we label as entitative thinking, where our subjective view of others gives primacy to emphasizing leaders over leadership, or to assuming that leadership and leaders are interchangeable terms. This primacy usually involves associating some form of exceptionalism to an individual, irrespective of her or his organizational role, with an expectation that this individual is able to influence others and is consequently labelled a leader. These leaders are assumed to be the catalyst for leadership practices and can be made even more distinct through labelling others – those not considered as leaders – as 'followers'.

We encourage you to think outside a 'box' that involves automatically 'personifying' leadership through entitative thinking. We want to encourage you to shift towards adopting process thinking, which avoids personifying leadership, by avoiding the assumption that leadership resides in a select group of exceptional individuals. Process thinking assumes that leadership emerges from practices involving two or more people, and these need not necessarily hold designated or recognized management or leadership roles. Evans sums up this viewpoint, 'leadership is pervasive and reciprocal' (2018: 251). This alternative understanding interprets leadership as an active verb, associated with direction-forming as a continuous process that is not restricted to an executive or management group at the apex of an organization's formal role structure. Within such a formal structure the notion of middle leader or middle manager emerges, and leadership is viewed as a formal role to which a person may aspire and so seek promotion. Such explicitly recognized roles make up the formal aspect of an organization. In addition to this is the informal aspect of an organization, where the nomenclature of leader, leading and leadership is not confined to formal role structure. Such informal leadership is decoupled from association solely with specific executive, senior and middle organizational management-focused roles.

The coming together of entitative thinking, process thinking, formal and informal aspects of an organization can help us understand and critique the notion of distributed leadership using a 2 × 2 matrix that reveals four perspectives (see Figure 13.1). **Entitative-Formal (EF)** and **Entitative-Informal (EI)** are based on the assumption that leadership

PROCESS THINKING
Leadership as process

Figure 13.1 Four perspectives of distributed leadership.

PROCESS-FORMAL (PF)

Leadership is a process that emerges from practices distributed amongst those in pre-defined groups of 'leaders'. These groups are based on formal organizational management/ leadership structures.

PROCESS-INFORMAL (PI)

Leadership emerges from practices. This leadership emergence may occur anywhere in an organization and is not restricted to the practices of any one group.

ENTITATIVE-FORMAL (EF)

Leadership is role-based and the aggregation of tasks and responsibility is governed by predefined groups of 'leaders'. These groups or managers can choose to distribute these 'leadership' role responsibilities to others.

ENTITATIVE-INFORMAL (EI)

Leadership is associated with individuals irrespective of role, who influence others. Here the notion of leader and follower is interchangeable for individuals distributed throughout an organization.

FORMAL ORGANIZATION
Leadership is associated with predetermined roles

INFORMAL ORGANIZATION
Leadership is not restricted to role type

ENTITATIVE THINKING
Leadership has material existence in individuals

has material existence in an individual, whereas **Process-Formal (PF)** and **Process-Informal (PI)** assume leadership is an emergent process.

Entitative-Formal (EF) and *Process-Formal* (PF) restrict the source of leadership to those in organizational roles usually labelled 'leader' and/or 'manager', and to teams that have leadership and/or management in their titles and/or imply expected collective responsibilities. *Entitative-Informal* (EI) and *Process-Informal* (PI) unhinge leadership from the role-based restrictions informing EF and PF.

Activity 13.3

To recap, compare your own definition of leadership with the four perspectives in Figure 13.1.

1   What perspective or perspectives are evident in your definition?
2   Have any of the four perspectives challenged your way of thinking about distributed leadership? If so, can you identify why this is so?

The conceptual development of distributed leadership

Distributed leadership originates in the leadership studies field and has been a mainstream concept in the education field since the turn of the millennium. Gronn (2008) reveals how leadership, as a dispersed rather than an individual property, had its origins in the research of group practices in the 1950s. This is important because power relations, practices and direction in an organization can differ from group to group. Simplifying and homogenizing distributed leadership to a one-size-fits-all concept in an organization results in glossing over the complexity of differing relations and practices in groups (Youngs, 2014). This is a point we will pick up on later in the chapter.

Most education researchers, when discussing the conceptual development of distributed leadership, refer to the works of Gronn (2002) and to Spillane (2006), who independently of each other published conceptual frameworks around the start of the millennium. These frameworks endeavour to bring a 'distributed perspective' (Spillane, 2006: 2) and unit of analysis (Gronn, 2002) to understanding leadership practice beyond leadership that is only attributed to those in formal organizational roles. An intention of their frameworks is to widen our understanding of distributed leadership from being limited to the functional distribution of leadership responsibilities by managers evident in the EF perspective of Figure 13.1.

Gronn's distributed framework has two components: the aggregation of leadership across more than one organization member, and conjoint agency as a form of distribution. The latter he describes (2002) as concertive action, in the form of:

- spontaneous collaboration;
  - anticipated through prior planning; or
  - unanticipated;
- intuitive working relations that emerge over time and are dependent on trust; and
- institutionalized or regulated practices.

Leadership activity is described by Gronn (2002) as being situated interdependently across at least two people whose responsibilities are complementary or overlapping. Spillane (2006) includes interdependencies in his description of distributed leadership practice that can be:

- collaborated distribution that involves reciprocal interdependencies;
- collective distribution where routines are pooled and co-performed but not at the same place or time; and
- coordinated distribution of sequentially arranged leadership tasks.

Spillane (2006) describes leadership as a distributed practice that stretches over the interactions of leaders, followers and the situation. Gronn has argued against one aspect of Spillane's conceptualizing, saying a leader–follower distinction is unhelpful because it implies there is less influence with the follower compared to the leader.

Activity 13.4

Consider your own thinking about distributed leadership.

1 Is your thinking reliant on the construction of some people as leaders and others as followers?
2 Is any distinct labelling of leaders and followers fixed to or associated with individuals, or is the labelling of leader and follower interchangeable across individuals?
3 To what extent does organizational structuring of roles sustain any distinct labelling of leaders and followers?

These questions are based in entitative thinking, where we locate leadership in an individual, so such thinking is associated with entitative perspectives (EF, EI) of distributed leadership (see Figure 13.1).

Since the publication of Gronn's unit of analysis for understanding leadership practice and Spillane's distributed perspective of leadership practice, there has been a proliferation of commentary and of research studies related to distributed leadership, especially in education. This increase can be attributed to four factors. As we explained in our introduction, distributed leadership is one of a number of post-heroic concepts, where theoretical concepts in the leadership studies field are no longer only distinguished by the elevation of individual leader figures and leader-centric thinking. The first factor is that distributed leadership has been part of the post-heroic evolution in the leadership studies field. Distributed leadership can imply a shift away from associating leadership only with an exclusive group and towards thinking of it as a more inclusive and organization-wide practice. Second, this implied inclusiveness can appeal to those who value democracy and assume distributed leadership can be a means to address inequalities and unjust power differentials (Woods and Roberts, 2018). Distributed leadership can then, albeit uncritically at times, be positioned as an antidote to the exclusion of organizational members in decision-making processes and direction-forming. The remaining factors are related to shifts in education.

The third factor is it was inevitable that distributed leadership, or some form of post-heroic leadership, should become popular in education. With the advent of New Public Management (NPM) reforms in the 1980s and 1990s, greater attention in education went on efficiency, effectiveness and economy. Education reforms included governments adopting, to differing degrees, the marketization of education and greater emphasis on performativity measures. The subsequent intensification of work for those in formal management roles at or near the apex of hierarchical organizational structures, with no increase of staffing, meant it was inevitable there would be a flow on of new work to others further down and across organizational structures to meet performative demands (Youngs, 2009). To some extent the delegation of the new work, sometimes labelled leadership, has contributed to the popularization of the EF perspective in Figure 13.1, especially in Ministry and Department of Education documents emphasizing improvement.

The fourth factor is related to the growing emphasis on collaborative work practices. These have contributed both to a wider, and sometimes new, distribution of leadership work due the coordination, direction and reporting associated with these practices, and to the rise of terms such as teacher leadership. For example, school networks have broadened their interpretations of leadership work beyond activity confined within the school to activity that involves collaboration with other schools. Teacher collective efficacy, where teachers believe their collective efforts improve student learning, and collaborative teacher inquiry, where teachers support each other with inquiries to improve student learning, also contribute to the emphasis on collaborative work practices. Collective and collaborative practice is also evident with the emphasis in some nations on developing and maintaining Professional Learning Communities (PLCs). In higher education, there is a growing hybridization of work carried out by professional and academic staff, along with the creation of roles that span professional and academic work (Youngs, 2017). The utilization of multiple teachers collaborating in one larger teaching space – as can occur in early-years education – is also becoming evident in schools, and is associated with terms such as Innovative Learning Environments and Flexible Learning Spaces. Collective and collaborative work practices can, on the one hand, provide opportunity for us to understand leadership as a phenomenon across and between multiple people, inclusive of and beyond positional leaders, especially in relation to the process perspectives (PF and PI in Figure 13.1). On the other hand, collaboration can become a mandatory practice through policies that expect organizations and education professionals to work together, where they have had little or no say in the configuration of such collaborative arrangements. The enactment of such policies may use inclusive terms like distributed leadership, and they may encourage the positioning of those in roles at the apex of an organization's structure as distributors of leadership work and as assumed enablers of collaborative practice. In such cases, distributed leadership is aligned to the EF perspective in Figure 13.1.

By now, you will see that there are various ways of understanding distributed leadership; no one definition encompasses the four perspectives we introduced earlier. The factors contributing to the popularization and conceptual development of distributed leadership are also diverse and sometimes contradictory. You may have read literature on distributed leadership – some conceptual and some research studies of practice. Our own reading of the distributed leadership literature shows that much of it is aligned to the entitative perspectives, EF and EI. In the following section, we argue that more research studies need to be informed by process thinking, with emphasis on the PI perspective.

Process thinking and distributed leadership

There are calls in the leadership studies field for a greater emphasis on processual studies of leadership. We have deliberately developed the two process perspectives (PF and PI) in Figure 13.1 so they are in contrast to most understandings of distributed leadership that assume entitative thinking. This brings us to the crucial question: what is leadership, and how can I recognize it when it is occurring? If our response gravitates towards entitative thinking we are then susceptible to focusing on the behaviours and traits of individuals, where leadership has its substance in an individual. Process thinking shifts our focus away from such 'personification' of leadership (Evans, 2018) and 'into a conceptual terrain of events, episodes, activity, temporal ordering, fluidity, and change' (Langley et al., 2013: 10). This shift of focus is best conveyed by a switch from 'leader' or 'leadership' as nouns, to the verb forms of terminology: 'leads', 'leading' or 'leadership' (as a verb). Active verbs bring our focus to the present.

Activity 13.5

1 What does leadership in action look like?
2 How do you recognize it when you 'see' it occurring in the midst of processes?
3 Does considering leadership as a verb rather than a noun alter your understanding of leadership?
4 How does such consideration impact upon your understanding of distributed leadership?

Note here the focus is on the present tense, rather than on past events or on what a person or a group says they *intend to do in the future*. Leadership, rather than being a constant, is temporal in nature. Employing a perspective informed by process thinking means you are receptive to seeing leadership in other places and circumstances. Utilizing particularly a PI perspective widens the parameters of what, to you, counts as leadership. Perceived thus, leadership becomes a temporal aspect and possible *outcome* of practice, rather than an *expected prerequisite for* practice.

This alternative to entitative thinking presents a nomenclature-related difficulty for those 'leader–follower' leadership studies. You may argue that leaders and followers are interchangeable, insofar as, as Evans (2018) points out, everyone assumes the role of both leader and follower, switching from one to the other – often multiple times – within the course of interacting with others (such interchangeability is highlighted in the EI perspective of Figure 13.1). Key questions, however, are: what or whom are people following, and do they follow from choice?

Let us return to consideration of how leadership may temporarily occur in processes and practices, in ways that Evans (2018: 60) likens to a scenario in which a ball is being thrown (sometimes rapidly) from one person to another within a group, as one person – through the agentic act of influencing others – assumes the temporary status of 'leader' and the others as 'the led', before the roles then switch repeatedly in an unsystematic way. In such situations, the possible interplay of leading and following may become so fluid and complex that the terms become redundant, for leadership under such circumstances may be described as 'fleeting, transient, temporary, momentary, intermittent, or precarious' (Evans, 2018: 60). Herein lies our reasoning for encouraging you to engage with process thinking when it comes to leadership. Leadership no longer is a constant, associated with (exceptional) individuals. Our focus shifts from practitioners towards practices. How then can we define leadership? Crevani (2018), for example, explores the ongoing production of direction in organizing. If leadership is associated with direction-forming and re-forming, then our attention turns to understanding the practices shaped by human and non-human elements that contribute to such (re)forming. These practices, however, do not occur in a vacuum. There are power relations in play as well as structures that enable and constrain practices. We now turn your attention to developing a social critical understanding of distributed leadership that can be applied to practice and research.

Applying a social critical understanding of distributed leadership

We start this section by introducing you to Critical leadership studies (CLS). CLS challenges the assumptions reflected in contemporary leadership studies, where mainstream theoretical viewpoints are leader-centric. As discussed above, post-heroic theoretical viewpoints emphasize the 'social, relational and collective nature' (Collinson, 2011: 184) of leadership. Embracing post-heroic theoretical viewpoints does not, however, mean that a critical understanding is taken, even though such viewpoints can challenge leader-centricity. Collinson explains that a critical understanding of leadership is one that critiques:

> the power relations and identity constructions through which leadership dynamics are often reproduced, frequently rationalized, sometimes resisted and occasionally trans-formed . . . Critical studies challenge hegemonic perspectives in the mainstream literature that tend to both underestimate the complexity of leadership dynamics and to take for granted that leaders are the people in charge who make decisions, and that followers are those who merely carry out orders from 'above'. *(2011: 181)*

Distributed leadership, despite the term's implicit suggestion of democratic and shared forms of practice, is not inherently critical unless it involves critique of power relations and of the structures that protect and/or perpetuate them. We also encourage you to take criticality further than this, so that you question what leadership is. We pick up on this later in this section. For each of the four perspectives in Figure 13.1 we provide statements that either question mainstream assumptions or probe deeper into understanding leadership practice.

Table 13.1 Examples of critically informed statements for distributed-leadership perspectives

		Examples of critically informed statements
Ways of understanding distributed leadership (see Figure 13.1)	ENTITATIVE-FORMAL Leadership is role-based and the aggregation of tasks and responsibility governed by predefined groups of 'leaders'. These groups or managers can choose to distribute these 'leadership' role responsibilities to others.	The distribution of more work labelled as leadership is primarily due to work intensification, not the development of inclusive practices. Leadership, leading and leader are attributed to an elite group who maintain power during a distributed process. The association of distributed leadership with organizational improvement and outcomes can be exaggerated in education policy.
	ENTITATIVE-INFORMAL Leadership is associated with individuals, irrespective of role, who influence others. Here the notion of leader and follower is interchangeable for individuals distributed throughout an organization.	A focus on power relations provides insight into why individuals have influence with and over other individuals, as well as why individuals yield to others. There are complementary and competing agendas across hierarchical and lateral role arrangements. A purpose is to develop democratic processes and address issues of social injustice.
	PROCESS-FORMAL Leadership is a process that emerges from practices distributed amongst those in predefined groups of 'leaders'. These groups are based on formal organizational management/ leadership structures.	The positioning of leadership at the top of a hierarchy of practices is contested and questioned. Collective (leadership) practice is present but usually restricted to a group so is exclusive rather than inclusive. The power relations that maintain the above-mentioned positioning and restriction are revealed and questioned.
	PROCESS-INFORMAL Leadership emerges from practices. This leadership emergence may occur anywhere in an organization and is not restricted to the practices of any one group.	Direction-forming and resistance are expected practices where meanings and process are contested. Other practices are not dependent on leadership practices. A purpose is to develop democratic processes and address issues of social injustice.

The statements presented in Table 13.1 are not exhaustive; rather, they are intended as a starting point for developing critical questions about distributed leadership practice and research. Examples of such questions are:

1 What are the 'implications for social justice and inequalities (power)' (Woods and Roberts, 2018: 32) with leadership distribution?

2 When distributed leadership is espoused in policy and other related documents, what perspective from Figure 13.1 is being promoted – and does this differ from the perspective-in-use? What research studies have been included and excluded in the related policy?

3 Does the rhetoric of distributed leadership in an organization align with how staff in non-management roles experience leadership?

4 Is distributed leadership a means to distribute power?

Question 4 is complex, implying an assumption that leadership distribution involves a distribution of power. This assumption produces two questions. First, *can* power be distributed from one entity to another? Second, to what extent does leadership distribution assume there are privileged managers in an organization who have access to a reservoir of power and may choose whom to distribute it to?

We also want to encourage you to question what (distributed) leadership is. Distributed leadership has become a mainstream theoretical viewpoint in ELMA usually situated in the entitative perspectives, EF and EI. By introducing you to process thinking, we are challenging the dominant entitative thinking that underpins most of the leadership studies field and ELMA. Process thinking, which has its roots in process metaphysics, is in direct contrast to the substantive ontology that informs entitative thinking. This contrasting sets up a possible paradigm shift with how you understand leadership and so sits at the 'radical' end of criticality (Evans, 2018). This process of contrasting can also help reveal and question the power that reifies leadership above other forms of practice and keeps leadership embedded in entitative thinking and a substantive ontology.

Introducing the case study: Rockville County Primary School

We now encourage you to apply what you have learned in this chapter to the case study, which draws upon findings of research carried out by Linda Evans into teacher morale, job satisfaction and motivation in English primary schools (see Evans, 1998). The research was a semi-ethnographic multisite case study, in which Evans gathered qualitative data both through loosely structured interviews with the teachers in three schools and, in what she describes as a 'teacher-cum-observer' role, through informal, unstructured and unsystematic observation (in the role of part-time class teacher and classroom-support colleague) of day-to-day life at the schools. The case study focuses on Rockville County Primary School (fictitious names of people and institutions are used throughout).

Case Study 13.1 Rockville County Primary School, part 1

Geoff Collins was the headteacher of Rockville County Primary School. He was seen by the teachers as a very affable, essentially well-meaning, but weak headteacher, provoking some teachers' derision. One described him: 'He's not directing the school – it's the tail wagging the dog! He's in the wrong job'; another said, 'Really, Geoff has very little influence on *me*', and many teachers remarked that they had no sense of what Geoff's views were on teaching and learning methods, curriculum development or, indeed, any educational issues. He conveys no impression of having applied any depth of analysis to any such issues, and he appeared oblivious to the activities going on in classrooms; he allowed teachers to teach precisely as they liked, unhindered and, to a large extent, unobserved by him.

Geoff nevertheless adopted a very hierarchical approach to leading and managing the school. He had established a senior leadership team of three: Geoff himself, Margaret, the deputy headteacher, and Alison, the next most senior teacher, who had been placed in charge of the school's Key Stage 1 department (for children aged four to six). Geoff's attitude to leadership seemed very clearly to be one of blind faith, non-intervention and unquestioning support in relation to those of his colleagues who held posts as desig-nated leaders, even at the lowest level of the formal leadership hierarchy, but particularly within the senior leadership team. This attitude was applied, without exception, to incumbents of designated leadership posts, not in a personal capacity, but in their capacity as leadership post-holders. It seemed to reflect Geoff's respect for authority and was applied irrespective of whether post-holders had been promoted by him, or whether he had 'inherited' them as leaders. His recognition of their authority ceased whenever a teacher who had held a designated leadership post relinquished it – as in the case of one who had been appointed to a middle-leadership post for coordinating the school's mathematics education, and who later relinquished the coordinator role when she reduced to part-time status on her return from maternity leave. Promotion to a desig-nated leadership role immediately secured Geoff's recognition of a teacher as a designated leader who was vested with authority that Geoff had not previously afforded the teacher.

Geoff manifested an apparently blinkered, 'head-in-the-sand'-type manner of refusing to accept criticism of the behaviour, policies and decisions of any designated leaders – particularly those who constituted his senior leadership team. Evans reports having overheard a teacher complain to Geoff about having been left alone to teach a large class of reception children (four- to five-year-olds) when her co-teacher was sick. The teacher who complained to Geoff had seen senior leadership team member Alison – who did not have responsibility for a class of her own – coming and going throughout the morning on seemingly routine, non-teaching tasks: filling flower vases, stocking bookshelves and trans-ferring the contents of one cupboard to another. Questioning Alison's self-deployment, the teacher had asked Geoff why Alison had not assigned herself to assist in what she (Alison) knew to be the understaffed reception class. Geoff's response was characteristically courteous, but unwavering: as a senior leadership team member, he said, Alison had the discretion to carry out her responsibilities as she saw fit; he would not make her accountable for her movements, nor would he assign her to help in the reception class. The issue was not debatable, and the message conveyed by Geoff, on this, and on many similar occasions, was clear; there was no right of appeal against decisions made by senior leaders.

Activity 13.6

1 To what extent does Geoff's approach to leadership represent distributed leadership?
2 Which of the perspectives presented in Table 13.1 reflects your response to question 1?
3 Can you identify what assumptions about leadership Geoff may be making in relation to his approach?

Case Study 13.2 Rockville County Primary School, part 2

We now introduce Amanda, who held a designated middle-leadership post as the coordinator of the school's religious education. An experienced teacher, Amanda was a recent appointee at Rockville. She soon established a reputation as an intellectual, reflective teacher whom Evans labels an 'extended professional'. One of Evans's Rockville teacher interviewees described Amanda: 'I respect what she does as a professional *immensely* . . . she's probably the most brilliant teacher – she's probably the most dynamic . . . the most energetic . . . the most gifted. I think she's fantastic!' Another teacher said, 'I've got a great deal of respect for Amanda – I've learned a lot, working with her . . . She's everything a teacher *should* be . . . Amanda questions development and the intellectual side of things . . . would consider content, children's needs, suitable assessment.'

Gradually, centred around Amanda, a subculture of intellectual 'extended' profession-ality emerged at Rockville as the focus of innovative teaching practice that many teachers began to buy into. This subgroup and the subculture that developed from it, implicitly challenged and undermined the authority of Geoff and his senior leadership team.

Activity 13.7

1 Do you consider Amanda's professional practice as a teacher at Rockville to represent distributed leadership? If so, in what respects?
2 Which of the four perspectives presented in Table 13.1 is reflected in your response to question 1?
3 Where is distributed leadership practice more in evidence – in Geoff's practice or in Amanda's?
4 Which of Geoff or Amanda seems to exert the more influence on the Rockville staff?
5 What assumptions about leadership are you making in your response to question 4?

Researching distributed leadership

For the final activity, we draw your attention to researching distributed leadership. If new to research, getting to grips with concepts such as ontology and epistemology, and with methodology and data-collecting methods, may be daunting. If so, we suggest you first think critically about how you understand leadership – particularly distributed leadership, since your thinking will help shape your research design and method.

If you favour the two entitative perspectives, EF and EI, you probably value individual, and perhaps collective, accounts of practice, and so the data-collection methods you choose should enable you to gather such accounts. Yet if you veer towards the process perspectives, PF and PI, you will wish to research leadership *practice* – leadership as a verb – so you may decide that, to gather data on leadership in action, you, as the researcher, need to be present as leadership emerges.

Activity 13.8

So, now consider the following questions:

1 What methodologies align to the two differing (entitative and process) ontologies that are represented in Figure 13.1?
2 What data-collecting methods and forms of data analysis are aligned to the methodologies you identified in your response to question 1?
3 How may your research aim(s) and research questions generate data and findings that contribute to a critical understanding of distributed leadership?
4 What mainstream leadership and distributed leadership claims do you expect to challenge in your literature review?

Conclusion

This chapter concerns distributed leadership in *education*, rather than in any *general* context. Education is primarily about learning – for the students, but also for the adults who, through their practices and the processes they engage in, directly or indirectly support students' learning. *Higher* education, as well as focusing on student learning, also encompasses research, knowledge production and critique. Learning, teaching – and in higher education, research – are the core purposes of education professionals. With this in mind, consider:

1 How may distributed leadership support or impede learning, teaching and/or research?

2 Which perspectives presented in Figure 13.1 seem most or least likely to underpin such support of these core purposes?

3 Consider the inequalities and barriers that may frustrate education professionals' enactment of these core purposes. What statements from Table 13.1 may provide a starting point in reducing these inequalities and breaking down these barriers?

We leave you with three key claims that summarize the chapter, and that we hope you will take forward in your own thinking. These are, first, how we view distributed leadership is associated with and reflects our own Implicit leadership theory; second, distributed leadership is not restricted to entitative thinking; and third, process thinking broadens and questions our view of leadership so that leadership can be understood as a consequence of practice.

Further reading

Gunter, H., Hall, D. and Bragg, J. (2013) Distributed leadership: a study in knowledge production. *Educational Management Administration & Leadership*, 41(5), 555–580.

Raelin, J.A. (ed.) (2016) *Leadership-as-practice: theory and application*. New York: Routledge.

Tian, M., Risku, M. and Collin, K. (2016) A meta-analysis of distributed leadership from 2002 to 2013: theory development, empirical evidence and future research focus. *Educational Management Administration & Leadership*, 44(1), 146–164.

Wilkinson, J. and Kemmis, S. (2015) Practice theory: viewing leadership as leading. *Educational Philosophy and Theory*, 47(4), 342–358.

Youngs, H. (2020) Distributed leadership. In: R. Papa (ed.), *The Oxford encyclopedia of educational administration*. New York: Oxford University Press. Available online: http://dx.doi.org/10.1093/acrefore/9780190264093.013.612 (accessed 3 August 2020).

References

Collinson, D. (2011) Critical leadership studies. In: A. Bryman, D. Collinson, K. Grint, B. Jackson and M. Uhl-Bien (eds), *The Sage handbook of leadership* (pp. 181–194). London: Sage.

Crevani, L. (2018) Is there leadership in a fluid world? Exploring the ongoing production of direction in organizing. *Leadership*, 14(1), 83–109.

Evans, L. (1998) *Teacher morale, job satisfaction and motivation*. London: Paul Chapman.

Evans, L. (2018) *Professors as academic leaders: expectations, enacted professionalism and evolving roles*. London: Bloomsbury.

Gronn, P. (2002) Distributed leadership as a unit of analysis. *The Leadership Quarterly*, 13(4), 423–451.

Gronn, P. (2008) The future of distributed leadership. *Journal of Educational Administration*, 46(2), 141–158.

Langley, A., Smallman, C., Tsoukas, H. and Van de Ven, A.H. (2013) Process studies of change in organization and management: unveiling temporality, activity, and flow. *Academy of Management Journal*, 56(1), 1–13.

Spillane, J.P. (2006) *Distributed leadership*. San Francisco, CA: Jossey-Bass.

Woods, P.A. and Roberts, A. (2018) *Collaborative school leadership: a critical guide*. London: Sage.

Youngs, H. (2009) (Un)critical times? Situating distributed leadership in the field. *Journal of Educational Administration and History*, 41(4), 377–389.

Youngs, H. (2014) Moving beyond distributed leadership to distributed forms: a contextual and socio-cultural analysis of two New Zealand secondary schools. *Leading & Managing*, 20(2), 88–103.

Youngs, H. (2017) A critical exploration of collaborative and distributed leadership in higher education: developing an alternative ontology through leadership-as-practice. *Journal of Higher Education Policy and Management*, 39(2), 140–154.

Educational and instructional leadership

Scott Eacott and Richard Niesche

14

What this chapter is about	222
Key questions that this chapter addresses	222
Introduction	222
A model of instructional leadership	223
The ideological, historical, political and organizational contexts of instructional leadership	224
What are the commonly held key features of instructional leadership?	226
What is the ideological, historical, political and organizational function of this model?	229
What are the effects of instructional leadership on professional practice?	231
What are the effects of instructional leadership on understandings of educational leadership?	232
Conclusion	233
Further reading	234
References	234

What this chapter is about

In this chapter, we present and discuss the relationship between educational and instructional leadership. We note that instructional leadership is one of the more commonly used and uncritically accepted labels in the field. As a result, it is rarely interrogated for its underlying assumptions and the implications of those for systems, schools and educators. Using John Hattie's (2009) *Visible learning* as a case study, we show how calls for instructional leadership over the last forty years are based on a lengthy history of research and practice in the field of educational administration and leadership, and draw heavily on developments in industry. In doing so, we show how, despite claims of integrating education into school leadership, instructional leadership overlooks the matter of context and decentres, if not removes, issues of race, gender, class and identity (the focus of many chapters in this textbook).

Key questions that this chapter addresses

1 What does instructional leadership mean?
2 How does instructional leadership relate to educational leadership?
3 What are the implications of the above for schools, systems and educators?

Introduction

Educational leadership is frequently queried with regard to what is *educational* about it. Going as far back as 1902, John Dewey noted 'it is easy to fall into the habit of regarding the mechanics of school organization and administration as something comparatively external and indifferent to educational ideals' (1902: 22–23). Instructional leadership is often seen as the potential missing link for integrating education into school leadership.

We acknowledge that there are many different terms and labels used around these topics, including, inter alia, instructional leadership, leadership for learning, pedagogical leadership, authentic leadership and many other forms of adjectival leadership. Two major labels, sometimes seen as synonymous, are instructional leadership and leadership for learning. The distinctions, and their implications, are important. The former, with a lengthy history primarily in the United States, concerns leadership that centres on instruction and therefore teachers and teaching. The latter, with a more recent history coming out of the UK, concerns leadership that centres on learning. Our focus in this chapter is instructional leadership.

We are also aware of Basil Bernstein's classification (1977) of the three key message systems of education: instruction (pedagogy), curriculum, and evaluation (assessment).

Although it is difficult to decouple these message systems as though they operate as separate entities, our focus in this chapter is instruction. The two key concepts for the chapter are therefore 'leadership' and 'instruction'. Bringing them together in a purposeful way, our attention is on the underlying logic of instructional leadership and its implications for educational leadership.

> **Instructional leadership:** an approach (style, model) to leadership that is explicitly focused on improving the instructional programme of the school.
>
> **Leadership for learning:** an approach (style, model) where leadership is focused on creating an environment focused on maximizing student learning.

A model of instructional leadership

> **Curriculum:** the selection of knowledge (that which is appropriate/legitimized) to be transmitted through education.
>
> **Instruction** (pedagogy): the selection and enactment of methods for how knowledge is to be taught.
>
> **Evaluation** (assessment): the means through which knowledge acquired by students is assessed.

There have been countless attempts to articulate what educational leaders should do in order to improve outcomes. With an intellectual heritage dating back to the foundations of the field of education, administration and leadership research has long sought the 'one best method', 'best practice' or similar in the pursuit of maximizing the outcomes of their organizations. However, given the contested nature of what the desired outcomes of education are, models of instructional leadership frequently sit across multiple subfields of education. Their genesis is just as likely to be located in school reform, instruction/pedagogy, curriculum and school systems research as it is in educational leadership. This means that what is presented as instructional leadership is not always immediately recognizable as a model of leadership. One such approach is John Hattie's *Visible learning* (2009) which we present and use now as a case study.

Case Study 14.1 Hattie's Visible Learning

Visible Learning is the product of a synthesis of 1,600 meta-analyses (over 95,000 studies involving 300 million students) relating to performance indicators and evaluation in education. It is claimed to be the largest-ever collection of evidence-based research into what works in schools to improve learning. It is based on a desire to understand which variables are most important, or have the greatest effect, for improving student outcomes. This variable-based approach to educational leadership has significant implications, to which we will return later in the chapter. Central to the argument of Visible Learning are effect sizes. Hattie calculated effect sizes for each identified variable in the mega-analysis based on their bearing on student learning and factoring in their cost to implement. The average effect size was 0.4, a value that has come to represent a year's growth per year of schooling for a student. Anything above 0.4 has a positive effect on student learning.

Hattie's Visible Learning website (visiblelearning.com) provides a list, updated regularly, of the practices that have the greatest impact on student learning. Based on adherence to the model, if an educational leader were to focus on the strategies of greatest impact, the maximum effect on student learning would be achieved. In other words, Hattie's Visible Learning provides a list of the instructional practices that work best for improving outcomes. It can therefore be used to make decisions regarding what to invest in (and what not to) and as a focal point for all decisions relating to school improvement.

Since the publication of the original book (Hattie, 2009), there is now an entire literature of 'visible' education in different curriculum areas, expanding into other aspects of education such as well-being and, not surprisingly, instructional leadership. In partnership with Corwin (a subsidiary of the Sage publishing house), there is an internationally delivered suite of professional-learning products and services, books and ebooks, digital professional-development products, institutes and on-site consultancies. As at the end of 2019, Visible Learning programmes are delivered in twenty-one countries (and growing) and have a major influence on the ways in which school systems, politicians and educators think about instructional leadership.

Visible Learning focuses on within-school factors for improving outcomes. It partitions the internal and external environments of schooling as though they are separate, even if related, entities. Hattie's justification for this separation is that we cannot control for factors outside of the school and therefore should focus our attention on what we can control. Consistent with orthodox claims in the field, Visible Learning considers the classroom teacher to be the most important factor for improving outcomes and that school leadership (particularly instructional) is second. In side-stepping the influence of outside-school factors, Hattie's model shifts attention away from larger societal inequities and the complexities of issues of race, gender, class and identity, with significant implications for who is responsible for outcomes.

The ideological, historical, political and organizational contexts of instructional leadership

Since its inception as a field of study, educational leadership, management and administration (ELMA) research research has sought to identify definitively the practices that generate the greatest impact on student outcomes. Schools and individual educators attributed with achieving the highest outcomes (either outright or value-added) have been the key empirical foci of ELMA research. Findings articulating lists of desirable traits, behaviours, practices, conditions and so on leading to improved outcomes have attracted the attention not only of scholars and researchers, but also of policymakers and systemic authorities.

Historically, instructional leadership has splintered in two main directions in the field. As a problem of practice, instructional leadership in the broadest sense has legitimized the contribution of clinical professors / expert practitioners. The heroic leader of the high-achieving school, or the inspirational turnaround leader who brought significant value-added outcomes to students in a disadvantaged community, were granted a status on the basis of their instructional achievements. Stories from the field, captured in case studies and narratives, became, and continue to be, a major source of knowledge in educational leadership, management and administration studies. At the same time, educational leadership researchers sought greater scientific credibility in the academy. Achieving this credibility required studies demonstrating more rigour and robustness in their designs, analysis and strength of evidence than narratives from the field. The work of Frederick Winslow Taylor, and his principles of scientific management, was highly influential during the early establishment of departments of educational administration, and its traces remain in our approaches to understanding instructional leadership.

Taylor's work took place in industry rather than education. But his goals were not dissimilar to those in educational administration and leadership. With a focus on efficiency, Taylor proposed to optimize productivity by simplifying jobs. He used observation-based 'time and motion' studies with stopwatches and clipboards to generate data on how long the various tasks took to complete. Collating these data, Taylor was able to identify the most efficient means, or 'one right method' for producing quality products. In doing so, managers could identify staff not working in the most efficient way, what Taylor labelled as soldiering (and Hattie labels as coasting), and this was the basis of his idea of a fair day's pay for a fair day's work (not too dissimilar to Hattie's one year's growth for one year of schooling). The significance of Taylorism for instructional leadership can be found in ideas of: (1) replacing rule-of-thumb methods with those based on a scientific study of tasks; (2) scientifically selecting, training and developing each worker rather than passively leaving them to train themselves; (3) cooperating with the workers to ensure that the scientifically developed methods are being followed; and (4) dividing work nearly equally between managers and workers, so that the managers apply scientific-management principles to planning the work and the workers actually perform the tasks.

A major turning point for instructional leadership was the 1966 Coleman Report (*Equality of educational opportunity*) in the United States. The Report argues that 'schools bring little to bear on a child's achievement that is independent of his background and general social context' (Coleman et al., 1966: 325). While consistent with more sociological descriptions of the role of schooling (see, for example, the work of Pierre Bourdieu), the idea that schools matter little compared to outside-school factors is a significant challenge for educational leadership research. However, the role of educational leadership was to be found also within the pages of the Coleman Report. With explicit attention to equity issues, the Report notes that schools in challenging contexts had a far greater influence on student learning. This paved the way for greater attention to school-reform efforts and school effectiveness/improvement.

> **Meta-analysis:** a statistical analysis that combines the results of a large collection of studies. It can be performed when there are multiple studies addressing the same question, with each study reporting measurements and being expected to have the same design features.
>
> **Mega-analysis:** a statistical analysis that combines the results of multiple meta-analyses in an effort to increase power (over individual studies and meta-analyses), improve estimates of the size of the effect and/or resolve uncertainty when studies disagree.
>
> **Effect size:** a quantitative measure of the magnitude of the difference between two approaches.

By the 1980s, and courtesy of the expanding attention to school effectiveness and school improvement, Hallinger claims that instructional leadership had become more theoretical and research driven than previously (see Hallinger and Wang, 2015). As is often the case in educational administration and leadership, Hallinger's claim arguably conflates exhibitionism of data and procedure for theory and research-driven scholarship. It does, however, highlight an important development in understanding instructional leadership. As statistical packages became more common (thanks to personal computers), instructional leadership research became more (if not exclusively) quantitative in nature. The small-scale case studies of heroic and turnaround leaders were replaced with validated scales, composite measures and statistical modelling.

At the turn of the century, the increasing influence of globalization created even greater calls for instructional leadership. Up until this point, there was little research outside of the United States focused on instructional leadership (Hallinger and Wang, 2015). The launch of large-scale testing programmes by the Organisation for Economic Co-operation and Development (OECD) such as the Programme for International Student Assessment (PISA), and Trends in International Mathematics and Science Study (TIMSS) generated a universal measure (test scores) and benchmarked nations on a previously unseen scale. PISA in particular established a league table that governments and systemic authorities could not ignore. Nations such as Finland rose to fame on the back of PISA, and other nations sought to find out what practices could be replicated (assuming that context was not overly important) to enhance performance at scale.

With increasing empirical evidence concerning instructional leadership, it became possible to undertake meta-analysis (e.g. Robinson, Lloyd and Rowe, 2008) and then mega-analysis (e.g. Hattie, 2009). The positive effect of instructional leadership against other approaches (e.g. transformational) led to instructional leadership becoming part of major policy reforms aimed at improving school outcomes. On an international scale, position descriptions, professional standards, and preparation and development programmes for school leaders became more centred on instructional leadership. To support principals in their role, many school systems even established specific roles entitled 'instructional leader' to support the instructional programme of schools. Unlike many adjectival approaches to educational leadership, those that quickly fade from memory, a focus on instruction – the very core business of educating – has remained an enduring focus.

What are the commonly held key features of instructional leadership?

Of all the adjectival approaches to educational leadership, instructional leadership has the most rigorous and robust empirical support (e.g. Hallinger and Wang, 2015; Robinson, Lloyd and Rowe, 2008). With increasing global pressure to raise student outcomes, the support for instructional leadership from systems, schools and educators has arguably never been greater. The strength of the empirical support is, however, the product of the underlying generative features of instructional leadership, a methodological artefact, rather than anything else.

As with all adjectival approaches, instructional leadership is based on a pre-existing normative orientation for how schools ought to be. There is no one single version of this normative orientation: however, high test scores in exit examinations (or large-scale national and international testing regimes) is a commonly held position. This pre-existing belief is rarely acknowledged in educational leadership, management and administration research, but remains a significant matter in dialogue and debates on the most appropriate way to lead schools. It is this orientation that serves as the criterion by which we judge the success/effectiveness of education. The purposes, processes and products of education are assessed against their coherence with our underlying beliefs of education. This pre-existing normative orientation is the first feature of any model of instructional leadership.

The second feature is the translation of the pre-existing orientation into a model of instruction. As Ladwig reminds us, 'you cannot improve pedagogy [instruction] without having some model of pedagogy as your guide, or your goal' (2005: 71). Two points are important here. First, it is impossible to not have a pre-existing orientation. You have a normative approach to education whether it is articulated or not. Second, despite what may appear as a subjective basis, any claim to a desirable model of instruction needs to be empirically defended in student (or organizational) outcomes. That is, any model of instruction should be directed to achieving a high standard and/or improvements in student outcomes. What remains challenging here is that the desired outcomes of schooling are highly contested (Ladwig, 2010).

Once a model of instruction has been articulated, it can then be used to audit existing practice. It is possible that any form of audit has a prerequisite of debating the merits of the model and (re)defining key terms. If that is the case, it is consistent with orthodox approaches to educational leadership that stress the importance of a shared vision or language to discuss practice. It also means that instructional leadership operates on educators as much as it does on students. However, auditing current practice does not necessarily require shared sense-making. It is equally possible that a model of instruction can be imposed on educators. Here is the complexity of instructional leadership: it is neither democratic nor prescriptive. Any auditing of current practice can be experienced very differently by educators. To undertake this audit may require observation of teaching (not too dissimilar to Taylor's approach), auditing of assessment tasks and/or analysis of curriculum materials. The important outcome of the audit is understanding how current practice(s) align with the desired approach.

Based on the evidence generated during the audit, the next aim of instructional leadership is to undertake an intervention designed to improve practice. Any intervention arguably has two purposes. First, there is the overarching goal of improving outcomes. The improvement will be achieved through advocacy of the desired model of instruction. This means that any intervention has an inbuilt advocacy function. For example, the Quality Teaching Rounds work by Gore and colleagues (e.g. Gore et al., 2017), which builds on earlier work on Instructional Rounds in the United States and before that medical rounds in hospitals, has the explicit goal of advocating for a particular model of instruction (Quality Teaching). This is not to say that the model of instruction does not improve

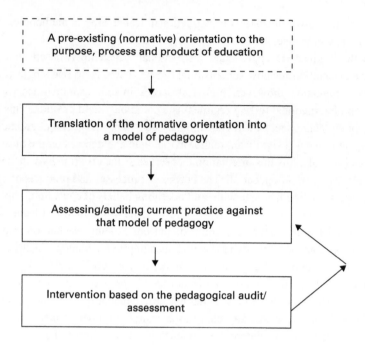

practice/outcomes, but it is to acknowledge that any model of educational leadership has an advocacy role. Second, the very purpose of the intervention is to bring practice into closer alignment with the desired model of instruction and by virtue, improve outcomes.

The cyclic nature of instructional leadership then continues. Following the intervention, there is a need to audit practice against the desired model of instruction. This continues as a self-referential cycle of improvement focused on teaching and learning. Figure 14.1 captures the key features of instructional leadership.

What is important to highlight in Figure 14.1 is that instructional leadership is not limited to quantitative measures of teaching and learning. It is about the underlying logic of educational leadership: a pre-existing normative orientation of the purpose of education, the translation of that orientation into a model of instruction (pedagogy, assessment or curriculum), auditing existing practice against that model and constructing appropriate interventions to address performance.

The pre-existing normative orientation means that the criteria used to assess the value of instructional leadership (desired student outcomes) are the very genesis of the model. Any argument for instructional leadership is therefore somewhat circular. The model is based on instruction that leads to the delivery of desired student outcomes and then those outcomes are used as evidence that the model works. Implications of this approach for educational leadership are that the model of instruction and its desired outcomes may narrow the outcomes of schooling and implicitly reduce leadership to the technical pursuit of those outcomes to the exclusion of all others. In doing so, matters of race, gender, class and identity become external variables to be overcome, if not dismissed, rather than part of schooling itself.

For educational leadership, there is also a belief that leadership matters. How it matters is through oversight of the instructional programme of the school (not too dissimilar to Taylor's approach) and through creating the conditions in which educators can achieve the highest quality of instruction. This is achieved by focusing attention on the strategies that have greatest impact on delivering desired outcomes (data that Hattie's Visible Learning provides). Through attention to within-school factors, this approach to instructional leadership generates a compensatory approach to school effectiveness. This means that educational leadership is conceived of as being able to compensate for any disadvantage that a child brings to school. In other words, high-quality instructional leadership is able to overcome context.

Activity 14.1

Thinking about your own organization, reflect on the following three issues:

- Many debates regarding schools come down to differences in the purpose(s) of education. In the absence of an explicitly identified purpose, others will assume a purpose and make judgements based on that. Reflect on whether there is *clarity* of purpose in your school and its instructional programme.
- Explicitly articulating the purpose(s) of education provides the basis from which to judge performance. That is, with clarity comes judgement based on the coherence of your activity against that purpose. Reflect on the level of *coherence* between activities at your school and its stated purpose.
- Having established the purpose(s) towards which you are working and for which you are demonstrating coherence, you generate the narrative for your own school. This need not be the same as other schools and instead is about crafting stories about the work of educators in context. Reflect on what the *narrative* is of your school.

What is the ideological, historical, political and organizational function of this model?

Instructional leadership requires an end in mind. As Figure 14.1 shows, the genesis of any model is a desirable set of outcomes, and instructional leadership (as it is commonly portrayed) is the systematic planning for delivery of those outcomes. What remains unexamined is who gets to decide on the desirable outcomes and the methods to achieve them? These questions are uncommon in educational leadership literatures. Instructional leadership functions such that it keeps educators busy on the technical delivery of an agenda set beyond the school. Drawing on the example of Hattie's Visible Learning, there is a list of the greatest impact strategies and the instructional leader's task is to implement those. At face value, it is impossible to refute claims that are grounded in maximizing outcomes for students. This is the ideological power of advocacy for instructional leadership. If we know strategies that improve student outcomes, why would we not want to implement them? In other words, ideas of instructional leadership shape how we come to understand education and educational leadership without ever drawing attention to their underlying assumptions.

Hattie's Visible Learning is, however, just the latest attempt to standardize through atomizing practice into its smallest measurable units. It contributes to a lengthy history dating back to the early integration of Taylorism in educational leadership preparation and development programmes (Eacott, 2017). Research has consistently shown that focusing on the core business of teaching and learning is the most effective strategy for improving student outcomes (Robinson, Lloyd and Rowe, 2008). However, by focusing on generic strategies there is little attention to context. Diverse social groups are rarely acknowledged or valued in decisions regarding instruction, curriculum and assessment. Context becomes just another variable for instructional leadership to compensate for, and overcome. The politics of who has the most to gain (and lose) from instructional practices is simply not asked. Instructional leadership functions by reducing these broader social questions to the external environment and by focusing on the technical delivery of teaching and learning programme as though they are apolitical.

By not asking questions regarding the acknowledging and valuing of diverse social groups and the politics of schooling, instructional leadership decouples schools from context. The artificial partitioning of the internal and external environments functions to sustain an insular research community. Insights regarding the role of schooling in broader social, economic and health aspects, among others, are moved to the periphery, if acknowledged at all. This generates a level of ahistorical reasoning for instructional leadership, where there is no recognition of why practices and outcomes are the way they are in context. Effective instructional leadership is seen as the pathway to improved outcomes. As a result, many strategies that are promoted align with contemporary fads and fashions (e.g. the latest edtech device or software) without any sense of whether it is offering something new or simply a different way of doing what educators already do.

Activity 14.2

Following on from Activity 14.1, to provide a framing to embed context into instructional leadership, consider the following five reflective questions for the instructional programme (or any reform/activity) in your current organization:

1 What educational benefits are sought through this activity?
2 Has a diverse range of social groups been recognized and valued in decision-making?
3 Who has the most to gain and lose in this activity?
4 How has the history of the school been recognized in this activity?
5 Is the programme offering something new, or just a better (more efficient/effective) way of doing what is currently done?

These questions enable educators to consider (use and interpret) multiple sources of information, evaluate alternate points of view, and develop a reasoned and defensible argument for action. Specifically, they focus instructional leadership on the educational, social, political, historical and future relations of schooling. In doing so, they provide a framing for a context-sensitive approach to educational leadership.

What are the effects of instructional leadership on professional practice?

As noted previously, instructional leadership has long been positioned as a problem of practice. As with any adjectival approach to educational leadership, instructional leadership seeks to focus schools on the delivery of desirable outcomes. In many cases, these outcomes are defined as improving students' test scores and/or exit examination results. At face value, this is difficult to argue with. However, what is obscured in such arguments is the advocacy for a particular purpose(s) of schooling without regard for other potential purposes. Given that the outcomes of schooling are contested (e.g. Ladwig, 2010), there is a need to publicly declare the purpose(s) of education towards which a school is working. Failing to do so, and therefore uncritically accepting the status quo, is how schooling reproduces societal advantages and inequities.

Orthodox ways of articulating a model of or resources for instructional leadership, such as Hattie's Visible Learning, atomize educational practice into the smallest measurable pieces. This takes us back to Taylor's approach to management, involving a clear demarcation of the work between task-operatives and task-overseers. Superficially, this is not problematic, as educational organizations operate with a hierarchy of roles. However, the implications are far greater. If research can identify high-impact strategies, then leaders do not necessarily require any discipline-specific knowledge. Through its focus on the core business of education – instruction – instructional leadership has the potential to de-professionalize the field and reduce the act of teaching to a technical exercise.

The question for practice is whether instructional leaders need instructional expertise or just the information of which specific strategies should be applied? It is possible to counterclaim that instructional expertise is a prerequisite for understanding if practices are being implemented with fidelity. However, better measures of high-impact strategies and greater precision in defining each strategy increase the possibility of non-educators overseeing instructional programmes. This is particularly the case in countries that adopt the title of 'principal' as opposed to 'headteacher'. The former does not require an educator, whereas the latter arguably does.

Co-opted into the neoliberal reform of education, instructional leadership is part of the shifting of responsibility for addressing large-scale social problems through schooling. With an embedded belief that leadership matters and (effective) schooling can compensate for social inequities, instructional leadership inadvertently shifts fault to schools, leaders and educators when outcomes are not achieved. If it is possible to identify high-impact strategies on the basis of what is believed to be rigorous and robust research (e.g. Hattie, Marzano), then it is not unreasonable to expect schools to be able to deliver on their promise. In other words, why cannot every school, leader and educator use these strategies to get great results? This belief shifts responsibility for the outcomes of schooling to those working in schools. It partitions schools from the contexts in which they are located. Attempting to generate statistically alike schools for comparison, or focusing on value-added data rather than raw outcomes does little to purposefully recognize and value social, economic and health distinctions across time and space. Instructional leadership, as commonly used in the educational leadership literatures, removes or reduces context to a variable, despite its long-standing recognition as arguably the most important factor in school outcomes (e.g. Coleman et al., 1966).

What are the effects of instructional leadership on understandings of educational leadership?

Teaching and learning are the core business of education. This means that instructional leadership is central to educational leadership as a field of inquiry. However, too often the focus on oversight of the instructional programme privileges the technical rather than larger questions about the purpose(s) of education and the impact of social relations. Lost in the discussion of models of instructional leadership are debates about whose knowledge is included in the curriculum, how that is reflected in the examinations that define the outcomes of schooling, and how education works for social justice or any issue beyond academic outcomes.

As a theoretical contribution to the field, instructional leadership is more about playing the current game of schooling better, instead of asking questions about the role of schooling in the ongoing constitution of society. Rather than embracing a transdisciplinary approach to understanding the role of schooling, a focus on instructional leadership narrows research to a subset of a field to the exclusion of all others. For advocates, any form of critique is dismissed as anti-progress and not wanting what is best for students without ever calling into question who decides what is best and for what.

Methodologically, instructional leadership research is very much a product of the field's pursuit of scientific credibility. The subjectivity of any model of leadership, even an enduring one such as instructional, means that empirical work is somewhat circular in logic. In this case, the very same data that is the genesis of the model is used to legitimize and validate the findings. The exhibitionism of data and procedure is conflated with scientific rigour and evidence from meta- and mega-analysis cannot escape the circular logic of leadership research.

Instructional leadership is a double-edged sword for understanding educational leadership. On the one hand, it provides the solution for which policymakers, systemic authorities, schools and educators have been searching: the strategies that lead to higher levels of student outcomes. Simultaneously, it narrows the focal outcomes of schooling with little regard for context.

Conclusion

Education is a social and political activity. Understanding instructional leadership requires acknowledging the rich web of social relations in which it is embedded and embodied rather than shifting them to the periphery. This is not beyond the core logic of instructional leadership, or any approach to educational leadership. Mitigating the issues, we have raised calls for a context-sensitive approach to instructional leadership, one where the impact of leadership is understood in context. We cannot assume that all schools are working towards the same goal. To achieve this, we need models of instructional leadership that focus less on the traits/behaviours of leaders, or the return on investment for particular strategies in achieving an agenda set elsewhere, and instead focus on how schools as part of communities articulate their purpose(s) of education, develop coherence in their programme of activities and generate their own narratives.

There is little doubt that context matters for educational leadership and there is no one way to do schooling (Eacott, 2019). This does not mean that every school is pursuing its own unique agenda. The work of schools, particularly given the considerable public funding that goes to them, needs to be defensible against an explicitly articulated purpose(s) of education. Here is the key connection of instructional leadership to educational leadership. Setting this direction is not done to schools but is achieved through context. Embodying democratic principles, establishing and sustaining any sense of direction for a school is a dialogue (and possibly debate) where educators and communities (including students) generate a context-sensitive version of what education can look like. It still needs to relate to curriculum, assessments and policy documents, but there is no one single version of what schooling can or even could be.

For the study of instructional leadership there is a need to reconsider the value of description. Too often, educational leadership researchers have sought to name the seven simple steps to improving outcomes. Schooling is far more complex than that. If it were not, arguably the field of educational administration and leadership would have solved the issue during the last hundred years or more of research. Attempts to outline the best methods for achieving outcomes, researchers have been quick to jump to the prescriptive. Rather than seeking prescription, there is a need for high-quality description regarding what is taking place in schools and relating activities to unfolding activities in the broader community. Then, we will be able to say something about the work of instructional leadership for improving outcomes.

TLeading the instructional programme is a, if not the, central task of an educational leader. Any idea of instructional leadership is intimately related to conceptualizations of educational leadership. This has considerable implications for systems, schools and educators. As we have shown through the illustrative example of Hattie's Visible Learning, and highlighting the core logic of instructional leadership, there are key assumptions that inform what we mean and how we go about it. Rather than having instructional leadership focus on the technical implementation of education, there is scope to ask bigger questions regarding the educational value of activities; how to recognize and value diverse social groups; the politics of education; and how to take into account the history of communities/

organizations while simultaneously offering something new. Substantial responsibility is thrust upon education for solving social problems. Asking questions of the instructional programme is a key way to generate the type of education that engages with issues of social justice, race, gender, class and identity.

Further reading

Callahan, R.E. (1962) *Education and the cult of efficiency*. Chicago, IL: University of Chicago Press.

Eacott, S. (2019) Taking context seriously: a relational approach to high-impact school leadership. *Australian Educational Leader*, 41(4), 28–30.

Gore, J., Lloyd, A., Smith, M., Bowe, J., Ellis, H. and Lubans, D. (2017) Effects of professional development on the quality of teaching: results from a randomised controlled trial of Quality Teaching Rounds. *Teaching and Teacher Education*, 68, 99–113.

Hallinger, P. and Wang, W.-C. (2015) *Assessing instructional leadership with the principal instructional management rating scale*. Cham: Springer.

Ladwig, J.G. (2005) Monitoring the quality of pedagogy. *Leading and Managing*, 11(2), 70–83.

Townsend, T. (ed.) (2019) *Instructional leadership and leadership for learning in schools*. Cham: Palgrave Macmillan.

References

Bernstein, B. (1977) *Class, codes and control: Volume 3 – towards a theory of educational transmission*. London: Routledge and Keegan Paul.

Coleman, J.S., Campbell, E.Q., Hobson, C.J., McPartland, J., Mood, A.M., Weinfeld, F.D. and York, R.L. (1966) *Equality of educational opportunity*. Washington, DC: National Center for Educational Statistics.

Dewey, J. (1902) *The educational situation*. Chicago, IL: Chicago University Press.

Eacott, S. (2017) School leadership and the cult of the guru: the neo-Taylorism of Hattie. *School Leadership & Management*, 37(4), 413–426.

Eacott, S. (2019) High-impact school leadership in context. *Leading and Managing*, 25(2), 66–79.

Gore, J., Lloyd, A., Smith, M., Bowe, J., Ellis, H. and Lubans, D. (2017) Effects of professional development on the quality of teaching: results from a randomised controlled trial of Quality Teaching Rounds. *Teaching and Teacher Education*, 68, 99–113.

Hallinger, P. and Wang, W.-C. (2015) *Assessing instructional leadership with the principal instructional management rating scale*. Cham: Springer.

Hattie, J.A.C. (2009) *Visible learning: a synthesis of over 800 meta-analyses relating to achievement*. Abingdon: Routledge.

Ladwig, J.G. (2005) Monitoring the quality of pedagogy. *Leading and Managing*, 11(2), 70–83.

Ladwig, J.G. (2010) Beyond academic outcomes. *Review of Research in Education*, 34(1), 113–141.

Robinson, V.M.J., Lloyd, C.A. and Rowe, K.J. (2008) The impact of leadership on student outcomes: an analysis of the differential effects of leadership types. *Educational Administration Quarterly*, 44(5), 635–674.

Educational reform and leading school change

Jill Blackmore and Rachel McNae

15

What this chapter is about   238

Key questions that this chapter addresses   238

Introduction   238

Approaches to leadership and change: ideological, historical, political and organizational contexts   240

Introducing Case Study 15.1: school redesign and innovative learning environments   244

Introducing Case Study 15.2: leading from the ground up   247

Power relations, structure and agency   249

What are the effects of these critical approaches?   249

What needs to change?   250

Conclusion   251

Further reading   251

References   252

What this chapter is about

This chapter is about leading school change: in it, we track how school reform has been viewed from different perspectives and how leadership as a contextualized practice has been constituted in each. We explain why leadership has become the focus of policy and research and with what effect on how school change occurs. We identify key shifts in understanding leadership and school change over time and illustrate through two case studies that schools are complex organizations, simultaneously powerful and vulnerable. We make the case for critical leadership practices which are contextualized, relational and purposeful with regard to social justice.

Key questions that this chapter addresses

1 What are seen as being the purposes of education and schooling, and hence of education reform?

2 What are the different key ways in which change can be understood?

3 Why and how might change be attempted in and to schools?

4 What is the function of leadership in effecting change?

Introduction

A functional approach to understanding school change: assumes linearity and causation between an intervention or policy and effects on students. School-effects research in the 1960s relied on quantitative input and output data, treating the school as a 'mystery' black box. This linear model used statistical correlations to compare schools. The question was about the size of effects of schooling based on measurable, standardized assessment while ignoring complex contextual features such as socio-geographical context, educational background of family, peers and community. Failure to achieve the desired outcome was blamed on implementation by school leaders and teachers.

Schools, like all organizations, have weaknesses and strengths that alter over time. While at one level, classrooms and schools look alike and are often compared on that basis, each school exists in a specific context shaped by location, size, student and local demographics, systemic and school governance, community resources, provider and policy frames. Schools are governed by education policies and different 'systems' (government, faith-based, private or NGO) that place certain constraints on school leaders. Schools and teachers are constantly adapting to contradictory external pressures – policies, new organizational forms, multiple interventions and programmes, escalating expectations and normalizing professional standards and accountabilities – with unpredictable and often counterproductive results.

Educational leaders (heads/principals and teachers) have little control over these externalities, yet are expected to manage efficiently and effectively, often without the necessary resources. Indeed, leadership has become the focus of policy and research in the context of greater devolution of responsibility and risk to individual schools in most anglophone countries over four decades. Internally, school leaders negotiate the microdynamics associated with changing everyday practices – among them teacher professional identity, student agency, parental expectations and resource differentiation. Thus, a tension exists between seeking, making and taking opportunities for innovation to generate change when often the risks and complexities required for sustainable change go unacknowledged by educational systems and governments.

In educational research, there are many different paradigms and ways of viewing and understanding the world. While the focus is increasingly on leadership, teachers, process and evidence as essential components of school change (usually equated to student learning outcomes), each approach comes from a different ontological, epistemological and political perspective.

Leadership is equally a contested, over-researched and overused concept. **Critical leadership** research has shifted from focusing on individual attributes (usually white and male) to viewing leadership as a relational practice that many undertake informally. **Relational leadership** recognizes that contextual factors (relationships to community, government, partners and colleagues) as well the social dynamics and cultural interactions of difference (race, class, gender, sexuality, disability) impact on what leaders do and how.

An interpretive approach to understanding school change: seeks to explain the context, actors and processes that bring about change in practice or improvement. This is about thick description of leadership and change practices, focusing on the journey. It questions the process, leadership role and specific context and conditions that are conducive to change and produced cases of hero leaders 'turning around' schools.

A critical approach to understanding school change: is reflexive, sees change as often performative, is about sense-making and contested as political understandings inform change and social dynamics. This means various actors experience and respond to change differently. Discourses of change are denaturalized and raise questions such as: What are the pressures and motivations for change? What is the purpose? Equity, efficiency, effectiveness? Who decides? With what effects?

Activity 15.1

Think about possible answers to the sorts of questions asked by those taking a critical approach:

- Why is school leadership and change the focus of policy and research now?
- How is leadership enacted in different situations and by whom?
- How do we understand successful change?
- How do we understand ethical leadership?
- How do leaders achieve socially just outcomes?

Approaches to leadership and change: ideological, historical, political and organizational contexts

The focus on school leadership arose as state-funded and managed government systems established in the late nineteenth early twentieth centuries in most Western nations were restructured from the 1980s onwards. This restructuring was achieved through policies promoting devolved governance and driven by neoliberal policies of marketization, managerialism and privatization. Following the United States and the UK, New Zealand and some Australian education systems moved to self-management. Self-managing schools were based on a business-focused, input/output user-pays model, leading to inequitable funding and greater accountability.

Leadership became the focus of policy and research in the 1990s. Education markets developed because funding based on enrolments and changed zoning policies encouraged schools within and between systems to compete. Given greater autonomy, the role of principals/heads became critical in positioning individual schools favourably. System-wide restructuring promoting parental choice was claimed to improve learning outcomes, as failing schools would close. This functionalist view of systemic and organizational change assumed linearity between policy, implementation and effect on practice. Self-management shifted the welfarist model of education as a universal entitlement for all children benefiting 'the public' towards one where 'the public' was constructed through the market as the aggregate of individual parental choices and individual schools.

Change is incremental

Moving towards increased school autonomy (charter schools in the United States, independent public schools in Australia, academies in the UK, free schools in Sweden), the dominant reform approach since the 1980s has been **school effectiveness and improvement** (**SEI**). SEI models focused attention on cycles of strategic planning, data, performance outcomes and evaluation. The SEI approach identified key characteristics of 'best practice' from researching successful schools: visionary leadership, consistent policy and focus on teaching and learning. The SEI paradigm focuses on formulaic approaches and frameworks about good leadership practices and what constitutes an effective school. SEI *assumes* continual linear improvement over time through an externally determined process-driven approach within the school. Many of the top-down external and internal approaches such as SEI reduce to one-size-fits-all, recipe-like and formulaic prescriptions. They assume one approach is of value for all classrooms regardless of language, culture or context, and therefore scalable and transportable globally. The SEI paradigm is now being mobilized by various philanthropic (Gates) and management organizations (McKinsey).

Government policymakers sought to scale up successful change across schools through an iterative exchange between achieving/failing schools without changing the conditions that created successful and failing schools. Leadership was a key aspect of SEI and leadership professional development frameworks were built into school-improvement plans, producing a repertoire of 'good leadership practice', a focus on teaching and learning and, by the 2000s, data-driven practices.

Change is unpredictable

School-change theorists since the 1990s (Fullan, 1993) have focused on the unpredictability of change, particularly when imposed externally, distinguishing between change that was deep-seated and sustainable rather than superficial. Change theory indicated that restructuring (e.g. devolution) did not change the cultures of schools and that change did not occur with continual incremental linear improvement, that it took time – often years – and that multiple new factors always came into play. Change theorists consider all educational reforms have unexpected outcomes and are unpredictable in terms of how they are enacted. There is a large evidence base of ethnographic and qualitative case studies that indicate how context matters (socio-economic, school location, policy, funding, demographics etc.) in terms of what leaders can do and how they do it (Hallinger and Heck, 2010), and that the micropractices of school improvement cannot be extracted from the macrofactors.

Such work recognizes the rapidly changing contexts, and the significance of conjuncture when leaders are more able to effect school change when they have multiple coinciding factors e.g. policy, resources and staff. School-change theorists identified resistance to change within and outside schools as part of the cycle of change and did not position teachers as being intrinsically resistant to reform as earlier models suggested. Rather, teachers judged and responded differently according to how reform initiatives impacted on their students (Hargreaves and Fink, 2012). Leadership was about dealing with uncertainty. School leadership was therefore critical in terms of identifying which external initiatives to adopt and adapt, which to reject and how to buffer staff against the avalanche of multiple top-down initiatives. Schools were conceptualized, drawing from management theory, as learning organizations that assumed more horizontal organizational forms encouraging teachers to share knowledge for reform.

Leadership is distributed

With choice policies in devolved systems producing greater inequality between schools, and the capacity of statistical models to focus on classrooms, the research and policy focus shifted to classroom practice, instructional leadership and teacher leadership. **Teacher leadership approaches** focused on the necessity for teacher professional development and collaboration as these are most likely to change everyday practice. Teacher ownership of change was considered fundamental to changing *and* sustaining new practices. Gronn (2008) argued that leadership responsibility in flatter organizations was *distributed* to teachers to focus on teaching and learning and share professional knowledge.

Change is a relational practice

Both change theorists and distributed-leadership approaches converged with the teacher professional-learning approaches. Both focused on the benefits of collaboration and professional-learning networks and communities of practice across schools in which teachers shared deep funds of professional knowledge related to content, pedagogy, discipline and of the learner. This relational approach to professional learning used multiple intellectual resources selectively rather than eclectically (Darling-Hammond and Bransford, 2005).

This view of teacher-led change also aligned with **action-research approaches** from the 1980s, which positioned teachers as researchers on and for practice through peer review and collaboration, drawing on notions of teachers as intuitive practitioners. Teachers worked together to identify a problem, collect evidence and work collaboratively with an external critical friend, and then evaluated and identified new issues and developed strategies – a form of school self-evaluation. This process of formative assessment through professional, relational and reflective practice positioned change as both incremental through everyday practice while managing different interventions arising from teacher research or external reform policies and refocus them towards student needs in context.

Diverse leadership for social justice

Critical approaches of leadership and school change from feminist, postcolonial, Black and Indigenous perspectives view schools as organizations socially constituted through gender, race, class, ethnic and sexual differentiation (Blackmore, 1999). Systemic and cultural forms of racial, gender and class discrimination play out in the dynamics of inter-personal relations in schools. Leadership, critical scholars argue, is embodied: perceptions and models of leadership are particularly open to stereotypes and biases based on race, class, gender, religion and sexuality impacting on leadership selection and practice (Tillman and Scheurich, 2014). Leaders should seek purposeful transformative change making schools and school systems more socially just. For example, the focus on gender-equity reform since the 1970s moved from changing girls and women, to changing curriculum and pedagogy in the 1980s, to changing school cultures in the 1990s and finally to changing masculinities in the 2000s. An important condition for equity is that governments are held responsible for policy and resources to enable schools to deliver equity as neither markets or local communities necessarily do so.

Change is an inclusive practice

Critical perspectives understand student learning outcomes broadly as physical, social and emotional as well as academic. To achieve these requires safe and inclusive school cultures facilitating a sense of belonging as emotional connectedness is a precondition to teaching and learning. Addressing bullying, discrimination and race- and gender-based harassment are critical to an inclusive school culture that also nurtures a diversity of approaches to and diversity of who leads. Leading school change, for Indigenous as postcolonial leaders, is about negotiating competing expectations of Eurocentric management top-down bureaucracies and local communities, challenging what is valued and what counts as success for schools and students. Indigenous leadership is understood and practised from a different worldview, with leaders representing and responsible to community and elders. Inclusive education is about valuing different forms of knowledge and knowing and understanding that leadership is a collective practice (Tillman and Scheurich, 2014).

The critical paradigms focus on issues of how class, race, gender, sexuality, religion and ethnicity (intersectionality) are factors in how leadership and change are undertaken, perceived and received. They see schools as sites of both social change and reproduction. Leaders should focus on equitable distribution of resources and programmes, recognition of difference and representation of all stakeholders as improved equity outcomes for marginalized groups benefit all students.

Activity 15.2

1 How do these leadership practices and processes of change align with or differ from your experience?
2 What are the commonly held key features of each approach?

Ownership of change is considered a key factor for sustainability of any reform and is most likely to occur with greater participation of all stakeholders – teachers, parents and students. Being involved in decision-making imparts a sense of agency and trust. Individuals are more likely to invest in rather than react against change. The pressure for greater **parental participation** coincided with increased parental choice, greater involvement on school boards and research arguing parental significance for early literacy and numeracy. Ownership frames the focus on **student voice and agency** with regard to decisions that impact on them. Students are considered co-producers in their learning as they bring funds of knowledge into school and schools need to cultivate their sense of belonging in a learning community.

Professional-learning theorists argue that school change is reliant on and driven by a well-educated and well-paid profession that has built with university researchers an evidence base, one that recognizes different stages of career and different professional development needs (Darling-Hammond and Bransford, 2005). Professional-learning networks between teachers and schools can enable sharing of initiatives that work, and hence scaling up innovation. Professional expertise includes not just using data, but an ability to make judgements and be adaptive to the changing context and student needs. The school leaders' role is to encourage staff to be innovative, develop strong internal peer review, protect their staff from overload and external pressures, and provide resources fairly as the overlay of multiple reforms can lead to contradiction and overload – reform fatigue and saturation.

The **emotional dimension of rapid and radical change** is now well recognized, but how this is understood varies. Those who are expected to change practice may feel their professional identity is threatened, their expertise ignored, or the initiative is not relevant and could be detrimental to their students. Earlier, the SEI paradigm saw emotional displays as a weakness and feminine. Now SEI, drawing from popular management literature, considers good leaders should acquire 'emotional intelligence' to manage deep-seated change. Critical perspectives view teaching as emotional work and leadership as about emotional management of the self and others (Blackmore, 1999). Feminists reject any emotionality/rationality binary and consider emotional displays are gendered, racialized and classed in terms of how they are enacted and perceived, and emotions often as symptomatic of the politicization of education. Schools' emotional economies draw on wider societal affective economies of anxiety (e.g. post-truth, terrorism and trolling).

Partnerships with universities, community organizations, industry or government have been a key thread in action research, teacher professional-learning communities of practice and most SEI. With growing inequality between rich and poor schools, communities and students, and the dismantling of public education systems, school leadership has focused on building collaboration with local health and welfare agencies and industry to support student health and well-being and create pathways into work and training. Partnerships can also inform school change. For example, creative practitioners can bring new sources of knowledge and imaginaries into a school in music and the arts (Hall and Thomson, 2017). Students and teachers can work in communities of practice with industry, community and in university research collaborations (Smyth et al., 2011).

Introducing Case Study 15.1: school redesign and innovative learning environments

The first case study is based on the Innovation Learning Environments (ILE) research study (learningspaces.edu.au) undertaken by Blackmore and colleagues (2012) in partnership with the OECD (Organisation for Economic Co-operation and Development) and Victorian Department of Education. The ILE study involved twelve Victorian schools (primary, secondary, community) across a representative sample of socio-economic profiles and locations (rural and urban).

We used the conceptual frame of redesign from Thomson and Blackmore's (2006) analysis of multiple case studies of leadership and school change. We argued that change as a concept suggests nothing necessarily or fundamentally new (as innovation suggests). Reform is an overused term and usually relates to system-wide initiatives. Redesign is about producing noticeable and fundamental changes in practice. This approach recognizes that schools as organizations are entangled in multiple interlocking sociocultural (community, demography), discursive (policy, media, governance) and material (location, buildings) environments and are deterritorialized due to outreach programmes, virtual communities, interagency services and professional networks.

Redesign is about reconfiguring the range of existing resources and attracting new ones (people, ideas, funds, buildings, community resources, policies etc.) to rethink what a school is doing for its students, thus adopting a critical perspective. Redesign means school leaders (principal/heads and teachers) need to attend to the cognitive, spatial, temporal, cultural, structural, communicative (face to face and virtual), aesthetic and semiotic practices of the school and its community in order to reorganize learning, rethink the use of time and space, how to communicate ideas, change the language, address relationships and involve all stakeholders, or relational leadership.

We argue that redesign recognizes that fundamental change is often contingent on a convergence of favourable factors – a new principal, a group of staff, or a policy – facilitating the opportunity to identify and agree on the need to do something differently. This agreement provides the warrant for purposeful change and who gets involved in the change process (ownership). Redesign is both process and product, requiring a formative process of self-evaluation set against desirable and achievable outcomes within a time frame. Evidence of the full range of student social, emotional, physical and cognitive outcomes can be acquired through multiple approaches and measures – student material artefacts (print, visual, aural), performances, observational data (students and teachers), behaviour and engagement, surveys, diagnostic and standardized assessments, parent involvement and personal relationships.

Case Study 15.1 Redesign – the Innovation Learning Environments study

In the ILE project, the Department of Education Leading Schools Fund invited clusters of schools in disadvantaged communities to rethink provision. In return, participant schools would gain additional funding, regional support and the capacity to work with architects, school councils and parents to plan innovative built environments. Multiple configurations resulted – multi-campus schools with senior/middle/primary years, community precincts and out-of-school spaces. Metaphors used to design the ILE, such as street or home, recognized the importance of relationships, belonging and place and the affective dimensions of learning. We researched student responses to these new environments using visual and digital techniques focused on safe places to be learn and play.

Who initiated change and the nature of the warrant varied. In an urban primary school in a well-off suburb, a Year 6 Anim8tion programme was introduced when student satisfaction surveys indicated that students were bored. The federal government Building the Education Revolution provided the opportunity to build a new learning space. Two teachers with computing and animation expertise initiated a one-day-a-week programme where Year 6 students working in self-selected teams, wrote storylines, drew and built stage settings, created and made animation characters and developed a five-minute video clip presented on graduation. Additional resources came from the school council, local Apple store and an Emmy-award-winning animation director. The students developed multiple interdisciplinary skills and an observable improved capacity for independent learning and social interaction. Team-teaching led to greater cross-discip-linary collaboration, and increased planning time encouraged teachers to share lesson plans. Due to excellent evaluations, other year levels reconsidered their programme, thus scaling up redesign.

At a large secondary college in a rural region with high school dropout, youth and intergenerational unemployment, the year level coordinators gained state funds to create an out-of-school ILE in the business centre. The focus was on students who found formal senior schooling difficult, including young mothers, who could learn online and/or in the new space, with teachers acting as adult tutors in a workplace environment. The initial aim of the 100 students was to return to complete Year 12, which many did. But success was redefined to include entering a vocational course or employment. Teachers circu-lated from the mainstream school to the ILE because they found it challenging and satisfying, leading them to critically reflect on teaching practice generally.

In a severely disadvantaged community, two primary schools were amalgamated despite parent protest. A community school with other agencies in childcare, welfare and counselling services on site was designed with the staff, parents and local government. Three separate learning spaces were built (Years 1–2, 3–4 and 5–6) around the central complex and a kindergarten. Each team of teachers was encouraged to focus less on standardized assessment and more on developing innovative and personalized pedagogies addressing student needs to make them feel successful. After six years, student academic achievement improved, as had student health and well-being. Parents volunteered to staff the front desk and the school hall and community facilities hosted a monthly market and sports events. The parent-volunteers told us they felt the school symbolized that they were respected by government and they wanted to reciprocate.

Thinking about Case Study 15.1: serial redesign

These vignettes indicate multiple factors about leading school change: the enabling policies (Leading Schools Fund, Leadership Development Framework), transitional funding and regional support. Teachers led innovation when opportunities existed. Leadership practices moved from being more directive to dispersed as collaborative practices and team teaching were consolidated with flatter structures and responsibility devolved to team leaders of learning centres. This imparted a sense of trust. All schools identified the importance of teacher autonomy, self-direction and agency. Ownership of change was critical – whether teachers, students or parents. Individuals invest in change if they see it has positive outcomes for the students.

Each school had a different warrant for redesign and adopted different foci: whole school, programmatic, year level or community. Importantly, principals/heads encouraged staff to take risks and experiment without blame for failure, and allocated resources to support the ILE. The new built environment was a catalyst, but did not lead to fundamental changes in practice without significant teacher professional development and experimentation pedagogically in open learning spaces. Leadership capacity-building resulted from experienced teachers mentoring next-generation teachers. After occupancy, open flexible learning spaces required constant reorganization (serial redesign) of time and space to sustain innovative pedagogies, as available resources need to be constantly reconfigured to meet the changing needs of staff, students and communities. Overall, what counted as success broadened to beyond academic achievement to include cognitive, social and emotional effects, health and well-being, while promoting belonging and enjoyment.

Introducing Case Study 15.2: leading from the ground up

New schools are critical sites of educational change, offering opportunities to present innovative curriculum approaches or (re)present existing ones. McNae and others examined how ten teachers, twenty-five students and two principals at Domaibest High School – a pseudonym – in New Zealand, as the foundation community, were agentic in establishing a school. Using Fletcher's (2008) Architecture of Ownership framework, and Phillips' (1990) categories of agentic behaviour – **control**, **bonding** and **meaning**, participants generated digital artefacts as indicators of decision-making (control), belonging (bonding) and meaning-making (meaning). In interviews, students and teachers shared reasoning for selecting certain images, and collaboratively explored how they made sense of, and forged, their agentic identities regarding relational, pedagogical, cultural and physical architectures within the overarching frame of ownership.

Case Study 15.2 Leadership architectures – distributive, disruptive and deliberative

At Domaibest High School (DHS) – a pseudonym – in New Zealand, the junior high was established in 2016, adding new student cohorts at Years 7, 8, 9 and 10 to meet demand. The senior high school (Years 11–13) had an innovative curriculum. The focus was on team-teaching and curriculum combinations, modular learning and integrated curriculum. Students tracked their project-based learning in time blocks with flexibility to earn credits and learning coaches in a vertical advisory system. In 2017, the schools combined with the expectation of greater staff flexibility, fewer transitional barriers for students and improved familial and professional collaboration. All principals had grown their school. Now their leadership approaches were renegotiated, requiring reflection on practice. The research interview with us became an occasion for peer reflection and talking about 'being', growing' and 'changing' as leaders were transformed by these experiences. The principals highlighted collaborative leadership practices within a 'power-sharing' context such as working together in open-plan offices, encouraging collaboration and adaptive help-seeking.

A distributed lens of leadership drew attention to how 'freedoms' were being 'distributed' in DHS. Space, choice and opportunities were evident with the sharing of skills, knowledge and power, a leadership 'presence' and the creation of leadership identities, agency and ownership. Each principal's leadership practice framed their leadership team, whose members then interpreted and implemented decisions according to delegated responsibilities. Each principal encouraged others to lead, extend their creative thinking and innovate pedagogically, demonstrating faith in their teams to make things happen: collaborative, relational and pedagogical leadership. Trusting others to lead means leadership is a **search for wholeness**.

Both principals demonstrated strategic and deliberative leadership actions by making purposeful appointments and employing teaching staff to fully complement the skills and abilities needed in teams. One principal created a diverse leadership team, appointing people to share leadership tasks which also required her to openly reflect on her own leadership skills, abilities and experiences. Involving specific teachers in decision-making about an integrated curriculum created new professional relationships in preparation for future timetable changes and workload allocation. Communicating a clear under-standing of why decisions were made and how decisions contributed to changing the educational landscape was essential. Both leaders sought to create sustained and embedded change by setting ambitious but achievable goals identified by teachers and students.

Their 'disruptive' leadership practice was seen to challenge traditional architectures and reshape relationships to suit the context. Leaders developed evaluative systems and processes to highlight taken-for-granted / residual practices no longer fit for purpose, thus disrupting unhelpful practices or historical discourses that did not align with the school vision. Both principals embraced risk-taking, engaged with constantly evolving practices, resources and staff combinations, particularly when creating learning modules. Both realized the importance of teacher and student involvement in deliberative decision-making processes, even with restricted timelines. A new school afforded different opportunities: multiple teachers working in one space shared with students and students addressing teachers by their first names. Reflecting on these ritualized practices was important, as was acknowledgement that everyone was a learner grappling with new topics. Students understood that teachers were making sense of their new teaching approaches and integrated curricula.

Team leaders could influence the pace of change, but required others to take risks and address professional discomfort. Leaders, teachers and students came to a shared under-standing of learning beyond narrow standards of success. They were supported in their experimentation and professional development, developing both capacity and self-efficacy, all precursors to sustainable change. Creating spaces for teachers and learners to find their place for **becoming** and **being** were important aims to build the relational architecture of a new school and leadership as a pedagogical relationship. Actions for change do not occur in a social vacuum.

Activity 15.3

Consider the theories of change in the light of these two case studies. Which have the most relevance? Why so?

Power relations, structure and agency

Much of the school-improvement literature ignores the politics of school reform and discursive context promoted in the media and politics about 'good' schools. They sideline how the market logic of neoliberal policies through choice and competition has increased social, economic and educational inequality. Focusing on school or teacher leadership as the solution distracts from wider sociocultural and economic factors impacting on schools. The SEI literature fails to address power inequalities of intersectional difference arising from gender, class, race, sexuality, ethnicity, disability or faith, which impact on how leaders are perceived and on leadership practices in different contexts.

The notions of redesign and relational leadership capture critical multidimensional aspects of how change works on, in and for schools, teachers and their students. There is no structure/agency or macro/micro binary, as schools are structuring structures which shape leadership agency. Critical approaches recognize the reality of teachers' and students' lives and how schools are social and community centres with multiple online and face-to-face interconnections locally and globally. Theories of school redesign that will make a difference to student learning, health and well-being recognize that students learn through multiple sources in and out of schools, through peers, families, popular culture, non-school activities of clubs, voluntarism, faith organizations and the internet.

What are the effects of these critical approaches?

Redesign and relational leadership approaches impart power to teachers and, in some cases, students, as leaders and keepers of various forms of knowledge – evidence from research, data and intuitive knowledge arising from experience. Parents and students are welcomed as co-producers of knowledge, which takes on multiple forms (for example, visual, digital, physical). These approaches recognize that innovation often emerges in schools facing the greatest challenges, that such schools need more systemic support and less surveillance, that innovation begins with teachers and school leaders, but requires professional freedoms to be experienced and enabling policies and conditions as teachers and schools cannot initiate and sustain innovation over time.

Educational leadership is a relational, contextual and social practice that belongs to everyone, rather than residing in an individual. It is a *way of being* and *becoming* rather than simply *doing*. Leadership is values-driven and draws on a capacity to display empathy and compassionate authority and to accept feedback, but always being reflexive with regard to one's own position and self-relative to others in terms of relations of power and difference. School leadership is about knowing your students, staff and community; having the capacity to listen and to encourage initiative; gathering and allocating resources; buffering staff against multiple conflicting policy agendas, deciding what to adapt, adopt or ignore to meet specific needs of school; mediating relationships between teachers and parents; providing a storyline using metaphors or examples to encourage innovation; supporting risk-taking; promoting interschool exchange and networking; and establishing deliberative decision-making and transparency as the norm.

A critical perspective of educational leadership questions all reform initiatives on the basis of expected social-justice outcomes (McNae, 2014). It views leadership as power to be shared and within networks of unequal relationships. The processes of redesign and relational leadership require leader and teachers to be reflective on and in practice as well as for practice, with a commitment not only to their students in a school, but also to developing a knowledge base and promoting the profession and education as a public good.

Activity 15.4

Have our arguments presented through these case studies altered your view of leading educational change? If so, how?

What needs to change?

These case studies are from highly devolved systems where leaders have some capacity to select staff and have one-line budgets, which imparts discretionary capacity. But schools are not 'autonomous'. Schools exist in policy, socio-geographical and governance environments, receive government funds and community support and have a legal, financial and moral obligation to society. Widening disparity between students and schools requires public funds to go to schools in most need and all schools, government and non-government, should be held accountable for equity outcomes.

Top-down models of school change driven by external universal standardized accountabilities implicitly undervalue and symbolize mistrust of both teachers and students. Redesign and relational leadership approaches put teachers and students first with 'the system' providing enabling policies within a social-justice frame and the necessary resources. School systems need to be adaptive, combining top-down and bottom-up supportive approaches to reform with feedback.

Often ignored in theorizing school change are the changing conditions of teachers' work – which are also the conditions of student learning. Trust in teachers must be rebuilt.

Just as it is difficult for students to learn if they are not healthy and well fed, have well-being, feel safe and that they belong in the school, similarly teachers working under stress – due to lack of resources, discourses of failure, performative displays that impact with long-term emotional and physical effects – cannot do their best. Collectively, leaders need to attend to the affective economy of the school to develop a sense of hope while addressing the realities, as schools cannot compensate for society.

Activity 15.5

What do these examples tell you about the governance of schools (government systemic, devolved, charter, free, academies etc.) and how this impacts on leading change?

Conclusion

In this chapter, we show that fundamental school change is not a fast or easy process. Often changes occur unnoticed merely through incremental shifts in ideas, routines and practices. More purposeful approaches can be whole of school, programmatic, year level or community focused. Reform can be externally imposed or principal- and/or teacher-, and sometimes student-initiated and led. Imposed or bottom-up reform can produce superficial change which quickly dissipates, or more fundamental and enduring change. Change is contingent, depending on whether leaders and teachers individually and collectively invest professionally and emotionally, on competing imperatives, adequacy of supports and resources, and leadership support. Critical leadership practice addresses power inequalities, difference, ownership, relationships, communication, recognition and resources and focuses on social-justice issues to improve the learning of all students across a wide range of social, physical and cognitive outcomes.

Activity 15.6

Do you see leadership and/or change differently? If so, how?

Further reading

Fuller, K. and Harford, J. (2016) *Gender and leadership in education: achieving against the odds*. Oxford: Peter Lang.

Hargreaves, A., Lieberman, A., Fullan, M. and Hopkins, D. (eds) (2009) *Second international handbook of educational change*. London: Springer.

Lingard, B., Hayes, D., Mills, M. and Christie, P. (2005) *Leading learning: making hope practical in schools*. Sydney: Allen and Unwin.

Wrigley, T., Thomson, P. and Lingard, B. (eds) (2012) *Changing schools: alternative ways to make a world of difference*. Abingdon: Routledge.

References

Blackmore, J. (1999) *Troubling women: feminism, leadership and educational change*. Buckingham: Open University Press.

Darling-Hammond, L. and Bransford, J. (eds) (2005) *Preparing teachers for a changing world: what teachers should learn and be able to do*. San Francisco, CA: Jossey-Bass.

Fletcher, A. (2008) Giving students ownership of learning: the architecture of ownership. *Educational Leadership*, 66(3). Available online: http://www.ascd.org/publications/educational-leadership/nov08/vol66/num03/The-Architecture-of-Ownership.aspx (accessed 4 August 2020).

Fullan, M. (1993) *Change forces: probing the depths of education reform*. London: Falmer Press.

Gronn, P. (2008) The future of distributed leadership. *Journal of Educational Administration*, 46(2), 141–158

Hall, C. and Thomson, P. (2017) *Inspiring school change: transforming education through the creative arts*. Abingdon: Routledge.

Hallinger, P. and Heck, R. (2010) Collaborative leadership and school improvement; understanding the impact on school capacity and student learning. *School Leadership and Management*, 30(2), 95–110.

Hargreaves, A. and Fink, D. (2012) *Sustainable leadership*. San Francisco, CA, Jossey-Bass.

McNae, R. (2014) Seeking social justice. In: C.M. Branson and S.J. Gross (eds), *Handbook of ethical educational leadership* (pp. 93–111). New York: Routledge.

Phillips, N. (1990) Wellness during childhood/adolescent development. *Prevention Forum*, 10(4), 1–10.

Smyth, J., Angus, L., Down, B. and McInerney, P. (2011) *Critically engaged learning: connecting to young lives*. New York: Peter Lang.

Thomson, P. and Blackmore, J. (2006) Beyond the power of one: redesigning the work of school principals. *Journal of Educational Change*, 7(3), 161–177.

Tillman, L. and Scheurich, J. (eds) (2014) *Handbook of research on educational leadership for equity and diversity*. New York: Routledge.

Part three

Critical perspectives and approaches to contemporary issues in educational leadership

16   Gender and educational leadership
   Jane Wilkinson, Anar Purvee and Katrina MacDonald   **255**

17   Sexual identity and educational leadership
   Catherine A. Lugg and Robin Roscigno   **269**

18   Race and educational leadership
   Mark A. Gooden and Victoria Showunmi   **281**

19   Socio-economic class and educational leadership
   Helen M. Gunter and Steven J. Courtney   **295**

20   Governance and educational leadership
   Andrew Wilkins and Brad Gobby   **309**

21 Performativity, managerialism and educational leadership
    Tanya Fitzgerald and David Hall   323

22 Corporatization and educational leadership
    Kenneth Saltman and Alexander J. Means   339

23 Leading in a genetics-informed education market
    Steven Jones, Steven J. Courtney and Helen M. Gunter   355

Gender and educational leadership

Jane Wilkinson, Anar Purvee and Katrina MacDonald

16

What this chapter is about	256
Key questions that this chapter addresses	256
Introduction	256
Gender and leadership in educational leadership scholarship and practice	258
Gender as a problem in educational leadership, and its effect on thinking and practice	260
How does thinking *intersectionally* illuminate this issue?	261
What needs to change?	263
Introducing the case studies: Rachael and Gegeen	264
Conclusion	267
Further reading	268
References	268

What this chapter is about

Since the 1980s, feminist scholars and those working in masculinity studies have focused on how gender as a category of social analysis historically has been ignored and/or sidelined in the field of educational leadership. In this chapter, we shed light on how this issue has been addressed in scholarship, particularly in contemporary accounts of educational leadership practice in the compulsory and post-compulsory education sectors. Taking a critical focus on power relations, structure and agency, we examine why these accounts are problematic, particularly in terms of how educational leadership is conceptualized and practised. We use case studies of women leaders (in an Australian school and a Mongolian university) to argue that thinking intersectionally enables the reconceptualization of how gender intersects with other social categories such as class and race. We thereby (re)construct educational leadership as practice and illuminate issues of power, agency and the politics of leadership.

Key questions that our chapter addresses

1 Why do we need to examine gender and educational leadership?
2 How are gender and educational leadership socially and culturally constructed?
3 What are the power relations that underpin these constructions?
4 How do these power relations work to reassert stereotypical ideas of gender and educational leadership?

Introduction

We are going to begin our chapter with some key definitions that we will be drawing on throughout our analysis and to answer the following question: how can stereotypical ideas about gender and educational leadership be interrogated and challenged to bring about societal change?

Before commencing this chapter, read the questions in Activity 16.1 and jot down your thoughts. At the end of the chapter, we will ask you to go back to your original thoughts and see whether and if so, how, they may have changed.

Educational leadership: Educational leadership . . . is about unequal relationships of power informed by multiple intersectionalities of gender, race, class, ethnicity, religion and sexuality and enacted into practice that is situated within a conjuncture of particular historical, social, political and economic moments. There is no universal or specific model of leadership that can ignore context. Nor is there a leader–follower dichotomy so often assumed in the conventional or hero-leadership imaginaries but rather a constant re/negotiation of leadership as a collective social practice immersed in relations of interdependence and intersubjectivity and under conditions not of any leader's own making. *(Blackmore, 2018: 208)*

Gender: 'Gender is the structure of social relations that centres on the reproductive arena and the set of practices that bring reproductive distinctions between bodies into social processes. . . . Gender concerns the way human societies deal with human bodies and their continuity, and the many consequences of that "dealing" in our personal lives and our collective fate' (Connell and Pearse, 2009: 11).

Masculinities: 'Masculinities are not equivalent to men; they concern the *position* of men in a gender order. They can be defined as the patterns and practice by which people (both men and women, although predominantly men) engage that perspective' (Connell, n.d., para. 1).

Feminisms: Feminist thought is old enough to have a history complete with a set of labels: liberal, radical, Marxist/socialist, psychoanalytic, care-focused, existentialist, postmodern, women of colour, global, postcolonial, transnational, and ecofeminist. To be sure, this list of labels is incomplete and highly contestable . . . Yet, feminist thought's traditional labels still remain serviceable. They signal to the public that feminism is not a monolithic ideology and that all feminists do not think alike.

The labels also help mark the number of different approaches, perspectives, and frameworks that a variety of feminists have used to shape both their explanations for women's oppression and their proposed solutions for its elimination. *(Tong, 2014: 11)*

Activity 16.1

1 Consider the stereotypes of gender and leadership you have encountered in your lifetime. What are the common media discourses in relation to leadership more generally and the gendered identities of leaders more specifically?
2 Do these stereotypes vary depending on the individual's class, sexuality and/or race?
3 Are there other forms of leadership you can identify which move beyond the stereotypical individual hero leader so often encountered in Anglo/Euro-societies?
4 What are these other forms of leadership and what do they suggest about how leadership could be differently conceptualized and practised?

Gender and leadership in educational leadership scholarship and practice

Traditional definitions of educational leadership tend to focus on leader–follower relations, an individual's influence on others, or a person's formal position in a hierarchy. For example, think of how *failing* schools that have a miraculous *turn-around* are portrayed in the media and by educators and educational systems. Too often, the complex work of changing educational practices is viewed as the primary task of individual hero headteachers / principals riding in on their metaphorical white horses to *save* struggling schools and students. The reality is far more complex than this. Yet these stereotypical ways of viewing and understanding leadership have a tendency to stick. They are part of a historical folklore embedded in deeply held societal attitudes about relationships between the genders, and what is *right* and *proper* work for men and women. Put simply, teaching has for a long time been regarded as women's work, whereas administration is men's work. In other words, educational leadership is still more typically associated with (white, able-bodied, heterosexual male) values and traits, such as competitiveness, assertiveness and individuality – the male hero/saviour. An increasing body of scholarship by gender scholars in studies of educational leadership and leadership studies more broadly has challenged this perspective. This scholarship has focused primarily on the gender binaries of masculine and feminine and this chapter explores these scholars' insights; however, it is crucial to recognize that the binary essentializing of gender may silence those whose identities do not fall within the masculine/feminine binary.

One of the key bodies of work that has challenged stereotypical views of educational leadership is that of feminist scholarship. Feminists have examined the puzzle of how and why women remain under-represented in leadership positions in female-dominated industries such as schools (and increasingly universities). Their research reveals that women's under-representation in leadership positions in education and leadership more broadly is a global phenomenon. It has been termed the **glass ceiling** or the *grass ceiling* (for women in agricultural leadership). The under-representation of women in educational leadership has been studied in a range of nations such as Australia, Canada, China, Finland, Hong Kong, New Zealand, Pakistan, the United Kingdom and the United States. The key reasons identified for this under-representation include:

> **Essentializing:** Essentialism entails the belief that those characteristics defined as women's essence are shared in common by all women at all times. It implies a limit of the variations and possibilities of change – it is not possible for a subject to act in a manner contrary to her essence. Her essence underlies all the apparent variations differentiating women from each other. Essentialism thus refers to the existence of fixed characteristic, given attributes, and ahistorical functions that limit the possibilities of change and thus of social reorganization. *(Grosz, 1995: 47–48)*

1   **Double burdens:** women encounter double burdens in their careers as they frequently juggle their caring roles (taking care of their children, partners and elderly parents) and professional demands. In traditional family structures in the West, fathers and husbands have not been expected to take on caring roles, thus leaving them 'carefree' to pursue careers without caring interruptions, and with the support of a female partner who carries out the domestic duties.

2 **Women as outsiders:** formal positions of power and authority such as headteachers /principals are historically viewed as highly masculinist forms of labour, i.e. *men's work*. Women face challenges because they are seen not to possess qualities typically associated with masculinist understandings of how leadership should be exercised, e.g. being assertive, commanding and in control. Yet for women, there is a double bind, for the same behaviours exhibited by males and females are often differently construed – assertive behaviour by a male may be applauded as a sign of leadership potential – condemned as *ball-breaking* behaviour if carried out by a female.

3 **Women as change agents:** historically, women have been viewed as outsiders in educational leadership. More recently, however, this outsider status has been harnessed by education systems as valuable in times of restructuring, for example, women may be brought in to challenge the status quo of schools, universities etc. In politics, women may be brought in as the new broom to clean up the mess left behind by traditional forms of governing that have failed (cf. the election of Theresa May as prime minister of the UK to usher in Brexit; the election of Prime Minister Julia Gillard in Australia when the previous prime minister was seen as too difficult to continue in his role).

4 **Gendered divisions:** in academia, women dominate in teaching and men in research. In schools, women are over-represented in teaching and males in administration. This historical gendered division of labour has further contributed to unequal opportunities of income, power and leadership for women.

5 **Vertical divisions:** in academia, fewer women receive postgraduate degrees and move into more elite research positions compared to males. Instead, there has been an increasing bifurcation of academia, with women concentrated in the less prestigious positions of middle management (e.g. head of school and dean) and males in more prestigious positions of research, which can attract large sums of funding and status. Therefore, gendered divisions in academia start early.

6 **Horizontal divisions:** academia is highly gendered. For example, women are over-represented in the less well paid, less elite and more feminized areas of study, such as the humanities and social sciences, whereas males as a group are over-represented in the so-called 'hard' sciences, and the better paid areas of engineering, medicine and information technology.

7 **Patriarchal institutions:** educational institutions employ highly masculinist notions of leadership that frequently reproduce and reward what is seen as more typical or characteristic male ways of behaving, and which are associated with leadership. Therefore, these practices are often reproduced and are seen as legitimate characteristics of leaders.

Focusing on how women are numerically under-represented in leadership roles in schools, further education and universities across the globe is a first and very powerful step in recognizing the global nature of this problem. If something is not measured, it becomes invisible and can be forgotten or ignored. However, there can be a number of problems with focusing on women leaders, their challenges and their numerical under-representation in leadership.

Gender as a problem in educational leadership, and its effect on thinking and practice

The first major issue with how gender and leadership are addressed in contemporary scholarship is that focusing purely on the under-representation of women leaders in education and/or their challenges may ignore other major issues about unequal power relations in society. Measuring women's under-representation in organizations such as schools and other education sectors and then documenting the challenges they face is vital.

However, if we stop there and assume that everything will be fine if only we can get equal numbers of women into leadership positions, then we ignore the complex reality that the under-representation of women is symptomatic of a larger issue of unequal/asymmetrical power relations in organizations and society more generally. Although in theory, a sector such as education might eventually achieve the same numbers of women and men in leadership, does this mean that equity (rather than equality which denotes everyone is at the same level) has genuinely been achieved? What of the ideologies, beliefs and values that may still pervade organizations and that are frequently misogynistic, racist and class-based? Would numerical parity for men and women leaders overcome these issues?

Second, a focus on women's under-representation and their challenges silences how leadership has traditionally been constructed as a masculinist enterprise. In other words, it constructs women as the problem to be solved whilst ignoring how particular qualities associated with more traditional ways of leading are valued and privileged in organizations. For instance, white, heterosexual males who are assertive are often viewed as leadership material, whereas males who do not fit these descriptors and women as a group may be sidelined, devalued or marginalized. To redress this issue, a growing field of scholarship known as masculinity studies has begun to challenge these heteronormative assumptions about how leadership should be understood and practised. Jeff Hearn and Raewyn Connell's scholarship in this area is particularly valuable.

Third, focusing on the numerical representation of women in leadership runs the risk of **essentializing** gender as a category. In other words, it may fall into the trap of reproducing binary divisions: classist, sexist, racist assumptions about *women* and *men* as groups, while failing to understand that there are critical differences not only between categories of gender but also within them. For instance, there is no such thing as a homogenous group of *women*. There are major differences between women depending on one's class, race, sexuality, able-bodiedness, etc. We explore these differences in our case studies. Likewise, the essentializing of gender as a category silences and 'others' those who feel they do not fit within the binarized suite of attitudes, behaviours, dispositions and practices attributed to the categories of male and female.

This is where understanding how gender is socially and culturally constructed is crucial. How leadership is practised, played out and understood looks very different depending on your subject location. For example, if you are an Indigenous woman leader in an Australian university, how you will be treated and how you will practise leadership may look very different from a Greek-background, working-class-background female leader in the same sector.

Fourth, focusing purely on women leaders and their numerical under-representation means that we frequently slide into arguments that become focused on female versus male leaders, e.g. do women and men enact different leadership styles? Is one leadership style better than the other? Do we need more women leaders in order to present a *softer* face of leadership to the world? Such arguments become essentializing, ascribing stereotypically gendered traits of masculinity or femininity to the sexes and reproducing fixed gender binaries that ignore a range of identities that do not correspond to durable ideas of what it means to '*do*' and '*be*' male and female. They ignore the reality that gender is not a fixed biological category but instead is about social and cultural differences ascribed to people who may identify as women or men.

This criticism does not mean that we should ignore or abandon studies of gender and leadership in education because they are critical in focusing the gaze on how social relations of gender are reproduced and constituted. Instead, critical feminists have shifted from solely documenting the challenges and barriers we have noted to also examining how educational leadership is socially and culturally constructed and produced. Feminist scholars have argued that leadership should not be defined purely as the possession of an individual (frequently white, able-bodied, heterosexual male) but rather can also be seen as a collective process encompassing not only power *over* others but power *with* others. These alternative definitions are crucial, for they highlight different types of power relations in leadership that are frequently ignored or overlooked – for example, how groups of people may work together in activist ways to promote causes that have a social good associated with them. To this end, Jill Blackmore, a major scholar in the field of critical feminist educational leadership scholarship argues that:

> Feminist analyses can no longer just focus on the shared experiences of women leaders in individual schools, nationally or cross culturally. Rather than focus on women leaders, feminist researchers need to focus on the social relations of gender and how these are reproduced/produce and constituted within globalized school systems. The feminist gaze needs to refocus on the wider gender restructuring of the social, political and economic in ways that they produce patterns of inequality that position women leaders and teachers in particular ways that limit or enable their leadership practices in specific contexts . . . This focus on the social and political relations of organizations means moving away from viewing women's disadvantage as an individualized problem addressed by changing women. Instead, the focus should be on how privilege is gained and retained by dominant perspectives and groups. *(Blackmore, 2013: 149)*

How does thinking *intersectionally* illuminate this issue?

Educational scholarship has been dominated by Anglocentric, American-centric and Eurocentric accounts and ways of conceptualizing and practising leadership. The

Intersectionality: 'Over three decades, social scientists have documented that gender does not exist in a universal form. Rather, gender is continuously shaped in relationship to other distinctions and in turn continuously affects those same – intersecting – distinctions. Intersectionality is a captivating concept whose applications have shown that inequalities are fashioned and orchestrated in complex, inconsistent, continuously changing, and historically varying ways' (Messerschmidt et al., 2018: 7).

unthinking imposition of Western-centric models of leadership such as distributed or transformational leadership on non-Western and/or Indigenous education systems that may be neither relevant nor appropriate to these cultural contexts is a contemporary version of colonization. This focus has been critiqued by scholars, yet such critiques overlook how other social categories such as that of gender, sexuality, race and class also intersect with cultural contexts to (re)produce essentializing and stereotypical constructions of leadership (see Chapters 17–19 of this textbook).

This domination of an Anglo/Eurocentric gaze extends to feminist scholarship. Although changing, when it comes to gender and leadership, much of the literature assumes an Anglocentric, white, heteronormative and middle-class female as its invisible and taken-for-granted subject location. Yet, emerging research for/with women from a range of equity backgrounds in 'Western' countries, 'non-Western' countries and Indigenous communities reveal both similar and very different conceptions and practices of leadership. This research challenges essentializing assumptions that lump women together in a homogenous (white, female) group. Women in the field of education may share similar trajectories; however, they face and encounter different types of marginalization and issues in regard to their diverse social and cultural backgrounds. Therefore, studies of leadership using an intersectional lens explore how gender intersects with different kinds of social categories, such as race, class, age, sexuality and cultural backgrounds. We sum up the key issues we have raised in Figure 16.1.

'Race' is one of the most commonly studied social categories (see Chapter 18 of this textbook). Many studies have found that women leaders from ethnic-minority backgrounds face numerous challenges because particular types of masculinities associated with whiteness have been privileged in educational leadership. For instance, women from marginalized backgrounds encounter systematic discrimination in educational leadership because of their race and gender, including being excluded from important networks and events that would be helpful for their career advancement. They frequently face triple burdens in regard to their caring roles as well as having to culturally adjust in order to enact leadership

Figure 16.1 Comparison of differing perspectives of women's under-representation in leadership.

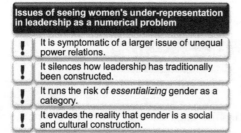

Issues of seeing women's under-representation in leadership as a numerical problem
! It is symptomatic of a larger issue of unequal power relations.
! It silences how leadership has traditionally been constructed.
! It runs the risk of *essentializing* gender as a category.
! It evades the reality that gender is a social and cultural construction.

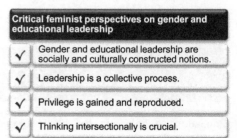

Critical feminist perspectives on gender and educational leadership
✓ Gender and educational leadership are socially and culturally constructed notions.
✓ Leadership is a collective process.
✓ Privilege is gained and reproduced.
✓ Thinking intersectionally is crucial.

in predominantly Anglo/Euro settings. Moreover, the intersection of gender and religion may have a powerful and disciplining effect as gendered religious discourses can negatively impact on how women leaders practise and experience their leadership.

Studies of/with Indigenous women leaders powerfully illuminate how alternative approaches to leadership may emerge and a collective and spiritual construct may be enacted. For instance, Benham and Murakami-Ramalho (2010: 78) put forward a collective and spiritual model of a **community of leadership** based on interviews with Indigenous Hawai'ian educational leaders. They identify principles of leadership derived from Indigenous Hawai'ian spiritual beliefs which incorporate 'Ha', the 'breath of life . . . that links all persons, past, present, and future', and the notion of place, 'land, sky, and sea' (Benham and Murakami-Ramalho, 2010: 81). This view of leadership challenges 'traditional epistemologies of Western leadership as a unidirectional, hierarchical and culturally neutral property of individuals' (Wilkinson and Bristol, 2018: 9). Instead, it: 'open[s] up epistemological, methodological and ontological spaces' through which Indigenous women leaders can speak back to these essentializing narratives (Wilkinson and Bristol, 2018: 9).

What needs to change?

With the continued impact of neoliberal orthodoxies on all aspects of social life, the effects are being felt within feminist movements. Catherine Rottenberg, in *The rise of neoliberal feminism*, argues 'a movement once dedicated . . . to women's liberation is now being framed in extremely individualistic terms, consequently ceasing to raise the specter of social or collective justice' (Rottenberg, 2018: 54). However, a new generation of young women feminist activists also suggests a consciousness-raising. For example, the #MeToo movement has sparked a worldwide reckoning, elevating the voices of women who have experienced sexual violence and harassment. Australian Clementine Ford, despite relentless online trolling from Men's Rights Activists, has been a strong voice in actively challenging of patriarchal systems that dominate and subjugate women. Her books *Fight like a girl,* and *Boys will be boys* address toxic masculinity and the importance for young women to embrace the feminist movement.

In America, young women such as Alexandria Ocasio-Cortez, a democratic socialist and a woman of colour was voted in to serve in the United States Congress in 2016. She uses her platform to challenge 'lazy tropes about women leaders' (twitter.com/AOC/status/1087758426615222274). In America, the Women's March on Washington, held the day after Donald Trump's inauguration as the US president, saw between 3 million and 5 million people participating in the United States with further participation across the world. The movement has since built a political movement called #womenswave with an agenda to fight for women's rights in the lead up to the 2020 presidential elections. The burgeoning fourth-wave feminist movements have much work to do in the face of the hegemony of neoliberal feminism that supports individualistic responses. New feminisms and consciousness-raising are required to challenge these hegemonies and also address the criticisms from women of colour concerning the lack of intersectionality.

Introducing the case studies: Rachael and Gegeen

Let us introduce two examples of how an intersectional analysis is crucial in examining diverse social categories. We choose two real-life cases. First, you will read about *Rachael* (all names pseudonymized), a principal / headteacher working in a primary school located in an area of concentrated social disadvantage in Australia. Her case is a good example of how class and gender intersect to influence the choices women make about aspiring to leadership positions. The second case focuses on *Gegeen*, who is a female university leader in Mongolia. Her case is a good example of how age, gender and sociocultural background intersect with each other when it comes to leadership practices.

Case Study 16.1 Rachael

Rachael was born in Northern Ireland in the late 1950s. Her parents were poor in Ireland and migrated with Rachael and her older brother to Australia during the Bring Out a Briton campaign (BOAB) under the Assisted Passage Migration Scheme in 1963. The BOAB campaign aimed to boost the numbers of white British immigrants to Australia in the face of post-war immigration and growing public anxiety about non-white immigrants. Rachael was five years old when they left Ireland and she notes that they arrived 'with nothing to their name'. Her family settled in the western suburbs of a large Australian city where her father worked as a carpenter and her mother in a dry-cleaning factory. Her memories of her working-class childhood reinforce the values that her parents instilled in her, telling her 'that anything is possible with hard work and knowledge' and that 'money doesn't necessarily solve any problems'.

Rachael's narrative around the lessons she takes from her working-class parents and her childhood reflect a classic meritocracy discourse: that education is a social equalizer. The idea that talent combined with effort affords all people the opportunity to navigate across social, cultural and economic boundaries is entrenched in meritocracy discourses around the world. In wealthy nations such as Australia, rising inequality coupled with stagnating social mobility belies meritocratic success.

Even though Rachael states that all she had ever wanted to be was a teacher, as a high-performing student, her secondary teachers encouraged Rachael to keep her options open and consider university rather than teachers' college. She began a science and economics degree at an elite university, while also working full-time at a fast-food restaurant where, at eighteen years old, she was already manager several days a week. Rachael's first attempt at university was short-lived. She reports that she was uncomfortable on campus and knew that economics and science were not for her, so she quit within six months to focus on her full-time work managing the fast-food restaurant, thinking that this was where her future lay. But she quickly realized that managing the shop was also not what she wanted, and that teaching was still her dream. To become a teacher was a respectable choice for a working-class girl in Australia in the 1970s. She went to teachers' college and became a teacher. She first worked in the same disadvantaged western suburbs where she grew up. And then through the next twenty-five years of teaching, she moved on to other, more advantaged, schools.

Rachael's principal encouraged her to apply for an assistant principalship, something she says she would not have applied for herself without a mentor. She believed that she was not ready, despite her years of experience as a teacher and literacy coach. After eighteen months as assistant principal in an advantaged suburb, the principalship became available in her current school in a highly disadvantaged suburb, a school where she had been a literacy coach. She has been the principal at this school for ten years and has no desire to be in any other school. The children remind her of her own childhood and her first years of teaching and she feels fit within this community and she remarks that she feels she can make a real difference to those children's lives. She remembers that when she began teaching she 'almost needed to be their mum and protector'. The idea of teacher-as-mother, evident in Rachael's comment, is a long-standing (white-saviour) maternal discourse associated with primary teaching. Rachael sees her role as principal in a different light from many of the other principals in her district. When describing her work as the headteacher/principal she comments, '[It's] compassion, common sense. It's not rocket science. It's putting yourself in that child's shoes. I just think it's so easy to do. And it's what we're supposed to do.' In Rachael's estimation, principals don't get a great deal of pressure from their line managers because, as she suggests, 'they don't care. They're just worried about their own jobs really. At the end of the day, no one cares about the kids [in this school] the way we do', so she actively resists external accountabilities that don't correspond with her own moral beliefs about what her school and community need.

Case Study 16.2 Gegeen

Gegeen was born in a large family in the countryside of Mongolia and now works as a director of a unit at a well-known public university in Ulaanbaatar, Mongolia. She chose to pursue her career in the male-dominated field of applied sciences, and so has studied and worked with men throughout her professional life. However, she has had diverse experiences because her age and gender interacted differently in these environments. For example, although she was the only female student in her class during her undergraduate studies, she was very well respected by her male classmates because she was older than them. As a result of her age, she was elected class leader. In this case, her age provided her with a measure of power in Mongolia, where age is highly respected.

However, when Gegeen commenced work as a lecturer at a Mongolian public university, she felt disempowered both because of her gender as well as the fact that she was the most junior member of her faculty. Thus, she started to learn some of the unwritten rules of the gender game in the highly masculine environment of Mongolian public universities. Gegeen received strong support from the few female colleagues she worked with on how to play the game and advance her career. She was advised by her mentor lecturer, 'to negotiate with men in a passive and stereotypically "feminine" manner, otherwise "they will grind you between their teeth" and not support you'. She found this advice troubling for it placed her in a challenging position: should she take their advice, pretend to be a demure woman and thus advance her career? What of her feminist inclinations which told her that by succumbing to these cultural and gender stereotypes she was reproducing the highly sexist norms which were keeping Mongolian women academics in their (submissive) place?

When interviewed, Gegeen reflected that the male-dominated nature of public universities in Mongolia is related to its politics. Unlike in many Anglo or European universities, senior leaders at public universities such as rectors/vice-chancellors are appointed by the government, not by a university council. As the governments are highly male-dominated, male leaders are mainly appointed as heads of public universities despite the fact that in Mongolia, women are, on the whole, far better educated than men. Thus, because men have the support at the political level, unequal power relations between men and women are played out at public universities in Mongolia. Gegeen reflects that ideally gender equality should exist in Mongolia because men and women have the same capabilities but women face a continual struggle as part of a broader societal system of unequal power relations reflected in leadership appointments in Mongolian public universities.

Activity 16.2

1 Identify the different intersections of social categories in each case study.
2 What does each case study reveal about how gender and intersecting categories are constructing differing understandings of educational leadership for Rachael and Gegeen?
3 Reflecting on these two case studies and your own history/understandings of gender and educational leadership, what understandings/conclusions have you now reached in regard to gender and educational leadership?
4 Go back to your answers to the questions in Activity 16.1 at the start of the chapter. How do you respond to these questions after reading the chapter?

Age/gender/sociocultural intersectionality in Mongolia

Mongolian culture and traditions have been greatly influenced by Buddhism; therefore, it is believed that if one has a long life, it is because they performed many good deeds in their previous lives. Thus, the elderly are respected in Mongolia and called 'virtuous seniors'. In the Mongolian language, there are two forms of the pronoun 'you': one is formal (*ta*) and one is informal (*chi*). Gegeen's classmates used to call her *ta* and show respect to her based on her age.

The socialist regime (1921–1990) in Mongolia brought significant changes in its culture and traditions, particularly in the country's governance. Mongolia had a highly centralized, hierarchical and masculinized governance similar to other Soviet Union countries during the socialist era. Leadership and appointment processes were in the hands of the male-dominated military and the Mongolian People's Revolutionary Party. Although Mongolia transitioned from socialism into a post-socialist era in 1990, the hierarchical practices from the previous era still exist. Thus, when Gegeen commenced work as a lecturer at a public university, she joined a hierarchical environment, where one's position and gender were what mattered the most.

Conclusion

In this chapter, we have explored how understandings and practices of educational leadership are inextricably linked to broader societal relations of power, particularly when it comes to issues of gender. We have examined how more traditional notions of leadership in education ignore or play down the reality that how societies think about, feel and experience leadership results from entrenched values, belief systems and ideologies associated with the social relations of gender. We have noted the critical role that feminist scholarship has played in raising consciousness of these issues and of reimagining and reclaiming other forms of leadership associated with collectivist and socially just forms of action and activism. Finally, our case studies reveal why issues of leadership and gender need to be considered in relation to other analytical categories such as race, class and sexuality in order to avoid reproducing binary divisions of power such as women versus men, Black versus white. We provide you with further reading to explore this key issue.

Activity 16.3

Look at your notes on your original thoughts of gender and educational leadership and discuss whether they may have changed after reading this chapter. The following questions might be helpful for you arrange your thoughts/discussion.

1   What are your thoughts of stereotypes of gender and leadership and the common media discourses in relation to this topic? Have your thoughts changed or stayed the same? Why?

2   What are your thoughts of gender and educational leadership concerning various social categories (e.g. class, sexuality, race and age)? What about conceptualizations and practices of gender and educational leadership in diverse societies? Have your thoughts changed or stayed the same? Why?

3   Was there any concept in this chapter that you were not aware of previously? Have you realized anything that changed your thoughts significantly and made you to think critically? What have you learned from this chapter?

Further reading

Blackmore, J and Sachs, J. (2007) *Performing and reforming leaders: gender, educational restructuring, and organizational change*. Albany, NY: State University of New York Press.

Connell, R.W. (1995) *Masculinities*. Sydney: Allen and Unwin.

Fitzgerald, T. and Wilkinson, J. (2010) *Travelling towards a mirage? Gender, leadership and higher education*. Mt Gravatt, Australia: Post Pressed.

Fuller, K. (2013) *Gender, identity and educational leadership*. London: Bloomsbury.

Husu, L., Hearn, J., Lämsä, A. and Vanhala, S. (2010) *Leadership through the gender lens: women and men in organizations*. Helsinki: Edita Prima.

References

Benham, M. and Murakami-Ramalho, E. (2010) Engaging in educational leadership: the generosity of spirit. *International Journal of Leadership in Education*, 13(1), 77–91.

Blackmore, J. (2013) A feminist critical perspective on educational leadership. *International Journal of Leadership in Education*, 16(2), 139–154.

Blackmore, J. (2018) Commentary: leadership as a relational practice in contexts of cultural hybridity. In: J. Wilkinson and L. Bristol (eds), *Educational leadership as a culturally-constructed practice: new directions and possibilities* (pp. 208–216). Abingdon: Routledge.

Connell, R. (n.d.) Masculinities. *Raewyn Connell*. Available online: http://www.raewynconnell.net/p/masculinities_20.html (accessed 7 March 2019).

Connell, R.W. and Pearse, R. (2009) *Gender: in world perspective*, 2nd edn. Cambridge: Polity.

Grosz, E. (1995) *Space, time and perversion: essays on the politics of bodies*. New York: Routledge.

Messerschmidt, J.W., Martin, P.Y., Messner, M.A. and Connell, R. (2018) *Gender reckonings: new social theory and research*. New York: New York University Press.

Rottenberg, C. (2018) *The rise of neoliberal feminism*. New York: Oxford University Press.

Tong, R. (2014) *Feminist thought: a more comprehensive introduction*, 4th edn e-book. Boulder, CO: Westview Press.

Wilkinson, J. and Bristol, L. (2018) *Educational leadership as a culturally-constructed practice: new directions and possibilities*. Abingdon: Routledge.

Sexual identity and educational leadership

Catherine A. Lugg and Robin Roscigno

17

What this chapter is about	270
Key questions that this chapter addresses	270
Introduction	270
History of LGB administrators and US public schools	271
LGB students and their shifting rights	273
Intersectionality and the politics of public schools	274
Who can lead?	274
How is this addressed in contemporary leadership practices and thinking?	275
Conclusion	278
Further reading	278
References	279

What this chapter is about

In this chapter, we present an overview of the issues involved with sexual identity and educational leadership, with particular focus on lesbian, gay and bisexual (LGB) adults in the United States. Regardless of locale, school leadership concerns navigating the context of your workplace. We identify and discuss two contexts of particular significance. First is the ideological context: we note heteronormativity as a durable and deeply influential power structure that positions heterosexuality as 'normal' and stigmatizes alternative sexual identities. This is connected to the second contextual feature – the political: we argue that state politics in the United States has been key to sustaining heteronormativity and gender norms in educational leadership, management and administration (ELMA). In that light, we examine the intersections of race, gender, class, ethnicity, dis/ability and sexuality in the construction of 'who' is seen as a leader. Finally, we explore briefly what it might mean to dismantle, or queer, the heteronormative foundations of ELMA.

Key questions that this chapter addresses

1 How have our understandings around sexual identity changed over the last sixty or so years?

2 What has been the history of ELMA in promoting or supressing sexual identity?

3 Are there differences in how public schools treat LGB students and LGB employees? If so, how? Why?

4 How might intersectionality and multidimensionality provide possible lenses to evaluating the needs and concerns of students and employees?

5 What measures could ELMA personnel take to ensure that their schools support LGB students, faculty and other school personnel?

Introduction

In this chapter, we explore the historical and political contexts confronting LGB people and US public schools. Since the turn of the century, the legal situation has radically improved in most, but not all, locales for lesbian, gay, and bisexual (LGB) adults who reside in the United States. That said, the progress has been much slower for public school educators. Beginning in the 1920s, LGB identities were criminalized, then medically pathologized, making it nearly impossible for public school teachers and administrators to be 'out' about their sexual identities (Lugg, 2016). The legal term for an LGB person was 'statutory felon' and, as such, LGB public school teachers and administrators were barred from holding professional licences, rendering them ineligible for employment. Additionally, under the rubric of community morals enforcement, ELMA as a professional and scholarly field has been and remains homophobic, sometimes dangerously so (O'Malley and Capper, 2015; Lugg, 2016). As the father of educational sociology, Willard Waller, wrote in 1932, 'Nothing is more certain than that homosexuality is contagious' (p. 147). Waller went on to explain that principals had a moral obligation to purge any and all 'homosexuals' from the public schools to ensure these institutions were free from moral taint and possible public scandal. Since that time, public schools have been both heteronormative and homophobic, with principals legally required to enforce rigid gendered expectations.

This chapter does not address the issues confronting transgender educational leaders, which are very complex and legally outrageous in the United States. As at 2018, transgender people had legal protections against employment discrimination in only eighteen states and the District of Columbia. In 2018, more than 200 municipalities also banned employment discrimination against transgender people. Nevertheless, the case law literature is full of cases where a transgender educational leader was fired or otherwise pushed from their public school position. Even when there is a rare success story (winning the case), the person involved typically will decided to take a financial settlement and does not return to their place of employment.

Sexual identity: how you see yourself as a sexual being. That is, with whom do you fall in love? Historically, ELMA has only accepted demonstrably heterosexual identities, though LGB people have always worked in public school settings.

Intersectionality: a term coined by legal scholar Kimberlee Crenshaw to address the experiences of Black women who experience employment discrimination. US law recognizes either discrimination because of race or gender, but not both – which is precisely the experience of many Black women. Extending this understanding of intersectionality to other policy venues, we can see that human beings have critical experiences because they have multiple identities at play in the school setting. We are not merely a race, or a gender or a sexuality identity etc. We are 'all of the above'.

Multidimensionality: this extends intersectionality in ways that provide ways to seek common ground across our multiple identities. It does not presume that any two people have absolutely nothing in common. Instead, you are to examine your own background/identities to seek commonalities with a new acquaintance, colleague, student etc. Once you determine what ground might be shared, work to build bonds of commonality, without neglecting or avoiding important differences.

History of LGB administrators and US public schools

After the Second World War, the situation facing LGB public educators actually deteriorated further, when sexual identity was conflated with Communism – which was portrayed as an existential threat to the nation state. LGB identity was repeatedly presented as a dangerous mental illness and, as such, states were then free to bar both suspected 'statutory felons' and 'lunatics' from working in public schools (Lugg, 2016). The slur that arose was 'Commie, Pinko, Queer' (Lugg, 2016). By the 1950s, full-scale witch hunts for suspected LGB public educators ensued (Lugg, 2016). Those LGB educators who were able to retain their positions largely did so by covering/hiding their identities and following the rigid gender expectations of the era (Blount, 1996). Men were to be 'manly men', and women 'womanly women' if they wished to keep working in the public schools (Blount, 1996). Of course, one odd issue is that, while heterosexual marriage was mandatory for men, it was disqualifying for women – since women could either serve their husbands or the school board – but not both (Blount, 1996).

By the late 1960s, spurred by the African American Civil Rights movement and the women's movements, LGB people began to push for greater civil rights and release from their criminalized status. In late 1973, the American Psychiatric Association 'de-classified' gay, lesbian and bisexual sexual orientations as mental illnesses, removing the mental health barrier to public school employment. Yet it would take an additional thirty years to completely decriminalize LGB identities, in the landmark US Supreme Court decision, *Lawrence v. Texas* (2003). Finally, in 2015, the US Supreme Court in *Obergefell v. Hodges* (2015) legalized same-gender marriages across the US – regardless of the individual state of residence.

While adult LGB status has not only been decriminalized, but actually given legal sanction in the areas of marriage, property and inheritance; the public schools remain the preserve of gender and (hetero)sexuality enforcement (Lugg, 2016). In 2018, only twenty-one states and the District of Columbia explicitly protected all LGB people from employment discrimination, although a total of eleven additional states barred discrimination against public employees (like teachers and school administrators working in public schools) for their LGB identity (see Human Rights Campaign, 2018). Additionally, in eighteen states, it remains perfectly legal to fire a public school teacher or administrator for their LGB identity. Furthermore, educational leaders and school boards can always employ the time-tested and ambiguous framing of 'fit' to remove suspected and actual LGB educators working in public schools (see Tooms, Lugg and Botch, 2010). Not surprisingly, while some public school teachers and a few administrators are 'out' about their LGB identities, the majority remain if not closeted (Adelman and Lugg, 2012), they are covered (Yoshino, 2006) – in that they will not publicly state their orientation, but will not lie about it if asked. While the legal restrictions targeting LGB people are falling away, employment in a public school setting remains fraught (Adelman and Lugg, 2012).

Activity 17.1

Thinking as a school leader:

1 Are there any legal and/or policy protections for minority educators in your district? Are minority groups completely 'enumerated'?

2 If not, what is your role in crafting these protections for your colleagues? What more might you do?

LGB students and their shifting rights

The current legal and political status of LGB students attending public schools is, perhaps, even more complex. Many of these students have both intersectional and multidimensional identities (Lugg, 2016) in that they are LGB *and* students of colour, and/or language minority students, and/or dis/abled, and/or poor. Consequently, they may experience ill treatment because of their identities as both a student of colour and LGB, or hold an 'Individualized Education Program' (IEP) and have an LGB identity, or all of the above. Additionally, trans students have and have *not* been protected under the US federal statue, Title IX of the Higher Education bill of 1973. Title IX forbids any gender discrimination in any public institution that receives direct or indirect federal assistance. At the time it was enacted, the legislation was designed to protect cis-gender women from discrimination in any educational setting that received direct or indirect federal aid (the latter in the form of tax-exempt charitable status; see Harvard Law Review Association, 2014). Since then, Title IX protections have been judicially expanded to sometimes cover LGBT people. That said, meaningful support for these expansions has waxed and waned, depending on which political party holds the White House. This judicial expansion was supported by the late Clinton Administration, then rescinded under the G.W. Bush Administration, supported and explicitly expanded to cover transgender identity during the Obama Administration, and promptly rescinded under the Trump Administration (see Miller, Mayo and Lugg, 2018). What this means on a very practical level is that generally, one's legal protections or lack thereof are a feature of state and/or municipal/district law and codes – not national/federal laws and regulations when it comes to LGB and T identities (Miller, Mayo and Lugg, 2018).

Activity 17.2

1 What are the legal rights for historically minoritized students in your public schools? Can you cite the statutory authority? Are these rights enumerated for all students?
2 Are there any statutes protecting students from abuse and harassment that explicitly enumerate diverse identities?
3 If there are no federal or state protections, are there any policy provisions at the local level protecting students from abuse and harassment? If so, what are they?
4 If not, what is your role in crafting these protections for your school and district?

Intersectionality and the politics of public schools

In the United States, the differing legal status of individuals, be they students, teachers or administrators, makes for very complex power relations within the walls of a given public school. And as we have noted, these vary from state to state, and in some instances, from district to district within a particular state. Different students are treated more or less justly along the lines of race, colour, gender, class, dis/ability, sexual orientation and so forth. Students have multiple marginalized identities, some of which are highly stigmatized. Consequently, we know both Black boys and girls are closely 'monitored' and assumed by many educators to be 'troublemakers'. Such assumptions are part of the structural racism of US public schools. But it becomes more complex when we start accounting for race *and* class *and* gender, and so on. The data is pretty robust that Black girls experience discrimination very differently from Black boys and white girls. Additionally, queer Black girls have different experiences from white girls (regardless of orientation); and being a disabled student often offers an increased level of surveillance.

What these experiences mean is that educators need to focus on attacking the structural (i.e. social, economic and political) factors that disadvantage certain children and clearly advantage other children. A quick example of the uneven distribution of privileges within a school is who is selected to participate in a school district's 'gifted and talented' programme – and who is not. While the criteria might be facially objective (test scores, grades, recommendations etc.), often the structural biases are woven in through the rubric of teacher or administrator recommendation. For LGB students of colour, they are at disproportionate risk for bullying and harassment – not only from their peers, but from educators, especially if they are attending a majority white school.

Who can lead?

Historically, ELMA in the United States has been of, by and for married Protestant white men who had to be in heterosexual marriages (Blount, 1996). While the principalship has greatly diversified along the lines of gender and race, the superintendency remain the province of married white males. And much of the change in the principalship has only occurred from the mid-1990s onwards. Still, the 'default' model for educational leadership remains overwhelming white, male and in heterosexual marriages. This situation places LGB public school administrators in exquisitely vulnerable positions, being closely surveilled by their communities and school boards while, concurrently, being expected to surveil their own teachers and students for any socially aberrant identities – which by definition, are not white, male and heterosexual, etc. (Lugg, 2016).

How is this addressed in contemporary leadership practices and thinking?

Generally, LGB identity is *not* addressed in leadership preparation programmes (O'Malley and Capper, 2015), nor with ongoing professional development (Payne and Smith, 2017), nor in public schools except in those states where it is mandated (like California, Illinois and New Jersey). Consequently, these silences allow the bigoted policies and practices from the past to shape contemporary policies and practices. This is particularly acute in those states that have yet to repeal their laws banning consensual same-sex behaviour and as well as laws that ban the promotion of homosexuality in public schools, better known as 'no promo homo' laws. As a consequence, in many locales, public school administrators are loathe to respond to anti-LGB bigotry, and even if they wish to respond, they fail to have the requisite knowledge, skills and experience to respond appropriate.

While the current state of affairs might be considered somewhat dismal, we think intersectional analyses open the epistemological door to queering the foundational knowledges of ELMA.

For example, by considering there might be multiple identities at play when it comes to establishing a potential policy on school dances, administrators should consider that some students will not be exclusively heterosexual. The resultant policies should treat students equally when it comes to identity and extracurricular activities – and acknowledge that the public school has both queer and

> **To queer:** to reconceptualize in a way that dissolves or disrupts socially constructed binaries, e.g. between the leader and the led, the subject and object of policy, etc.

non-queer students. Similarly, the curriculum should be examined so that it is factual when it comes to sexual identity across the disciplines, making sure that LGB people are represented and not 'closeted' (e.g. failing to discuss Whitman's and Lorde's identities when examining their poetry). Furthermore, the staff and faculty handbook should be updated to reflect current and queerer understandings of how race, gender, sexual identity, dis/ability, religion etc. can shape how a given employee views both their understandings of what it means to professional and how to best serve students.

While 'queering' has been used to refer to the inclusion of queer individuals into hegemonic structures, queering also is a broader methodological tool. Queering – as it is understood in the broader Queer Theory literature – deconstructs binaries and hierarchical power relations in order to unseat established structures of oppression. In a policy context, queering can refer to challenging established procedures, boundaries and identitarian categories. In other words, queering demands a renegotiation of the very foundation of educational policy work. Similarly, queering the curriculum might work to dissolve the binary between the deviser and the recipient of the curriculum in order to better represent the interests of the latter.

That said, employing 'queerer' analyses *will* make ELMA professional lives more complex – which is the point. We all live complicated lives and tend to favour more simple analyses to reduce potential cognitive and emotional burdens. However, many of these analyses are actually simplistic, and by definition do harm to both our students and staff

– and even ourselves. Consequently, queering our assumptions and foundational understandings will benefit all, while providing ELMA professionals paths forward in devising policies and then enacting them.

Activity 17.3

Queering educational-leadership practice

Think about an example of educational-leadership practice that you have enacted or encountered. What assumptions underpinned this practice, e.g. concerning roles, purposes and/or methods? What sorts of possibilities for different practice are created by changing or removing these assumptions?

We now turn to a case study that underscores just how complex these issues are for one particular public school principal. This particular case study, while a hypothetical, is drawn from our collective experiences as educators and researchers, and Robin's particular expertise as a special education teacher working in both suburban and urban public schools. This case is deliberately designed to cause students a fair amount of discomfort given the complexities involved. That said, it invites a strong intersectional and even multidimensional analysis given the case's sheer complexity.

Case Study 17.1 Steven Hopewell's dilemma

Steven Hopewell is the principal at Westside High School. He has been in the district for twelve years as a high school social studies teacher, served two years as assistant principal and was promoted to principal two years ago. As a well-respected member of the school community, Steven is known to be personable, trustworthy and a competent leader. Steven has lived with his long-time partner, Miles, for sixteen years, and the couple has been legally married for two years. While Steven does not consider himself closeted in his personal life, he does not make mention of his spouse while at Westside High and his sexuality is somewhat of an 'open secret'. Stephen drives a considerable commute to school each morning, as he does not want to be seen in the community with his partner or to see any students from school outside of school hours. In particular, Steven has been scrupulous with social media. He does not have a visible presence on any sites under his professional name and only has contact with a few trusted colleagues on any social media.

On some weekends, Steven and his partner volunteer at an LGBT youth centre in their city. The centre provides social programming, health services and counselling to local LGBT youth. The centre is very important to both Steven and Miles as they met there in college, when both men were active in local LGBT organizing. Steven is conflicted because his position within the school district has forced him to neutralize and conceal his political identity, so his volunteer work is especially important to him.

One day, while Steven is volunteering to chaperone an event for LGBT teens at the centre, one of his students, Melissa Street, enters the room. Melissa and Steven exchange glances, then Steven greets her and welcomes her to the space. Being an out lesbian and outspoken advocate, it is not surprising to Steven that she would attend such an event, however, he purposefully had chosen to do this work at a considerable geographic distance from Westside. Melissa approaches Steven and said, 'I didn't expect to see you here, Mr Hopewell. My mom drove me here because she had an appointment in the area, and I thought this event sounded cool. But, don't worry, I won't tell anyone I saw you here.' Steven breathes a sigh of relief. It was not so much that he was worried about his sexuality being uncovered, but the fact that he could be accused of having biases or political leanings related to his identity that troubled Steven. Westside was a very conservative town, with a large majority of the families in the town being stationed at the nearby military base. As an administrator, he often had to assuage the anxieties of the parents who claimed the curriculum had 'liberal biases' or was 'anti-American'. He was worried that his purported impartiality would be called into question, along with his sexuality. Stephen was also worried he would be in breach of his contact, which had stipulations about engaging in political activity as a public employee. The event concluded, and Steven and Melissa both went their respective ways.

Two months passed by, and Steven was even more careful about his extracurricular activities. Melissa passed Mr Hopewell in the hallway and always smiled warmly, but never made any mention of the day she saw him at the centre. This was the case until January, when the school counsellor, Mrs Cipolla, paged Mr Hopewell. 'Mr Hopewell, I have a parent on the line who would like to open an HIB [harassment, intimidation and bullying] investigation.' Mr Hopewell was familiar with these calls, as it was part of his job to investigate such instances. He instructed Mrs Cipolla to transfer the call to him. The woman on the other end of the phone identified herself as Mrs Street, Melissa Street's mother. She wanted to report an incident that happened to Melissa outside of school. Another student, whom Melissa had previously been friends with, had taken a picture of Melissa at practice and put it on social media with the word 'dyke' written over her picture. The image had circulated among many of the girls on the team and Melissa was devastated. Mr Hopewell assured Mrs Street that it would be investigated.

Mr Hopewell began investigating the incident and methodically and calmly called each girl named by Mrs Street into his office, with the counsellor present, to interview them. He discovered that the creator of the image was Angela Hays, one of the children of one of the most vocal parents in the community. Mr and Mrs Hays were well-respected, as Mr Hays was a retired police sergeant, and Mrs Hays was involved in the Parent–Teacher Association and Boosters association for Westside. Additionally, Angela had an IEP for a learning disability and Mrs Hays was also very active in the special education parents' community. Historically, the Hays family had been very influential in the school district, and Mr Hopewell remembered other times that they had led informal campaigns against certain other administrators, and their curriculum decisions and policies that did not meet their strict moral and religious code.

Mr Hopewell had found that Angela was bullying Melissa; however, he feared repercussions from the Hayses, particularly because he was unsure how, if at all, Angela's behaviour was a manifestation of her disability. He feared that holding Angela accountable may be a violation of her IEP, or that her parents would influence his reputation in the community. He also feared that not acting on this incident might prompt Melissa to publicly out him to the community, should he not rule the incident bullying.

Conclusion

In the United States, the legal constraints, coupled with lingering animosity and ignorance, greatly constrain the ability of administrators to respond in protective ways in serving their LGB teachers and students, much less advocate and lead in proactive ways to better serve those who teach and learn under their care. Additionally, these contexts can be highly variable, with some locales strongly supportive, while others just a few kilometres away, are utterly toxic. Consequently, it is incumbent on practising administrators to be well-versed in understanding what their legal and political constraints actually are. That said, this does not mean administrators should be merely passive and accept hostile educational environments. Instead, they should carefully seek out like-minded educators and community members and build for policy changes at the local level to provide a better, and hopefully queerer, environment for their students and teachers.

One point to consider is that the US Constitution sets 'minimums' on civil rights, beneath which no state nor municipality may fall. However, school districts, municipalities and states are free to enact *greater* protections if they wish. For example, the state of South Carolina does not explicitly protect LGB or T identities. But the city of Columbia, South Carolina does. This means that *all* public educational institutions within the boundaries of the city of Columbia must conform with the municipal code, although the state remains silent on these protections. While this is a brief example, clearly there are opportunities for policy creativity on the part of ELMA personnel once they are conversant with the local policy context.

Further reading

American Civil Liberties Union (2018) Know your rights: transgender people and the law. Available online: https://web.archive.org/web/20180824210608/https://www.aclu.org/know-your-rights/transgender-people-and-law#close (accessed 23 September 2018).

Blount, J.M. (1998) *Destined to rule the schools: women and the superintendency, 1873–1995*. Albany, NY: SUNY Press.

Blount, J.M. (2005) *Fit to teach: same-sex desire, gender, and school work in the twentieth century*. Albany, NY: State University of New York Press.

Graves, K. (2009) *And they were wonderful teachers: Florida's purge of gay and lesbian teachers*. Urbana, IL: University of Illinois Press.

Mayo, C. (2014) *LGBTQ youth & education: policies & practices*. New York: Teachers College Press.

Tooms, A. (2007) The right kind of queer: fit and the politics of school leadership. *Journal of School Leadership*, 17(5), 601–630.

References

Adelman, M. and Lugg, C.A. (2012) Public schools as workplaces: the queer gap between 'workplace equality' and 'safe schools'. *Law Journal for Social Science*, 3, 27–46.

Blount, J.M. (1996) Manly men and womanly women: deviance, gender role polarization and the shift in women's school employment, 1990–1976. *Harvard Educational Review*, 66(2), 318–339.

Harvard Law Review Association (2014) Developments in the law: sexual orientation and gender identity. *Harvard Law Review*, 127(6), 1680–1814.

Human Rights Campaign (2018) State maps of laws & policies: employment. Available online: https://www.hrc.org/state-maps/employment/ (accessed 7 October 2018).

Lawrence v. Texas, 539 U.S. 558 (2003).

Lugg, C.A. (2016) *US public schools and the politics of queer erasure*. New York: Palgrave Macmillan.

Miller, s.j., Mayo, C. and Lugg, C.A. (2018) Sex and gender in transition in US schools: ways forward. *Sex Education*, 18(4), 345–359.

Obergefell v. Hodges, 576 U.S. ___ (2015).

O'Malley, M.P. and Capper, C.A. (2015) A measure of the quality of educational leadership programs for social justice: integrating LGBTIQ identities into principal preparation. *Educational Administration Quarterly*, 51(2), 290–330.

Payne, E.C. and Smith, M.J. (2017) Refusing relevance: school administrator resistance to offering professional development addressing LGBTQ issues in schools. *Educational Administration Quarterly*, 54(2), 183–215.

Tooms, A.K., Lugg, C.A. and Bogotch, I. (2010) Rethinking the politics of fit and educational leadership. *Educational Administration Quarterly*, 46(1), 96–131.

Waller, W.W. (1932) *The sociology of teaching*. New York: Wiley.

Yoshino, K. (2006) *Covering: the hidden assault on our civil rights*. New York: Random House.

Race and educational leadership

Mark A. Gooden and Victoria Showunmi

18

What this chapter is about	282
Key questions that this chapter addresses	282
Introduction	282
Race in UK and US society	283
Race and educational leadership: definition and points of difference	284
Race, organizations and leadership	285
Educational leadership, race and power	288
What needs to change?	291
Conclusion	292
Further reading	293
References	293

What this chapter is about

As the fields of research and practice start to recognize the need to move towards a more diverse understanding of leadership, it is crucial to encourage more dialogue on race to highlight its importance in educational leadership. We intend doing that here by using two different countries, the United States and the UK, as contextual lenses through which to illuminate racialized power dynamics in education and its leadership. A primary aim of this chapter is to promote race-based reflections upon and discussions about educational leadership in the respective contexts of the United States and the UK. Thinking about leadership from a critical perspective will help properly situate race within analyses of leadership practices, as well as within education research and theories.

The key questions that this chapter addresses

1 Why is race important to educational leadership in the US and UK?
2 How do race and educational leadership interplay conceptually and in practice in these two countries?
3 How might using the case study clarify some of the concepts and issues in studying race and educational leadership?

Introduction

We will use these questions as a framework through which to articulate our respective perspectives as racialized US and UK citizens on issues of race. (Regarding terminology, Black Minority Ethnic (BME), Black, people of colour and African American are used interchangeably throughout the chapter.) First, we introduce ourselves as the two authors. Dr Mark Gooden is a professor at Teachers College, Columbia University. His work focuses on anti-racist leadership, culturally responsive school leadership, and the law. Dr Victoria Showunmi is a researcher and lecturer at University College London in the Institute of Education. Her work focuses on gender, identity and race and how they interconnect with educational leadership and it is grounded in the use of auto-ethnography. Both authors use narrative to think through their work in educational leadership.

The notion of race has been addressed in the UK largely under the banner of leadership and diversity (see the definitions box). The emergent research field in diversity and educational leadership in the UK focused primarily on gender (e.g. Ozga, 1992), challenging the status quo in research. More research has since been conducted on the sociology of leadership and the need for leadership to reflect the diverse communities in the UK (see Chapters 16, 17 and 19 of this book). Before we go further, a note on terminology: the UK is a nation state comprising (in 2020) four home nations with distinctive compulsory-phase, or K–12 education systems. Education is politically devolved to the National Assemblies in Wales and Northern Ireland and to the Scottish Parliament. England has no discrete parliament, so the UK Secretary of State for Education rules on education in England.

Research on race in the United States confirms its inter-relationship with multiple aspects of American life but defines almost nothing singularly. Still, because race is so prevalent in the United States, we should centre it in leadership (Gooden and Dantley, 2012), since responses to it impact several outcomes in schools, mainly 'achievement indicators', discipline, curriculum, recruitment and place-ment of teachers and principals. Only then do we then become conscious of race and how it also influences leaders' practices.

Understanding diversity as integral to social science means recognizing that individual attitudes and practices concerning difference occur in the context of historically, culturally and socially embedded realities, beliefs or frame-works. Like race, these function to hierarchize groups of people according to constructed categories. Our racial awareness and identities as authors prompt us to centre race in our discussions of educational leadership. Before we continue with the chapter, we briefly discuss race in our two national contexts, drawing on key statistics.

> **Diversity:** the way in which differences between people are recognized, understood and given social meaning. Certain differences are more socially meaningful than others, particularly including perceived race, or skin colour, owing to arbitrary but durable power relations and structures. Groups may be constructed of people perceived to have characteristics deemed to be unlike those held either by the majority, or by a power-ful minority. Diversity discourses therefore operate under a proliferation of (white) cultural norms often taken to be (race) neutral. These dynamics are produced and reproduced through multiple societal institutions and technologies, including education.
>
> **Equity:** the fair treatment of those who have been historically and legally deprived of resources, access, opportunity and power. Such treatment may be differential in order to achieve fairness. Equity is ultimately a means of making the marginalized equal.

Race in UK and US society

In the United States, there are differential social and economic experiences between Hispanic, African American, Asian and white ethnicities, among others. Typically, African Americans are disadvantaged in employment, health, housing and education (Plaut, 2010). The ethnic-group distribution differs between the United States and the UK: in the United States, the largest racial minority group is Black (African Caribbean, African or African American; 12.6 per cent). In contrast, the largest minority ethnic group in the UK is the South Asian population (5.9 per cent). Context-sensitivity is therefore necessary for all locations in which diversity research is conducted and speaks particularly to a critical approach (see the Introduction to this book).

Our primary focus here is on race. However, multiple dimensions of diversity intersect to (re)produce (dis)advantage differentially, including gender. In the UK, between 1997 and 2006, almost all Vice-Chancellors (VCs) appointed were white, 23 per cent had studied at

Race: a constructed dimension of human difference that is deployed to obscure the way in which human beings belong to a single species and share a common origin. Those in or with power determine so-called racial categories based ostensibly on skin colour and other physical characteristics: these take little or no account of how such features are spectral and inherently socially, intellectually and dispositionally meaning-less. Racial categories nonetheless have social significance imposed upon them, and are deployed to deny humans' equality in dignity and as members of humanity. Racial categories may also be reappropriated by the marginalized as resources for identifica-tion and as the basis for claims to equality – we will be using Black as a descriptor in this way. All peoples of the world possess equal faculties for attaining the highest level in intellectual, technical, social, economic, cultural and political develop-ment, with any differences between their achievements entirely attributable to geographical, historical, political, economic, social and cultural factors. Race is often used to mask these factors and provide an alternative, stereotype-based explanation for any difference.

Oxford or Cambridge universities, and 85 per cent were male. Until 2011, there had only ever been one VC from a BME background – a male and non-UK national. However, between 2017 and 2019, there were three new BME VC appointments in England, two female and one male. In the United States, 70 per cent of college presidents were men in 2016, while 17 per cent represented racial minorities. Specifically, only 8 per cent of those identified as Black, 4 per cent Hispanic/Latinx, 2 per cent Asian or Asian American, 1 per cent American Indian, 1 per cent Middle Eastern, 1 per cent Multiple races. The remaining 83 per cent of these presidents were white (ACE Data Explorer, 2019).

In English schools, in 2018, white British people comprised 85.9 per cent of classroom teachers, but 92.9 per cent of headteachers (Department for Education, 2020). As student diversity increases in the United States, the teaching and leading workforce remains largely white (80 per cent white and 76.6 per cent female; and 78 per cent white and 54 per cent female, respectively) (McFarland et al., 2019).

In 2012, women held 15 per cent of directorships of Financial Times Stock Exchange (FTSE) 100 companies (Sealy and Vinnicombe, 2012) – a 2.5 per cent increase from a three-year plateau. However, only 9.9 per cent of female FTSE 100 company directors are from minority ethnic groups, and only one a UK national. In the UK, career progression in business, higher education and politics reflects ethnic and gender penalties. In the United States, the consistently low number of Black executives leading Fortune 500 companies was at a high of seven in 2007, when it included a woman. However, that number dropped to six in 2013 and five in 2015. By October 2019, today the number of CEOs leading Fortune 500 companies is four, with no women (Dingle, 2019).

These statistics resonate with Acker's characterization of organizations as 'inequality regimes' with 'loosely interrelated practices, processes, actions and meanings that result in and maintain class, gender and racial inequalities within particular organisations' (2006: 443).

Race and educational leadership: definition and points of difference

This section unpacks the range of concepts used when talking about race and leadership. We aim to shed light on those frequently used terms that communicate the differences in leadership, including **racially conscious**, **white racial dis-consciousness** and

white privilege. Individually, this terminology appears empowering; however, when used to describe race and leadership in contrast to white leadership, the terms and practices in many cases lead to detrimental outcomes for race and leadership.

There is ample evidence to demonstrate that Black leaders are always working against the negative images and stereotypes presented in the media (Osler and Webb, 2014). Black leaders are subjected to double-minority discrimination along with micro-aggressions which 'are the subtle verbal and nonverbal slights, insults, and disparaging messages directed towards an individual due to their gender, age, disability, and racial group membership often automatically and subconsciously' (Prieto et al., 2016: 36). What happens when an individual occupies more than one of these categories, for example, is both gay and Chinese or both female and Black? Leaders like these exist at an intersection of recognized sites of oppression.

More recently, research suggests that the social-identity group to which a leader belongs is considered a significant factor in leader effectiveness and the extent to which a leader may feel able to enact that identity (van Knippenberg, 2011). From a sociological perspective, this is explained by the extent to which the leader and the group see themselves as part of a collective or share the same social identity. This is a concern in educational leadership too, where the reification of a corporatized leader 'class' increases dis-identification with the led or practising teachers (see Chapter 22 of this book).

> **Inclusion:** a process of and disposition towards sharing power with previously excluded and/or marginalized people. Power-sharing forms of inclusion aim to provide marginalized people with a sense of belonging and ownership, helping them feel welcome and understand that they are important members of the organization.
>
> **Institutionalized racism** (also known as systemic racism): a form of racism expressed in the practice and structure of social and political institutions. It is reflected in disparities regarding wealth, income, criminal justice, employment, housing, health care, political power and education, among other factors.
>
> **Racial and ethnic consciousness:** the awareness of membership of a racial or ethnic group that is displayed by both group members and the larger society in which they reside. The concept embodies both popular and social-scientific understandings of classification, identification and membership.

Race, organizations and leadership

Organizations are microcosms of the societies within which they are embedded, and work cannot be understood outside the context of the sociocultural arena in which it

> **Racism:** any action or attitude, conscious or unconscious, that subordinates an individual or group based on race or its proxies, skin colour or particular configurations of physical features. It can be enacted individually or institutionally. Racism is a historical, social, cultural, political and institutional relationship between white people and people of colour. The relationship is built into the fabric of society.

is enacted. Organizational dynamics often mirror societies' structures, beliefs and tensions, including less favourable outcomes for minority ethnic individuals and women in many Western societies. As such, ethnicity scholars need to acknowledge the socially constructed and contextual nature of ethnicity in organizations. Many scholars, such as Acker (2006), have noted that hierarchies are gendered, racialized and classed, especially when it comes to leadership in Europe and the United States.

Dominant leadership theories, however, have traditionally suppressed and neutralized 'difference', including gender and race/ethnic dimensions. Much of the data generated in early leadership research was gathered in business, military and government settings, from white Anglo-Saxon men in so-called leadership (i.e. hierarchical authority) positions. Leadership publications have reflected this bias. Osler (2006) points out that textbooks aimed at aspiring school leaders published in the 1980s and 1990s in the UK seldom referred to equity, even though by then minority ethnic communities were well-established in this country. This omission was mirrored in academic journals and educational-management courses, where race equality was rarely a focus, even though ethnicity was known to matter in student achievement (see, however, Johnson, 2017).

Similarly, many US school leaders and preparation programmes have embraced a race-neutral, post-racial or colour-blind approach to leadership. Unchallenged views assume that sixty years after the famous American Supreme Court case, *Brown v. Board of Education* (1954), all have equal access to education and schools are welcoming places. Here we introduce the *Williams v. Port Huron School District* (2012) (hereinafter *Williams*), which, along with contemporary US literature, challenges those assumptions by showing an explicit occurrence of how racism impacts leadership in contemporary times, in egregious, but subtle ways (see *Williams*). In fact, the *Williams* case reveals how whites not only can and do maintain control over districts, but also how they use their power to ignore or redefine power relationships in schools, actions that lead to what we refer to as white racial avoidance (see definitions box).

> **White racial avoidance:** an exertion of privileged power within a white supremacist system to employ an authority with the effect or purpose of avoiding discussing race. It redirects the conversation away from race or ignores it altogether. People of colour might practise it even with limited systemic power.
>
> **White privilege:** the legitimization of one's perceived entitlement as a white person to preferential access to resources and positional superordination over people of colour. It does not require awareness or agreement by benefiting whites to exist.

Case Study 18.1 The *Williams* case

We now illuminate white racial avoidance by presenting a case study of the *Williams* decision in the US context. This legal case was appealed from a federal district court to a higher federal court of appeals. It demonstrates how white racial avoidance surfaces, builds momentum and continues unabated. The lower court had found that the school officials were entitled to qualified immunity – this is where US public officials 'can be held accountable only insofar as they violate rights that are "clearly established" in light of existing case law' (Ali and Clark, 2019, para. 5).

In *Williams,* a 6th-Circuit Court of Appeals ruled that school administrators and school board members were entitled to qualified immunity from a suit brought by a group of Black students whose parents alleged that school officials in the district had violated their children's Fourteenth Amendment equal protection rights by acting with deliberate indifference to student-on-student racial harassment.

The school, Port Huron Northern High School, is predominantly white (approximately 89 per cent). There are about 3 per cent Black students. One Black administrator, Ms Marla Philpot, works at the school.

The Black students claimed their white classmates subjected them to constant peer racial harassment that ran the gamut from name-calling, especially frequent use of the word 'nigger' and displays of the Confederate flag on campus, to several instances of vandalism on school grounds involving racial slurs, including graffiti.

The assistant principal was also being racially harassed and bullied. For instance, when Ms Philpot was hired in 2003, within her first week she found Ku Klux Klan paraphernalia and white supremacist literature placed on or around her desk. Before the year ended, both students and parents had blatantly and repeatedly called Ms Philpot a 'nigger.' In fact, one parent showed up at the school spewing racial slurs with the expressed intent to assault Philpot after she disciplined her son, presumably as a requirement of her job as an assistant principal.

Cheryl Wojitas, the principal during the first two years of this harassment, did nothing to address an unwelcoming and unsafe environment. Perhaps Principal Wojitas was unprepared to address racial issues at the school, afraid, or simply unwilling to do so. Regardless, she did not launch any investigations into the troubling behaviour. In a puzzling but not uncommon display of power, district officials promoted Wojitas to a central office position.

The district then hired Principal Dahlke. Unlike Wojitas, he acknowledged the school's racial issues. Dahlke initially aimed to take action and installed surveillance cameras in an attempt to catch those students who committed infractions and plastered the school with racist graffiti. Strangely, after one year of trying, Dahlke was unable to find any students guilty of wrongdoing. For three years (2003–2006), school leaders did not punish a single white student for serious infractions that undoubtedly impacted the climate of the school, especially for Black students.

Why not? Officially, the court of appeals concluded that the Black students failed to establish a violation of their constitutional rights based on the school administrators' deliberate indifference to the harassment because they could not show that the administrators' response 'to the harassment or lack thereof [was] clearly unreasonable in light of the known circumstances'. As noted in the case, at one point in these events, Principal Dahlke appeared to justify white students' use of racial slurs when he expressed confusion while implying that African American students who refer to themselves using the N-word may be contributing to the issue.

The *Williams* case illustrates some troubling realities as a case of educational leadership. First, the school administration's response to the racial harassment by the white students was obviously ineffective. Is it reasonable to expect school leaders to protect these Black students from student-to-student racial harassment, or racial bullying?

This case also reifies and explains two major issues in race and leadership. First, school principals can use power to invoke racial avoidance and even go unpunished when they fail to fulfil this part of their responsibilities. Second, it shows how leaders who have not explored racial issues, including learning how to respond to them, can very well respond in detrimental ways. Their conduct can have the consequence of maintaining the safety of unruly white students at the cost of creating an unsafe and unwelcoming environment for other students. For instance, the non-compliant white students were presumed innocent for three years, even as the Black students, presumed to be partially complicit in the harmful, discriminatory incidents because of their use of the N-word at a point, found no justice. The case provides a clear example of oppression, and the administrators' response would be commonly referred to as 'blaming the victim'.

While it might be easy to conclude that the US principals in this situation were just an exceptional case of incompetent leaders and/or bad people who refused to act, we argue that there is another truth here that probably supports their invoking of racial avoidance. Our study of education leadership as practised in schools and as taught in leadership-preparation programmes in the United States teaches us that racial avoidance, though not expressly named, is commonplace in many educational K–12 settings and higher education campuses. Another way to consider racial avoidance is to recognize it is an attribute where school leaders and/or their teachers fail to adroitly, intentionally or routinely engage in conversations about race, racism or racist occurrences in schools, and therefore take no action. This separation of race from leadership work can be generally learned from society, but it is often reinforced by faculty, albeit tacitly, who teach these students in leadership-preparation programmes.

The school leaders in this case study are asserting white racial avoidance as a form of power, which is supported by their positional power as white administrators who can virtually ignore the safety and welfare of the Black students in the school. Additionally, they are failing to ensure the safety of a Black assistant principal, Ms Philpot, on their leadership team, and the other students in the school as they witness this behaviour with no consequences at first, and only minor admonishment subsequently.

Activity 18.1

Let's take a moment to critically reflect on the case study. Look back at the words and phrases defined in the five definition boxes so far.

1 Which of them are relevant to this case study?
2 How have they been operationalized or enacted?
3 What do you think this case study might say about racism in the US education system?
4 What might educational leaders have done better?

Educational leadership, race and power

In what follows, we will use the case study to demonstrate how power is constructed in contemporary thinking and practice in educational leadership through three commonly used terms: **diversity**, **equity** and **inclusion**. In addition, we will show how even with these terms in play, those whites who wish to are able to use their power in particular ways to control the narrative and how it operates within organizations, including schools.

In the United States, **racism and racialization** play out across these three terms that are intended to be helpful to address historic inequities. However, power dynamics mean that the uses of the terms diversity, equity and inclusion are easily co-opted and thus become weakened and even used against people of colour, who are supposedly intended as beneficiaries. The three terms are generally used when addressing challenges stemming from racism, such as discrimination and historic inequities. However, we have found instances where the terms fail to engender impactful conversations and stop short of bringing about large-scale changes. Why? Because all of these terms gather different meanings, especially relative to the power of the actors involved, who have various degrees of agency within the system. For us, race is ultimately about power arrangements in society and leadership, and next, we draw on the case study to illuminate both race's foundation in power, and also the need for a critical approach to interrogate it.

Let's start with **diversity**. (White) cultural norms have influenced everything in education from housing patterns, schooling arrangements, distribution of resources and hiring patterns. Consequently, these norms influence and create very measured diversity approaches, which have supported the maintenance of homogeneity, causing well-meaning whites to realize that a lack of difference is problematic in multiple, serious ways. Diversity as currently widely conceptualized and practised, along with racial avoidance, reifies existing beliefs about *who gets access*. Diversity becomes limited to adding a small percentage of people of colour. So, who controls diversity and who benefits from it?

In the case study, Black students were not the only ones subjected to racial harassment. Assistant Principal Ms Philpot was also left unsupported by her principal. Why would the principal allow such egregious behaviour?

Instead of Ms Philpot's fellow assistant principals arguing that more teachers and leaders of colour should be hired to make her feel less isolated, they largely ignored the racial animus directed at the only Black administrator. Again, the term diversity has been defined in the context of racial avoidance and the school leaders take it no further than hiring one Black school leader. The pride that educational leaders may feel when they hire one Black teacher or one Black principal must, we argue, be tempered with empathy for such appointees. What must life be like for those individuals? The prerequisite for such empathy is a profound and sustained reflection upon race, or the risk is that harmful racialized power dynamics are reproduced even through well-meaning action. Using diversity or difference in this way undermines true, self-reflexive efforts to achieve equity and does little to disturb the taken-for-granted power structure.

Diversity in American schools is usually considered a forced goal to consider because demographers continue to state that students in US school districts are becoming increasingly more racially and culturally diverse, especially those learning in the urban context. That means the leaders in Port Huron, like those across the United States, have to work intentionally to recruit teachers of colour, a goal that is easily undercut by using race-neutral or racial-avoidance techniques. What else does it mean? While white teachers are not necessarily ill-prepared to teach children of colour, many are unacculturated. Therefore, the teachers are often culturally very different from their students. Hence, diversity in the US context around race becomes challenging because there is a cultural mismatch between those educators and their students.

This leads to **inclusion**, which essentially refers to making marginalized people feel welcome through enabling access and sharing resources and ideally power. While some school districts have attempted to be more inclusive and invite more teachers of colour into their schools, those districts have failed to achieve more inclusive environments. Before we elaborate, let us recognize that in the US, a number of teachers of colour were fired soon after the *Brown v. Board of Education* (1954) decision. This history is important because it gives us an example of how school boards used their power to demonstrate their dissatisfaction with the *Brown* decision and to again punish the supposed beneficiaries of the edict to desegregate schools. When teachers of colour were retained, many were reduced in job status and often not given teaching positions at all. What happened to Assistant Principal Philpot next demonstrates that history is not too far from the present for Black educators because as the only Black administrator she indeed experienced diminished status. Moreover, her inclusion in the process of decision-making, that is, the dynamic power structure, was very limited. For example, Philpot was the target of multiple racially charged attacks from white parents that openly and irreverently undermined her authority and her leadership. Though it is hard to imagine she received absolutely no support, there is little evidence of her principal defending her against her attackers.

Assistant Principal Philpot had to work at the school and withstand the abuse from white students and their parents. Her situation, a single instantiation of a common story in US history, is an example of a Black educator being demeaned by students, and gaining insufficient support from the principal. Hence, inclusion, when considering impact is more salient than diversity alone. In this case, inclusion benefits the school district more than the Black educator. In other words, the school district can claim that it has included a diverse (difference of one) principal on its administrative team, but it has not provided her with power or truly recognized her authority (inclusion) to serve as a school leader. In essence, few benefits came to the assistant principal in this arrangement, so one has to wonder, is this an example of inclusion or of tokenism?

Finally, we address the notions of **equity** and power. Equity reminds us that marginalized people have been historically and legally deprived of resources, access and power for many decades. Equity, then, requires what is understood as the fair treatment of those individuals, ideally (but not necessarily) ultimately to raise them to equal status. From the perspective of a person of colour, Ms Philpot would like to be included with full privileges, to be recognized and respected as a leader in her own right. From the perspective of the white administrator, he gathered the benefit of her presence and set out to treat her equally. However, without critically reflecting upon and foregrounding questions of race in his work, and specifically concerning how this might influence his support for Ms Philpot, he perhaps inadvertently, though equally harmfully, reproduced a racialized power dynamic. Principal Dahlke may have genuinely wanted Ms Philpot to be there, but he offered no solution for the racially motivated issues that cropped up and threatened the quality of her experience and even her safety and well-being. Recall that equity is about providing people with what is commonly deemed to be fair given unequal starting points, even if that means that people are treated differentially. Even though Ms Philpot was situated differently because of her racist mistreatment, the principal treated her 'equally', i.e. in the same manner as her white counterparts. The actively engaged quest for equity is a stronger action than diversity and inclusion, as it assumes power is truly being shared as a result of historical, legal and social deprivations. Principal Dahlke's intention of equity failed.

Using the concepts of **diversity**, **equity** and **inclusion**, we have tried to demonstrate with a critical lens the crucial forms of power that whites hold in this paradigm, especially if they are socialized to choose racial avoidance. White leaders are not required by US society to admit that they possess power within the system, or even assert they have power and activate it, for it to work. In fact, most do not do so unless they feel threatened, or deprived because of 'unfair independent actions' in the system. Accordingly, in the *Williams* case, white leaders decided to use their power of 'silence' to say little to criticize the racial harassment initially. It is technically inaccurate to say they are doing nothing. Principal Dahlke observed the occurrences, taking some steps, but ultimately stopped short of sufficient meaningful actions. Less can be said about the actions and deduced about the intentions of Wojitas and others. Still, despite the transparent bullying behaviour that took place at the school, the court still found that the principals, superintendents and the board were all entitled to qualified immunity (protection) from the threat of being sued for student-on-student racial harassment. After all, racial avoidance is not illegal and it can be and is performed frequently by whites without social penalty. In other words, the school leaders exercised their power without taking a single impactful action to combat the harassment and protect Black students.

Activity 18.2

Applying your learning from the case study to considerations of race and educational leadership more widely, please respond to these questions:

1 With a critical focus on power relations, structure and agency, how is the construction of race problematic in educational leadership?
2 What is the effect of this treatment of race on leadership practice and conceptualizations?
3 What can you do to change the current state of affairs in your school setting relative to race and leadership?

What needs to change?

Encouraging leaders to engage in conversations that critically examine their practice can help them develop a proactive approach that incorporates race meaningfully. The aim of such conversations is to enable leaders to better grasp some of these issues before challenges emerge, such as those discussed in the case study. The growing racial and cultural diversity in schools in these two national contexts of the United States and the UK provides an opportunity to engage leaders in these conversations and related training.

These conversations should be included in the training of aspiring principals or headteachers, meaning in the United States those who are in graduate school working to obtain their principal certification, and in the UK, those who are in universities undertaking master's programmes in educational leadership. However, those who are currently practising in the field, in senior-leadership (but sub-principal) or middle-leadership roles, can also benefit from this type of professional learning. Therefore, we recommend making changes to cultural and structural conditions in education such that the postgraduate degree and leadership-preparation programmes that are available to school leaders are actually taken up by them. On these programmes, anti-racist conversations, curricula and ethos should be foregrounded.

Specific changes are needed to mitigate the issues of racial avoidance. First, racial avoidance can be thought of as a broader scheme of white responses to race and racism. We want to clarify that in the United States, this response is not just limited to white actors, though it is greatly influenced by a system where white is regarded as the superior cultural norm. For example, in the case study, the assistant principal responded to racial incidents, but she had to respond within the paradigm that was (re)constructed within the school by the white school leaders, white children and their parents who were responsible for helping create the racially hostile environment and community. It is important to note that these actors all drew their power from a system of white supremacy. We acknowledge that the *Williams* case in some ways appears to be an extreme case study, but we hasten to add that there are two relevant nuanced points to recognize and honour in its useful explanatory power.

First, the *Williams* case represents a pronounced illustration of what happens in much subtler, but no less powerful, ways each day in schools and society. Second, we have found that in the subtle cases that often are not broadcast loudly or covered by the media, or that make it to court, white cultural norms remain powerful factors in controlling resources, limiting access and in the diminishing growth of children and professionals of colour.

Conclusion

We want to finish by highlighting four key messages from our chapter. First, exploring how racial avoidance is a form of implicit racism can develop understanding of how a leader's unconscious negative evaluations of racial or ethnic minorities can be realized by a persistent avoidance of complex multiracial interactions. Second, racism is complex and requires an understanding of how it works on a systemic level in order to properly address it. Third, in a world that is becoming more racially and culturally diverse, it is irresponsible to train leaders without relevant engagement with race and culture. Finally, it is possible to address race and leadership in a manner that is positive, productive and supportive of leaders' development.

Further reading

Curtis, S. and Showunmi, V. (2019) Black women leaders: intersectional and present in the field of education 'hear our voice'. In: P. Miller and C. Callender (eds), Race, education and educational leadership: an integrated analysis (pp. 261–286). London: Bloomsbury Academic.

Gooden, M.A. and O'Doherty, A. (2015) Do you see what I see? Fostering aspiring leaders' racial awareness. *Urban Education*, 50(2), 225–255.

Miller, P. (ed.) (2016) *Cultures of educational leadership: global and intercultural perspectives*. London: Palgrave.

Showunmi, V. (2018) Interrupting whiteness: an auto-ethnography of a Black female leader in higher education. In: R. McNae and E.C. Reilly (eds), *Women leading education across the continents: finding and harnessing the joy in leadership* (pp. 128–135). Lanham, MD: Rowman & Littlefield.

References

ACE (American Council of Education) Data Explorer (2019) College presidents, by race and ethnicity. Available online: https://www.aceacps.org/minority-presidents-dashboard/ (accessed 1 February 2020).

Acker, J. (2006) Inequality regimes: gender, class, and race in organizations. *Gender & Society*, 20(4), 441–464.

Ali, A.H. and Clark, E. (2019) Qualified immunity: explained. *The Appeal*, 20 June. Available online: https://theappeal.org/qualified-immunity-explained/ (accessed 14 January 2020).

Department for Education (2020) *School teacher workforce*. Gov.UK. Available online: https://www.ethnicity-facts-figures.service.gov.uk/workforce-and-business/workforce-diversity/school-teacher-workforce/latest (accessed 16 January 2020).

Dingle, D.T. (2019) There are only 4 Black CEOs at Fortune500 companies. Here is how the ELC plans to change that. *Black Enterprise*, 16 October. Available online: https://www.blackenterprise.com/elc-increase-number-black-ceos-nation-largest-public-companies/ (accessed 1 February 2020).

Gooden, M.A. and Dantley, M. (2012) Centering race in a framework for leadership preparation. *Journal of Research on Leadership in Education*, 7(2), 237–253.

Johnson, L. (2017) Interpreting historical responses to racism by UK Black and South Asian headteachers through the lens of generational consciousness. In: S.J. Courtney, R. McGinity and H.M. Gunter (eds), *Educational leadership: theorising professional practice in neoliberal times* (pp. 124–137). Abingdon: Routledge.

McFarland, J., Hussar, B., Zhang, J., Wang, X., Wang, K., Hein, S., Diliberti, M., Forrest Cataldi, E., Bullock Mann, F. and Barmer, A. (2019) *The condition of education 2019*. Washington, DC: National Center of Education Statistics. Available online: https://nces.ed.gov/pubsearch/pubsinfo.asp?pubid=2019144 (accessed 28 July 2020).

Osler, A. (2006) Changing leadership in contexts of diversity: visibility, invisibility and democratic ideals. *Policy Futures in Education*, 4(2), 128–144.

Osler, J.E. and Webb, R.L. (2014) An in-depth qualitative and quantitative analysis to determine the factors that affect the existence of African American Women superintendents in the North Carolina K–12 public school system. *Journal on School Educational Technology*, 10(2), 17–40.

Ozga, J. (ed.) (1992) *Women in educational management*. Buckingham: Open University Press.

Plaut, V.C. (2010) Diversity science: why and how difference makes a difference. *Psychological Inquiry*, 21(2), 77–99.

Prieto, L.C., Norman, M.V., Phipps, S.T.A. and Chenault, E.B.S. (2016) Tackling micro-aggressions in organizations: a broken windows approach. *Journal of Leadership, Accountability & Ethics*, 13(3). Available online: https://www.articlegateway.com/index.php/JLAE/article/view/1906 (accessed 28 July 2020).

Sealy, R. and Vinnicombe, S. (2012) The female FTSE board report 2012: milestone or millstone? Cranfield University. Available online: https://dspace.lib.cranfield.ac.uk/handle/1826/7050 (accessed 31 January 2020).

Van Knippenberg, D. (2011) Embodying who we are: leader group prototypicality and leadership effectiveness. *The Leadership Quarterly*, 22(6), 1078–1091.

Williams v. Port Huron School District, No. 10-1636, 6th Cir., 9 January 2012.

Socio-economic class and educational leadership

Helen M. Gunter and Steven J. Courtney

19

What this chapter is about 296

Key questions that this chapter addresses 296

Introduction 296

The meaning of socio-economic class 297

The impact of socio-economic class on leaders, leading and leadership 298

The impact of socio-economic class on educational leaders, leading and leadership 299

Breaking through the 'class' ceiling 304

Conclusion 307

Further reading 307

References 308

What this chapter is about

In this chapter, we present and discuss the relationship between socio-economic class and educational leaders, leading, leadership and leaderability. We note that socio-economic class is an under-researched area in the field of educational leadership yet suggest that present and aspiring leaders' backgrounds may be an important factor in subsequent 'leaderful' practice. We draw on a research case study as well as on research from related fields to suggest that socio-economic class may interplay with educational leadership in multiple ways. For example, access to leadership roles is probably classed, as in other fields; constructions of leader and leading conceptually foreground middle- and upper-class qualities and features; and yet socio-economic class may also be a factor prompting leaders to work with disadvantaged followers in what we call transformative, rather than transformational ways, that privilege social justice.

Key questions that this chapter addresses

1 What does socio-economic class mean?
2 How does socio-economic class intersect with educational leader, leading, leadership and leaderability?
3 How might this play out in schools?
4 What are the possibilities for a declassed, transformative educational leadership?
5 In what ways might knowledge production in and about educational leadership be classed?

Introduction

Socio-economic class is a major structuring process in civil society, in which wealth and family determine educational and occupational opportunities. There is little research into the impact of socio-economic class on educational professionals in regard to their career aspirations and achievements, or certainly in regard to promotion into school principal and university president roles. We use the available research to outline the key issues concerning socio-economic class, and we locate our case-study analysis in the UK as a whole and England in particular as an example of a highly class-structured society and economy. We consider the implications of our analysis concerning how the field is classed for what leader, leading and leadership is assumed to mean, and we consider how knowledge production for research and professional development is inflected with socio-economic class assumptions of what is normal.

The meaning of socio-economic class

Socio-economic class is a hierarchized and stratified classification of people, as we describe in the definitions box.

This definition by Parker et al. (2003) shows that the grouping of people into separate socio-economic classes is a human construct designed to structure agency by creating advantage and disadvantage through social (family, networks, symbols) and economic (earned and inherited wealth) factors. Hence, we tend to use the short-hand of 'socio-economic' to signify both the way that people position themselves, and are positioned.

Socio-economic class is a power structure designed to enable and/or thwart agency through framing values, identity and practice according to societally agreed indicators. Some indicators are tangible and/or material, such as housing, consumption and income, and others are subtle, including family name, accent, deportment and taste. Socio-economic class is recognized, attributed and judged through objective exchange relationships from how people are addressed through to whom they marry. For example, low socio-economic neighbourhoods can be described as 'disadvantaged' or even 'ghettos' compared to more 'favourable' areas that are 'up and coming',

> **Socio-economic class:** In class systems people are collectivised into classes, that is, objective positions of relative economic and political advantage constituted by mechanisms which distribute important material and cultural resources for action. Classes differ according to their relative material advantages and the opportunities and methods open to them to maintain or improve their access to resources. Class positions of individuals tend to be shaped by what can be inherited, that is, property, wealth, income-earning occupations and education, and are heavily influenced by the state's legal protection of private property, inheritance and tax law and educational policies (*Parker et al., 2003: 205*)

'gentrified', 'classy' and inhabited by 'people like us'. Gentrification illuminates how an area's classed status is attached to its inhabitants rather than to any innate property of the architecture.

Socio-economic class is intergenerational through legal protections, the enculturation of inheritance, and the normalization of eugenics in regard to certain class 'types' having a 'natural' right to rule compared with those who are 'born to follow' (see Chapter 23 of this book). Historically, there is a tendency to group into 'higher' classes (e.g. aristocracy, corporate CEOs), 'middle' classes (e.g. professions, business owners), and 'working' classes (e.g. wage labourers). Research analysis can recognize but also trouble such divisions through examining the political, social, economic and cultural context in which socio-economic class practices are located and reworked. Consequently, degrees of segregation and permeability between classes may be enabled through the rejection/acceptance of the idea of social and economic mobility combined with views and actions regarding the law and cultural norms. Socio-economic class is reproduced and evident in people's imagining of the world, their aspirations and their practices regarding what is normal and achievable. Bourdieu (2000) articulates these elements through his concept of **capital** that is embodied, recognized and organizational, and can be invested in seeking and attributing acclaim. Hence the social and economic order and a person's place within it are based on the complexity of symbolism (e.g. credentials, titles, buildings, dress, accent) interplayed with the relational (e.g. family, networks) and cultural (e.g. discernment about what is regarded as distinction and worthy of attention and approval).

The impact of socio-economic class on leaders, leading and leadership

Socio-economic class intersects with race, gender, ethnicity, faith, sexuality and age in ways that generate and sustain both approved and disapproved-of values, identities and practices. This is embedded in social, economic, political and cultural structures, where top jobs in government, media, corporations, military and the arts are dominated by people from particular family and education backgrounds that demonstrate historically rooted socio-economic advantage that, additionally, is raced and gendered. This is what Jones identifies in the UK as 'the Establishment' that 'includes politicians who make laws; media barons who set the terms of the debate; businesses and financiers who run the economy; police forces that enforce the law which is rigged in favour of the powerful' (2014: 5). Distinction is evident in what is said and done in ways that are approved of (or at least not challenged). Jones (2012), for example, identifies 'chavs' as the normalized and often 'mocking' label for the working classes who are poor and have the worst features of society (i.e. criminality, violence, welfare-dependency) attributed to them.

The way that socio-economic class works within organizational structures has implications for those who aspire to and who formally take on senior roles in public services (e.g. politics, law, military and police), corporations (e.g. media and business) and interest groups within civil society (e.g. faith institutions, business and arts). Socio-economic class legitimates the identification of those who 'stand out from the crowd' as the **leaders**, who do **leading** and exercise **leadership**, and who demonstrate that 'certain something' as illuminative of **leaderability**, collectively the '**4 Ls**'.

Education combined with family and wealth is recognized as central to these 4 Ls regarding the preparation and status related to attendance at private school and elite universities (known as Oxbridge in the UK). For example, only 7 per cent of UK children attend private school but they dominate the professions and the arts. Kirby (2016) reports that 71 per cent of top officers, 61 per cent of top doctors, 32 per cent of MPs and 50 per cent of the Cabinet, 48 per cent of senior civil servants, 51 per cent of leading journalists, 34 per cent of CEOs, 67 per cent of British Oscar winners, 42 per cent of BAFTA winners, and 63 per cent of British Nobel prize winners had been privately educated.

Leader: an individual who inherits (e.g. monarch) or is appointed (e.g. an organizational role) or who is listened to (e.g. has charisma) in regard to a role, and who is formally entitled and/or recognized as *the* leader of others who are followers.

Leading: what a leader says and does as the leader in a role, and how that is recognized and accepted (bodily gestures such as curtsey, and the use of titles) by followers.

Leadership: how power is exercised by the leader who does leading, through enabling followers to say or do or not to say or do.

Leaderability: how the leader who is leading and exercising leadership demonstrates authority and legitimacy through how what they say and do is related to assumptions and expectations of the role.

The impact of socio-economic class on educational leaders, leading and leadership

The data just provided about the UK does not include headteachers or principals, and at the time of writing there is no major study of the socio-economic class composition of the education workforce or the impact on educational leaders, leading and leadership. Pioneering research by Fuller (2013) uses interview data to examine socio-economic class awareness by headteachers of the workforce and school students in England, where she identifies the impact of social and economic location on background experience, social mobility and professional dispositions. Such research demonstrates that we do not know enough about the challenges for educational professionals from 'working-class' backgrounds who enter 'middle-class' educational institutions dominated by those educated in private schools and at elite universities. Research about higher education demonstrates that even if someone from a working-class background is appointed to a post in a university, 'they must still negotiate an alien, emphatically middle-class cultural setting, not to mention sustain themselves during the various periods of low or no income that early career academics typically have to endure' (THE, 2018: 41).

Schools and universities are sites where there are socio-economic class barriers to progress for staff and students, particularly concerning access to a school/university place to study or for employment, not least through how a potential applicant may self-exclude through thinking that this is not a school or university for them. If an application is made, then the personal profile that shows which school or university has been attended can be read in different ways, and at an interview a person's socio-economic status can be visible through dress, accent, language and demeanour. Educational professionals do classed work, particularly in neighbourhoods undergoing change and population shifts. Such barriers are integral to the design of reforms to schools in England, where we will focus our subsequent case analysis in this chapter. Here, a focus on staff within organizational roles demonstrates that publicly owned and funded schools tend to be structured and operate in ways that mimic socio-economically classed structures and cultures in private fee-paying schools. For example, there are vertical structures regarding job descriptions and pay scales, and cultural practices regarding titles and deference. Globalized reforms regarding privatization, competition and entrepreneurialism have led to the 4 Ls

School leader: an individual appointed to a formal role with a formal title e.g. headteacher//principal, deputy/vice-principal, heads of department or curriculum, where delegation with accountable reporting and performance evaluation enables unity of command of the leader over teachers and support staff, who are followers.

School leading: what a headteacher says and does regarding organizational purposes and practices that tends to concern control through visioning and organizational advantage through performance evaluation of followers.

School leadership: power is exercised by the headteacher//principal as leader regarding the purpose and location of the school in the market place, where the role and contribution of the 'school workforce' as followers is defined and regulated.

School leaderability: the headteacher//principal leader demonstrates authority over and legitimacy attributed by followers through compatibility with accepted beliefs about the role, and is evidenced in dress, posture, language and general practices.

being labelled 'educational' in England but in reality, the focus has been less on *educational* purposes, curriculum design and pedagogic practices, and more on *organizational* efficiency and effectiveness as a privatized business that may be secular or faith-based. This business restructuring has enabled organizational efficiency to be designed and equated with preferred socio-economic class backgrounds for attracting the right type of staff and students. Consequently the 4 Ls in a school context can be characterized according to the definitions in the box.

While the focus is on the school as an organization, increasingly autonomous schools are linked in chains through 'ownership' by faith, business and/or conglomerates. For example, in England there has been since 2010 a rapid proliferation of school types (e.g. academies, studio, university technical colleges, free), where the linking of schools through multi-academy trusts (MATs) is generating new types of corporatized 4 Ls where 'executives' outside the school control the school leader and followers. Changes to the middle classes within and external to the nation state and the intense development of a globalized 'travelling' managerial class that undertake 'on-the-hoof' work in corporate contexts impacts on how these new forms of organization are designed and professional practice enacted.

The school 4 Ls are classed socially and economically in a range of ways and are historically located in certain national systems. For example, in England there is a long-established 'headmaster' tradition that is classed (and intersects with race and gender):

> In an hierarchical and class-stratified society such as England, whole institutional leadership could not be expected from or entrusted to a headteacher who, however carefully selected and trained, would be in origin working class or petty bourgeoise at best. Institutional leadership, which involved setting the goals, ethos and values of the school; establishing its 'mission'; allocating resources available; and determining the mode of organization necessary to achieve this mission – all of this was a function of class position in English society, not of professional status. School leadership in this sense could not be trusted to a mere elementary school headteacher, male or female. *(Grace, 1995: 9)*

Organizational and moral leadership of the staff, students and parents as a function of a classed society meant that preparation for the role was located in the class system of birth, private schooling and elite universities. However, the development of professionalism in the post-1945 period regarding official training, accreditation and licensing alongside increased access to public education by the working and middle classes meant that classed forms of authority and legitimacy where threatened. While Grace demonstrates the advancement of democratic purposes and structures in public education, he also shows how the 'headmaster tradition' has endured and been reworked through the modernization of the educational professional where 'its culture of headship as personal, powerful, controlling, moralizing and patriarchal has become an important constituent in the subsequent discourse and practice of school headship especially in the secondary school sector' (1995: 11). This is certainly evident in the leader-centric victory narratives of and by headteachers, where trained conformity and delivery processes enables socio-economic class co-option to take place.

While publicly accredited leadership training in England suggests an open and aspirational system for professionals, in reality, the indicators of socio-economic class such as family name, place of school attendance, and accent, operate in ways that only allow those who conform to the 'known ways of doing things' or 'fit in' to be successful: first, the focus on personal 'attributes' linked to claims for transformational leadership are presented as neutral but are connected to trait theories, where such qualities may be classed; second, the corporatization of the role and equivalence with commercial leaders regarding status, pay and conditions, where, as we have shown, leaders in the corporate sector are more likely to be middle or upper class; third, and related, the adoption of corporate methods for selection, mentoring and performance management, combined with the widening of the pool of potential applicants by removing the need to be a qualified teacher; and fourth, the school as a business required the use of entrepreneurial forms of the 4 Ls whereby the profession is trained and inspected in regard to organizational management and leadership.

Much of this is veiled but can be evidenced in accounts by headteachers of their struggles with the reforms to their work and identities. For example, a major study in the school sector in England by Gewirtz (2002) provides a detailed account of how change has produced contextually layered responses by the profession. Evidence is provided about Ms English who led the school at a time of welfarist social democracy, while the successor headteacher, Mr Jones, is a product of more recent school business autonomy:

> What I have been able to show, by focusing on the individual headteachers, is that the new languages of enterprise, quality and excellence grate against existing and embedded welfarist languages but may still encompass aspects of the welfarist project, even if the possibilities for the realisation of the project are altered significantly. Headteachers bring with them into this transformation personal qualities, complex histories and social positionings which mean that a straightforward totalising fit within a dominant discourse is unlikely. For example, Ms English's welfarism is intermingled with an apparent elitism in that her warm and mutually respectful relations with students do not extend to her relationships with staff, a number of whom complained that she treated them in a dismissive way. At the same time, Mr Jones' energetic new managerialism appears to be underlain by a genuine commitment to working-class youth. Thus, social positionings, like gender and social class, can interrupt or inflect the acting out of dominant discourses.
> (Gewirtz, 2002: 47–48)

There are accounts of what it means to experience such a contradictory personal and professional context, which exposes what happens when teachers are socially and economically positioned differently from the children and communities where the school is located (Gordon, 2008), where social-justice agendas are complex to enact and can, in Bourdieuian (2000) terms, be misrecognized.

In the next section, we present a research case study from a wider project that one of us carried out (Courtney, 2015) into school leadership in diversified provision in England. Nine headteachers or principals were interviewed, and a range of socio-economic class positions was evident across the sample. These participants' socio-economic class was not a focus of the study, and yet it was a consistent, if sometimes implicit feature of how they saw themselves, their motivation to practice and their identities. For this case study, we are drawing on narrative data from one headteacher who self-identified as working class. Our intention is not to make a general statement about how such leaders lead, but to present an empirical instantiation of the possible regarding agency in the context of socio-economic class as a structural feature, and to invite you to reflect on what it reveals of that structure and of the practice recounted here.

Case Study 19.1 Ellen

Ellen (a pseudonym) is headteacher of a Pupil Referral Unit (PRU) in a socio-economically disadvantaged, post-industrial urban community in northern England. As well as being working class, Ellen is Black, with African Caribbean heritage, a woman and she is also a second-generation immigrant. We ask that you bear in mind as you read this account the ways in which dimensions of (dis)advantage never operate singly, but must be considered together: this is commonly attempted through using intersectional approaches.

A PRU is a state-funded school for pupils who are unable to access mainstream provision, either temporarily or permanently, perhaps because they have been excluded from such provision, or because they are ill or pregnant. PRUs tend to be smaller than mainstream provision, and since many of their pupils have been excluded from other schools, these children may present particular challenges concerning behaviour and/or learning difficulties. Since most exclusions affect working-class children, these make up the majority of PRU pupils. No research has been conducted into the socio-economic class of those who teach and lead in PRUs. What follows is a crafted narrative account that we have created from extracts of Ellen's interview data: our changes concern mostly reordering for chronological coherence and editing for clarity and confidentiality: we have inserted no substantive details.

Ellen's story

When I was seventeen, I was pregnant at school . . . I didn't come from a family who went to university, so I didn't really know what to do, basically. And I think a lot of people thought, right, that's it, my career was over. But I had a really supportive mum, so what I basically did . . . I had my child at eighteen, had a year off, and then went back into doing A levels. Didn't know what to do.

When I started doing my A levels again, I was twenty. I had to do it on my own to be honest with you and I had to put the work in, because I'd failed when I was younger, when I was eighteen. And that meant that I had to grow up; I had a baby. You know, I had to. The long goal for me, was what the life chances that I was going to give for my child. So. . . it was going home, doing the research, doing the work and coming back and making sure that, you know, homework was on time. And it had to be self-directed. So, it was about having a goal, and the goal was for my child and the goal was what I wanted to do for my career.

Passed two A levels, and I thought 'Ooh, I'll become a teacher!' And I trained as being an English and Drama teacher. And it was at that period of time where I couldn't get a job, so, for the first year, I did quite a few supply [substitute] jobs. And then I ended up applying for a post that was funded through a pot of money to help Black or ethnic-minority children that were underachieving. So, that was how I got into teaching, so I couldn't actually get into doing what I was trained to do, which was English and Drama. And a post, a really unusual post came up. And that was to do with, again it was to do with Black underachievement. So, I did that for about two or three years. Alongside that I also ran a Saturday school so a lot of my focus was on Black underachievement. So, I ran a Saturday school for about five or six years. And then, eventually, I just thought, the focus of what I wanted to do was teach, and it wasn't just about Black children, it was about teaching all children who'd had, who'd probably had to face some kind of adversity, basically, so I went to work as a youth offending officer, education, which was very interesting at the time, but not what I wanted to do. And then I got a post in a Pupil Referral Unit. So, it was for students who'd been permanently excluded but were going back into mainstream school. Did that for a year, and then landed a post as a Key Stage 3 Deputy. And that was for a Pupil Referral Unit. And eventually I did that for about four years and then ended up as Head of a Pupil Referral Unit. And then came here as Deputy. And the reason why I came here, because I wanted a traditional Pupil Referral Unit, basically, where I've got the children, I could take them through. Got the post as Deputy for two years and then 2010, I took up the post as Head. So that's my career path, so it's always really been with working with disadvantaged children, children who are facing some kind of adversity and might have behaviour problems, complex families, a range of different agencies that we work with. So, it's not just about teaching.

I mean, one of the things for me about applying for jobs, when I look for jobs, it's what could I do to improve, not just about, not just about education, it's about life chances as well. And I think in the Pupil Referral Unit it's very much about the education and life chances come along the same side. You have to work on self-esteem, so for me, from becoming a Deputy, it was well, yeah, I can do that, and you know, I've got the leadership. And I can do that. I've got an understanding; I know what the systems are. And also, what has come alongside the job has been able to understand about education and how education functions and how it is very important, especially in the field that I've been working in, a lot of Pupil Referral Units are either in youth clubs, and the focus was around vocational etc. My drive has been around education and aspirational sort of attainment targets, and stuff like that. So that's the change in Pupil Referral Units, as they've evolved. You know, not many of them used to offer GCSEs. For me, it was if you were excluded, then that's what we need to do and develop that curriculum further. So, any student who comes here now has access to five GCSEs. And that's really all they need if they're going to go to move on, even if they want to go to university etc. When you walk around the school, there's an ethos in the school which has to be created, not just by myself, but by my staff. So it is very, very nurturing. And that has to be, that's the focus of a Pupil Referral Unit. It's very, very small. So, we know those children. We have, sort of, relaxed relationships with those students but the boundaries are still in there. But I want children to come and be happy. They've all had negative experiences in school where no one's believed in them and you know, they're not expected to do well but my drive with these students is that we are a school, there's aspirations, where do you want to go?

I suppose I share very much a similar lifestyle, upbringing to a lot of these children here, where I've come from a council estate, low aspirations, etc., and their parents have low aspirations. So, it's very easy for me to say well, yeah, hold on a minute, I know what you're doing, I know this, that and the other, but, you know, if you want a house, if you want a car, you need to move on that next step. So, it's about not having that self-fulfilling prophecy. I remember one of the children when I'd bought a car, and he went, 'did you get that on disability?' [i.e. from the state's welfare provision] I thought, 'nah!' [laughs]. No, you can actually buy a car! You can get a loan! So, it's, you know, how you, sort of change that culture and that culture of thinking that, you know, yes, I can go to university if I want to.

Activity 19.1

1 Narrative data is considered useful in allowing research participants to construct causal relationships in their accounts as they make sense of their lives. How does Ellen attribute causality between her working-class background and her present-day leadership practice and dispositions?

2 What discourses and assumptions about socio-economic class and education does Ellen draw on in her account?

3 What other discourses and 'stories' of socio-economic class might Ellen have drawn on? How might these have changed her narrative?

Breaking through the 'class' ceiling

Socio-economic class is one issue in a range of interrelated structural injustices affecting the education profession workforce, and while important research is underway on issues of gender and race (see Chapters 6, 16 and 18), there is little known about the realities of socio-economic class in everyday leadership practice. Nevertheless, we have identified that there is consistent analysis over time that socio-economic class impacts in negative ways on people and educational organizations, where the growth in preparation and training programmes and postgraduate study for professionals suggests that there is a move towards the understanding and development of practice that challenges class-based enculturation. However, the questions we need to ask about the growth in accreditation and leadership centres for education is whether the evidence base and conceptual tools used actually replicate and modernize socio-economic class distinctions through models such as **Transformational Leadership**, or whether there are opportunities for more **Transformative Models**.

What we mean is that the behaviourist Transformational Model dominates in education policy reform and training programmes, and that this is an approach to professional purposes and practice that enables socio-economic class structuring to be evident but in a modernized and seductive way. Notions of transformation are about enabling the school or university to shift from a public institution to a private business, and the focus on entrepreneurial impact requires top-down and class-informed 'capitals' that are social, cultural and, as Bourdieu (2000) argues, symbolic. Transformative Models are different because they relate the professional to wider social-justice agendas within the community, whereby the focus is on equity and working against the denial of educational opportunities and in favour of fair access. There is a range of research and theorizing in the field of educational leadership that challenges social injustice in regard to the workforce composition and the impact of reforms on identities, purposes and practices (see Chapter 9). The insights gained from this work present a different, *transformative* approach to the 4 Ls where, in addition to the formal leader who does leading and leadership, and displays leaderability, there is an inclusive and democratized approach (see definition box).

> **Leader:** *a* leader can be in the wider workforce and who makes a contribution that is listened to and recognized.
>
> **Leading:** *a* leader from the wider workforce can say and do to contribute to debate and decision-making.
>
> **Leadership:** is a *relational* resource that *all* can access and where power is shared and used by the professional community and the students they work with and for.
>
> **Leaderability:** authority and legitimacy are demonstrated by *every* member of the workforce, where the worth of a contribution is not judged in relation to structural and cultural dis/advantage.

This approach to the 4 Ls not only recognizes the value and impact of the headteacher or principal in regard to a social-justice agenda, but also disconnects the 4 Ls from organizational hierarchy that is likely to be classed. In other words, if the 'class ceiling' is to be broken, as the THE (2016) suggests, then the solution lies in how the 4 Ls are no longer conceptualized in terms of a leader–follower binary whose power dynamic reflects and reproduces socio-economic class distinctions. Here, followers are agentic voids and know their place until the leader – whose role is superordinate in the organizational hierarchy – motivates and inspires. In order to do this, the field needs to actively engage with the intellectual and empirical resources that do not rely on class distinction rooted in socio-economic capitals, but rather enable a social-justice agenda.

Such resources are evident in the field, and are available through a critical focus on the 4 Ls in studies that illuminate and present alternatives regarding:

- **Values:** focused on the realities and opportunities located in the educability of all children and disconnected from parental socio-economic resources.

- **Power:** a shared resource for all to access and use through communal approaches to decision-making, with notions of democracy and participation that are shared within the organization.

- **Curriculum:** designed to secure access, recognition and the realization of human potential through relating knowledge production to communities and families.

- **Teaching and learning:** the prime focus of an educational institution, and so for leadership to be educational then it has to be located within and oriented towards teacher–student activity.

- **Localized systems:** accounts of educational provision that challenge segregation and demonstrate professional and community control over decision-making.

- **National systems:** comparisons across national borders and within national system studies show that socio-economic class does not dominate the conceptualization and conduct of professionalism.

- **Research:** challenges to knowledge-production purposes, design and outcomes are needed in regard to what is known and worth knowing in order to disconnect 'powerful knowledge' from socio-economic class interests and domination.

Accessing and developing these resources is directly related to the research agenda for the field and to the need for projects that not only map the socio-economic class composition of the education profession, but also develop models for educational professionals that do not replicate such distinctions. We consider the research agenda through Activity 19.2.

Activity 19.2

1 Think back to the case study about the headteacher in England. What questions and issues does this account raise for you concerning the potential role of socio-economic class in influencing leadership practice and dispositions?
2 How might you investigate these?
3 What theoretical resources might you use? Why these?

An important element of the research agenda is to investigate the ways in which knowledge production in the field of educational leadership may itself be classed in regard to social and economic structures and cultures. There are a number of avenues to explore, focusing usefully perhaps on different sites of knowledge production. For instance, universities, particularly in the United States, the UK and Australia, are decreasingly accessible to those without sufficient economic, cultural and social capitals to enter or survive what can be years of precarity at the beginning of a career. This may both encourage middle-class entrants to the academy and normalize what might be understood as middle-class dispositions and/or performances, such that those from working and lower-middle-class backgrounds learn to adapt to, mimic and internalize *being middle-class*. Or they and their work may remain a dissonant presence in the academy, never quite attaining legitimacy. Second, the question of whether knowledge produced in the field of practice, e.g. by school leaders themselves, is (1) more likely to derive from working-class positions and actors, and (2) more likely to gain wider currency and/or legitimacy than that produced in universities, is in urgent need of empirical attention. Knowing this will enable us to conduct more nuanced analyses concerning how socio-economic class may intersect with the types of knowledge more commonly produced in given sites. For instance, there may well be humanistic knowledge, focusing on the lived experience of a range of socio-economic class positions owing to its primary production in schools. However, criticality may be located in experience, but the codification of critical knowledge that describes, explains, theorizes and seeks to disrupt power relations in the field of educational leadership may be more likely to be produced in universities, and so reflect middle-class assumptions. One way forward is for activist professional researchers in universities and researching professionals in schools to work in partnership on projects and on postgraduate study, and as Apple (2013) has argued, elite knowledges are relevant, owned by everyone and are a resource for all to access and use. The problem we currently face is that there are few investigations, and so a disposition of alertness to various possibilities and of critical self-reflexivity is required.

Conclusion

In this chapter, we have established a series of propositions and questions concerning the interplay between the notions of socio-economic class and of educational leader, leading, leadership and leaderability. Whilst the focus through our illuminative research case study has been on schools, we invite you to reflect on the ways in which our argument holds and does not hold concerning other sites, for example, higher education. We have made the argument that socio-economic class is likely to mediate or influence what and how knowledge concerning educational leadership is produced; how leading is done; who gets to lead; and what counts as leaderability. We conclude by urging the field to undertake empirical studies to address the questions we have raised, and we have suggested some principles and issues that might be taken into account in taking forward this research agenda.

Further reading

Apple, M.W. (1993) *Official knowledge: democratic education in a conservative age*. New York: Routledge.

Côté, S. (2011) How social class shapes thoughts and actions in organizations. *Research in Organizational Behavior*, 31, 43–71.

Martin, S.R., Innis, B.D. and Ward, R.G. (2017) Social class, leaders and leadership: a critical review and suggestions for development. *Current Opinion in Psychology*, 18, 49–54.

Reay, D. (2017) *Miseducation: inequality, education and the working classes*. Bristol: Policy Press.

Savage, M. (2015) *Social class in the 21st century*. London: Pelican Books.

References

Apple, M.W. (2013) *Can education change society?* New York: Routledge.

Bourdieu, P. (2000) *Pascalian meditations*, trans. R. Nice. Cambridge: Polity Press.

Courtney, S.J. (2015) Investigating school leadership at a time of system diversity, competition and flux. PhD thesis, University of Manchester, Manchester.

Fuller, K. (2013) *Gender, identity and educational leadership*. London: Bloomsbury Academic.

Gewirtz, S. (2002) *The managerial school: post-welfarism and social justice in education*. London: Routledge.

Gordon, J.A. (2008) Community responsive schools, mixed housing, and community regeneration. *Journal of Education Policy*, 23(2), 181–192.

Grace, G. (1995) *School leadership: beyond education management*. London: Falmer Press.

Jones, O. (2012) *Chavs: the demonization of the working class*. London: Verso.

Jones, O. (2014) *The Establishment and how they get away with it*. London: Penguin.

Kirby, P. (2016) *Leading people 2016: the educational backgrounds of the UK professional elite*. London: The Sutton Trust. Available online: https://www.suttontrust.com/our-research/leading-people-2016-education-background/ (accessed 29 July 2020).

Parker, J. with Mars, L., Ransome, P. and Stanworth, H. (2003) *Social theory: a basic tool kit*. Basingstoke: Palgrave Macmillan.

THE (2016) The class ceiling: why aren't there more academics like me? *Times Higher Education*, 20 October. Available online: https://www.timeshighereducation.com/comment/the-class-ceiling-why-arent-there-more-academics-like-me (accessed 29 July 2020).

THE (2018) Being working class in the academy. *Times Higher Education*, 25 October. Available online: https://www.timeshighereducation.com/features/being-working-class-academy (accessed 29 July 2020).

Governance and educational leadership

Andrew Wilkins and Brad Gobby

20

What this chapter is about	310
Key questions that this chapter addresses	310
Introduction	310
Governance	312
Educational leadership	315
Conclusion	320
Further reading	321
References	322

What this chapter is about

In this chapter, we critically analyse the relationship between educational leadership and governance through an examination of key trends in global education reform. Through adopting two perspectives of governance as 'instrumental-rational' and 'agonistic-political', we demonstrate how governance can be used to enrich studies of educational leadership, where educational leadership is understood as 'governance-in-practice'. To evidence the application and value of governance to studies of educational leadership, we draw on case-study material from England and Australia. Finally, we use this material to consider some of the implications of studying educational leadership through the lens of governance.

Key questions that this chapter addresses

1 What is governance?

2 What is the relationship between governance and educational leadership?

3 In what ways are different formulations of governance more or less dominant to enactments of school leadership and management?

4 To what extent is governance implicated in linking practices of school leadership and management to wider political and economic projects and possibilities.

Introduction

In this chapter, we describe and critically analyse the relationship between governance and educational leadership. The aim of making explicit such a relationship is to show the application and value of governance to the study of educational leadership. Taken in its widest sense, governance can be loosely characterized as a political and economic strategy aimed at perfecting the design of accountability relations and structures. Decreased government involvement in the running and monitoring of education provision means that public servants, be they school leaders or school governors, are called upon to make themselves accountable to stakeholders and evaluation and funding bodies, typically through horizontal and vertical relations of accountability that rely on performance bench-marking, external inspection and high-stakes testing. Governance (broadly conceived) concerns the extent to which these relations and structures of accountability function successfully within a narrow definition of rational self-management.

By implication, educational leadership (and management) is a function and condition of governance, since it provides a set of vital relays for linking the formally autonomous operations of schools with the political ambitions of the state and the interests of the wider public. The relationship between governance and educational leadership, we argue, is therefore crucial to mapping the current political moment, namely to detail the specific rationalities and configurations that bear upon the development of schools as organizations and the different interests served or excluded by these configurations.

A further, related aim of the chapter is to trace empirically the application and value of governance to the study of educational leadership so that other researchers may use similar or adapted and revised analytical strategies. To achieve this, we deploy two distinctive formulations of governance to show how governance-in-practice (in this case, educational leadership practices) can be differently conceptualized and understood. These two **formulations of governance** are **instrumental-rational** and **agonistic-political**. In a pragmatic sense, governance can be understood as a blueprint or model for producing schools that are 'publicly accountable' (narrowly conceived) – properly audited and monitored, high achieving, financially sustainable, law compliant and non-discriminatory. Governance, in this sense, can be considered a technical, even apolitical dimension of the leadership and management of schools as organizations – it is about striving to generate critical mass to meet certain strategic and operational priorities that enhance the quality and standards of schools. This is an *instrumental-rational* formulation of governance. But educational leadership, as an expression of governance, is deeply politicized in this sense. For educational leadership to be considered legitimate for example, it must, for the most part, conform to a dominant account of what educational leadership and its purpose is (to be discussed later). But who gets to decide the purpose and design of educational leadership?

We therefore require a second formulation of governance: *agonistic-political*. Such a view is important to contesting the supposedly politically neutral aims and language of governance and opening up analytic spaces in which the politicized nature of governance, and by implication educational leadership, reveals itself through the different interests served and excluded by such programmes. Later in the chapter we draw on two case studies of education reforms taken from two national policy contexts – the academies programme in England and the Independent Public Schools (IPS) programme in Australia – to illustrate how the same phenomenon can be analysed differently using these two formulations of governance.

> **Governance:** the ways in which government and non-government entities intervene, both formally and informally, to shape the way organizations and individuals conduct themselves. These interventions are designed to facilitate certain kinds of change (change in individual behaviour or organizational structure) or limit the possibilities for change in order to maintain the status quo. In both cases, governance is designed to improve conditions by which change can be affected or limited to serve different political, economic and environmental aims.

> **Leadership:** defined here as discourse. It is a dynamic and culturally and historically specific body of knowledge and practices that are concerned with influencing the conduct of others and one's self to specific ends. The meaning, practices and effects of leadership (including educational leadership) are shaped by social and political interests and power, and therefore the field and exercise of leadership are both sites of contest and struggle.

We have structured the chapter as follows. In the next section, we offer a historical account of the development of the concept and practice of governance through an examination of the changing role and responsibility of government. Following this we illustrate the significance of governance to educational leadership through a consideration of key global education trends and reforms, notably school autonomy and the relentless drive for self-improvement and self-management within a context of devolved education service planning. The subsequent section draws on case-study material taken from England and Australia to show the value and application of governance to educational leadership research, specifically how governance can be traced empirically and conceptualized differently through educational leadership practices using two distinct formulations of governance: *instrumental-rational* and *agonistic-political*. In the final section, we draw together these various perspectives and insights to reflect on some of the dilemmas and tensions inherent to theorizing governance in the context of educational leadership research.

Governance

The political and economic significance of governance can be richly theorized and understood when analysed in the context of the recent history of the development of government. In this section, we provide a definition of governance by way of a brief economic and political history of the changing role and responsibility of government, specifically the transformation of government in some Western countries during the 1980s and the subsequent reconfiguration and repurposing of different governments around the globe. These changes in the formation of government have direct implications for the configuration of state practices as well as the relationship between citizens and the state. As we intend to show, governance can be understood as both a condition and response to these changes.

The late 1970s and 1980s represent a watershed moment in the history of politics and economics. Spearheaded by the free-market principles of liberal economists and political conservatives, the 1980s ushered in a new era of government for many Western countries – a model of government that would later be replicated by countries around the globe. Against a background of high inflation and economic stagnation during the 1970s, the post-war social-democratic state came under fierce opposition from right-wing economists and politicians, who declared policy initiatives and redistribution programmes underpinned by strong government intervention to be oppressive, cost-ineffective and demoralizing. Instead, the role and responsibility of government was gradually reimagined and repurposed during the 1980s to complement a new vision of welfare, citizenship and the economy, one in which the vitality of market forces, the circulation of capital and the rights of individuals as consumers took precedence over previous social and economic goals, specifically the need to protect individuals and groups against the unintended consequences of capitalism and to secure the unconditional welfare rights of citizens.

Proposals for a small state underpinned by deregulated industry, decreased public spending, conditional citizenship and individual responsibility attracted widespread support among right-wing think tanks, politicians and economists during the late 1970s. It was not until the 1980s with the rise of Thatcherism in England and Reaganism in the United States that proposals for a small state were transformed from a collection of ideas into a governmental programme. The institutionalization of 'economic liberalism' under Thatcherism and Reaganism was integral to this mobilization, as it helped to carve out a new role and responsibility for government in the macro-economy, one that gave legitimacy to the small state. The post-war social-democratic state, with its emphasis on economic protection and government-subsidized mass social programmes, was effectively curtailed to make way for new government priorities: global alignment, capital mobility and fiscal responsibility. These same economic and political imperatives continue to shape the role and responsibility of governments today. The scaling back of the welfare state and the contracting out of public utilities and resources to private companies and charities capture the essence of a small state.

Yet despite reluctance among governments to own and manage their public utilities and resources, governments appear no less active in setting rules and managing expectations intended to shape and inform how public organizations govern themselves – what Cooper (1998: 12) calls 'governing at a distance'. These rules and expectations are enshrined through the formulation of professional guidelines, performance targets, strategic objectives and contractual obligations against which public organizations are compared and judged to be efficient, cost-effective, consumer-responsive, industry-facing and high-performing. Designed to make organizations more knowable and governable, these technologies and techniques enhance the capacity of governments and other non-government bodies to exercise control over the internal operation of public organizations or, at the very least, limit the choices public organizations have in terms of how they self-evaluate. Consider the important role played by test-based accountabilities, comparative-competitive frameworks and data management systems at the level of the school. These forms of punitive intervention and self-management are typically carried out by school leaders and governors on themselves and others, yet they are principally designed to make schools more amenable to scrutiny by external authorities and evaluation bodies, especially national para-government agencies like the school's inspectorate, the Office for Standards in Education, Children's Services and Skills (Ofsted), who evaluate schools on behalf of government and the consumer public.

On this understanding, a useful definition of governance offered by Rhodes (1996: 652) is 'government without governing'. In other words, governance can be used to characterize both the absence and presence of state power: the weakening of traditional structures of government and the strengthening of the continuation and exercise of state power over and through organizations. It is therefore misleading to characterize government and governance as separate forces or technologies since governance can be understood to be a form of 'government': 'modes of action, more or less considered or calculated, which were destined to act upon the possibilities of action of other people' (Foucault, 1982: 790).

While the term 'governance' lacks a precise meaning, it is typically used in political science, public policy and sociology literature to describe societies and economies in which vertical structures of top-down government are replaced (or supplemented) by the development of horizontal, flexible networks of bottom-up government. Here the term 'governance' is used to capture the ways in which key roles and responsibilities for service planning – specifically the appraisal, monitoring and budgeting of public services – have shifted from government entities to para-government organizations, management groups, leadership teams and even communities. These new forms of bottom-up government, sometimes called small government or devolved government, are often celebrated within policy documents and political speeches as levers for community empowerment and downward accountability since they work to shift power away from national governments, even local governments, to produce contexts in which service planning and delivery is managed through the 'spontaneous' interaction, cooperation and co-influence of multiple stakeholders rather than the planning committees of political authorities and their 'vested interests'. In 2011, the former British prime minster David Cameron set out a vision of a 'Big Society' in which he made similar claims about the strong relationship between devolution and community empowerment, the idea being that devolution enriches opportunities for community and citizen participation in service planning and delivery.

Viewed from a different perspective, governance is designed to weaken the influence of traditional structures of government and bureaucracy, even democratic processes, so that opportunities arise for improved public–private partnerships and the management, delivery and monitoring of public services by non-government, 'non-political' entities, such as charities, businesses and social enterprises. Governance therefore refers to qualitative changes to the design, management and ethos of public services, specifically the use of narrow, instrumental definitions of quality and accountability to measure the cost effectiveness and impact of public services. The shift from government to governance also signifies something unique about the exercise of modern forms of state power, namely the desire to govern through improving conditions for self-organization and self-improvement. Not to be confused with government and at the same time not to be analysed separate from it, governance can be described as a political and economic strategy aimed at supporting contexts in which the governing of the health, happiness, wealth, education and welfare of the population is achievable in the absence of any direct, coercive government intervention.

Related to this concept of governance is a very specific understanding of the nature and exercise of responsibility. No longer exclusively the domain of state intervention and protection, matters of public interest including duties of care and responsibility for others and to the self (broadly conceived) are purposefully reimagined under governance as matters of private interest and individual responsibility. Economic stability and job security emerge as goals and moral obligations to be satisfied by individuals and organizations, for example. Governance therefore signals the abrogation of state responsibility and its reluctance to protect individuals and organizations against some of the worst excesses of unregulated markets. At the same time, governance can be viewed as a political strategy or policy programme designed to foster the adaptive capacities of citizens and communities to operate within this new risk environment and the vulnerabilities and insecurities it engenders. Governance is concerned with improving conditions in which individuals and organizations are best placed to navigate and respond to these uncertainties and their attendant calculations and risks. Governance therefore operates at the intersection of two distinct processes: 'dis-embedding' and 're-embedding' (Keddie and Mills, 2019). Take schools in England for example. Under proposals to improve conditions for a self-improving school system, many schools are granted autonomy and flexibility to function outside the bureaucracy and politics of local government as administratively self-governing entities or 'state-funded independent schools'. Yet this process of 'dis-embedding' requires those same schools to anchor themselves more rigidly to new relations and fantasies of market discipline and competition as well as complimentary state-mandated directives, provisos and obligations – a process of 're-embedding' that strengthens relations of accountability between schools and central government through the prism of a market logic (see Wilkins, 2016).

Activity 20.1

Every person occupies different roles in their daily life: citizen, employee, parent, student, teacher, consumer, activist, patient, carer, leader, community member.

Consider the different roles you occupy, either voluntarily or involuntarily, and reflect on:

1 What kinds of responsibilities underpin that role?
2 Do you choose these responsibilities, or have you been chosen to perform them?
3 Who or what compels you to perform these responsibilities?
4 How and why did you learn to perform these responsibilities effectively?
5 How can you be sure you have inhabited and performed these responsibilities?

Educational leadership

Informed by positivist scientific approaches, the mainstream field of Educational Leadership, Management and Administration (ELMA) is construed here as contributing a scientific understanding of administration and the structures and functions of organizations. More recent scholarship on leadership has refocused on the desirable traits and behaviours of leaders, characterizations of heroic and exceptional leaders and organizational change in the context of universally prescribed categories of 'best practice'. Increasingly, this field is inhabited by critical voices that stress, rather than diminish, ELMA's relationship to wider political, social and cultural forces and their continuing impact on education (Bates, 2010). The mainstream field of ELMA has been critiqued for its instrumentalist and individualist models of leadership, its lack of theoretical and philosophical engagement, and the epistemological realism that leads it to accept the dominant education reform context as a mere uncontested backdrop of leadership. We now direct our attention to the critically informed analysis of leadership's relationship to politically driven structural and performative reform.

As discussed earlier, the rationale of 'government without governing' has engendered models of self-directed service planning and delivery. In education, this has taken the form of school autonomy and self-management. Imagined by its proponents as a condition of school improvement, school autonomy is endorsed by global governance bodies like the Organisation of Economic Co-operation and Development (OECD) and the World Bank, although there is no conclusive evidence that school autonomy improves educational outcomes for students. Nevertheless, the centralized and hierarchical coordination and management of schools has given way to local decision-making and network governance, framed by economic logics that model schools on the corporate competitive enterprise (Courtney, McGinity and Gunter, 2017). Through the process of contractualization, the freedom accorded to schools as service providers is disciplined by market competition and the requirement to demonstrate improved performance to governing bodies and other regulatory agencies. This means that school autonomy is largely conceptualized and exercised through the logic of competitive performativity; that is, through systems of accountability that evaluate and report school, student and staff performance, often narrowly measured through quantifiable performance benchmarking and testing.

Educational leadership is a strategy of this New Public Management (NPM) reform project. While adherence to (and the efficient administration of) centralized policies and procedures were valued in the case of bureaucratically managed school systems, different kinds of principal agency are required for the autonomous school. Governance promotes and compels new kinds of visionary, empowered, innovative leaders equipped to independently and strategically lead and solve organizational problems in flexible, rapidly changing and insecure market and policy settings. Such a corporate model of leadership and its associated notions of 'best practice' has been successfully operationalized by a cadre of bureaucrats and policy entrepreneurs who promote the use of private consultancies, certain popular books, governmental agencies and reports, and school leadership bodies like the National College for School Leadership in England.

In this sense, leadership performs governance-in-practice. Notions of leadership and the practices of leading are refashioned around this system of governance that diminishes state-directed, hierarchical forms of power by facilitating the conditions of local empowerment and self-governance. With private business and corporate leaders being models for school governance, principals are charged with creating strategic and business plans, collecting and evaluating data and performance, monitoring and managing teacher performance, managing school finances, diversifying income streams and promoting schools to users as consumers. School leaders are expected to establish and manage external partners and stakeholders to improve performance and accountability. In England, for example, school governors have been spotlighted as integral to school leadership by holding school leaders to account for financial and educational performance (Wilkins, 2016).

Viewed within the discourse of governance, educational leadership is a largely technical, universal and politically neutral know-how for optimizing organizational processes, calculability and outputs. This is the dominant view of the mainstream field of ELMA, which advances ahistorical, apolitical and functionalist accounts of leadership. Socially critical scholarship, however, brings into the analysis of educational leadership the historical and cultural relations of power 'which shape and pattern school leadership in particular periods and in various cultural settings' (Grace, 1995: 3). For this knowledge-base – which is concerned with politicizing the technical – educational leadership represents a vital relay that links the changing political objectives of the state to the management of schools. Leadership, as both a body of knowledge and practice, is therefore constituted through governance and tactically deployed in political strategies of 'governing at a distance'.

Activity 20.2

Leadership is often trapped in the discourses of organizational efficiency, performance and accountability.

Consider your ideas about leadership by engaging with the following:

1 Are leaders born or made?
2 What makes a 'good' school leader?
3 Where do your ideas about leadership come from?
4 How might the social and cultural context of a school influence what 'good' school leadership is?
5 To what extent can and should school leaders challenge the dominant ways of thinking about and doing educational leadership?

Case Study 20.1 England

Experiments in market-based reforms to education in England since the 1980s have not only strengthened the status and importance of educational leadership to schools but carved out normative spaces in which certain kinds of educational leaders and leadership styles are, by choice or necessity, more widely practised. Borrowing from business practices and scientific management theory more generally, the internal operation of the school now more closely resembles a business with all the trappings and incentives that accompany setting up and running a business, namely output controls, performance indicators and private-sector styles of management practice. The imprint of business ontology on school culture is nowhere more visible than in the use of standardization and testing. Standardization and testing function, on the one hand, are tools for defining and measuring self-improvement, the principal means through which school leaders and governors (those tasked with the responsibility of holding senior leaders to account for the financial and educational performance of the school) evaluate pupil's educational performance and make judgements about the quality of teaching. On the other hand, standardization and testing are tools for satisfying performance benchmarks and baseline assessments defined by the national school's inspectorate (Ofsted), external regulators and international assessment bodies (see Programme for International Student Assessment, PISA).

From this perspective, educational leadership can be considered a tool of governance to the extent it recalibrates schools as navigable spaces according to data management systems that register their explicitness and transparency as performative entities. As we demonstrate in this section, the movement towards greater devolved management and school autonomy in England, as exemplified through the academies programme, means that large numbers of schools operate as managers and overseers of their own provision with professional discretion over funding allocation, admissions and staff pay and conditions. This raises the issue of a 'regulation gap' with local government no longer acting as the principal management group for schools. Unwilling to concede too much control to schools, central government and para-government agencies have intervened by compelling school leaders and governors to adopt certain roles and responsibilities in order that their actions are knowable and governable from the perspective of external funders and regulators. Participation in school leadership and governance therefore tends to be limited to those who are technicians of 'best practice' or 'what works' and those who are effective translators for the realization of government-mandated initiatives and performance-driven objectives (Courtney, McGinity and Gunter, 2017).

Since the 1980s, both Labour and Conservative governments in England have continued (much less discredited or disrupted) the ideological work of creating an education system in the image of the market. This includes new legal arrangements to improve conditions for privatization management of education services. City Technology Colleges (CTCs) introduced under the terms of Education Reform Act 1988 and the Local Management of Schools (LMS) enabled some publicly funded schools to pursue such an arrangement, that is, a form of administrative self-governing unimpeded by the politics and bureaucracy of local government. Later, in the 2000s, the New Labour government introduced the City Academies programme to enable alternative providers, specifically charities, universities and social enterprises set up as private limited companies, to oversee management of underperforming schools in disadvantaged, urban areas, thus removing certain schools from local government jurisdiction. In 2010, the Coalition government (a cooperation between the Conservative and Liberal Democratic parties) revised the academies programme to enable all schools to convert to academy status by joining or creating their own foundations or trusts (see the Academies Act 2010). At the time of writing, statistics released by the Department for Education (DfE) indicate there are 8,973 open academies in England representing 33 per cent of the total number of primary schools and 68 per cent of the total number of secondary schools (DfE, 2019).

Research suggests that the conversion of local-government-run schools into academies (or 'academization') has implications for the way schools are organized internally, especially among 'sponsored academies' that are run by large management groups called multi-academy trusts (MATs). Key changes include a stricter focus on performance management, centrally mandated contractual obligations and market discipline to enhance upward accountability to funders and regulators with restrictions placed on who gets to participate in school governing bodies, usually determined by skills audits and competency frameworks (Wilkins, 2016). Against a background of diminishing local government support, school leaders and governors increasingly find themselves entrenched by bureaucratic-managerial roles and responsibilities spanning oversight of premises management, succession planning, budget control, resource allocation and employment disputers.

As already alluded to in the introduction, we propose two ways through which to interpret these changes to educational leadership. On the one hand, educational leadership can be understood from the narrow rational perspective of an **instrumental-technical** account of governance. A key role for school leaders and governors in the current education landscape is to maintain the long-term sustainability of the school as a high-reliability, high-performing organization, one that maintains reputational advantage in the local education marketplace and strengthens accountability upwards to funders and regulators. On the other hand, these approaches to educational leadership typically fail to acknowledge the different sets of political and economic interests served and excluded through these configurations of the school, key among them being the smooth function of the school as a corporate competitive entity. NPM techniques, such as the ones already outlined, help to render the internal operation of the school more amenable to the scrutiny of others and more readily calculable in the context of webs of 'commensurability, equivalence and comparative performance' (Lingard, Martino and Rezai-Rashti, 2013: 542). Viewed from an agonistic-political perspective, governance as a strategy in rational self-management serves to strengthen relations of accountability between central government and schools, making governance a 'key fidelity technique in new strategies of government' (Rose, 1999: 152).

Case Study 20.2 Australia

Australia's system of education is composed of a public system of schools which educates approximately 65 per cent of the nation's school students, and a government-subsidized private system made up of Catholic and independent religious and non-religious schools. Each of Australia's states and territories is constitutionally responsible for their education system, with each having their own education departments and regulatory bodies. Since the 1960s and 1970s, federal governments have increasingly exerted influence over state education policy and practice, often using funding to tie the states to national political priorities. This control has tightened over the 2010s with the establishment of mandatory national curriculum and testing, and professional standards and accreditation agencies. At the same time, federal governments have endorsed an agenda for greater principal and school autonomy.

For over a century, Australia's systems of public education have been highly centralized, with state-based education bureaucracies planning and coordinating compulsory school education across Australia's vast geography. This orthodoxy was challenged in the 1990s by the Kennett Government's decentralization agenda for the state of Victoria. The Kennett Government devolved administration, planning and resource allocation to schools. It introduced stakeholder governance through school councils and facilitated competition by deregulating student enrolments. Business planning, managing school budgets and the recruitment and employment of staff became key responsibilities of school leaders. Despite these reforms, most Australian states remained largely resistant to school self-management reform until the late 2000s with the introduction of the Independent Public Schools (IPS) initiative in Western Australia (WA) and its subsequent adoption in the state of Queensland.

The WA Government and Department of Education promote IPS as a tool for empowering schools and the local community through improved conditions for devolved decision-making. For schools that opt into the programme, principals assume responsibility for recruiting and employing staff, determining a staff profile/positions, financial and resource management (a 'one-line budget'), managing small contracts, and developing business and strategic plans. This autonomy however is disciplined by contractual accountability, whereby each school signs a Delivery and Performance Agreement (DPA) with the Director-General of the Department. This agreement stipulates the responsibilities of the school and the Department, and the performance targets to be achieved and reported on as part of a three-year cycle (through a Department review). Overseeing the school's progress towards its performance goals is the school board, which provides input into the school's business plan and signs off on the DPA. The board does not intervene in or manage the school, nor does it exercise authority over or performance manage school staff. Rather, it performs an accountability function that strengthens the align-ment between central government objectives and schools.

Importantly, IPS does not accord schools full autonomy. Schools are subject to union-negotiated industrial agreements, must teach the mandated curriculum, must submit themselves to external accountabilities, have their student enrolments regulated by 'catchment zones', and must comply with Department and public-sector policies and standards. Nevertheless, responsibility for the management of performance has been devolved to schools and this freedom to self-manage has proved so appealing that, at the time of writing, more than two-thirds of public schools (575) have opted into the programme over the past decade (DoE, 2019). Over the years, criticism of the unfair advantages gained by IPS schools has resulted in the Department extending some key features of IPS to non-IPS schools, including full responsibility for financial management.

Approached from an agnostic-political perspective, a critical issue for school autonomy reforms like IPS is how governance transforms the meaning and practices of principal autonomy and leadership. The promotion of corporate knowledge, and the stress placed on demonstrating improved performance in the context of competition for resources and students, is resulting in some principals modelling their professional identities on the chief executive officer role of private enterprise (Gobby, 2013). This corporatized and entrepreneurial form of leadership, along with the increased administrative burden associated with self-management and accountability requirements, is resulting in a values-drift. In this situation, corporate, financial and resource objectives, management and processes are prioritized over pedagogical and curriculum leadership. Therefore, when undertaken in the context of performative and market-based relations, school autonomy does not induce freedom but instead compels the exercise of entrepreneurial, corporate and accountable forms of self-governed conduct.

While this governance approach to the management of schools was promoted in the rhetoric of school and community empowerment, this has not materialized for many stakeholders. For principals and teachers, schools are operating according to the logics and priorities of central governments, their regulatory bodies and the forces of market competition, regardless of the needs of local contexts. There is limited opportunity for principals, teachers and other stakeholders to act outside of these legitimated ways of conceiving and leading schools. School boards, for instance, are being used by principals to select members with business and expert knowledge to shore up the corporate and governance know-how of schools. The effect is that boards avoid discussing substantive issues about educational purpose, curriculum and pedagogy, and those without governance know-how are excluded from school decision-making.

Conclusion

In this chapter, we have introduced the concept of governance as an analytical tool through which to interpret and understand educational leadership, but also to engage with the field of educational leadership research more generally. In order to nuance our analysis of what educational leadership is (or what different people claim it to be or should be) and complement a multidimensional conception of educational leadership, we provided two formulations of governance: instrumental-rational and agonistic-political. Each formulation offers a specific orienting position to framing the concept of educational leadership as governance-in-practice, as evidenced in our discussion of the academies programme in England and the Independent Public Schools (IPS) programme in Australia.

The first formulation of governance offered here – instrumental-rational – lends itself to a functionalist account of educational leadership, by far the more dominant framing of the two in terms of its impact on education policy and practice globally. Global discourses of 'good governance', where they relate to the strategic management of organizations according to the explicitness of performance indicators and output controls, communicate a view of organizations as necessarily governable, answerable and transparent. A requirement of 'good governance' is not only that organizations make themselves accountable in this way, but more importantly, that there are universally prescriptive conditions and indicators by which organizations can be judged and compared as accountable, usually within a framework of market discipline that values corporate, performative and contractual measures of accountability. Where educational leadership performs this function, an instrumental-rational account of governance is appropriate. Yet certain techniques and technologies are required to flourish on the ground and among frontline staff, especially among those responsible for leadership and management, in order for organizations to be 'recognizable' as exemplars of good governance. It is here, then, that an agonistic-political formulation of governance is necessary, one that attends to the intrinsic links between governance and governmental programmes more generally.

When theorized through the lens of an agonistic-political formulation of governance, educational leadership can be conceptualized as sites of struggle over meaning as morally charged requirements to make decisions 'locally' and in the best interests of students sometimes conflict with compulsory, government-mandated requirements to make the internal operation of the school more business-like in terms of its value structures and normative commitments. The idea here is that governance is a process of abstraction or reification by which schools and related educational organizations are de-socialized from their immediate contexts to serve wider political and economic interests, usually through tools and technologies of performance and compliance checks. This process of abstraction does not always succeed in the way that government entities and intergovernmental organizations would like it to, however, as educational leadership is the everyday labour of socially situated actors. Yet, the prevalence of images and discourses of 'heroic', entrepreneurial, corporate, managerially adept leaders, both in England and Australia, should be a reminder that educational leadership is vulnerable to capture from a market determinism that produces opportunities and legitimacy for the state to intervene in the running of schools.

Further reading

Gunter, H.M. (2009) *Leadership and the reform of education*. Bristol: Policy Press.
Stevenson, H. (2018) Transformation and control: what role for leadership and management in a 'school-led' system? In: A. Wilkins and A. Olmedo (eds),

Education governance and social theory: interdisciplinary approaches to research
(pp. 209–226). London: Bloomsbury Academic.

Stoker, G. (1998) Governance as theory: five propositions. *International Social Sciences Journal*, 50(155), 17–28.

Wilkins, A. and Olmedo, A. (2018) Introduction: conceptualising education governance – framings, perspectives and theories. In A. Wilkins and A. Olmedo (eds), *Education governance and social theory: Interdisciplinary approaches to research* (pp. 1–20). London: Bloomsbury Academic.

References

Bates, R. (2010) History of educational leadership/management. In: P. Peterson, E. Baker and B. McGaw (eds), *International Encyclopedia of Education, volume 4*, 3rd edn (pp. 724–730). Oxford: Elsevier Science.

Cooper, D. (1998) *Governing out of order: space, law and the politics of belonging*. London: Rivers Oram Press.

Courtney, S.J., McGinity, R. and Gunter, H.M. (2017) Introduction: theory and theorising in educational leadership. In: S.J. Courtney, R. McGinity and H.M. Gunter (eds), *Educational leadership: theorising professional practice in neoliberal times* (pp. 1–11). Abingdon: Routledge.

DfE (Department for Education (England)) (2019) Open academies and academy projects in development. Last updated October 2019. Available online: https://www.gov.uk/government/publications/open-academies-and-academy-projects-in-development (accessed 21 July 2020).

DoE (Department of Education (Western Australia)) (2019) *Department of Education Annual Report 2018–2019*. Available online: https://www.education.wa.edu.au/web/annual-report (accessed 4 August 2020).

Foucault, M. (1982) The subject and power. *Critical Inquiry*, 8(4), 777–795.

Gobby, B. (2013) Principal self-government and subjectification: the exercise of principal autonomy in the Western Australian Independent Public Schools programme. *Critical Studies in Education*, 54(3), 273–285.

Grace, G. (1995) *School leadership: beyond education management*. London: Falmer Press.

Keddie, A. and Mills, M. (2019) *Autonomy, accountability and social justice: stories of English schooling*. Abingdon: Routledge.

Lingard, B., Martino, W. and Rezai-Rashti, G. (2013) Testing regimes, accountabilities and education policy: commensurate global and national developments. *Journal of Education Policy*, 28(5), 539–556.

Rhodes, R.A.W. (1996) The new governance: governing without government. *Political Studies*, 44(4), 652–667.

Rose, N. (1999) *Powers of freedoms: reframing political thought*. Cambridge: Cambridge University Press.

Wilkins, A. (2016) *Modernising school governance: corporate planning and expert handling in state education*. Abingdon: Routledge.

Performativity, managerialism and educational leadership

Tanya Fitzgerald and David Hall

21

What this chapter is about	324
Key questions that this chapter addresses	324
Introduction	324
Performativity	325
Managerialism	326
Introducing the case studies	328
Using the case studies to think about performativity, managerialism and power	334
Conclusion	336
Further reading	336
References	337

What this chapter is about

In this chapter, we begin by presenting an outline of the principles of performativity and managerialism. Specifically, we trace the historical roots of these concepts and highlight ways in which they have been transferred into practice in educational settings. We then examine and critique the underpinning knowledge claims and present an illustrative case study to reveal and explain the power structures inherent in both performative and managerial cultures. We consider the role of educational leaders and leadership and in doing so stress the importance of an anti-performative stance. We offer a number of concluding questions to assist the reader to critically engage in a level of reflection about their own workplaces and work practices.

Key questions that this chapter addresses

1 How can performativity be understood and what is its impact on professional practice?

2 What are the origins of managerialism and why is this important to understand?

3 In what ways do performativity and managerialism encourage/discourage productive work practices?

4 How might educational leaders and practitioners work against performative and managerialist practices and why might this be important?

Introduction

Performativity and managerialism are two concepts commonly used by critical scholars to capture ways in which workplace policies and practices have shifted, and been influenced and reworked by specific political and economic ideologies. Both performativity and managerialism are increasingly prevalent in organizational settings where private-sector practices are incorporated into the workplace and there is increased control and regulation of work and workers by managers and management.

The widespread reforms of the public sector that occurred in the 1980s were ostensibly designed to change ways in which public-sector organizations operated. The shift was very much from public-sector *administration* to management, and as such was radical in both its scope and purpose. The New Public Management (NPM) agenda was influenced by economic principles that placed primacy on efficiency, decentralization, cost-effectiveness and global competitiveness (Clarke and Newman, 1997; Clarke et al., 2000). The two main ideological strands within NPM were neoliberalism and managerialism. Driven by New Right ideologies, neoliberalism emphasized the importance of the free market, consumer choice, accountability and performance. As we highlight in this chapter, both perform-ativity and managerialism are now deeply embedded in the everyday understandings and work of school leaders and teachers. This is not to suggest that teachers and leaders have acquiesced to these demands but, increasingly, as the case studies illustrate, resistance presents numerous personal and professional challenges.

Performativity

Performativity is a term first used by Lyotard in 1984, when he suggested that postmodern society is obsessed with efficiency and effectiveness. This has led to all kinds of businesses (and more recently schools themselves), being judged in terms of outcome and performance. Thus league tables, exam results (national and international) and inspection reports are increasingly the measurements by which schools and teachers are judged. Performativity is linked with the increased accountability and surveillance under which teachers find themselves and their schools being judged in terms of outcome and performance. Ball (2003) notes that a performativity discourse currently pervades teachers' work. It is a discourse that relies on teachers and schools instituting self-disciplinary measures to satisfy newly transparent public accountability and it operates alongside a market discourse.

The term 'teacher performativity' has been identified in relevant literatures as referring to targets, evaluation and performance indicators, quality assessments, and teachers accounting for their own performance (Ball, 2003). Performativity emphasizes audit and self-reporting procedures that make use of comparisons between individuals, institutions and nation states. The performance of an individual or institution such as a school or university provides a measure of their productivity or output which can then, in turn, be utilized to make further judgements about value or worth. It is mechanisms such as an inspection report, examination results or research league tables that can then be further used to gain a competitive advantage by marketing these successes. Accordingly, profes-sional discourses have now shifted as terms such as inspection, control, regulation, objectives, performance measures, performance management, performance indicators, supervisor or line manager, accountability and audit are now readily used across the public sector.

The core aspects of educational performativity are comparison and commodification. Comparison of data on institutional or individual performance provides information to consumers within the education marketplace. These public data can then be used in different ways to make institutions more responsive to their consumers thereby increasing the choices available. This is not to suggest that institutions present transparent data as, increasingly, institutions use data to serve their own needs in a competitive educational marketplace. There is, we would suggest, a complex interface between information-giving, impression management and promotion. The version of the individual or institution presented for public viewing and consumption is itself a performance to demonstrate adherence to expected norms, values and practices.

Performativity requires individuals to be accountable for their performances, constantly record what has been achieved, take accountability for actions and activities, and ensure they are doing the 'right thing'. New structures, work activities and roles have emerged to implement and manage policy, audit, regulation and the management of individual and institutional performances. Within the microlevel unit of a classroom, department or office, individuals are encouraged to think about themselves, calculate their own achievements and re-present themselves in the best possible way. Thus, the emphasis has shifted from the professional individual working as part of a collective and collaborative group, to the managed individual responsible and accountable to her/his manager and the institution. Crucially, management has been rendered an almost ubiquitous, if not invisible, part of the institution or organization and accepted as routine and necessary.

> **Performativity:** requires individuals to identify their work routines, practices and achievements in relation to the expected outcomes of the institution or organization. This is achieved through the production of data that reports performance against predetermined targets thereby making judgements about that individual and her/his worth possible.

Ball (2003) has argued that performativity has de-professionalized the work of teachers as their work is now increasingly regulated and prescribed. Teachers are now required to perform in certain ways and simultaneously manage their own performances. We sum this up in the definition box.

Performativity is just one aspect of the changing dynamics that impact on the ways schools are led and arranged and the intense pressure teachers face as they account for themselves and their work. A much wider concept than performativity is managerialism, to which we now turn our attention.

Managerialism

Managerialism permeates the educational leadership literature in much the same way as it is said to have pervaded educational institutions. Yet, despite its ubiquity and importance, managerialism largely remains an under-theorized and elusive concept that has multiple definitions and blurred boundaries. There is no single agreed definition. Hood (1991) for example, emphasizes the adoption of private-sector practices and concerns, notably efficiency, effectiveness and excellence, whilst Pollitt and Bouckaert (2000) highlight management reform and changes to structures and processes. Flynn (2002) suggests that managerialism is the pursuit of management ideas and as such places importance on the role of managers, management and managerial practices. Simply put, in a managerial organization, management is deemed to be important and managers are given the legitimacy to manage. And since management can only be undertaken by managers, there is an accompanying belief that managers must be in control and exercise their authority over the managed (workers/employees). Thus, workers are accountable to managers, and it is managers who make the difference in an organization. Perhaps confusingly, management and managers are often referred to as leadership and leaders in a number of contexts, not least educational institutions. In public-sector organizations such as schools, hospitals and

Table 21.1 The twin pillars of managerialism and neoliberalism

Managerialism	Neoliberalism
Organization adopts business and private-sector practices such as strategic planning, key targets and accountabilities, performance measurements	A shift from collective (public) interests to the (private) individual and an emphasis on choice, quality and the consumer
Management culture permeates organization	The commodification of services (e.g. university degrees now called 'products') and an emphasis on the market
Management viewed as a rational and top-down process	A focus on effectiveness and efficiency (value for money) and adoption of an entrepreneurial culture
Introduction of line management (supervisors, managers and performance-management processes)	Central regulation and control
Human-resources policies and processes such as induction used to secure commitment of staff	Growth of contractual relationships and use of consultants; emphasis on employment flexibility (for the employer)
Measurement and quantification of outputs as evidenced by use of league tables and test results	Blurring of boundaries between the public and private sectors

universities, it is generally believed that private-sector practices are superior and when adopted, enhance the efficiency, performance and competitiveness of that organization.

The difficulty of defining managerialism is compounded by blurred boundaries with cognate concepts such as NPM and neoliberalism. Drawing on the work of Gewirtz and Ball (2000), Pollitt and Bouckaert (2000) and Ward (2011), we illustrate in Table 21.1 how the twin pillars of managerialism and neoliberalism underpin NPM.

In essence, what these two pillars indicate is that there has been a significant change in the role of the state in services such as education, health, welfare and an increasing emphasis on the performance of the public sector. As illustrated in Table 21.1, managerialism and neoliberalism have distinctive characteristics and trajectories. In a managerial environment, the basic social unit is the organization itself whereas a neoliberal climate promotes the primacy of the individual. Managerialism holds that all problems have managerial solutions (Klikauer, 2015) and neoliberalism, inextricably linked with economic and political theories, upholds the guiding principle of the free market and individual choice.

As we see it, managerialism is an ideology that positions better management as transformative. It is management that, in the public sector, will deliver more with less, and in the private sector, will ensure competitiveness in the global marketplace. It is management that will stimulate greater innovation right across government and the business sector. It is management that will direct and channel professional skills so as to focus on the highest priority goals and therefore bring about successful outcomes for the organization (Clarke and Newman, 1997). It is management that will turn broad political aspirations into measurable outputs and outcomes. As Drucker, one of the first advocates of/for manageri-alism noted: 'it is managers and management that make institutions perform. Performing, responsible management is the alternative to tyranny and our only protection against it . . . For management is the organ, the life-giving, acting, dynamic organ of the institution it manages' (Drucker, 1974: x).

In terms of specific ideologies and practices, managerialism exhibits considerable and sometimes rapid change (Clarke and Newman, 1997). But each new model, package or fashion retains the under-lying belief that it is managers who are the key to a transformed public sector. Managers are the focal point, not politicians, nor professionals, nor front-line staff. Managers make things happen. In addition, manageri-alism has stimulated new work place identities and, consequently, positions such as 'business manager', 'strategist', 'marketing advisor', 'contractor', 'customer service advisor' and 'consultant' have been created to further demonstrate that the managerial organization is competitive, effective, efficient and accountable. See the definition box for an apt summary of the major emphasis that managerialism promotes.

> **Managerialism:** associated with managerial techniques that have been imposed on public-sector organizations or institutions and which require a focus on efficiency, effectiveness and the measurement of outcomes and performance (staff and the institution). A core feature of a managerial organization is the adoption of 'for profit' values and competitive practices to secure the best advantage possible. In a mana-gerial organization, professional autonomy and direction are largely absent.

Introducing the case studies

This section of the chapter seeks to link the wider themes of managerialism and perform-ativity in education as explored above to the working practices of education professionals. The material in the two case studies is based upon extracts from research funded by the UK Economic and Social Research Council (Hall, Gunter and Bragg, 2011) that invest-igated the widespread phenomenon of distributed leadership in schools in England. Selected findings from two of the schools sampled as part of the research are offered in these case studies. Both the names of the schools and those working within them have been anonymized in order to protect the identities of research participants. A more detailed account of this research and its relationship to the themes explored in this chapter can found in a related journal article (Hall, 2013) in the further-reading section at the end of this chapter.

Case Study 21.1 Birch Tree School

Birch Tree is a school for eleven- to sixteen-year-olds that serves a socio-economically disadvantaged inner city area located within a metropolitan area of northern England. It opened as an academy following the closure of two local schools. At the time of the research inspections by the national inspection agency Ofsted (Office for Standards in Education, Children's Services and Skills) had noted 'improvements' in the quality of leadership and management at the school, but had also highlighted a number of areas where further 'improvements' in both student attainment and teaching quality were required.

Since the creation of Birch Tree in 2006, there had been a significant turnover of staff, so that two years after the school had been formed only 25 per cent of the teaching staff remained from the two predecessor schools. Comments from Sally, the principal, and other colleagues in senior positions within the school offered strong clues as to the reasons for this high turnover:

I absolutely 100 per cent knew that I was not taking all them shit people out of the predecessor schools . . . I wasn't prepared to have them because I know that if you give me two rusty sheds at the bottom of the garden and excellent people, I'll give you a school. You can't give me a building like this and crap teachers, the kids will wreck the building. *(Principal)*

We've only been together a few years, lots of the really negative people either didn't come and also to be fair your traditional skivers, you know the ones who always seem to have quite a few Mondays off or don't do their reports ever or skive meetings, Sally won't tolerate . . . I can think of twenty people who have started here but are no longer here for that very reason . . . you know staff had to get in but just not, just didn't fit into the ethos. We have a big think on ethos but we always call it the EDS for Ethos Deficiency Syndrome or message, or they just weren't on. *(Senior leader)*

Associated with the high turnover of staff at Birch Tree was the presence of large numbers of young and newly qualified teachers; a situation linked, according to Sally, by the difficulties those who have worked in other schools have in adjusting to the new vision of the school.

To be successful here, you've got to buy into the vision. *(Administration manager)*

I think it's come from her [Sally's] vision and how she's got there but I also think with the staff that's involved as well, I think that's very important. I think you could have maybe a strong leader but if you've not got the right staff sharing that vision then I think it might not necessarily work and again obviously its down to her [Sally] and whoever has been interviewing to pick the staff that probably share that vision. *(Teacher)*

Interpreting Case Study 21.1

Leadership at Birch Tree was commonly defined in terms of hierarchy, a notion that was referred to by both the principal and other staff in terms of legitimizing, accepting and normalizing Sally's dominant position within the school and its decision-making processes:

> sometimes I'll say the problem you've all got is you think this is a democracy and it ain't because frankly I get paid a lot of money and the reason I get paid a lot of money is because the buck stops here. . . . It is impossible for me, for the one and a half days that I'm in, not to be a charismatic hero because I can't do it. I can't not go around touching people and asking questions and dominating situations and such, because I can't do it because, actually, that's what I am. *(Principal)*

When teachers were asked to discuss leadership, they commonly began with the principal and then worked their way 'down' the school hierarchy. So, for example, a teacher when asked to describe his/her understanding of distributed leadership responded: 'From what I understand of it, it kind of comes from a leader kind of letting go a little bit and from what I see from what happens here, you know kind of chunks of leadership or elements of it are given out to different people.'

There is also a strong sense of a traditional 'top-down' approach to leadership both in terms of the way in which those at various points in the school hierarchy describe their own roles and those of their more senior colleagues and of how the principal herself describes her own work.

> Everyone knows exactly what to do, they know where the issues may arise and the senior leader team, the middle leader team and all the teachers know that they can rely on everyone above them and everyone below them. *(Teacher)*

> She's a very strong and effective leader. *(Teacher)*

> The remit I've been given from Sally is that at the next Ofsted we have outstanding at teaching and learning, so basically my job description is to get us there. *(Senior leader)*

A further feature of the school was the manner in which validation from external bodies, Ofsted in particular, was so important to many of the respondents. Indeed this feature of the school appears to be at the heart of the vision and acts as one of the seemingly unquestionable tenets of its modus operandi.

Case Study 21.2 Lime Tree School

Lime Tree Grammar School is a larger-than-average academically selective school for boys aged eleven to eighteen, situated in a relatively affluent location with a very low turnover of teaching staff. The school draws its pupils from a range of social backgrounds but the proportion from socio-economically disadvantaged backgrounds is low. National test data showed pupil attainment as being at least twice that of local and national averages.

The current headteacher at Lime Tree, Malcolm, has been in post for three years and described his plans to 'move the school forward' in terms of meeting the potential of all its pupils. In part at least this was linked to an Ofsted inspection describing the school as outstanding with pupils' prior attainment as being exceptionally high, but proposing that even more could achieve the highest levels at national tests at age sixteen. Malcolm described the leadership structure at Lime Tree as follows when he took over the school.

> Originally the structure was very traditional, comprising a team of three, a head teacher, two deputies; one role was deputy curricula (mainly timetable) and the other was deputy responsible for boys' discipline . . . lots of people doing other things but in a managerial capacity tied back, in terms of accountability, to the job descriptions of the two deputies. So, not leading in their own right, but managing tasks that were part of the deputies' job description.

He felt that there was a degree of under-performance and a general acceptance that attainment could not be taken beyond a certain level. In terms of challenging this Malcolm was keen to change the organizational structure of the school. Within eighteen months of his headship, the leadership model had changed to incorporate a layer of assistant headteachers with responsibilities in the following areas:

- assessment and achievement;
- student welfare and support;
- staff development and learning;
- business and enterprise (school specialism); and
- head of sixth form.

The headteacher and the original two deputy heads (one with responsibility for the curriculum, teaching and learning, and timetable, and the other responsible for school organization and student welfare) were also part of these new organizational arrangements. At the time of the research Malcolm indicated that the new structure was 'quite well established'. Following the reorganization of the school's leadership structure the Senior Leadership Team (SLT) comprised the headteacher and two deputy heads. The newly established Extended Leadership Team comprised the SLT plus five assistant head teachers, the school business manager and the ICT strategy leader (a non-teacher who works at a strategic level in ICT). The SLT and ELT meet alternate weeks.

> We needed an expanded team of ten. So having the senior leadership team and the extended leadership team provides that. It's provided that pathway through a changed process from traditional to more dispersed. (Malcolm)

Interpreting Case Study 21.2

Central to Malcolm's approach to restructuring the school was his idea of 'taking people with you'. So, whilst he may have been tempted to opt for more wholesale change at the school he adopted a measured approach taking account of the need to 'value' those, not least two long-serving deputy heads, who had been working significantly longer at the school than himself:

> The whole concept there was trying to keep the people who were there in the first place valued, not wanting to sort of go for a radical revolution where suddenly their views didn't count.

> It was all about taking people with you and making the people who were in post originally feel a part of the rationale for why you're moving in a certain direction and, to be fair, I mean they have been the greatest champions of it. They see the value of it and there are times when they'll say things to me like, 'You know, I don't know how we managed to do all that we did.'

For Malcolm the capacity to 'take people with you' is linked to what he describes as 'empowerment' and giving to others the capacity to lead:

> For me it starts with empowerment and it's a feeling of being able to apply your creative energies to see a development through and therefore it's not necessarily linked to a formal structure in a school. It's facilitated by a formal structure; there is leadership at every level. There is leadership in the classroom. There is a culture here of student leadership and students working with staff on things like cross-curricular projects and the boys are taking the lead so its providing that capacity to, it's providing that scope to empower people to develop either themselves or the work they do in whatever way is appropriate to the needs of the organization and the individual.

The research team focused upon the decision-making process in relation to particular school developments where, according to the headteacher, the staff had been consulted as part of this. One of the key forms of staff consultation used at Lime Tree were Twilight Sessions. These involved the entire teaching and support staff being divided into small groups of five or six, each group containing staff at different levels. Malcolm's rationale for this model, located within his ideas about empowerment, was to encourage contributions from more junior teachers and those more reticent about expressing their views in larger forums. Malcolm described it as a 'tried and tested' method that they have used for a number of different developments, and for what he has described as some 'quite substantial changes'. Malcolm believes staff find the Twilight Session forum: 'genuinely consultative, in that you start with broad avenues of inquiry and statements of intent but then you allow the detail to be fashioned by the discussion'. Malcolm claims 'there is genuine bottom-up involvement' and unlike an open whole-staff meeting, where he believes that often only the voice of the minority is heard 'everyone gets a say . . . everyone feels they can contribute to the discussion and ultimately you see your contribution being fashioned in terms of the creation of the final policy'. This justification for a consultative approach accords with his view that leadership needs to be emotionally engaged opening up possibilities for getting 'to places' that would not otherwise be possible:

> I suppose what does resonate with me, and it runs through all aspects of leadership, is an emotional leadership approach . . . because I think it gets you to places that without it, and without considering it, other forms of leadership don't, just being able to read people and understand where people are coming from. It's everything from mood, time of day, type of personality, what actually will incentivize someone to want to do something and you have to be really tuned in, I think, to how people will read situations.

Malcolm finds this method of consultation secure and he believes it leads to more lasting outcomes because people can't say they have been railroaded into something that they disagree with:

> no one can say they haven't been consulted and, at the end of the day, while you will always get criticism and a cynical view, no one hand on heart can say 'this had been done to me' . . . It's quite powerful to be able to say 'as we discussed', 'as we've agreed', so in terms of making the policy work then there is a feeling that you've got the critical mass of opinion that is very much for it.

It is clear from this that Malcolm is embracing a form of leadership in which consultation plays a key role. Implicit within this approach, from Malcolm's perspective, is a form of contract whereby those who have engaged in the consultative process, in effect all teachers at the school due to the compulsory status of Twilight Sessions, are not from Malcolm's perspective legitimately able to subsequently complain about the nature of the decision-making process or by implication the decision itself. Those dissenting from this perspective are identified by Malcolm as critics and cynics and their participation in the consultation process means that they are not able to question the nature of this consultation process or to view decisions as having been 'done to' them. Malcolm sees this consultation model as empowering, 'quite powerful', in terms of making 'policy work' and thus enabling the school to make progress in those directions that he or Ofsted regard as desirable.

Malcolm's view of the school's decision-making process and the central importance of a consultative model is shared by many staff at Lime Tree, in particular those in designated leadership positions. Further insights into the responses of teachers to Malcolm's style of leadership were offered by research relating to the creation of a new house system. Niamh, associate assistant headteacher, was given responsibility by Malcolm for the creation of a new house system. During interviews, Niamh was clear that she had been given a high degree of autonomy in terms of her leadership with regard to this matter. Other staff interviewed interpreted this in different ways:

> It definitely came across to me, at least, that he [Malcolm] wanted it to happen but if the staff were against it we would have to revisit it – but the staff weren't negative so it went ahead. *(Support staff member)*

> Initially I suppose it was a directive from the head, 'this is what we would like to try, we would like to dip our toe in the pool of vertical tutoring and see how it goes'. *(Associate assistant head)*

This suggests a different view of the consultations in which the school had been engaged than suggested by Niamh. Here the respondents perceived less room for manoeuvre in terms of contributing to the new house system accompanied by the view that the decision to move to a new house system had already been made by Malcolm.

Using the case studies to think about performativity, managerialism and power

We now ask and address a series of important questions of our case studies in relation to the chapter focus. First, how are performativity and managerialism constructed in contemporary thinking and/or practice? The case study of Birch Tree School illustrates the unconscious way in which performativity and managerialism are integral to the everyday practices in the school. The headteacher and teachers are conscious of the importance and impact of external audit by Ofsted and align their own behaviours and the vision of the school with this, and other, accountability regimes. Both the headteacher and teachers are aware of those who are productive and those who are not. Labelled 'skivers', these are the teachers who have apparently not bought into the vision and are therefore not wanted in the school. There is a leadership hierarchy in place and teachers are labelled as 'senior' or 'middle' leaders to denote their authority as well as their place in the hierarchy.

A flatter organizational hierarchy was put into place at Lime Tree Grammar School following an organizational restructure with teachers expected to participate in consultative meetings (Twilight Sessions). Those who do not participate and opt out were labelled 'critics and cynics' by the headteacher. While Lime Tree Grammar espouses the importance of collaboration and consultation, evident in the case study is the uncompromising view of the headteacher that change, driven too by external audit and pupil performance, is required. In subtle ways, while the headteacher at Lime Tree Grammar heralds the importance of teacher empowerment; on the other hand, he is not reticent in making known his own managerial agenda.

Our second question is, what is the critical focus on power relations, structure and agency? At Birch Tree School, this critical focus is to ensure that all members of the school, including support staff, are aware of the vision, the outcomes expected and possible consequences of non-compliance (as evidenced by the denigration of the 'skivers'). The 'vision' expounded does not appear to be linked with student learning or the school as a learning community, but focused on external validation by audit. At Lime Street Grammar there is explicit attention to student learning and the centrality of the school leadership and teachers working collaboratively towards a common goal. Further evident is the headteacher's view that leadership is both the answer and solution to any problems of practice.

Our third question is, what is the effect on practice and conceptualizations? The teachers at Birch Tree, and indeed many of those designated as leaders or senior leaders remain in largely subjugated positions in which they are mainly responsible for implementing that which has been agreed and decided upon elsewhere. In some respects this applies to Sally herself who remains highly dependent upon external judgements of the school's success. The capacity for Birch Tree School and its teaching staff to generate sustainable, creative and locally authentic responses remains constrained by the limited conceptualization of schooling as viewed through the lens of Ofsted inspections.

At Lime Tree Grammar a more participative approach as represented by the consultative meetings was welcomed by many staff, in particular by those in more senior positions who we might speculate perceived greater opportunities for active involvement in the shaping of decisions. A danger with this approach is that teachers at Lime Tree are being invited by Malcolm to develop a sense of involvement and ownership that is ultimately not matched by the actual processes and practices in place at the school. The sense of some teachers as described in the case that 'decisions had already been made' before they had been consulted is a clear example of this danger surfacing.

Fourth, we ask what needs to change to mitigate the issues? At Birch Tree, it can be argued that current leadership practices are dominated by autocratic practices linked to the performative and managerialist environment dominated by Ofsted and Sally as their local-ized representative. Schools in socio-economically disadvantaged areas in England not uncommonly find themselves vulnerable to the disciplinary power of Ofsted intervening in their situation. This is especially the case given their capacity to declare schools as failing and ultimately to force the closure or redesignation of individual schools, something that has happened frequently in this context. It therefore seems likely that spaces for signi-ficant changes in practices are most likely to open up in the wake of either shifts in the external regulatory environment in the form of more sensitive treatment of such schools, successful and mobilizing resistance to this regulatory environment and/or the capacity of the school to raise attainment levels in difficult circumstances.

Malcolm has clearly signalled his desire to engender more participative approaches to leadership and management at Lime Tree and this has been welcomed by many of the teaching staff and by his senior colleagues. Nevertheless, as discussed previously, a danger is that this becomes perceived as a thin performance of collegiality. Efforts by a range of colleagues to expand the scope and range of participative decision-making at Lime Tree, a move that would be enabled by the advantageous position of the school both academ-ically and socially, would appear to offer significant promise in this context. That said, any moves in this direction that were perceived as threatening the market position of Lime Tree and, in particular, its 'outstanding' status with Ofsted could be judged as less likely to gain wider support.

Activity 21.1

Reflect upon the two case-study schools, Birch Tree and Lime Tree.

1 Where are performativity and managerialism evident within these accounts?
2 To what extent do these accounts resonate with your own experiences of working (or studying) in educational institutions?

Conclusion

This chapter has overviewed the key concepts of performativity and managerialism, and offered to readers a working definition of each. Two case studies have been presented to illuminate the workings of both performativity and managerialism. While we have offered a reading of these concepts against the research evidence, it is anticipated that readers may bring their own understandings to these case studies of professional practice and leadership. To this end, we have sketched a number of questions to further assist readers to reflect on their own professional practice. Importantly, we have shown that leaders can and do resist what appears to be an overwhelming performative and managerialist agenda, and that professional autonomy is possible.

Activity 22.2

1   How do you understand the terms performativity and managerialism?
2   In what ways do you see these in operation in your own institution and to what effect?
3   What tools or apparatus, language or terms, and policies or practices support managerial practices?
4   How might performativity and managerialism be viewed from the perspective of a leader or a practitioner (e.g. teacher)?
5   Performativity is, in essence, a form of accounting of the self. How might you account for your work that meets performative norms and expectations? What is it that you do that is counter to a performative climate or culture?

Further reading

Dunleavy, P. and Carrera, L. (2013) *Growing the productivity of government services*. Cheltenham: Edward Elgar.

Gunter, H., Grimaldi, E., Hall, D. and Serpieri, R. (eds) (2018) *New Public Management and the reform of education: European lessons for policy and practice*. Abingdon: Routledge.

Hall, D. (2013) Drawing a veil over managerialism: leadership and the discursive disguise of the New Public Management. *Journal of Educational Administration and History*, 45(3), 267–282.

Pollitt, C. (2013) 40 years of public management reform in UK central government: promises, promises. . . . *Policy and Politics*, 41(4), 465–480.

Power, M. (1999) *The audit society*, 1st paperback edn. Oxford: Oxford University Press.

References

Ball, S.J. (2003) The teacher's soul and the terror of performativity. *Journal of Education Policy*, 18(2), 215–228.

Clarke, J. and Newman, J. (1997) *The managerial state: power, politics and ideology in the remaking of social welfare*. London: Sage

Clarke, J., Gewirtz, S and McLaughlin, E. (eds) (2000) *New managerialism, new welfare?* London: Sage.

Drucker, P.F. (1974) *Management: tasks, responsibilities, practices*. London: Heinemann.

Flynn, N. (2002) *Public sector management*, 4th edn. Harlow: Pearson.

Gewirtz, S. and Ball, S. (2000) From 'Welfarism' to 'New Managerialism': shifting discourses of school headship in the education marketplace. *Discourse: Studies in the Cultural Politics of Education*, 21(3), 253–268.

Hall, D., Gunter, H. and Bragg, J. (2011) *End of award report: distributed leadership and the social practices of school organisation in England*, Economic and Social Research Council, UK. Available online: http://reshare.ukdataservice.ac.uk/851924/2/EOA_Report_RES-000-22-3610.pdf (accessed 29 July 2020).

Hood, C. (1991) A public management for all seasons? *Public Administration*, 69(1), 3–19.

Klikauer, T. (2015) What is managerialism? *Critical Sociology*, 41(7/8), 1103–1119.

Lyotard, J. (1984) *The postmodern condition: a report on knowledge*, trans. G. Bennington and B. Massumi, Manchester: Manchester University Press.

Pollitt, C. and Bouckaert, G. (2000) *Public management reform: a comparative analysis*. Oxford: Oxford University Press.

Ward, S.C. (2011) The machinations of neoliberalism: New Public Management and the diminishing power of professionals. *Journal of Cultural Economy*, 4(2), 205–215.

Corporatization and educational leadership

Kenneth Saltman and Alexander J. Means

22

What this chapter is about 340

Key questions that this chapter addresses 340

Introduction 340

Pre-Fordist phase: 1837–1890 – common schools 341

Fordist phase: 1890–1973 341

Neoliberal phase 1973–present 344

Digital phase 2010–present 350

Conclusion 352

Further reading 353

References 354

What this chapter is about

In this chapter, we discuss a key term that every educational leadership scholar should know: corporatization. Corporatization refers to the ways that public education – and more specifically educational leadership – has been refashioned according to the model of the private business corporation. Drawing largely on the US context, in what follows we provide an overview of the relationship between the corporatization of schools and educational leadership in terms of its impact on economics, politics and culture of schooling. We do this by discussing four historical phases of corporatization and educational leadership: pre-Fordist 1837–1890, and its common schools; Fordist 1890–1973, where corporatization intensified through Taylor's factory model, or scientific management; neoliberal 1973–present, whose political and cultural agenda is achieved through the mechanism of the market; and digital 2010–present, which is characterized by the student as data engine and by philanthrocapitalism.

Key questions that this chapter addresses

1 What are the origins of the corporatization of education? How has it been developed, and with what purposes and effects?

2 What is the relationship between the corporatization of education and eugenics?

3 How has positivism influenced the corporatized, Fordist model of schooling?

4 How has resistance to corporatized education been expressed?

5 What does corporatization in the neoliberal era look like? What is the role of venture philanthropism?

Introduction

In this chapter, we will describe how public education and its leadership in the United States have been corporatized in a range of ways and according to conceptually distinct, but sometimes chronologically overlapping, phases: pre-Fordist, Fordist, neoliberal and digital. The United States offers a particularly stark example of corporatized educational leadership, with singular historical features and conditions. However, we invite you whilst reading to reflect on similar processes and/or outcomes in nation states globally, owing to the influences of international ideologies and/or other structural conditions.

Pre-Fordist phase: 1837–1890 – common schools

The origins of the corporatization of education can be traced back to the development of mass industrial schooling in the mid-nineteenth century. Horace Mann was the most prominent educational leader in the United States during this period. From 1837 to 1848, Mann used his position as Secretary of the Massachusetts Board of Education to advocate for a universal system of common schools, secular schools that would be funded through public tax revenue and accessible to the public. These schools were conceived specifically as a means to address the class conflicts and social tensions associated with capitalist industrialization.

While Mann viewed common schools as a means of moral uplift, he also spoke to the interests of business and economic elites. His salary was paid by Dwight Clark, a wealthy industrialist, and he opposed workers' rights to organize. Mann viewed common schools as a sphere for providing the right moral training for the poor so that they would develop proper respect for authority and the habits and dispositions necessary for the demands of industrial labour. Ultimately, such inculcation was to serve corporate interests in the early US industrial economy. For Mann, common schools were to be the 'balance wheel of the social machinery' imbued with the capacity to 'disarm the poor of their hostility toward the rich' (1849: 59, 60). Furthermore, and despite claims to universality, common schools systematically excluded Native Americans, African Americans and other minorities.

> **Corporatization:** the ways that public education and, more specifically, educational leadership have been refashioned based on the model of the private business corporation. It encompasses a number of aspects, including the ability of business interests to influence changes in educational policy and curriculum, changes in the ownership and control of schools, changes to the labour force of schools, changes to the culture of schools and the culture of school leadership, and changes to how people are taught to think about schools.

Fordist phase: 1890–1973

The factory model of schooling

Horace Mann represented an early educational leader who premised the development of mass schooling as means to serve the corporate interests undergirding nineteenth-century US industrialization. Such a model of educational leadership persisted and expanded in the early twentieth century and was instrumental in the conception and development of the modern public school system. This era is often referred to as **Fordism**, a mode of economic and social regulation centred on the factory within national systems of production and consumption. During this period, new educational leaders emerged who believed that schools should not only function as an adjunct to industry, but sought to transform educational organization on the model of the factory and the industrial corporation. This was an era of monopoly capitalism embodied in figures like J.P. Morgan,

John D. Rockefeller and Andrew Carnegie, and was powered by revolutions in industry rooted in the 'scientific management' principles of Frederick Winslow Taylor.

What is scientific management?

Scientific management was derived from Taylor's time-motion studies, which sought to measure and increase efficiencies in factory production through the rationalization of production techniques and the organization of the labour process within capitalist enterprises. Armed with Taylor's theories of scientific management, new industrial educational leaders emerged such as Franklin Bobbitt, David Snedden and Ellwood Patterson Cubberley, who sought to retool the public educational system as a means of sorting populations for roles in the economy. In the Fordist industrial era, the educational leader was increasingly modelled on the corporate business manager and factory foreman responsible for increasing quantified outputs of student learning.

Activity 22.1

One early educational leader who believed strongly in Taylorism and scientific management was Elwood Cubberley (6 June 1868–4 September 1941) who served as Dean of Stanford School of Education. He argued forcefully that schools should resemble industrial factories.

1 What do you think about Cubberley's view on schools as described in the following quote?
2 Do schools today resemble the factories envisioned by Cubberley? Why or why not?

> Our schools are, in a sense, factories in which the raw materials (children) are to be shaped and fashioned into products to meet the various demands of life. The specifications for manufacturing come from the demands of the twentieth century civilization, and it is the business of the school to build its pupils to the specifications laid down. This demands good tools, specialized machinery, continuous measurement of production to see if it is according to specifications, the elimination of waste in manufacture and a large variety of output. *(Elwood Cubberley, twentieth century educational leader, qtd in Callahan, 1962: 97)*

The influence of educational leaders like Cubberley was fundamental in the expansion of large public-school bureaucracies, vocational and academic tracking, compulsory primary and secondary schools, the introduction of standardized subject areas and testing, and the standardization of teacher work (Kliebard, 2004). Within mass compulsory public schooling, heavy emphasis was placed on drill, routine, control, discipline, standardization and examination so that schools could efficiently sort students into their proper roles in the industrial economy (Bowles and Gintis, 2011).

Eugenics and the hidden curriculum

The emphasis on routine, standardization and sorting students for the economy was heavily influenced by the **eugenics movement**, a pseudoscientific movement that attempted to establish a genetic basis for class, race, and gender inequality (see Chapter 23 of this textbook). IQ testing became the central tool for sorting students of different class, gender and ethnic backgrounds into their supposedly 'proper' place in the industrial hierarchy. Corporate titans like John D. Rockefeller, who created Standard Oil, and Andrew Carnegie, who dominated the steel industry, established private foundations that invested millions into such testing services. They looked to the school system to promote their economic interests while stabilizing existing divisions of wealth and power and diffusing radical movements. While always couched in the language of civic virtue and the public good, corporate models of educational leadership imagined public schools largely in terms of producing an exploitable workforce to serve the private sector. Sociologists of education have termed this **the hidden curriculum** of schooling, which refers to all of the embedded practices, routines, rituals, assumptions, values and dispositions within schools.

Positivism and the hidden curriculum

The ideology of positivism was central to the 'hidden curriculum' of Fordist schooling (Giroux, 2001). Capitalist aims for education such as skills for work and the reproduction of social and economic relationships were occluded by seemingly disinterested, supposedly universally valuable, and allegedly objective scientific measures such as IQ testing and grades. **Positivism** is a form of instrumental rationality (means-ends calculation) that frames truth as accumulated facts. That is, facts are presented as objects without history. Facts, in this view, speak for themselves, are meaningful on their own, and do not require interpretations or theoretical assumptions. For example, the assumptions of positivism saturate standardized testing in schools. Standardized tests produce numerical 'truths' that are falsely claimed, first, to be universal and neutral, whereas in fact they are partial and based on class and culture, and second, to constitute learning. Testing obscures the values, assumptions, interests and social location of real human beings who make decisions as to what to include and exclude from the curriculum. It also serves as a crucial instrument of the powerful by obscuring the ways that ruling groups educate subordinate ones into language, ideologies, common sense and ways of seeing that maintain the social order. Positivism in education through, for example, testing and grades, naturalized and depoliticized the unequal distribution of life chances by misrepresenting the means of exclusion and inequality as the result of neutral disinterested mechanisms. Positivism also obscures the cultural politics of knowledge and curriculum by framing truth claims as uncontested, conflict-free and beyond practices of interpretation. That is, it suggests that knowledge can be comprehended outside of ideological discourse that mediates it through false assertions of objectivity and value-neutrality. While models of corporate educational leadership significantly impacted the organization of public education in the early twentieth century, pockets of opposition also flourished.

The advent of progressive education

A new form of **progressive educational leadership** emerged, based on the idea that public schools were not simply efficient mechanisms for producing workers, but sites for promoting full human development and democratic capacities. Published in 1916, John Dewey's monumental *Democracy and education* offered a powerful rebuke of corporate leadership. It positioned the public school as a vehicle for transmitting the values, principles, aspirations, shared concerns and critical dispositions necessary for democratic participation. Influenced by such ideas, public schools became sites of reform and struggle. Teachers unions like the New York Teachers Union, founded in 1916 and later destroyed by McCarthyism in the 1950s, waged campaigns to fight corporate management and end poverty and racial discrimination in schools and communities. In the 1930s, the socialist educational theory of George Counts and the reconstructionists experienced a brief but formative influence. Such movements laid the foundation for later civil rights struggles to abolish racial segregation in the 1950s and to promote decentralization, local control and other democratic experiments in public education in the 1960s and 1970s.

Neoliberal phase 1973–present

From Keynesianism to neoliberalism

Neoliberalism: a concept that is mobilized to explore a multitude of transformations over the last few decades.

At the level of policy, neoliberalism is associated with the rejection of post-war Keynesian economics and welfare-state compromises in favour of reliance on neoclassical economic theories, market mechanisms and forms of entrepreneurial individualism. This includes the defunding of the public sector and privatization of public services, attacks on organized labour (such as through the passage of right-to-work laws), corporate 'green washing' of environmental protections, deregulation of capital mobility and finance, 'colour-blind' interpretations of racial equality and civil rights, and the general management of societies through policies and logics of marketization, responsibilization, militarization and criminalization.

The corporatization of education and the concomitant refashioning of educational leadership took a significant turn from the 1980s to the present. Financial crisis in the 1970s called into question the liberal Keynesian views that had dominated the United States and the UK since the great depression. **Keynesianism** held that the nation state ought to play a significant role in modulating the vicissitudes of the business cycle by using welfare-state mechanisms to assure adequate consumer spending and employment.

In response, in the late 1970s in the United States and the UK, neoliberal ideology became prominent. **Neoliberalism** is the dominant cultural-ideological framework, economic programme and political ideology of the last four decades. Neoliberalism has advanced a radical economic programme benefiting the ruling class that called for privatization of public goods and services, the deregulation of markets, capital and labour, allowance of foreign direct investment, monetarist management of the economy, and attacks on labour unions.

Neoliberalism's political agenda

Neoliberalism advances a political agenda that seeks to collapse the distinction between public and private spheres by framing all public goods and services as private ones to be governed through market logics. Neoliberalism also promotes a post-politics, post-ideology view typified by Blair and Clinton and deepening what Margaret Thatcher termed the **TINA thesis** – There Is No Alternative to the market. Neoliberal post-politics frames democracy as no longer a struggle for emancipation, equality and freedom so much as now a matter of properly administering and managing institutions in accordance with corporate culture and market imperatives. This has been termed the **new managerialism**, which applies corporate managerial practices to schools.

Neoliberalism's cultural agenda

Culturally and ideologically, neoliberalism propagates a social Darwinian, survival-of-the-fittest, view of the individual as primarily a competitive worker-entrepreneur and consumer and not a citizen. It promotes a view of the social as primarily a market rather than a social collectivity. It furthers a view of the public sphere as always bureaucratically encumbered and inefficient and therefore in need of private markets.

At the level of governance, neoliberalism is associated with a hegemonic constellation, a cultural project, and distinct sociotechnical rationalities aimed at remaking the state and citizen through the extension of market logics into every aspect of social life. This includes the realm of educational leadership, where new market forms of managerialism have emerged emphasizing privatization and commodification of educational services, an emphasis on standardization of curriculum and accountability through high-stakes testing, and the role of education as an economic driver of growth and innovation.

At the level of power, neoliberalism is associated with the fracturing of the post-war social compact between capital and labour, the reassertion of ruling-class authority and the uniting of traditional centre-left and centre-right parties under the rubric of elite corporate and financial control. This has been propelled by a richly funded infrastructure of neoliberal think tanks and right-wing billionaire donor networks like the Koch network.

Neoliberal education

In education, the neoliberal view has come to colonize dominant forms of educational leadership and schooling by modelling them on corporate organization and culture. This has framed public schools as hopelessly inefficient and bureaucratic and in dire need of radical experimentation particularly with private, corporate-sector reform. Guided by neoliberal ideology, corporate educational leaders have significantly impacted the ownership and control of schools. They have privatized public schools through charter schooling (academies in the UK) that shifts management of schools from the public to private control. They have also promoted voucher schemes that use public tax dollars for private schooling and scholarship tax credits that use tax incentives to encourage the use of public dollars for private schools.

In emphasizing the economic uses of education, corporate leadership has framed students and parents as consumers of private educational services. Schools in this business framing are supposed to compete in markets. In addition to 'competition' and 'choice', the business metaphors include that the public schools have to be 'allowed to fail' like corporations, that schools ought to be subject to 'creative destruction' (Saltman, 2012). Corporate educational leaders have framed the individual uses of schools for economic ends and the social uses of schools for global economic competition.

Corporatization in the neoliberal era has included the expansion of school commercialism and corporate culture in schools. Administrators have been imagined as business managers, teachers as service workers, and students as both customers and workers. School and district leaders began to be modelled on business leaders, taking the moniker 'CEO', while schools increasingly dropped the word 'public' and refashioned their names to emulate private schools.

Following business in the neoliberal era, radical market-based reformers have sought to capitalize on disaster, both natural and human-made disasters, to implement privatization schemes that could not be put into place through normal political and policy means. The dismantling of public education and creation of four charter networks in New Orleans after Hurricane Katrina, the closures of vast numbers of public schools in Chicago and Detroit and their replacement by charters, along with the razing of public and private housing and community dispossession are but a few examples of neoliberal capitalizing on disaster.

Activity 22.2

Make a list of common contemporary practices and/or features of schooling in a system that you know well. Although neoliberalism is not the same everywhere, its reach is significant and so there is a strong chance that elements have reached your country or region. For each item on your list, think of the extent to which it may represent a neoliberal, market-based logic.

For instance, predicting individual students' future attainment from data generated from previous assessments constructs children's learning and development as a rational, evenly linear process of measurable inputs and outputs. What others can you think of?

Neoliberal educational leadership

Leadership in this context turned to corporate management models (Courtney, McGinity and Gunter, 2017). Long-standing values based on industrial standardization took a neoliberal turn with movements to standardize the curriculum and pair deregulation of school models with increased 'accountability' on outcomes. Accountability meant a wholesale embrace of standardization of curriculum and standardized testing. Here, corporate imperatives for homogenizing and scaling up product met with the ideologies of business efficiency.

The intersection of corporatization, standardization and new managerialism is exemplified by some of the largest for-profit educational contractors such as cyber school K12 Inc. and Edison Learning. Both sought to standardize curriculum and school models to decrease costs and increase profits. Both companies failed to come through on what they promised – namely increased test scores, yet they did generate enormous profits by redirecting educational resources from public schools to the private bank accounts of the owners. For instance, Chris Whittle, the owner of EdisonLearning, has made hundreds of millions of dollars in his career as an educational entrepreneur.

Case Study 22.1 Venture philanthropy in education

We are going to present a thematic case study to illustrate the arguments and points that we are making about corporatized educational leadership. To do that, we have selected the thematic case of venture philanthropy in education. Billionaire venture philanthropists such as Bill Gates, the Walton family, Mark Zuckerberg and Eli Broad have emerged as key educational leaders, propagating a neoliberal remaking of philanthropy, designed to privatize different aspects of the public school system (Saltman, 2010, 2018). Gates has championed the creation of charter schools, the Waltons have promoted vouchers and scholarship tax credits, while Broad has spearheaded the corporatization of educational leadership. Zuckerberg has promoted private digital learning services. All of them have aimed to undermine university and state control over teacher and leader accreditation and shift preparation and accreditation to private organizations such as charter school organizations.

The venture philanthropies have redefined charitable giving by allowing donors to retain control over the use of money and requiring the recipients to compete to aggressively embrace privatization and corporatization initiatives. Venture philanthropists are shifting policy governance and priorities from the public to super-rich individuals such as Gates, Broad and the Walton, Dell and Fisher family members.

Activity 22.3

1 In what ways might venture philanthropists be argued to be educational leaders?
2 How do you think their activities might influence what educational leaders at other points in the system are able to do?
3 What is the extent, role and impact of venture philanthropy in education systems that you know?

Social and cultural reproduction in education

Social and cultural reproduction changed in the neoliberal era in ways that reflected the new corporate educational leadership. In the industrial era, schools created the conditions for corporate profit in part by teaching knowledge and skills in forms that were designed to teach different classes of students the knowledge, tastes and dispositions for their role in the workplace. In Fordism, working-class schools largely taught working-class children basic skills, but also docility and obedience to authority, readying them for the hierarchical forms of authority of the workplace. Professional-class children learned different dispositions. Professional-class schools encouraged greater curiosity, dialogue, dissent and debate as they prepared students to take their place in leadership roles in the public and private sectors.

In the neoliberal era, reproduction changed. Neoliberal deregulation by the 1980s and 1990s resulted in the closure of factories and the decimation of industry and the economy was financialized and retooled for service work. A growing number of working-class and poor people have in turn been marginalized from the labour process altogether. The increasingly marginal role of workers to the work process has meant that business increasingly views schooling less as a long-term public investment in an industrial workforce and more as a short-term profit opportunity through corporate contracting and privatization of educational services. That is, in the neoliberal era the rapid expansion of privatization advocated by corporate leaders like Gates, and for-profit contracting schemes, including testing and textbook making, and technology contracting, represented a short-term opportunity for corporations. Moreover, the neoliberal era saw expanded forms of educational repression as controlling and commodifying the bodies of youth became prominent.

Corporatization targets the body

Learned self-regulation of the Fordist era gave way to direct control of bodies. As working-class factory jobs disappeared, an increasing part of the workforce became redundant to the economy. Schools were less necessary to replicate social relations for work through time-intensive forms of learned self-regulation. Increasingly, business owners could profit in the short term by commercializing students and schools. As in for-profit prisons, bodies themselves became the new means of profiting through contracting.

Large educational management organizations privatized public schools by cutting overheads (teachers, texts), standardizing models, union-busting to drive down teacher pay and drive up management income, contracting, homogenizing corporate curriculum products and replacing teacher labour with technology products. The ideology of corporate culture and corporate educational leadership became overt by the 1990s. The hidden curriculum was no longer hidden. Capitalism was now openly the justification for all aspects of schooling. In this era, positivism expressed through heavy and frequent standardized testing and standardized curriculum is at the core of a multibillion dollar business itself (McGraw-Hill, Pearson, Houghton Mifflin, ETS, Kaplan) and proclaimed test failure is used by neoliberals as a justification for turning schools into businesses in the form of charters, vouchers and a plethora of corporate reform initiatives.

The dictates for learned self-regulation or direct bodily control follow a class-based pattern in the neoliberal era of the corporatization of education. Schools have subjected working-class and poor students to intensified levels of repression and direct forms of control, as their use for capital does not involve learned self-regulation for the labour force so much as being commodified objects in an increasingly commercialized educational system that merges with for-profit communications and media sectors. Professional-class students are hailed as entrepreneurial subjects of learned self-regulation taught to self-manage the body, the brain and affect. These students learn to manage their own bodies for academic competition with smart drugs – such as amphetamines, anxiety-control drugs such as Xanax (alprazolam) and antidepressants – in order to compete on positivist tests to hopefully exchange academic rewards for economic ones.

Smart drugs

Technologies of physical control include not just the increased modelling of schools on the prison and military, but massive overdiagnosis and prescription of ADHD attention and anti-anxiety drugs, behaviourist grit pedagogies and employment of biometric instructional technology (Saltman, 2017). Standardized testing and declarations of educational failure grounded in test outcomes are used to justify these corporeal controls. The exponential increase in ADHD prescriptions of children coincided with the advent of high-stakes standardized tests as teachers and parents began drugging kids to game the tests and increase the chance of ongoing school funding or to drug the kids out of distracting other test-takers.

Grit pedagogy

Grit pedagogy, a neoliberal form of character education, employs behaviourist strategies of conditioned response to teach in ways that avoid reflection and dialogue (Saltman, 2017). Biometric pedagogies use real-time webcams to measure the faces of students and translate bodily stature into claims about student attention, interest and alleged learning. Biometric pedagogy alleges to measure and translate body movement into student learning and teacher performance. The pharma and media technologies make learning into a material impact on a body evacuating mediation, thinking, critical consciousness and knowledge production through dialogic exchange (Saltman, 2017).

Digital phase 2010–present

Control, data and learning analytics

The digital phase of corporatization has many components. Learning analytics, 'Pay for Success' and grit pedagogies all merge corporeal control with surveillance and measurement of bodies. Scripted lessons, a kind of quasi-religious practice of indoctrinating dogma, have continued to expand for teachers. They are now widespread, imposed under the guise of 'best practices' accountability and standards with the profits flowing to the large publishing companies. What is significant is that dialogue between teachers and students, the relationship between student subjectivity and social context, and consciousness play no part in this concept of learning. Learning is what is done to a body. Data gleaned from surveillance of bodies appears to seamlessly translate to the control and measurement both of student learning and of teaching as a scripted performance.

The student as data engine

Although we would argue that we are still living in an era of neoliberal corporatization of schools and educational leadership, there are signs that new forms are emerging, particularly through the integration of new technology and forms of financialization. The digital phase of corporatization involves the rapid expansion of media and technology corporations taking over curriculum, school time and teacher work. The digital phase of corporatization of education brings together privatization and commercialization of public schools with the making of students into data producers whose data can be captured and sold for profit. The digital phase also tends to treat learning as something that is done to a body rather than seeing learning as a process involving dialogue and exchange, reflection, interpretation and consciousness. The digital phase of corporatization is characterized by the making of student data and students themselves into investment securities whose selves and activities are becoming the basis for speculation in financial markets.

Philanthrocapitalism

The digital phase of educational leadership has been promoted by corporate philan-thropy / for-profit business that goes by the name **philanthrocapitalism**. Since philanthrocapitalism muddles the line between for-profit business and charity while hiding the financial operations it is hard to see these organizations as philanthropies at all. The big three philanthrocapitalists are the Chan Zuckerberg Initiative, the Emerson Collective and the Omidyar Network. These philanthrocapitalists are merging for-profit and non-profit activity together and have organized as limited-liability companies in order to avoid public scrutiny over the use of and movement of their money. We would suggest that a few key reforms are converging that typify this phase of the corporatization of schools: Pay for Success, Adaptive Learning Technologies and Social Emotional Learning.

Pay for Success/Social Impact Bonds

Pay for Success or Social Impact Bonds, which are promoted in the Every Student Succeeds Act (the latest iteration of the US Elementary and Secondary Education Act), bring together banks with philanthropic foundations with governments in order to privatize public services. This is justified on the basis that measurement provides accountability and the public will not have to pay if the metrics do not show success. Schooling, juvenile justice, recidivism reduction and childcare are some of the services targeted for Pay for Success. Banks such as Goldman Sachs largely finance an already established public service to limit the risk of not getting paid; the service is measured; and if the programme 'succeeds' then the bank can double its money at public expense. Banks aim to influence the selection of programmes and the evaluation. This public-skimming scheme is sold under the guise of innovation, cost savings and accountability. The privatization of the service is made into an investment bond that can be securitized by an investment bank. Increasingly the surveillance of clients in Social Impact investing is done through data technology. In Pay for Success ventures, new modes of positivism, privatization, surveillance and corporeal control merge as quantitative measurement and cost–benefit becomes the justification for the value of a public project (Saltman, 2018).

Adaptive Learning Technology

Another scheme of the digital phase, **Adaptive Learning Technology**, which is promoted as a part of the Personalized Learning movement, has been referred to as the 'Netflixing' of education (Roberts-Mahoney, Means and Garrison, 2016). In this scheme, teachers are imagined as facilitators and curriculum software on screens is the teacher. Students choose lessons based on interest and test performance. Adaptive Learning Technology is a kind of new techno-tracking in which a case of the student is built over time out of data collected by the students' use of the software. The numbers then falsely appear as a neutral disinterested and objective record of the student and their performance. Adaptive Learning Technology builds standardized testing into lessons, deepening and expanding on the positivist legacy of excessive testing and teaching to the test (Saltman, 2018). Teaching and test preparation merge.

Proponents of these schemes claim that such technologies are 'personalized' because students can move at different speeds. However, under the guise of personal student choice, the subjective experiences and the particular context are disregarded, as is the relationship between knowledge, experience and the social world. As such, Adaptive Learning Technology represents a deepening and expansion of the positivism that has defined the era of test-based accountability in the neoliberal phase of corporatization. What is also new about Adaptive Learning Technology and Pay for Success is that the capture and commodification of student data is becoming the basis for corporate profit. Adaptive Learning Technology projects, such as the Chan Zuckerberg Initiative's (CZI) Summit Learning, are being widely implemented in schools without a fee, but Summit/CZI, which is financially interwoven with Facebook and other for-profit education companies, is able to take student data and use them for other corporate educational projects. CZI's other educational projects include pay-for-fee services as well as advertising-driven platforms with profit models like Facebook's. These trends are converging. Pay for Success profiteers are moving to use Adaptive Learning Technologies to measure and justify further Pay for Success projects.

The digitalization of Social Emotional Learning

The digital phase includes **Social Emotional Learning** schemes such as the teaching of grit pedagogy that are promoted through the Every Student Succeeds Act. These projects aim to make resilient individual subjects who can withstand the disinvestment in schools and communities, and who can withstand poverty and the ill-effects of it. Grit, for example, is a kind of neoliberal character education in the age of austerity that has been popularized in privatized charter schools. Like biometric pedagogy, it aims to replace learning through dialogue and student questioning and thinking with automatic response to rapid-fire scripted teacher lessons. Grit emphasizes physical control and measurement of that control as a means of learning. Learning in this view does not involve dissent, dialogue, questioning and curiosity, but learned dispositions for obedience to authority. There is an industry in selling grit pedagogy, and grit has been promoted through privatizing of schools. The digital phase allows media corporations and philanthrocapit-alists to hijack educational governance decisions about pedagogy and curriculum from teachers and communities, representing a hollowing out of the nation state's sovereignty over one of the last large-scale public institutions. Positivism allows the values and ideologies of the corporations to be concealed under the guise of disinterested objectivity and neutrality, numerical quantification, the ideology of technological innovation and an alibi of accountability.

Conclusion

The corporatization of education and educational leadership ought to be comprehended as a long-standing yet varied project of ruling-class interests and understandings imposed on public schools and their leaders. Corporatization represents the stripping of wealth from public institutions, the imposition of hierarchical and authoritarian organizational forms, and the displacement of public values with private ones. It is also through that positivist emphasis on 'data driving' leadership that corporatization delinks knowledge and the process of teaching from crucial concerns with the social context, the experience of students and the broader social import of learning.

There has been a great deal of academic and public criticism of the neoliberal form of corporatization. As well, growing social movements including teachers and teachers unions have become organized and mobilized to resist corporate school reform and reassert the values for public education. Criticism and rejection of such corporate reform schemes as teacher pay for performance, chartering, vouchers, and excessive testing and standardization have become mainstream and are being linked to traditional demands for teacher autonomy, school funding and community forms of control.

It is crucial to recognize that public schools are sites and stakes of struggle for school models and social organization, curriculum and knowledge, pedagogical practices, ideologies and politics. Public schools can model democracy and foster democratic approaches to teaching and learning, and propagate democratic cultures. Democratic cultures in schools counter the authoritarian and hierarchical organization of the corporatization with vibrant dynamic and dialogic forms of knowledge-making practice. Democratic cultures in schools foster forms of school governance that are defined through power-sharing, are inclusive of community and support educational projects that provide the intellectual tools for students to comprehend broader social forces and contests and intervene to collectively address them. Democratic cultures in schools recognize that knowledge is subject to interpretation and struggle and that democratic pedagogies involve the process of helping students to comprehend how claims to truth relate to broader material and symbolic interests, structural and systemic forces and struggles. While corporatized education promotes identifications and identities with corporations and their owners, democratic education promotes identifications and identities with a public constituted by difference and empowered for collective self-governance throughout all social institutions. In other words, the struggle against the corporatization of schools and for democratic schooling has to be comprehended as part of a broader struggle to build a democratic society.

Further reading

Bowles, S. and Gintis, H. (2011) *Schooling in capitalist America: educational reform and the contradictions of economic life*. Chicago: Haymarket Books.

De Lissovoy, N., Means, A.J. and Saltman, K.J. (2016) *Toward a new common school movement*. Abingdon: Routledge.

Means, A.J. (2018) *Learning to save the future: rethinking education and work in the era of digital capitalism*. New York: Routledge.

Saltman, K.J. (2007) *Capitalizing on disaster: taking and breaking public schools*. New York: Paradigm.

Saltman, K.J. (2012) *The failure of corporate school reform*. New York: Paradigm.

Saltman, K.J. (2018) *The swindle of innovative educational finance*. Minneapolis: University of Minnesota Press.

Saltman, K.J. (2018) *The politics of education: a critical introduction*, 2nd edn. New York: Routledge.

References

Bowles, S. and Gintis, H. (2011) *Schooling in capitalist America: educational reform and the contradictions of economic life*. Chicago: Haymarket Books.

Callahan, R.E. (1962) *Education and the cult of efficiency*. Chicago: University of Chicago Press.

Courtney, S.J., McGinity, R. and Gunter, H.M. (2017) *Educational leadership: theorising professional practice in neoliberal times*. Abingdon: Routledge.

Dewey, J. (1916) *Democracy and education: an introduction to the philosophy of education*. New York: Macmillan.

Giroux, H. (2001) *Theory and resistance in education: towards a pedagogy for the opposition*. Westport, CT: Bergin & Garvey.

Kliebard, H. (2004) *The struggle for the American curriculum: 1893–1958*, 3rd edn. New York: RoutledgeFalmer.

Mann, H. (1849) *Twelfth annual report to the Secretary of the Massachusetts State Board of Education (1848)*. Massachusetts: Commonwealth of Massachusetts, Board of Education. Available online: https://archives.lib.state.ma.us/handle/2452/204731 (accessed 7 August 2020).

Roberts-Mahoney, H., Means, A.J. and Garrison, M.J. (2016) Netflixing human capital development: personalized learning technology and the corporatization of K–12 education. *Journal of Education Policy*, 31(4), 405–420.

Saltman, K.J. (2010) *The gift of education: public education and venture philanthropy*. New York: Palgrave Macmillan.

Saltman, K.J. (2012) *The failure of corporate school reform*. New York: Paradigm.

Saltman, K.J. (2017) *Scripted bodies: corporate power, smart technologies, and the undoing of public education*. New York: Routledge.

Saltman, K.J. (2018) *The swindle of innovative educational finance*. Minneapolis: University of Minnesota Press.

Leadership in a genetics-informed education market

Steven Jones, Steven J. Courtney and Helen M. Gunter

23

What this chapter is about   356

Key questions that this chapter addresses   356

Introduction   356

Genetic personalization and education   358

What critical educational leaders need to know about educational genetics   361

Critical intellectual work and educational leadership   364

Conclusion   367

Further reading   368

References   368

What this chapter is about

Most previous discussions of education systems, policy and practices highlight the ways in which the quasi-market has come to dominate internationally. This means that education is no longer understood as a public good, but rather as supply (i.e. provision at compulsory or post-compulsory level) and demand (i.e. young people see themselves as agentic consumers of that provision).

In this chapter, we focus instead on a shift in the discourse: we have identified a disquieting turn to genetics. This resurgent discourse builds on marketized foundations, claiming to be a scientifically neutral means of determining through DNA one's place in differentiated and hierarchized provision. We call attention to the ways in which such thinking may both reinforce existing segregation in provision, and also foster new forms. Genetics-informed education policy is, and will be, mediated by educational leaders, and so we offer critical tools to help them navigate this dangerous terrain.

Key questions that this chapter addresses

1 What is marketization in the context of education systems, policy and practices?

2 How does genetics fit into that framing?

3 What is the claimed relationship between genes and educational achievement?

4 What might this proposed new role for genetics look like in the case of university admissions?

5 What does this mean for educational leaders and leadership, no matter where they lead and what their role is?

Introduction

The restructuring of education internationally is based on changes to supply and demand. The education market produces changes in supply, where owners offer distinctive educational products (for example, charter schools in the United States, free schools in Sweden and academies in England). The market also manipulates access to those products through consumer demand and ability to meet entry requirements (e.g. fees, passing a test), where inequitably available products can be bought to enable access to the 'best' place. For example, parents might pay for tutorial support to help their child pass an entrance examination to a 'better' school. The trend for autonomy in, and competition between provision means that restructuring has been concerned with two major interconnected strategies, both aiming at market distinctiveness: how to *provide* the best place and how to *win* the best place in education institutions of all phases. These strategies are operationalized through marketing based on *traditionalism*: 'children in our family always go there', or *aspiration*: 'I want my child to have the opportunity to go there'.

Educational services can brand their offer through regulating and restricting admission *formally* through faith, sex, tested ability or parental income; or *informally* through how race and class operate within civil society and organizations. They seek to demonstrate the benefits of purchasing that brand through, for example: student outcomes in tests and league tables; the social capital of 'winning' a place in a coveted school or elite university; and the persistent social-networking advantage of having attended. While the rhetoric concerns parental choice, in reality, *schools choose children*: in a competitive context, the focus is on choosing the right type of children, and developing in those children their sense of entitlement based on their family, blood and status.

So, a question is to what extent are places in school and university related to *nature*, or what is inherited genetically, or *nurture*, or what is developed through the environment? Is nature or nurture causally linked to intelligence and achievement? If it is nature, then how does the debate avoid eugenics? The definitions box provides the key definitions of three important features.

We encourage you to read about the debates concerning the meanings outlined in the definitions box, but here we are concerned with the notion of predictability. Is it possible to predict a child's intelligence and achievement, and so for education provision to be arranged on that basis? What are the implications for those in charge of schools, universities and education policy?

Historically, educational segregation has been premised on **eugenics**, which, while discredited, remains normalized within societies. In eugenics, the fact that people are born into advantage and disadvantage is used to justify social, health and education policies that perpetuate these inequalities. While the growth of public-services education based on universal access and the educability of all children has continued in a range of nation states, with evidence of success (see Sahlberg, 2015), the acceptance of biological determinism, or nature over nurture, continues in everyday notions of social mobility and judgements about who deserves an education (see Chitty, 2007).

The relationship between science, intelligence and achievement is currently being modernized following huge developments in genetics. The fit between the educational product and customer genetics is increasingly promoted as the means through which a

---

Intelligence: the label given to the demonstration of a range of cognitive processes and capacities, including memorization; the ability to think in abstract ways; to make new links between ideas; or derive new meanings from empirical observations; to learn quickly or deeply; or to show particular ability in a discipline such as music, foreign languages or maths. Intelligence is deeply contested: some see it as influenced by the environment and susceptible to growth, if indeed it exists at all; others see it as consisting in innate, fixed abilities, measurable through an IQ test. Eugenics is based on the latter.

Achievement: the attainment of one or more goals. In the genetics discourse, the goals are extrinsically set and reflect elite interests. For example: high attainment in external examinations; entry to schools where such high attainment is statistically more likely; entry to elite universities; the development of durable, economically productive social networks; and high earnings.

Eugenics: the combination of ideology and pseudo-science regarding human reproduction and status. Eugenicists identify socially and economically censured conduct (e.g. criminality, prostitution, poverty) as behaviours eradicable through selective breeding, particularly amongst poor and/or people of colour, based on a claimed biological link between person, class, race, intelligence and behaviour.

personalized education can be identified, planned and delivered, and causally connected to the predictability of outcomes. Those who are aspiring or serving educational leaders, who are exercising leadership, must address this matter and critically engage with the claims and evidence. We are therefore using genetics as a way of thinking critically about both the evidence base for professional practice and the morality of professional choices.

Genetic personalization and education

How many times have you used descriptors of students such as: they are very bright, or they struggle with mathematics, or they are talented in music? Such phrases can be commonplace in educational communications and everyday decision-making, but beyond anecdote and the adoption of preferred attributes, they are largely professionally indefensible. However, the tendency to think in this way matters deeply when designing and enacting the curriculum, considering pedagogy and undertaking assessment. Educators have a major responsibility to plan for what is shared (e.g. whole-group lecture) and what is individual (e.g. differentiated learning opportunities, resources and outcomes). Increasingly, **personalization** has become more widely accepted as the means through which individuals should have their specific learning needs met in the education market of provision.

Personalized learning is about enabling a closer fit between the student's needs with both access to particular education institutions and also to an experience of teaching and learning strategies deemed appropriate. Those needs may be determined by parents, for example in homeschooling; choosing a faith or single-sex school; or in considering a school's social mix and choosing one based on class and/or race – particularly using personal resources in order to move house or pay fees for a private education. Or those needs may be manufactured by professionals who offer places based on IQ and other approved-of talents such as sport, music or academic prowess: such claims are legitimated through publicly recognized alumni who embody intelligence, achievement and attainment. The major current trend is to more securely fit the child to the education provision and content through genetics, where DNA can be tested and used to design personalization. But what is the scientific justification for this?

A much-publicized recent scientific 'breakthrough' is the genome-wide association study (GWAS). Following this, in 2018, a group of eighty genetics researchers published a paper establishing a link between genes and educational attainment (Lee et al., 2018). This paper – drawing on research undertaken in collaboration with a California-based personal genomics and biotechnology company called '23andMe' – was said to represent 'a significant step forward for the emerging field of educational genomics' (Williamson, 2018).

Lee et al.'s (2018) analysis claimed to offer a genetic explanation for 11–13 per cent of the variance in educational attainment and 7–10 per cent of the variance in

> **Genomics:** the field of study concerned with genomes, or how all genes within an organism interrelate and contribute to that organism's development.

cognitive performance. A related paper by Smith-Woolley et al. showed how such research begins to offer ways of changing educational practice. Claiming to offer the first 'genetically sensitive' study of university success, its findings highlighted 'the potential for DNA-based predictions of real-world outcomes' (2018a: 1). Being able to genetically identify 'naturally bright kids' (Asbury and Plomin, 2014: 55) is presented as beneficial to educators, educational leaders and education systems.

Asbury and Plomin presented a 'genetically sensitive approach' (2014: 186) through which they called for a shift from one-size-fits-all education to a provision based on genetics and personalization. We would like to focus on this through a specific example of the fit between DNA and university admissions. The research indicates that universities are the most likely site for pressures on educational leaders to manifest concerning the use of genetic information upon which to base decisions about admission to their provision. We turn now to a consideration of some of that evidence and of the claims that arise from it.

Case Study 23.1 A new role for genetics in accessing and offering places in universities?

Could genetics help selective universities to choose the brightest and best candidates? Given the known correlation between elite institutions and graduate outcomes, such as earnings, this question is of significance not only to individual universities but also to the general population. Those with the highest status in society tend to be educated at the most prestigious universities (Kirby, 2016). So who enters the door of those institutions has substantial influence on who governs future generations. With Plomin characterizing DNA as a 'fortune teller' (2018: 134), the possibility for gene-based assessment of an individual's educational suitability for particular 'providers' within the market across all phases is clear.

In this research case study, we are drawing on a study reported in an article by Smith-Woolley et al. (2018a), who argue that DNA can help in university admissions. Their evidence involves a study of over 3,000 pairs of twins and, in their paper, both a 'twin analysis' and a 'DNA analysis' are offered. The twin analysis is not found to predict achievement at university, but it does predict both participation likelihood and the 'quality' of institution attended. The DNA analysis, however, is found to predict achievement. It explains up to 5 per cent of variance across indicators of university success.

University 'success' is constructed with the help of four indicators, all of which are problematic. The first, entrance-exam achievement (e.g. A levels in England), is actually an indicator of pre-tertiary success. The second, participation in higher education, is generally a consequence of the first. The third, institution quality (measured crudely using a single league table) is also a consequence of the first. However, the indicator also assumes that a high ranking always trumps a low ranking, despite evidence that some young people choose their institution according to other criteria (e.g. because of background characteristics, such as wanting to live at home for cultural reasons, or because a particular university has a strong research reputation in a particular field). The final indicator, achievement, is the most appropriate proxy for success. Smith-Woolley et al. (2018a) measure it on a scale from first-class honours (five points) down to a non-honours degree (one point).

Smith-Woolley et al. (2018a) are careful to discuss only the potential for DNA-based predictions of university outcomes. However, it is perhaps telling that their paper on university 'success' follows another suggesting that selective schools are effective at sifting the genetically able from the genetically less able. In this other paper, Smith-Woolley et al.'s (2018b) main contribution is to plot a genome-wide polygenic score against school type to show that pupils at grammar schools and private schools have higher scores than pupils in state schools. However, once a control for factors involved in student selection is introduced, no significant genetic differences between school types remain. In other words, the process of selection is validated on genetic grounds. In this way, the analysis within the paper is based on challengeable assumptions. For example, in the paragraph below, the authors unproblematically conflate higher socio-economic status (SES) with 'educationally relevant genes'.

> Traditionally, the relationship between the factors involved in school admission and later achievement have been thought to operate environmentally. For example, parents with higher SES may invest more time in their children's education and can afford more resources (e.g., more books or private tuition), which in turn may lead to better opportunities and improved achievement. However, a less frequently invest-igated factor influencing both selection factors, as well as achievement, is genetics. In the example above, parents with higher SES are not only passing on educationally relevant environments, but they are also passing on educationally relevant genes, a concept referred to as gene-environment correlation. *(Smith-Woolley et al., 2018b: 3)*

On one hand, the possibility of DNA-informed selection in higher education suggests a step towards equity in admissions (as the most genetically able can be matched against the highest-performing institutions). On the other hand, even if applicants were considered holistically with genetic indicators used alongside a range of other academic and non-academic indicators, it could usher in selection cultures that value what students are born with. It also raises questions about predictive accuracy where the stakes, at an individual level, are so high.

As Richardson (2017) notes, a higher-education admissions test that could identify raw intelligence is seductive. And, since entry tariff is explicitly rewarded in external league-table indicators, it is conceivable that university managers contract private companies to bypass expensive candidate-selection processes.

Activity 23.1

Imagine you are head of admissions for an elite university. One of your genetics researchers asks why you don't use the latest research to ensure that the students selected for entry are the very best that apply. What is your response? Why?

What our case study allows you to do is to engage with the evidence but also to recognize the challenges involved in developing evidence-informed practice in education, particularly for those in leadership roles who have responsibility for developing others' practice as well as for the creation and enactment of policies concerning access, admission and within-institutional student/pupil treatment. We suggest that using critical approaches in thinking about and acting on these matters is crucial, and so it is to this that we now turn.

What critical educational leaders need to know about educational genetics

Engaging with the research evidence and claims about the unfolding findings and progress in DNA is challenging for busy professionals, and certainly those who do not have a natural-science background. Integral to taking up a critical approach by educational leaders is that educational leading is based on intellectual inquiry into what is presented as 'good practice' and that leadership is about the exercise of power that is educative or open to ongoing learning. In order to facilitate this, we intend outlining the issues that critical educational leaders need to engage with:

Eugenics

Critical educational leaders need to know that while the word eugenics may not be used, the ideas are embedded and implicit. In Chitty's terms, 'personalisation' is how an education system is designed and developed according to 'a belief in genetic determinism in the area of human intellectual capacity' and how this 'grew out of a set of ideas about sustaining and improving the quality of the human race – broadly covered by the term "eugenics"/' (2007: 6). Historically, we note the rejection of 'human educability' (2007: 7) in favour of personalized heritability regarding gender, class and race, and how forms of 'biological distinctiveness' underpin the design of and access to educational services (Gunter, 2018). This is evident in contemporary politics regarding arguments for intelligence testing for entrance to academically selective schools (called grammar schools in England) through to broader arguments about whether too much money is wasted on educating children who cannot benefit from it (Young, 2018). It seems that we are witnessing a shift from the conflation of ideology and science in the form of eugenics, towards ideologically neutral scientific claims about how genes can predict educational achievement.

Winners and losers

Critical educational leaders need to know that one reason that DNA-based explanations for intelligence are gaining recognition is because, as Saini (2018) points out, it has always been useful for the winners in society to find an extrinsic basis for their success. Her examples range from the divine right of kings to Victorian hymns. Few willingly attribute their success to luck or social advantage. The worst aspects of the human condition can secure and underpin the protection of winners, from genocide through to embedded segregation. To explain why sensitivity is needed, we need to position such research in its appropriate historical context, revisiting books such as *The bell curve* (Herrnstein and Murray, 1994), in which the case is made that human intelligence is determined by both inherited and environmental factors, leading to the emergence of a 'cognitive elite'. The authors also wrote about racial differences in intelligence, following earlier research by Jensen (1969), who argued that genetics could explain reported IQ gaps between African Americans and white people. While it is claimed that genetic science has 'begun to escape the dark biological politics of twentieth-century eugenics' (Williamson, 2018: 1), it is the case that genetic determinism can be used to reproduce and legitimize a DNA-based meritocracy in which 'personalized' education keeps children in their birth-determined place. Genetics offers a ready explanation for the stubborn tendency of generations to remain socially immobile. It is a narrative upon which the right-wing seizes, not least because it carries with it a ready-made rationale for defunding. Higher education becomes a 'right' for those with elite genomes, already branded 'intelligent' by a DNA test. Instead of universities being places for the curious, the open-minded and the disenfranchised, access is decided by birth.

Communication

Critical educational leaders need to know how important it is to consider the discourses of genetics because they are crucial in mediating the science for public consumption. Proponents of DNA-based approaches to education tend to make appeals to common sense. The science is presented as neutral and non-threatening through such framings as 'one way of helping each and every child to fulfil their academic potential is to harness the lessons of genetic research' (Asbury and Plomin, 2014: 3). Often the tone is inclusive and pragmatic: 'It's time for educationalists and policy makers to sit down with geneticists to apply these findings to educational practice' (2014: 3). The language of personalization takes this further: 'even the most basic understanding of genetics tells us that schools would serve their pupils – and society – better by developing their unique talents and interests; by finding methods of teaching that allow Sam to be Sam and Sarah to be Sarah,' claim Asbury and Plomin (2014: 9).

Counterarguments are difficult to articulate (because who wouldn't want children to be themselves?) but little evidence is presented of whether a fuller understanding Sam's or Sarah's genes would aid their educational progress. Indeed, if polygenic scores are probabilistic at population level, should educational decisions for individual children ever be based on their results? But geneticists' discourses nonetheless seek to oppose what they identify as one-size-fits-all models of education and focus on the individual talents of each child: 'by personalizing education, schools, through embracing the process of genotype-environment correlation, should draw out natural ability and build individual education plans for every single child, based on pupils' specific abilities and interests rather than on arbitrary hoops set in place by partisan, vote-counting governments' (Asbury and Plomin, 2014: 11). Nods toward more progressive government spending can occasionally be found in the literature ('extra funding must be provided to help those children who struggle . . . This may be one way in which we can start to tackle the challenge of improving social mobility' (Asbury and Plomin, 2014: 6)), but counterpositions are misrepresented as environmental determinism ('great swathes of education policy militate against taking genetics into account, fostering herding methods and making personalization virtually impossible' (Asbury and Plomin, 2014: 12)). Genetic determinism is rejected by Asbury and Plomin ('that way lies the madness of Nazi sterilisation' (2014: 96)), but only sporadically and unconvincingly.

Positioning

Critical educational leaders need to understand the political and values positioning that underpins methodological design and hence the claims being made about nature over nurture. Plomin (2018) argues that the blueprint for our intellectual capacity lies in the 1 per cent of DNA that differs between people. Such 'advances' are framed as benignly apolitical. One reviewer summarizes the science as follows: 'let your child go with his or her genes, taking up those opportunities to which they are genetically suited' (Mithen, 2018). This feeds into a narrative of 'personalization' which distracts from a narrative of education segregation that is likely to accompany it. Mithen continues to note that:

> I am happy to bow to Plomin as a psychologist and a geneticist, but I found his sociology rather lacking, in fact quite baffling. He describes how instead of genetics being antithetical to equal opportunity 'heritability can be seen as an index of opportunity and meritocracy'. How can that be? . . . Plomin writes that 'opportunities are taken, not given' and that education is when 'children can find out what they like to do and what they are good at doing, where they can find their genetic selves'. But how can a child whose polygenic scores provide a rare talent for music find his or her genetic self in an underfunded state that has removed music from the curriculum?

It is questions such as this that geneticists, when writing about educational heritability, fail to address. The science is presented as though societies are otherwise perfectly meritocratic and offer equal opportunities for all young people to fulfil their academic potential. But a key question for educational leaders in arranging their provision is whether the science base is overstated. For Asbury and Plomin, 'the ability to learn from teachers is, we know, influenced more by genes than by experience' (2014: 7). Genetic influences are said to increase over time until, in later life, cognitive ability is almost as heritable as height. And Asbury and Plomin claim that a significant proportion of the difference between individuals in how well they can read is explained by genetic influence, leaving as little as 20 per cent to be explained by the environment (2014: 24). However, polygenic scores are probabilistic, not deterministic, as Plomin (2018) makes clear. Plomin stands accused of 'spreading a lot of outdated misinformation in the media that is not supported by the latest science of genetics, including his own work' (Kaufman, 2019). The twin-based approach involves environmental factors being simplistically measured as 1.0 minus the genetic factors, and the conclusions reached by Plomin and his colleagues are not accepted by all researchers in the field.

Asbury and Plomin are clear that our aptitude for intelligence and achievement is not hardwired, and that the understanding of a child's genetic inheritance 'simply helps us figure out which buttons to push to help realise that child's potential' (2014: 97). The stated goal is raised educational attainment: 'if we're serious about figuring out how to raise mathematics achievement – and we should be – we need to begin by taking genes into account and by deciding whose mathematic ability achievement we want to raise' (2014: 55). But the question is whether this betrays a naivety, wilful or otherwise, in overlooking other consequences? As we have noted, it is difficult to counter such a position without appearing to place political concerns ahead of children's progress. However, the problems of education are not genetic. Richardson points to the problem of 'self-fulfilling labelling' (2017: 321), which arises when children are told they have lesser cognitive ability and adjust their expectations to meet their diagnosis. There is also that danger that educators regard learners differently in light of DNA evidence, perhaps not understanding fully that genome scores have – even in the view of their strongest advocates – very little predictive value at the individual level.

Richardson also questions conclusions drawn from studying twins, exposing the vagueness that muddies results (2017: 342), talking about the 'bad science' engendered by genetic and brain reductionist approaches (2017: 346), and highlighting the way in which ideologies of inequality are perpetuated rather than challenged. Attention is drawn instead to the 'increasing number of studies that show the inhibiting and distorting effects of class structure on the development of individuals' potential' (Richardson, 2017: 346).

Activity 23.2

Go back to the response you drafted in relation to Activity 23.1.

Review your response and consider any changes you would now make in regard to your original text.

How and why is it the same or different?

Critical intellectual work and educational leadership

Our case study is important because it connects professional identity, decision-making with emerging and challenging evidence. It is also a highly contentious area where professionals may find themselves caught up in debates full of accusations. Advocates of genetics and personalization are quick to dismiss those who dissent from their dominant narrative, generally as 'those whose political beliefs depend on the blank state hypothesis' (Young, 2018), and where comparisons can be made with creationists and anti-vaxxers (Young, 2018). So how can caution about genetics be legitimately sounded? How does one express concern for, say, policy ramifications in an age of austerity? Or show the usefulness of such 'evidence' to right-wing arguments that education has limited impact in the face of genetic factors or that there are clear links between IQ and economic growth?

Where genetics is concerned, science is positioned as a matter of truth, with scientists untroubled by whether or not the facts they discover cause offence. Opponents are positioned as emotional, anti-science or politically motivated. However, a review of *Blueprint* (Plomin, 2018) in *Nature* (Comfort, 2018) notes that although the author uses more civil, progressive language than his predecessors, the content remains 'vintage genetic determinism'. Scientists like Plomin particularly attract the hostility of education-alists, as Toby Young (2018) and others note. This is because the implication of Plomin's research is that schools and school-based interventions will do little to reduce the attainment gap. Genes trump education.

In such ways, Plomin and his colleagues are positioned as radical and bold truth-speakers, with the rest of the scientific community framed as backward-looking. By dismissing 'elite Harvard professors deciding what's for the people' (qtd in Wakefield, 2013), Plomin taps into populist anti-expert sentiment. According to Williamson (2018), wealthy foundations buy into these discourses. The Wellcome Trust and the Jacobs Foundation now offer educational genomics research awards. Plomin's team is funded by research grants totalling £30 million, and links are also made with private companies seeking to monetize DNA technology. Indeed, Plomin's work allows for the privatization of genetic material – companies selling polygenic scores direct to consumers or, more alarmingly, to education providers.

The prospect of machinery allowing individuals to better understand their own intelligence and that of their children is welcomed by Asbury and Plomin: 'the technology will soon be available, for example, to use DNA "chips" to predict strengths and weaknesses for individual pupils,' they say (2014: 12). In addition, they contend that 'the same technology is already used in heart medicine and immunology; it's only a matter of time before it can be adapted for education' (2014: 12). All children are predicted to have a Learning Chip that will predict their cognitive ability and academic achievement. The implications of screening – 'practical, ethical, moral, legal, political and educational' are later described as meriting further consideration (2014: 19).

The idea of well-trained and well-paid teachers working in well-funded schools to educate future generations is undermined. After all, environment matters little. The danger is that social policy becomes regressive. Why spend on education when outcomes are predetermined? Why widen participation at selective universities when it is what lies inside the student that really counts? As Comfort (2018) says, it is 'live ammunition for those who would abandon proven methods of improving academic achievement among socio-economically deprived children'. On the other hand, Kaufman (2019) notes that there is consistent evidence for the beneficial effects of education on cognitive abilities – approximately 1 to 5 IQ points for each additional year of education – and lists the many ways that educators make a difference in students' lives.

Debates about genetics and education must not be distorted by those whose primary goal is to bait liberals. Nor should research be compromised by the substantial entrepreneurial opportunities that arise within a new and emerging market. The issue is not one of science versus denialism. Rather, to develop Saini's (2018) dichotomy, it is one of humans as simple biological machines versus humans as complex, social beings. Add to this the global trend to cut public spending, and the danger is that headline scientific innovations are used to legitimate regressive social policy.

Valid fears exist that a DNA-driven model of education would be wide open to privatization in a deregulated environment, with claims for an elite education based on recourse to DNA testers supplied by profit-making companies. Entry to elite university is an obvious first step. But the reality is that right-wing governments need little excuse to defund education further and to restrict learning opportunities for those less privileged. In reality, the promise to 'personalize' needs to be seen in this context.

Critical educational leaders must therefore draw on intellectual resources to make sense of these matters in relation to their role. To help, we propose using Apple's (2013: 41) nine tasks for critical educationalists: we will first show through Table 23.1 how Apple's nine tasks may be used to think and act critically about genetics and educational leadership, thinking particularly about our case study concerning university admissions above.

Those professionals constructed in policy and organizational culture as 'educational leaders' are found in a multitude of roles, sites and phases. Our example in Table 23.1 pertains to the university admissions officer, but we want to open the debate through Activity 23.3 to different sorts of education leaders who are required to respond to genetics-based structural reforms.

Activity 23.3

Use Apple's nine tasks for critical educationalists (Table 23.1) to plan actions in response to genetics-based education structural reform. Do this for the following 'educational leaders':

Principal or headteacher of a public school committed to non-selective admissions, but who is in competition with neighbouring schools targeting specific groups of students;

A teacher who is an acknowledged subject expert, with no formal 'leadership' role but considerable influence. She feels under management pressure to adapt her teaching according to an implicit genetic ceiling for her poorer and/or non-white students and to focus her energies on those deemed genetically gifted;

Regional Education Officer, who is responsible for delivering 'efficiency savings' handed down from the central ministry, and who is working in a policy environment where 'rationalization' dominates.

Table 23.1 Relating critical principles to leaderful action on university admissions

Apple's (2013) nine tasks for critical educationalists	How educational leaders in higher-education admissions might use these to act on genetics
1 Bear witness to negativity	Make explicit how education policies that draw on genetics negatively affect certain groups
2 Point to contradictions and to spaces of possible action	Discuss how DNA-based individual achievement predictions derive from statistical probabilities for whole populations. Design your system differently
3 Act as critical secretaries to those engaged in activism	You might be the activist in this scenario: contact and get help from critical researchers in your institution
4 Contribute to understandings of what counts as important knowledge	Think about your role as policymaker: your interpretation of policy matters as the version to be locally enacted
5 Keep radical/progressive traditions alive	Ask who has asked these questions before and in what ways they engaged in activism. Pass them on
6 Speak about them in different registers for different audiences	Have these conversations in diverse ways with professional colleagues, students, parents, state officials and the media
7 Act with progressive movements	Find out who else is enacting policy as you are and build an intellectual and moral case together
8 Be a mentor and role model	Model inclusive understandings of human educability in your policy formulation
9 Use one's privilege to open spaces for those without	Use the authority of the role to admit those with 'unfit genomes' and celebrate their success

Conclusion

In this chapter, we have sketched out the major debates concerning the resurgent turn to genetics in operationalizing markets in education. We have demonstrated how positions are variously taken up; imposed or assumed, and so straw men are plentiful in what little dialogue is currently taking place between geneticists and social scientists. As critical scholars, we hold that knowledge of the social world that is free of standpoint, subjectivity or politics is impossible, and so we are explicit in our own positioning: we insist that genetically determined educational achievement at the level of the individual is not currently supported by the scientific evidence, and so claims that an individual's DNA provides a 'blueprint' for their future attainment are ideological scientism. The fact that such claims are so prevalent in the global education reform movement speak to the seductiveness of a scientific legitimation for a sort of resource rationalization that maintains and reproduces existing elite structures and groups under a facade of objectivity.

We note how these processes are enabled by the global marketization of education provision, where it is a small step from conceiving of children as distinct markets meriting discrete provision to constructing a genetic foundation and justification for those differences.

Educational leaders, in whatever role they occupy, are vital in either reproducing or disrupting this intensifying discourse. Our case study of the university admissions tutor was selected to illuminate the potential power of individuals in constructing and enacting policy that may affect thousands of people's present opportunities and future possibilities. Such power also lies with other educational leaders. Any discourse is most meaningful and also most vulnerable in the moment of its social enactment, and so human agency, empowered through critical tools, offers the most powerful means of achieving social justice for all.

Further reading

Kline, W. (2005) *Building a better race: gender, sexuality and eugenics from the turn of the century, to the baby boom*, 1st paperback edn. Berkeley: University of California Press.

Meloni, M. (2019) *Impressionable biologies: from the archaeology of plasticity to the sociology of epigenetics*. New York: Routledge.

Morton, A. (2018) The purpose of education is to give people skills for life. And we have lost sight of it. *Conservative Home*, 5 September. Available online: https://www.conservativehome.com/thecolumnists/2018/09/alex-morton-the-purpose-of-education-is-to-give-people-skills-for-life-and-we-have-lost-sight-of-it.html (accessed 24 January 2020).

Williamson, B. (2018) Postgenomic science, Big Data, and biosocial education. *On Education: Journal for Research and Debate*, 1(2). Available online: https://doi.org/10.17899/on_ed.2018.2.7 (accessed 30 July 2020).

Zimmer, C. (2018) Genetic intelligence tests are next to worthless. *The Atlantic*, 29 May. Available online: https://www.theatlantic.com/science/archive/2018/05/genetic-intelligence-tests-are-next-to-worthless/561392/ (accessed 31 May 2019).

References

Apple, M.W. (2013) *Can education change society?* New York: Routledge.

Asbury, K. and Plomin, R. (2014) *G is for genes: the impact of genetics on education and achievement*. Chichester: Wiley.

Chitty, C. (2007) *Eugenics, race and intelligence in education*. London: Continuum.

Comfort, N. (2018) Genetic determinism rides again. *Nature*, 561, 461–463.

Gunter, H.M. (2018) *The politics of public education: reform ideas and issues*. Bristol: Policy Press.

Herrnstein, R.J. and Murray, C. (1994) *The bell curve: intelligence and class structure in American life*. New York: Free Press.

Jensen, A.R. (1969) How much can we boost IQ and scholastic achievement? *Harvard Educational Review*, 39(1), 1–123.

Kaufman, S.B. (2019) There is no nature–nurture war. *Scientific American*, 18 January. Available online: https://blogs.scientificamerican.com/beautiful-minds/there-is-no-nature-nurture-war/ (accessed 24 January 2020).

Kirby, P. (2016) Leading people: the educational backgrounds of the UK professional elite. Sutton Trust. Available online: https://www.suttontrust.com/wp-content/uploads/2019/12/Leading-People_Feb16-1.pdf (accessed 3 August 2020).

Lee, J.J., Wedow, R., Okbay, A., Kong, E., Maghzian, O., Zacher, M. et al. (2018) Gene discovery and polygenic prediction from a genome-wide association study of educational attainment in 1.1 million individuals. *Nature Genetics*, 50(8), 1112–1121.

Mithen, S. (2018) Blueprint by Robert Plomin review. *The Guardian*, 24 October. Available online: https://www.theguardian.com/books/2018/oct/24/blueprint-by-robert-plomin-review (accessed 24 January 2020).

Plomin, R. (2018) *Blueprint: how DNA makes us who we are*. London: Allen Lane.

Richardson, K. (2017) *Genes, brains, and human potential: the science and ideology of intelligence*. New York: Columbia University Press.

Sahlberg, P. (2015) *Finnish lessons 2.0: what can the world learn from educational change in Finland?* New York: Teachers College Press.

Saini, A. (2018) Why scientists must fight off the DNA determinists. *Prospect*, 12 December. Available online: https://www.prospectmagazine.co.uk/magazine/why-scientists-must-fight-off-the-dna-determinists (accessed 24 January 2020).

Smith-Woolley, E., Ayorech, Z., Dale, P.S., von Stumm, S. and Plomin, R. (2018a) The genetics of university success. *Scientific Reports*, 8(1), art. 14579. Available online: https://www.nature.com/articles/s41598-018-32621-w (accessed 30 July 2020).

Smith-Woolley, E., Pingault, J.-B., Selzam, S., Rimfeld, K., Krapohl, E., von Stumm, S., Asbury, K., Dale, P.S., Young, T., Allen, R., Kovas Y. and Plomin, R. (2018b) Differences in exam performance between pupils attending selective and non-selective schools mirror the genetic differences between them. *npj Science of Learning*, 3(1), art. 3. Available online: https://www.nature.com/articles/s41539-018-0019-8 (accessed 30 July 2020).

Wakefield, M. (2013) Revealed: how exam results owe more to genes than teaching. *The Spectator*, 27 July. Available online: https://www.spectator.co.uk/article/revealed-how-exam-results-owe-more-to-genes-than-teaching (accessed 31 July 2020).

Williamson, B. (2018) Postgenomic science, Big Data, and biosocial education. *On Education: Journal for Research and Debate*, 1(2). Available online: https://doi.org/10.17899/on_ed.2018.2.7 (accessed 30 July 2020).

Young, T. (2018) Is sociogenomics racist? *Quillette*, 15 October. Available online: https://quillette.com/2018/10/15/is-sociogenomics-racist/ (accessed 24 January 2020).

Conclusion
Putting critical approaches to work in educational leadership

Helen M. Gunter, Steven J. Courtney,
Richard Niesche and Tina Trujillo

What this chapter is about	372
Key questions that this chapter addresses	372
Introduction	372
Knowledge actors and activity in critical educational leadership	377

Conclusion	380
Further reading	381
References	381

What this chapter is about

In this final chapter we raise some questions for you to address regarding your practice as a researcher of and/or as a professional within educational services. The researchers who have reported their projects and analysis in this textbook have provided you with access to critical ways of thinking about, within and for professional practice and research. In doing so, and as a reminder from the Introduction, we have located our approach in Smyth's (1989) critical scholarship: to take the context seriously, to address issues of power, and to work for empowerment. We realize that this is important but also challenging, and so we therefore present this textbook as a case study for critical educational leadership studies, where we focus on how you have read and engaged with the projects and analysis as a form of intellectual practice.

Key questions that this chapter addresses

1 What intellectual purposes do you have as a practitioner?
2 What do these mean for your practice?
3 What counts as knowledge in educational leadership?
4 Who are the knowledge producers?
5 How does thinking with Arendt's conceptualizations of labour, work and action help you to think about critical educational leadership?

Introduction

Critical educational leadership requires educational professionals in kindergarten through to universities to engage with intellectual matters. Criticality is not opinionated fault-finding where you might support or oppose, but is based on understanding knowledge production in two main ways: first, as a professional who wants to practise critical educational leadership in their everyday work; second, as a student of professional practice who wants to understand critical educational leadership in everyday work. Some readers will be professionals who aspire to be students, some will be students who want to become professionals, and some will be both at the same time – doing a job and studying part-time. In this final chapter, we will refer to you as possibly a student and/or a professional, where following Smyth (1989) you will need (1) to take the context that you are in seriously – doing and studying that job means that the context will be examined from the position of practice and from the position of research; (2) to address issues of power – exercising power yourself in a job and using theories of power to understand the job means that power will be examined from the standpoint of your agency interplayed with professional, political, economic, social and cultural structures; and (3) to work for empowerment – examining what it means for you to be empowered in your role and researching theories and strategies for relational empowerment with others will be examined in regard to yourself, colleagues and the organization within a wider context. Consequently, there will be a relationship between what you know as an educational professional and as a student, how you exercise judgement regarding what is worth knowing as a professional and as a student, and how and why that knowledge from practice and research is vital for educational services. While our authors are mindful of your need to 'run' a service or organization, we move the agenda away from the 'what works' imperative of functional improvement and effectiveness, towards questioning and resolving the 'socially just' opportunities of professional improvement and effectiveness. We enable you to ask and resolve questions such as: Who says it works? What is the evidence? Might it work differently? So, this textbook helps you to think professionally by treating your reading as a case study that enables you as reader to consider what you have read and how you have engaged with that reading, and how that reading will be a resource that you can come back to over time.

The intellectual activities that are integral to educational professionalism in practice and in study are focused on **ideas** and **people**.

The definitions box presents ideas as a part of a suite of important issues for how we practise and study practice. In our everyday lives, we may have ideas about family, community, wider society and ourselves, and we may have ideals where we want to bring about change and improvement to create a different, better world. We may also think ideologically, subscribing to right- or left-wing ideas and ideals about people, society, the state and the economy. Where we obtain our ideas, ideals and ideologies from is complex and can be based on inherited traditions,

> **Idea:** a thought or suggestion that describes and gives meaning to a situation and may lead to a course of action.
>
> **Ideal:** an imaginary situation that is normatively presented as desirable and worth working for.
>
> **Ideology:** a system of ideas and ideals that can form the basis of a theory about the economy, society, politics and governance.

it 'is about narrating "one idea after another" as a form of descent from then to now with both continuities and breaches' (Gunter, 2016: 31). Ideas in the present can be accepted faithfully and/or reworked in the present as modern. Importantly, we may well have opinions and beliefs that are based on our family, community and nation that are received and accepted. Power structures from faith organizations, corporations, the military and influential people can determine our knowledge, and we may not have evidence (or power) to challenge. In the busyness of our everyday lives, we may not give thought to what is considered normal and ordinary. In reading and engaging with this textbook, we would encourage you to move beyond the everyday notions that you may think and chat about, and to challenge your commonplace certainties and attitudes. Importantly, ideas, ideals and ideologies do not necessarily descend from the past to the present, but are located in power structures that write people and their intellectual contributions into and out of history.

Taking a critical approach to educational leadership therefore means that we ask questions about the knowledge that exists (in the library, in a training manual, on a

PowerPoint slide) and the knowledge that is marginalized or even forgotten, and consider the people who are recognized as knowers, who are in the know and who are knowledgeable. For example, why do we remember Mozart but not his sister Marianne? So, as a student and/or practitioner in the field, you need to be asking questions about what is included and excluded. Whose work is there, and who is written out? What recognition is given to certain methodologies and methods? In whose interests does this work? In order to support such inquiries, we intend presenting you with the idea of being and doing practice and research as a **knowledgeable user**, **producer** and **actor**.

As an educational professional, you will engage with the first definitions box through trained and developed knowledge about pedagogy and assessment through to organizational structures and cultures for the provision and funding of educational services. As a student, you will engage with those definitions through trained and developed knowledge about the purposes of research, research design and theorizing, and so think about whose ideas, ideals and ideologies you are examining, and how they are historically located. Consequently, the textbook as a case study is about the use of knowledge that you may read or hear about as an educational professional in thinking and doing your job, and/or as a student in thinking and doing your research. We therefore identify a **knowledge user**.

Activity C.1

Look back at your reading and notes, and consider:

1 What are the key ideas and ideals about critical educational leadership that you have identified and used?
2 Focus on one or two examples from your reading and thinking, and consider the purposes of using that knowledge.

When we use knowledge we also tend to generate new knowledge. This new knowledge may be the insights gained about teaching and learning in your professional context through to new ways of theorizing pedagogy through research. We therefore identify a **knowledge producer**.

Activity C.2

Look back at your reading and notes, and consider:

1 What new insights have you developed as an outcome of using knowledge to think about practice and/or the research of practice?
2 Focus on one or two examples from your reading and thinking, and consider the purposes of producing new knowledge.

When we use and produce knowledge for and about practice within critical educational leadership, then we engage in cerebral activity where we read/listen and think, and we may go on to talk and write. We therefore relate with and for others, whether that is our colleagues, our students, and/or our university tutors and dissertation/thesis supervisor. In doing so, we share knowledge and ways of knowing through practice and/or research, where we not only know how to do something but also know why we are doing it. If we do not know, then we have the knowledge to find out and to decide what is known and is worth knowing, and how we might go about knowing differently. We also know what is possible and safe within a context, and so we can exercise judgement about what is contextually appropriate and secure. This relationality means that we act and take action, and we therefore identify a **knowledge actor**.

Activity C.3

Look back at your reading and notes, and consider:

1 What critical educational leadership projects have been undertaken (could be ongoing) in your practice and/or in your research?
2 Where might a new contribution be made to practice and/or research? What makes this contribution desirable and acceptable?

Ideas, ideals and ideologies are crucial to educational professionals as **knowledge users** and **producers**, and many professional and research training sessions focus primarily on this. Building on the work of Smyth (1989) and others, we also focus in this textbook on the **knowledge actor** as an **intellectual** and potentially a **public intellectual**. In other words, ideas in books (talks, webpages, journal articles) do not exist outside of the objective relationships between **people**. A focus on this relationality generates questions about the power of ideas, ideals and ideologies, and the tension between autonomy and accountability regarding what a knowledge actor thinks, says and does.

The second definition box presents two approaches for knowledge actors: first, as an isolated and abstract thinker and, second, as a relational communicator.

If we focus on the first example of a knowledge actor, then there is the opportunity to consider the place of the intellectual within practice and research in education. You may distance yourself from people in order to have some time to read, take notes, imagine and think. That may be a formal space, such as a library, or you may do it more informally, while sitting on a bus or working in the garden. Such an approach is seen as necessary but also problematic: the expertise developed is helpful for academic activities, but seen as potentially irrelevant for what is regarded as the *real* world.

Intellectual: 'an intellectual focuses on autonomous thinking and within practice reveals a scholarly *habitus*' (Gunter, 2016: 34, original emphasis).

Public intellectual: 'someone who applies intellectual activities for a whole community, or nation, in a way that is open and accessible to the members of that community, or nation, however defined' (Lyon, 2009: 70).

Activity C.4

Review your intellectual experience of studying and consider what you regard as important for:

1 thinking *about* practice and/or study;
2 thinking *for* practice and/or study.

If we now focus on the second example in the second definitions box, then taking on a public intellectual role by coming out of the library (or your reverie) requires professionals and researchers to focus on how thinkers engage with and produce ideas with and in relation to others. This requires the knowledge actor to think with and for the public, and speak about issues that the public needs to engage with. Such thinkers may be individuals, but they can also be part of groups or networks who locate according to their dispositions and activities. For professionals, this can be subject associations, or trade unions, or a group of school principals in a locality, or a business group of school owners. For researchers, this can be those who undertake research in regard to a particular issue (e.g. leadership in higher education), or within a particular context (e.g. nursery, rather than school leadership), or who take a particular approach (e.g. functional improvement/effectiveness), where there can be special interest groups that meet and share research findings and analysis.

Activity C.5

1 Review your experience of being a public intellectual in the sense of *sharing ideas about and for critical educational leadership* in your role as: (a) a professional (e.g. in a meeting); and/or as (b) a student (e.g. at a conference). What do you regard as important about communication in these roles?
2 What is your experience of 'being listened to' or 'ignored'? What do you think affects how ideas are received and acted upon (or not)?

The entitlement to speak in public and for the public as a knowledge actor is an important matter, and can be based on expertise and professional credentials, but can also be a power structure located in class, race, gender, age and sexuality. The modes of communication through various forms of media influence greatly who has and/or is given a platform to speak, and influence also how messages can be received supportively or with ridicule. There is a need to relate knowledge use and production to who present themselves and who are acclaimed as intellectuals in critical educational leadership.

Activity C.6

Look back at your reading and notes, and consider:

1 Who are the intellectuals in critical educational leadership?
2 What knowledge claims are made about critical educational leadership, what debates are taking place and how are disputes resolved?
3 Which intellectuals (researchers, writers, teachers) are missing from this textbook and why do you think that is the case?
4 What evidence do you have of public intellectual activity in critical educational leadership?

Knowledge actors and activity in critical educational leadership

Intellectual activities interplay ideas and people in regard to critical purposes and practices. It is this approach we have taken in this textbook, where we have positioned the reader as a knowledgeable user, producer and actor who is committed to developing their knowledge purposes and practices in relational engagement with others.

Consequently, we conceptualize knowledge production 'as not only located in the library and/or the special work of an elite caste, but is an intellectual activity open to all' (Gunter, 2016: 37). This *opening to all* means that we locate knowledge production in a field of study and practice that is plural in regard to the knowledges that are available as intellectual resources, and in regard to field membership that includes children and families, and professionals, through to taxpayers and government ministers. Mapping the field enables field members such as the authors and readers of this textbook to recognize the purposes and activities within knowledge production. Such mapping can be focused on examining knowledge traditions within the field (e.g. Gunter, 2016), and can record the experiences of those who live and contribute to knowledge production. For example, educational professionals who have undertaken master's work have written about their experiences of doing both the job and research (e.g. Tomlinson, Gunter and Smith, 1999). Doctoral students have reported on their experiences of doing research (e.g. Anyon, 2009), where professionals as doctoral researchers have reflected on the interplay between research, identities, values and the reality of the day job (e.g. Rayner et al., 2015).

Such accounts require a focus on the meaning of **purposes** and **practices** by and for knowledge actors. Purposes are the proposed intentions with rationales, and practices are what a person thinks, says and does. Following Arendt (1958), this may be framed as **labour**, **work** and **action** (see Table 24.1).

The intellectual requirements of **labour** are to exercise agency that has been trained with skills and know-how and imbued with a survival imperative to deliver what is

Table 24.1 Thinking with Arendt about purposes and practices

	Purposes	Practices
Labour	Maintain and survive	Deliver and measure
Work	Create and sustain	Craft and make
Action	Understand and learn	Question and change

required; to measure and be measured. As an educational professional, this may mean that you enact predesigned lessons and produce data about student text outcomes, and as a researcher, this may mean you transcribe and code data. Importantly, labour requires relational monitoring, evaluation and feedback adjustments according to predetermined plans. Labour is about functionality, and tends to be associated with forms of organizational leadership that is about securing delivery management.

The intellectual requirements of **work** are to exercise agency in ways that are beyond the consumption of labour (data production is automatically out of date and requires ongoing calculation), and so the outputs of work require design, are durable and can outlive the creator in ways that may not be able to be measured. As an educational professional, work may mean tangible 'things' such as the production of textbooks, restructuring of organizational roles and structures, and involvement in school architectural design, but it can be less tangible: a conversation in the corridor, for instance, may impact in ways that relationally shape lives beyond that moment. Work is about the experiential reality of doing a job, and tends to be associated with forms of transformational leadership that is about creating cultures that link isolated work with others in a common vision and mission.

Labour and work are worthwhile, but the intellectual requirements of **action** are to exercise agency to 'make a difference', in ways that are beyond labouring to survive, and working. Action is based on our capacity to do something new, based on our uniqueness as human beings (Arendt, 1958): we begin by understanding the context that we are located in; we can interrogate that context relationally with others and spontaneously consider issues and strategies. As an educational professional, this may mean using speech to question the way students are organized and segregated within and between educational organizations, and it could lead to new professional-development opportunities to think about the organization of learning. Action is political in the sense that it concerns the exchanges between people within civil society, and so it emphasizes social-justice agendas regarding power, the access to education and to knowledge production.

Building on Arendt's conceptualization, Gunter (2020) argues that educational professionals can undertake action as critical educational leadership in six main ways. The first three are forms of action in the public domain that educational professionals have undertaken in their jobs:

- **Biographical:** using narration to present a synthesis of key insights from doing the job (e.g. Clark, 1998)

- **Hierarchical:** presenting a think piece that sets up a 'friend–enemy' distinction in order to justify/oppose an argument and/or reform strategy (e.g. Astle and Ryan, 2008);

- **Entrepreneurial:** packaging exhortations for change with how-to-do-it problem-solving technologies (e.g. Goddard, 2014).

Activity C.7

Reflect on these three forms of action, and consider:

1 What evidence do you have of these forms of action within educational organizations:

   a   from your practice; and/or
   b   your data; and/or
   c   your reading?

2 What are the implications of these forms of writing for how you design and conduct a research project?

The second three are forms of critical primary research used by knowledge actors:

- **Functional:** the provision of empirical and conceptual evidence to justify 'getting the job done' improvement, effectiveness and efficiency (e.g. Leithwood, Jantzi and Steinbach, 1999).

- **Realistic:** the identification of values, dispositions and practices within organizations in order to produce accounts of a working life (e.g. Evans, 1999).

- **Activist:** the questioning of field purposes and practices, and the development of research methodologies and conceptual tools in order to undertake communal and relational social-justice projects (e.g. Anderson, 2009).

Activity C.8

1 What evidence do you have of these forms of critical research about educational organizations:

   a   from your practice; and/or
   b   your data; and/or
   c   your reading?

2 What are the implications of this critical primary research for how you design and conduct a research project?

Conclusion

Critical educational leadership is premised on the ongoing democratization of knowledge production, and the contributions to this textbook not only present evidence of the current situation, but also note the debates and contestation that is taking place. Our activities as intellectual knowledge users, producers and actors are therefore subject to ongoing critic-ality: you as a reader are actively involved in this. Consequently, there are issues that need to be on our agenda, and if we are serious about inclusive approaches to intellectual activ-ities, then we need to ask: whose knowledge matters and why? What do we do about it? Such questions return the discussion to matters regarding the endurance and violence of class, gender, race, age and sexuality as power structures, the dominance of elite knowledge and the legacies of colonialism (Blackmore, 2010).

Activity C.9

1 Go through all your notes so far and consider your knowledge gains.

   a   Which of it resonates with knowledge you already had?

   b   Which of it has moved your thinking in a completely new direction?

2 Who or what controls your access to knowledge, and what does this mean for your research project?

These are ongoing issues in how and why we work for and about critical educational leadership as students and as professionals. We therefore can address but cannot resolve these matters and must continually focus on developing ways of thinking and practising that enable productive contributions. At this stage of the textbook process, we will take a pause while you continue to engage with the use, production and action for and about knowledge. Here are some questions that you might want to take forward regarding criticality:

- What counts as knowledge in critical educational leadership? Why?
- What does critical educational leadership assume the purposes of education to be? Why?
- Who funds knowledge production in critical educational leadership? Why?
- What methodological innovations are there in critical educational leadership? Why?
- What is the relationship between critical educational leadership and education policymaking? Why?

Such questions will enable you to think about an emerging and dynamic map of use, production and action, and to generate new questions for thinking about the field and your location.

Further reading

Bogotch, I.E. (2012) Who controls our knowledge? *International Journal of Leadership in Education*, 15(4), 403–406.

Connell, R. (2007) *Southern theory: social science and the global dynamics of knowledge*. Cambridge: Polity Press.

Fitzgerald, T., White, J. and Gunter, H.M. (2012) *Hard labour? Academic work and the changing landscape of higher education*. Bingley: Emerald.

Greenfield, T. and Ribbins, P. (eds) (1993) *Greenfield on educational administration*. London: Routledge.

Gunter, H.M. (2013) On not researching school leadership: the contribution of S.J. Ball. *London Review of Education*, 11(3), 218–228.

References

Anderson, G.L. (2009) *Advocacy leadership: toward a post-reform agenda in education*. New York: Routledge.

Anyon, J. with Dumas, M.J., Linville, D., Nolan, K., Pérez, M., Tuck, E. and Weiss, J. (2009) *Theory and educational research: toward critical social explanation*. New York: Routledge.

Arendt, H. (1958) *The human condition*, 2nd edn. Chicago: University of Chicago Press.

Astle, J. and Ryan, C. (eds) (2008) *Academies and the future of state education*. London: CentreForum. Available online: https://www.bl.uk/collection-items/academies-and-the-future-of-state-education (accessed 31 July 2020).

Blackmore, J. (2010) Disrupting notions of leadership from feminist post-colonial positions. *International Journal of Leadership in Education*, 13(1), 1–6.

Clark, P. (1998) *Back from the brink: transforming the Ridings School – and our children's education*. London: Metro Books.

Evans, R. (1999) *The pedagogic principal*. Edmonton: Qual Institute Press.

Goddard, V. (2014) *The best job in the world*. Carmarthen: Independent Thinking Press.

Gunter, H.M. (2016) *An intellectual history of school leadership practice and research*. London: Bloomsbury Academic.

Gunter, H.M. (2020) A short history of criticality in the field of educational administration. In: R. Papa (ed.), *The Oxford Encyclopedia of Educational Administration*. New York: Oxford University Press.

Leithwood, K., Jantzi, D. and Steinbach, R. (1999) *Changing leadership for changing times*. Buckingham: Open University Press.

Lyon, E.S. (2009) What influence? Public intellectuals, the state and civil society. In: C. Fleck, A. Hess and E.S. Lyon (eds), *Intellectuals and their publics: perspectives from the social sciences* (pp. 69–87). Farnham: Ashgate.

Rayner, S., Lord, J., Parr, E. and Sharkey, R. (2015) 'Why has my world become more confusing than it used to be?' Professional doctoral students reflect on the development of their identity. *Management in Education*, 29(4), 158–163.

Smyth, J. (ed.) (1989) *Critical perspectives on educational leadership*. London: Falmer Press.

Tomlinson, H., Gunter, H. and Smith, P. (eds) (1999) *Living headship: voices, values and vision*. London: Paul Chapman.

Index

Page numbers: Figures are given in *italics* and tables in **bold**.

'4 Ls' 298, 299–300

academic positions, women 95, **96**
Academies Act 2010 33, 34
academy schools 300, 317–18, 345
accountability 144, 310, 318–19
    business-management approach 114
    GERM approach 123
    high-stakes 32
    neoliberalism 346
    organizational 321
    performance 129, 132, 326
    school principals 70
    system strategic leadership 82
    US education 19–20
achievement
    definition 357
    heritability 364
    personalized learning 358
Acker, J. 284–5
action, requirements 377, 378–9
action-research approaches 242
activist learning communities 149
activist research 379
Adaptive Learning Technology 351–2
ADHD diagnoses 349
adjectival approaches 226–7
administration
    ELMA research 155–69
    historical meaning 140–1
    LGB people 271–2
advocacy 38–41, 181, 227–9
affective justice 52, 56
age–gender intersection 266–7
agency 143–4, 247
    change ownership 243, 249
    definition 31, 142
    distributed leadership 208
    labour and 377–8
    researchers 195

    socio-economic class 297
    structure interplay 5, 30
aggression studies 191–3, 199–200
agonistic-political governance 311, 319, 320
AITSL *see* Australian Institute for Teaching and
    School Leadership
Allan, Julie 167
Alvesson, M. 34
America *see* United States
Anderson, G.L. 21, 22
Anderson-Nathe, B. 3–4
Anyon, Jean 156–7
apartheid regime, South Africa 60–2
apathy studies 191–3
Apple, Michael W. 6, 42–3, 307, 366, **367**
applied research 23
apprenticeship model, principals 47
Arendt, H. 377, 378, **378**
Asbury, K. 359, 363–5
aspirational leadership 303–4
assessment systems *see* evaluation . . .
attainment and genetics 358–9, 364–5
auditing practices 227–8
Australia 45–58, 95, 240, 260–1, 264–5, 319–20
Australian Institute for Teaching and School
    Leadership (AITSL), 'the Standard' 46–8,
    49, 50–1, 55
authoritarian leadership 189, *190*, 191–3, 197–200
authority as agency 5
autocracy 63, 68
    democracy opposition 197–200
    group structure 191–3
autonomy
    definition 32
    principals 68, 70
    school governance 315–16, 319–20
    SEI models 240

Ball, S.J. 123, 325–7
Banksia College, Australia 52–5

becoming, spaces for 248–50
behaviourist biometric pedagogies 349
behaviours
    categorization *190*
    definition 189
    experimental studies 191, 194, 199–200
    group studies 190, *190*, 192
    leader 141–2
being, spaces for 248–50
belonging, sense of 242
Bernstein, Basil 222–3
'best practice', SEI approach 240
biases
    embodied leadership 242
    experimental studies 189, 194–5, 198–9
Billig, M. 198–9
biographies 195–6, 378
biometric pedagogies 349, 352
Black leaders 285, 290
Black Minority Ethnic (BME) peoples 282, 284
Black students 60–2
    sexual identities 274
    underachievement 303
    white racial avoidance 286–9
Blackmore, Jill 68, 93, 244, 261
BME (Black Minority Ethnic) peoples 282, 284
Bobbitt, Franklin 342
body, corporatization of 348–50
bonding category, agency 247
borders, theoretical frameworks 161
bottom-up approaches 250, 313–14
Bouckaert, G. 326–7
boundaries 142
Bourdieu, Pierre 162–5, 297, 301, 305
Broad, Eli 347
Brooks, J.S. 22
Brown v. Board of Education (1954) 286, 290
Buddhism 266
bullying 274, 277, 287, 291
Bush, T. 78
business-management approaches 114–15
business sponsorship 33
businesses, schools as 300–1, 316–17, 346

Campbell, D.T. 193–4
capital concept 162, 297, 305
capitalism 341–2, 343, 348
career ladder systems 80
caring roles 52, 56, 258
Carnegie, Andrew 342–3
Carroll, B. 6
case studies
    research methods 175
    subjectivity 179
casualization of work 93
centralized systems
    Australia 319

China 79–80, 87
Centre for Training, Experimentation, and Research in Pedagogy
    (CPEIP) 130–1
change
    as inclusive practice 242–4
    incremental nature 240–1
    ownership of 243, 245–6
change agents 259
change theory 241–4, 249
charter schools 345–7
Chile 121–35
China 75–89
Chipkin, I. 64
Chitty, C. 361
choice
    GERM approach 123
    logics of 163
    marketization 357
    research projects 167
City Academies programme 318
City Technology Colleges (CTCs) 33, 318
civic purposes, schooling 26
civil rights movement 18, 24, 272, 278
Clark, Dwight 341
class 295–308
    corporatization and 348
    gender intersection 264–5
    learned self-regulation 349
'class' ceiling 304–7
CLS (Critical leadership studies) 212
cognitive ability 363–4
Cohen, M.I. 22
coherence principle 181–2, 184
Coleman, James 18
Coleman Report 225
collaborative work practices 210, 247
collective practices 38–9, 210
collectivism 78, 80, 85
Collinson, D. 212
Comfort, N. 365
commodification of performativity 325
common schools 341
communication and genetics 362–3
community governance 314
community of leadership model 263
community partnerships 244
community power-sharing 150
comparison aspect, performativity 325
compatibility thesis 173
competition
    logics of 163
    schools 19–20, 33, 123–4, 316
competitive performativity 316
*Complementary research methods for educational leadership
    and policy studies* (Lochmiller) 182–3
comprehensive school system, Scandinavia 108
concept–theory distinction 157

confirmation bias 198–9
confounding effects 195
Confucianism 77, 87
conjoint agency 208
Connell, Raewyn 158–9, 260
Constitution of South Africa 1996 60, 64, 71
constitutive practices 128
consultative approaches 332–5
context
    change theory 241
    critical approaches 4–5
    cultural dependency 78, 88
    direction-forming process 233
    diversity research 283
    instructional leadership 231
    schools decoupling from 230
    social ideas 196–8
    theory/method partitioning 180, 183
contractualization 316, 319, 347, 348
control
    agency for 247
    corporatization 350
    experimental studies 189
    logics of 142
Cooper, D. 313
corporatization 300–1, 316, 339–54
Courtney, Steven J. 7
CPEIP (Centre for Training, Experimentation, and Research in Pedagogy) 130–1
credibility 173–4, 176, 180, 225
Crevani, L. 212
critical, use of word 2
critical approaches
    case studies 140
    definitions 4–6, 31
    functionalist research differences 5
    impact of 34
    importance 36–7
    interpretations 4
    leader/leading/leadership 144, 146–8, 150
    micropolitics 152
    school change 239, 242, 249–50
critical feminism 96–7, 261
Critical leadership studies (CLS) 212
critical perspectives
    definition 2, 31
    impact of 34
    theoretical work 38
Critical Race Theory 21–2
critical realism 151
critical research approach, definition 17
critical social theory 157–60, 162–3, 166
critical thought, emergence of 21–3
CTCs see City Technology Colleges
Cubberley, Ellwood Patterson 173, 342
Culbertson, Jack 174
cultural justice/injustice 51–2

cultural norms, diversity 289
cultural reproduction 348
cultures
    China 76–8, 85, 88
    criteria 143–4
    definition 141
    of evaluation 145–6
    gender issues 94, 98, 100
    group behaviour 192
    neoliberalist agenda 345
    racial diversity 291–2
    schooling 26, 242–3
    social ideas 196–8
    of testing 147
curriculum design, class 305
curriculum reforms
    Chile 123
    China 80
curriculum systems 222–3

data comparisons 325
'data driving' leadership 352
data forms, separation of 175
data generation 23–4, 173, 175, 177, 179, 350
decentralization, definition 32
decentralized centralism 79–80, 87
decision-making
    agency 248
    consultation 332–3, 335
deliberative leadership 247–8
democracy
    autocracy binary 199–200
    group structure 191
    Lewin's respect for 197–9
democratic cultures 353
democratic leadership 17, 22–3, 27
    confirmation bias 198
    experimental studies 189, *190*, 191–2
    shared leadership distinction 99
    South Africa 63, 68
democratic welfarism 106
density of leadership 47
description, value of 233
devolved governance 240, 314, 320
Dewey, John 222
digital phase, corporatization 350–2
digitalization of learning 352
direction-forming process 206, 233
'dis-embedding' process 314–15
disadvantaged communities 245–6, 335
discipline 164
discourse 164–5
discrimination prohibition 62
discursive policy frames 31–2, 42
discursive politics 142
'discursive struggle' 31
disruptive leadership 247–8

distributed leadership 35–6, 47, 56, 203–19, 330
    conceptual development 208–10
    framing of 112–14
    in-service training 130
    master's programmes 131
    perspectives *207*
    school change 241–2, 247–8
diversification
    definition 32
    school-type 33
diversity
    definition 283
    race 282–4, 286, 288–92
    schools 46–7
    social justice 242
division of labour 97–8, 259
DNA-based evidence
    intelligence 361–4, 366
    personalized learning 358
double burden, women 258
doxa concept 162
Drucker, P.F. 328
dysfunctions 3, 145

economic justice/injustice 51–2, 55
economic liberalism 313
economic programmes 344
economic purposes, schooling 26
Edison Learning contractor 347
education as context 217
Education Reform Act 1988 (ERA) 32–3, 318
education reforms 87, 112, 209, 237–52, 311
educational administration *see* administration
educational leadership, definition 107, 257
educational leadership, management and administration (ELMA)
        research 155–69, 184, 214, 224, 270–1, 274–6, 315–16
educational management *see* management
EF leadership *see* Entitative-Formal leadership
effect size, definition 225
effectiveness
    functionalist research 35
    identifying 3
    scientific 143
    US legacy 18–19, 21
efficiency
    identifying 3, 225
    modern cult of 19–20
    schools 300
    US legacy 18–19
EI leadership *see* Entitative-Informal leadership
elite universities 298, 300, 359, 366
ELMA research *see* educational leadership, management and
        administration research
embodied leadership 242
emotional dimensions of change 244
emotional leadership approach 333
empiricism 179, 226–7

empowerment
    critical approaches 6
    decision-making 332
    organizational requirements 151
    professional work 373
    women 95, 98, 101
England 29–44, 163, 214–16
    class structure 296, 299–301
    governance 312–13, 317–19
    managerialism 328–34
    race 283–4
Englund, T. 116
entitative thinking 204, 205–7, 209–11, **213**, 214, 217
Entitative-Formal (EF) leadership 204, 206–7, 209–10, **213**, 214,
        217
Entitative-Informal (EI) leadership 204, 206–7, 210, **213**, 214, 217
entrepreneurial action 379
entrepreneurial leadership 320
epistemology 175, *178*, 181
equality 64–5
equity
    definition 283
    gender relations 98
    policy reforms 31–2, 110
    race and 288–91
    school change 242–3
    social justice 65, 70
ERA *see* Education Reform Act 1988
essentialism 258, 260–2
ethical assumptions 173
ethnic consciousness 285
ethnic groups 283–4, 286
ethnicity in organizations 285–6
ethnographic studies 24
eugenics 343, 357, 361–2
evaluation, culture of 145–6
evaluation systems 126–7, 129, 222–3
Evans, Linda 206, 211, 214, 216
Every Student Succeeds Act 351–2
evidence-based practice 178
excluded pupils 302
experimental mortality 194
experimental studies 188–94, 196–7, 199–200
external
    criteria 143–4
    definition 142
external validity 193, 195

face (*guan xi*) 77–8
factory model, schooling 341–2
facts 343
fairness concept 64–5
feminine leadership qualities 93
femininity–masculinity binary 258
feminisms, definition 257
feminist leadership 93–4
feminist movements 263

feminist theories 96–8, 258, 261
feminization of labour 98
field-based practices 184
field concept 162, 163
Finland 226
Fisher, R.A. 193
Fletcher, A. 247
Flynn, N. 326
follower–leader distinction 205, 208, 211, 305
Ford, Clementine 263
Fordism 341–4, 348
formal admissions 357
formal leadership structure 206
formative assessment 242
Foucault, Michel 162, 164–5, 167
frames
    definition 160–1
    theory 160–2
Fraser, Nancy 46, 51–2, 55
free schools 110
Freire, Paolo 157
Fuller, K. 299
functionalist approaches 2–4, 6
    critical research differences 5
    educational organizations 140, 144, 145–6
    effectiveness 35
    governance 321
    knowledge 31–2, 379
    micropolitics 152
    power 150–1
    school change 238, 240
funding cuts, schools 39, 42

Gadamer, Hans-Georg 166
Gates, Bill 347–8
Gauteng Ministry of Basic Education, South Africa 66
gender 255–68
    definition 257
    diversity dimensions 283–4, 286
    Indonesia 94–5, 98
    leadership interconnection 92–104
    queer theory 22
    South African schools 63
gender equity 242
gender parity 65
generative principles 176–7, 178, 180–1, 183
genetic determinism 361–3
genetics-informed market 355–69
genome-wide association study (GWAS) 358
genomics 358
gentrification 297
GERM see Global Education Reform Movement
Germany 196–8
Getzels, J.W. 188–9
Gewirtz, S. 301, 327
Gharabaghi, K. 3–4
Gibbs, Paul 166–7

'glass ceiling' 95, 98–9, 258
Global Education Reform Movement (GERM) 122–5, 133–4
global–local processes 79
'good governance' discourse 321
Gooden, Mark 282
Gore, J. 227
governance 309–22
    definition 311, 313
    formulations of 311, 321
    government distinction 312–14
    neoliberalism 345
'governance-in-practice' 311, 316
government–governance distinction 312–14
government partnerships 244
Grace, G. 3, 300
Greenfield, Thomas Barr 141–2, 174
Griffiths, D.E. 141
grit pedagogy 349–50, 352
Gronn, P. 208–9, 241
ground-up leadership 247–9
group behaviour studies 190, 190, 192
group practices, distributed leadership 208
group randomization 193
group structure studies 191–2
Gunter, Helen M. 7–8, 34, 378
GWAS (genome-wide association study) 358

habitus concept 162–3
Hallinger, P. 77, 226
Halpin, A.W. 141
harassment, racial 287, 289–91
Hargreaves, A.P. 131
harmony, culture of 78
Harwood, Valerie 167
Hatcher, R. 42
Hattie, John, Visible Learning 223–4, 229–30
'headmaster' tradition 300
headteachers
    Chilean system 122, 124
    class and 299–304
    education reforms 238–9, 240, 245–6
    England 38–9, 42
    in-service training 130
    performance commitments 125–7, 128–9, 132
    principals distinction 231
    selection/evaluation 126–7
    structural change 331
    see also school principals
Hearn, Jeff 260
heritability 363–4
Hernstein, R.J. 362
heroic leadership 112–14, 224–5, 226, 258
heteronormativity 270
Heystek, J. 70
hidden curriculum 343, 348–9
'hierarchical answerability' 143
hierarchical approach

to action 379
    gender importance 267
    senior leadership 215
hierarchy
    criteria 143–4
    definition 142
    distributed leadership 330
    labelling staff 334
high-stakes accountability 32, 33–6
higher classes 297
higher education
    distributed leadership 217
    gender aspects 92–104
    see also universities
history variable, experimental studies 194, 195, 197
homophobia 271
homosexuality 275
Hood, C. 326
horizontal divisions, gender 259
Horsford, S.D. 21
Hoyle, E. 151
Huang, Z.J. 79

ideals
    definition 373
    importance 375
ideas
    definition 373
    importance 375
ideological context
    instructional leadership 224–6, 229–31
    research methods 173–5
    school change 240–4
    sexual identity 270
ideology
    China 79
    definition 373
    importance 375
IEPs *see* Individualized Education Programs
ILE (Innovation Learning Environments) 244–7
in-service training 80, 130
inclusion
    definition 285
    race and 288–91
inclusivity, change 242–4
incremental change 240–1
Independent Public Schools (IPS) initiative 319–20
Indigenous peoples
    community model 263
    gender construction 260–2
    school change 243
    South Africa 60–2, 69
Individualized Education Programs (IEPs) 273, 277
Indonesia 91–104
industrial corporation models 341–2, 348
Industrial Revolution 17
industry partnerships 244

inequality in organizations 284
inequity, policy reforms 31
inferential factors, experimental studies 194–5
informal admissions 357
informal leadership structure 206
injustice
    forms of 51–2
    recognition-based 55
Innovation Learning Environments (ILE) 244–7
innovative practice 216
institutional leadership 103, 300
institutional logics 93
institutionalized racism 285
instructional leadership 81, 83–5, 221–35
    definition 223
    effects of 232
    historical context 224–6, 229–31
    key features 226–9
    logic of *228*
    model of 223–4, 227–31
    see also distributed leadership; pedagogical leadership
instrumental-rational governance 311, 321
instrumental-technical governance 318
instrumentalization 3
instrumentation variable, experimental studies 194
intellectual activities, knowledge actors 377–9
intellectuals
    definition 375
    role 376
intelligence
    definition 357
    DNA-based evidence 361–4, 366
    genetic studies 364–7
    heritability 364
    personalized learning 358
    racial differences 362
interaction effects, experimental studies 195
internal
    criteria 143–4
    definition 142
internal validity 193, 195
International Successful School Principalship Project (ISSPP)
    112–13, 175
interpretive approach, school change 239
intersectionality 261–7, 271, 273
invisible power 94, 96, 99
IPS (Independent Public Schools) initiative 319–20
IQ testing 343
ISSPP *see* International Successful School Principalship Project
Italy 145–8
ivory basements 98

Jensen, A.R. 362
Jones, K. 42
Jones, O. 298
journals 173, 176, 178–9, 199
justice 70

see also social justice
'justice as fairness' concept 65

Kaufman, S.B. 365
Keynesianism 344
Kirby, P. 298
knowledge
    context 4–5
    positivism 343
    power and 249
    questioning 373–4
knowledge actors 374–5, 377–9
knowledge producers 374
knowledge production 175, 178, 180–1, 372
    conceptualization 377
    definition 31
    functionalist 31–2
    social justice 42
    socio-economic class 306–7
knowledge users 374, 377

labour 97–8, 259, 377–8
labour-market model 108
Ladwig, J.G. 227
laissez-faire leadership 189, *190*, 191–2, 197, 199–200
language gaps 66
leader
    approaches to 144–9
    behaviours 141–2
    definition 298, 305
    disconnections 142
    framing 143
    historical meaning 141
    manager distinction 205
    power 150
    role 141
    socio-economic class 298–304
leader–follower distinction 205, 208, 211, 305
leader-centric narratives 300
leader-centric theories 204–5, 212
leaderability, definition 298–9, 305
leaders/leader distinction 142
leadership
    approaches to 144–9
    definitions 212, 298, 305, 311
    disconnections 142
    framing 143
    historical meaning 141
    power 150
    recognition of 210–11
    values underpinning 142
leadership architecture 247–8
leadership for learning 222, 223
Leadership Profiles, AITSL 46, 48, 50
Leadership Requirements, AITSL 48
leadership style 187–202, 261
leading

approaches to 144–9
definition 298, 305
disconnections 142
framing 143
historical meaning 141
power 150
socio-economic class 298–304
league tables 33–4, 226
learned self-regulation 348–9
learning
    language of 109
    leadership for 222–3
    positivism 352
    socio-economic class 305
    visible 223–4, 229–30
learning analytics 350
Lee, J.J. 358–9
legal rights, LGB students 273
legal sanctions
    LGB identity 272
    same-sex behaviour 275
legitimacy of research 179–80
Leithwood, K. 175
lesbian, gay, and bisexual (LGB) people 270–9
Lewin, Kurt 188, 189–92, 194, 195–8, 200–1
LGB (lesbian, gay, and bisexual) people 270–9
LGBTQ populations 22
Lippitt, Ronald 189, 199–200
Local Management of Schools (LMS) arrangements 318
localized systems 305
Lochmiller, C.R. 182–3
logics of field 163
López, G.R. 21
Lynch, Kathleen 52, 56
Lyotard, J. 325

McNae, R. 247
macro-level agendas 164
Madimbo, M. 70
maldistribution-based injustice 51
male domain, higher education as 92–3, 98
management
    educational organizations 139–53
    ELMA research 155–69
    leadership encompassing 141
management theory 18
manager–leader distinction 205
managerial approaches
    constraint of 142
    Nordic countries 111–12, 114–15
    US schools 19–20, 22, 24, 27
managerialism 6, 17, 143, 323–38, **327**
mandated policies, China 82
Mann, Horace 341
marginalization
    Australian schools 50, 52–3
    equity and 243

feminist theories 96
   neoliberalism and 348
   race construct 21, 262, 290
   reproduction/disruption 22
   women 262
market-based reform, privatization 346
market forces
   neoliberalism 345
   school governance 312, 317–18, 320
marketization
   definition 108
   genetics-informed 355–69
   Nordic countries 107, 109–10, 115, 116–18
   school change 249
masculinities
   definition 257
   femininities binary 258
   feminist theories 97
   labour forms 259
   power connection 92–5
   race–gender intersection 262
   women's leadership traits 100
masculinity studies 260
mass schooling 341–2
master's programmes 130–1
matriarchal cultures 94
MATs see multi-academy trusts
maturation variable, experimental studies 194
meaning category, agency 247
mega-analysis 225, 226
mental illness 271–2
mentoring 85, 86, 131
Meny-Gibert, S. 64
merit, culture of 146
merit pay 114
meritocracy 98
message systems, classification 222–3
meta-analysis 225, 226
methods
   conception of 182–3
   context partitioning 180, 183
   practice connection 176
   theory relationship 172–85
micro-aggressions 285
micro-level agendas 164
micropolitics 151–2
middle classes 297, 299–300, 306–7
middle leaders 206
minority communities 18, 22–4, 284, 286
misrecognition-based injustice 51
misrepresentation-based injustice 51
mixed-methods approach 23, 173
Mongolia 265–7
monopoly capitalism 341–2
morality 77, 82
Morgan, J.P. 341
multi-academy trusts (MATs) 300, 318

multidimensionality 271, 273
multiple-treatment inference 194–5
municipal schools, Chile 124, 126–9, 131–2
Murray, C. 362

Naples schools 145–8
A Nation at Risk report 19
nation states 41
National College for School Leadership 36
national systems, socio-economic class 300, 306
nature–nurture debate 357
neoliberalism/neoliberal reforms 17
   Australia 50
   Chile 123
   corporatization and 344, 350
   definitions 31, 107, 344–5
   England 30
   feminist movements 263
   instructional leadership 231
   logics of 41, 249
   Nordic countries 106–10, 115
   within NPM 324–5
   pillars of 327
   policy reforms 32
   restructuring policies 240
   US education 19–20, 25–6, 27
networks 142, 376
New Labour policy 36
new managerialism 345, 347
New Order regime, Indonesia 94–5
New Public Management (NPM) 108–11, 114, 209, 316,
      318–19, 324–5, 327
New Zealand 240
Niesche, Richard 8–9
Nixon, Jon 166–7
Nkondo, G.M. 69
Nordic countries 105–19
normative assumptions, research methods 173
normativity
   femininity 93
   functionalist approaches 2
   gender relations 99
   instructional leadership 227–8
   social justice 42
   theory and 38
Norway 106–12, 114
NPM see New Public Management
Nussbaum, Martha C. 166

objectivity 173
'obligations' 144
Ocasio-Cortez, Alexandria 263
OECD see Organisation for Economic Co-operation and
      Development
Ofsted inspections 330–1, 334–5
ontology 162, 173, 178
open-access education 62

open learning spaces 247
Organisation for Economic Co-operation and Development
    (OECD) 111–12, 114, 226, 244
organizational dynamics 140, 145, 285
'organizational professionalism' 114
organizations
    accountability 321
    components of 141
    construct 141–2
    efficiency 300
    empowerment requirements 151
    inequalities 284
    instructional context 224–6, 229–31
    purpose 141
    race and 285–8
    research context 173–5
    school change context 240–4
outcome-based evidence 228–9, 231
outsider status, women 259
Overvaal School, South Africa 66
ownership of change 243, 245–6

paradigm wars, definition 175
paradigms of research 174–5
parallel leadership 47
parent–school power relations 111
parental participation 243, 246
parenting responsibilities 53–5
parity of participation 51–2, 55, 56
Parker, J. 297
participation
    criteria 143–4
    definition 142
    parity of 51–2, 55, 56
    performativity and 335
partnerships 244
patriarchal culture 94, 98, 100
patriarchal institutions 259
Pay for Success 350–2
pedagogical leadership 81, 85–7, 222–3
    see also instructional leadership
people, definition 141
people-focused work 373, 375
performance commitments 125–7, 128–9, 132
performative reforms 315–16
performativity 32, 33–6, 323–37
personal relationships 77–8
personality tests 191
personalization, genetic 358–61, 362–4
Personalized Learning movement 351
'personification' of leadership 204, 206, 211
Peterson, M.F. 195
PF leadership see Process-Formal leadership
philanthrocapitalism 350–1
philanthropy, corporate 347
Phillips, N. 247
PI leadership see Process-Informal leadership

PISA see Programme for International Student Assessment
plan–pilot–implement–reflect–revise process 79
Plomin, R. 359, 363–5
policies
    criteria 143–4
    principles 62
    reforms 31–2, 110
    school principal activities 68
policy contexts
    educational organizations 150–1
    neoliberalism 344
    social/psychological theories 160
policy frames 31–2, 42
policy transformations, China 79
political context
    instructional leadership 224–6, 229–31
    neoliberalism 345
    research methods 173–5
    schools 117, 240–4
    sexual identity 270
    university leaders 266
    US public schools 274
political economy 118
political justice/injustice 51–2
politicization 133, 311
Pollitt, C. 326–7
positioning and genetics 363–4
positive research approach 17, 19, 21
positivism 343, 348–9, 351–2
post-heroic concepts 204–5, 209, 212
power
    critical approaches 5, 6
    distribution 214
    educational services 150–2
    feminist theories 96
    gender and 99
    managerialism 334–5
    masculinity connection 92–5
    neoliberalism 345
    performativity 334–5
    professional work 372–3
    race and 288–91
    socially-critical approaches 148, 150
    socio-economic class 305
    theory 164, 167
power relations
    critical approach 4
    distributed leadership 212
    gendered 261, 266
    organizational 151
    parent–school 111
    school change 249
    US public schools 274
    white racial avoidance 286
practices
    criteria 143–4
    definition 142

knowledge actors 377, **378**
leadership as 217
methods connection 176
theory distinction 157, 178
praxis 157–60, *158*
predictability 357, 359–60
pregnancy at school 52–5
primary schools 46–7, 86, 214–16, 264
primus inter pares leadership 111, 113
principals
    accountability 70
    Australian schools 46–58
    autonomy 319
    Chinese schools 76, 78, 80–1, 83–5
    corporatized leadership form 320
    education reforms 238–9, 240, 245–6
    gender issues 265
    headteacher distinction 231
    instructional leadership 81, 83–5, 226
    Nordic countries 106, 111–14, 115, *116*, 117–18
    policy activities 68
    South African schools 63–4, 68, 70
    top-down approaches 330
    see also headteachers
private good, education as 107, 115–17
private schools 124–5, 298–9
private sector managerialism 327
private services, neoliberalism 345
privatization 107–10, 115–17, 345–8, 365–6
privatization, standardization, testing and accountability (PSTA) 124, 132–3
'problems' 167
process thinking 204, 205–7, 210–12, **213**, 214, 217
Process-Formal (PF) leadership 204, 207, 210, **213**, 217
Process-Informal (PI) leadership 204, 207, 210–11, **213**, 217
professional-class schools 348, 349
Professional Emphasis, AITSL 48
professional groups/networks 376
professional learning 80, 85, 87, 242–4, 292
Professional Practices, AITSL 48, 50
professional work 372–3
Programme for International Student Assessment (PISA) 109, 226
progressive educational leadership 344
PRUs (Pupil Referral Units) 302–4
PSTA *see* privatization, standardization, testing and accountability
psychological theories 159–60
psychopathology 167
public education/schools
    Australia 319
    Chile 124
    corporatization 352–3
    Fordist system 342
    'headmaster' tradition 300
    neoliberalism 345–7
    positivism 343

US 20, 271–2, 274–5
public good, education as 107, 116–17
public intellectuals 375, 376
public organization governance 313
public sector managerialism 324, 326–8
public services
    governance 314
    neoliberalism 345
Pupil Referral Units (PRUs) 302–4
purposes
    criteria 143–4
    definition 142
    knowledge actors 377, **378**

Qiang, H. 78
qualitative data 175, 177
quality of education 61, 65, 67–8
quality judgements, research methods 177
Quality Teaching Rounds 227
quantifiable-output-based concepts 3
quantitative data 175, 177
Queer Theory 22, 275
queering 275–6

race 281–94
    construct of 21–2
    definition 284–5
    gender intersection 262–3
    intelligence and 362
    LGB intersection 274
    representation in schools 63
racial avoidance 286–8, 289, 291–2
racial consciousness 284–5
racial discrimination 60–1
racial harassment 287, 289–91
racial parity 65
racialization as power 289
racism 274, 285–6, 289, 292
radical change 244
Ranson, S. 143–4
rapid change 244
Rawls, J. 65, 67
're-embedding' process 314–15
reactive effects, experimental studies 195
Reagan, Ronald 19
Reaganism 312–13
realistic research 379
reality, framing 3
recognition-based injustice 55
redesign of schools 244–7, 249, 250
reductionist theories 21
reflexivity 38–9, 163
reform
    critical approaches 250
    use of term 244
    see also education reforms
regulation

by testing 128
  GERM approach 124
  hierarchy/participation 142
relational leadership 239, 242, 249–50, 375
relationship-building culture 77–8, 85
religion–gender intersection 263
representation and participation 56
representativeness *see* external validity
research
  context of 195–6
  generative principles 176–7, *178*, 180–1, 183
  legitimizing 179–80
  socio-economic class 306
research methods 171–85
  distributed leadership 217
  historical context 173–5
  mitigation of issues 181–3
  professional practices effects 180
  theory connection 182–3
research tradition 173, *178*
researcher bias 195
researcher biography 195–6
resilience 67–8
resistance
  importance of 42
  theory for 38–41
responsibility, exercise of 314
restructuring policies/strategies 240, 356–7
results-based accountability 19
Rhodes, R.A.W. 313
Richardson, K. 364
Rockefeller, John D. 342–3
Rorschach tests 191
Rottenberg, Catherine 263

Saini, A. 361–2, 366
same-sex behaviour 275
SASA *see* South African Schools Act 1996
Scandinavia 108, 111–12
  see also Norway; Sweden
school autonomy 315–16, 319–20
school-based professional learning 85
school boards 319–20
school change 237–52
school-change theory 241
school choice *see* choice
school effectiveness and improvement (SEI) models 240–1, 244, 249
school leader, definition 299
school leaderability, definition 299
school leadership, definition 299
school leading, definition 299
school principals *see* principals
schools inspectorate 33–4
schools/schooling
  apartheid legacy 61–2
  business sponsorship 33

competition 19–20, 33, 123–4
context decoupling from 230
corporatization 341–54
direction-forming process 233
discourses 164–5
diversification 33
diversity 46–7
factory model 341–2
funding cuts 39, 42
genetic selection 360
governance 310–22
improvements 18, 164–5
instructional programmes 226
managerialism 328–34
multiple purposes 26–7
outcome-based evidence 228–9
psychopathology in 167
social contexts 19
social problems and 231–2
socio-economic class 298–304
visible learning 224
science–intelligence–achievement relations 357
science–values relationship 142, 148
scientific credibility 173–4, 176, 180, 225
scientific dynamics 145
scientific effectiveness 143
scientific inquiry 179
Scientific Management 17, 20, 173, 225, 342
Scott, J. 25
scripted lessons 350
secondary schools 80–1, 95, 109, 148, 300
segregation, South Africa 60–1
SEI models *see* school effectiveness and improvement models
selection bias 194–5
selection–maturation interactions 194
self-governing schools 314, 320
senior leadership
  hierarchical approach 215
  innovative practice 216
  women 93, 95–6, 99–103
Senior Leadership Teams (SLTs) 331
serial redesign 246–7
service planning 313–14
SES (socio-economic status) 360
sexual identity 269–79
Shanghai, China 76, 79–81, 83, 87
shared leadership 99
Shields, C. 69–70
Shirley, D.L. 131
Showunmi, Victoria 282
SLTs (Senior Leadership Teams) 331
small state concept 312–13
smart drugs 349
Smith, P.B. 195
Smith-Woolley, E. 359–60
Smyth, J. 4–6, 142, 372, 375
Snedden, David 342

social Darwinism 345
Social Democratic parties 107–8, 110
social-democratic welfarism 106–8
Social Emotional Learning 352
social epistemology 181
social groups, instructional leadership 230
social ideas, culture/context 196–8
social identity, race 285
Social Impact Bonds 351
social justice 51–6
    accountability and 35–6
    AITSL Standard 50–1
    definition 51, 64
    ELMA research 159
    leadership for 17, 20, 22, 24, 27, 242
    normativity 42
    pillars of 64–5, *65*
    policy reforms 31–2
    quality of education 67–8
    socio-economic backgrounds 63–4
    South African context 64–6, 69–71
    Transformative Models 305
social problems 231–2
social relations 260–1
social reproduction 348
social theory 157–60, 162–3, 166
socially-critical approaches 140, 144, 148–9, 150, 152, 316
socio-cultural intersection, gender/age 266–7
socio-economic backgrounds, South Africa 63–4, 67
socio-economic class 295–308
socio-economic status (SES), genetic links 360
solidarity 52, 56
South Africa 59–73
South African Schools Act 1996 (SASA) 62, 67
Spillane, J.P. 208–9
standardization/standardized testing
    Chilean system 122, 124–5, 127, 129
    GERM approach 123
    neoliberalism 346–7
    positivism 343
    school governance 317
Stanley, J.C. 193–4
State Ibuism, Indonesia 95
state power, characterizing 313–14
statistical regression 194
stereotypes 242, 258
strategic leadership 81–4, 87
strategic thinking 77
'street teachers' 148
strong leadership concept 112–14
structural factors
    critical approaches 37
    English schools 331
    US public schools 274
structural policy frames 31–2, 42
structure(s)
    agency interplay 5, 30

criteria 143–4
definition 31, 141, 142
school change 249
theoretical frameworks 161
structuring context, research 195
student rights 273
student voice, change ownership 243
'style'
    concept establishment 189
    criteria 188
subjectivity 164, 173–4, 179, 232
subsidized private education 124–5
success
    constructing 359–60
    framing 112
Sun Tzu, *The Art of War* 77, 81
surveillance, LGB people 274
Suryakusuma, J. 95
Sweden 106–12, 115–16
system leadership 81–3, 87, 114
system thinking 84
systemic change 240
systems, definition 141

Taoism 77, 81–2
Taylor, Frederick Winslow 17, 173, 225, 231, 342
Taylorism 173, 176, 180, 225, 230
Teach for America (TFA) programme 25–6
teacher collective efficacy 210
teacher-development systems 80
teacher leadership approaches 241
teacher pedagogical leadership 81, 85–7
teacher performativity 325–6
teaching
    as respected profession 82
    socio-economic class 305
team-teaching practices 246, 248
technical skills 179–81
technological determinism, intelligence 365
temporality, leadership 211
test-based accountability 123
testing
    Chilean system 124–5, 127–8
    corporatization 343
    Italy 147
    neoliberalism 346–7
    reactive/interaction effect 195
    school governance 317
testing variable, experimental studies 194
TFA (Teach for America) programme 25–6
Thatcherism 312–13, 345
Theoharis, G. 22
theoretical frameworks 160–2
theory
    for advocacy/resistance 38–41
    context partitioning 180, 183
    definition 156

methods relationship 172–85
    practices distinction 178
    research methods connection 182–3
    as thinking/acting resource 162–3
    use of 37, 155–69
Theory Movement 141, 174, 178, 180
Thomson, P. 176–7, 244
TINA thesis 345
top-down approaches 240–1, 243, 250, 330
totalitarianism 6
traditionalism 357
training programmes 24–6, 111–12, 130–2, 176, 304
trait theories 301
transformational leadership 378
    see also distributed leadership
Transformational Leadership models 304
transformative leadership 65, 69–71
Transformative Models 304–5
transgender people 271, 273
Trujillo, Tina 9–10, 25
trust, rebuilding 250–1
turnaround leaders 225, 226, 258
turnover of staff 329

Ubuntu leadership 65, 69
United Kingdom (UK) 240
    class structure 296, 298–9
    governance 314
    Keynesianism 344
    neoliberalism 345
    race contexts 282–4, 286, 291–2
    see also England
United States (US) 15–28, 240
    contemporary models 19–20
    corporatization 340–54
    educational leadership programmes 24–6
    effectiveness/efficiency legacies 18–19
    feminist movements 263
    governance 312–13
    LGB people 270–9
    methodological constraints 23–4
    race contexts 282–4, 286–9, 291–2
universalization 3
universities
    gender case studies 264–6
    genetics for admissions 359–60, 362, 366, **367**
    institutional logics 93
    master's programmes 130–1
    partnerships with schools 244
    restructuring effects 97–8
    socio-economic class 298–9, 306–7
    women senior leaders 95, 99–102
unpredictable change 241
urban centres, US 20
US see United States

validity factors 193, 195
values, socio-economic class 305
values-driven leadership 250
values-oriented models 26
values–science relationship 142, 148
'values turn' 146
variable-based approaches 223
VC (Vice-Chancellor) appointments 283–4
venture philanthropy 347
vertical divisions, gender 259
Verwoerd, H.F. 61
Vice-Chancellor (VC) appointments 283–4
visible learning 223–4, 229–30
visible power 94, 96, 99
voucher system 124, 125, 345

Walker, A. 77
Waller, Willard 271
Walton family 347
Ward, S.C. 327
welfarism 106–10, 117, 301
Western-centric models 262–3
'what works' rhetoric 24–6, 175–6
white privilege 285, 286
white racial avoidance 286–9, 291
white racial dis-consciousness 284
White, R.K. 199–200
Whitty, G. 3
wholeness, search for 248
Williams v. Port Huron School District (2012) 286–8, 291–2
Williamson, B. 365
Willmott, H. 34
women
    apartheid repression 61
    empowerment 95, 98, 101
    in higher education 92–104
    minority ethnic groups 284
    queer theory 22
    school roles 63
    state definitions 95
    under-representation 258–61, 262
    US public schools 271–2
work 93, 377–8
working classes 297–9, 302, 306, 348, 349
Worth Less? campaign 38–9, 40

xenophobia 17

Young, M.D. 21
young parents 52–5
Young, Toby 365
youth centres 276–7

Zuckerberg, Mark 347